THE PARTY FAMILY

THE PARTY FAMILY

Revolutionary Attachments and the Gendered Origins of State Power in China

Kimberley Ens Manning

CORNELL UNIVERSITY PRESS   ITHACA AND LONDON

Photographs in chapter 8 by John Manning, June 1958, China.

First published 2023 by Cornell University Press.

Library of Congress Cataloging-in-Publication Data

Names: Manning, Kimberley Ens, 1970– author.
Title: The party family : revolutionary attachments and the gendered origins of state power in China / Kimberley Ens Manning.
Description: Ithaca : Cornell University Press, 2023. | Includes bibliographical references and index.
Identifiers: LCCN 2022051753 (print) | LCCN 2022051754 (ebook) | ISBN 9781501715518 (hardcover) | ISBN 9781501771415 (paperback) | ISBN 9781501715525 (epub) | ISBN 9781501715532 (pdf)
Subjects: LCSH: Families—Political aspects—China—History—20th century. | Interpersonal relations—Political aspects—China. | Women—Political activity—China. | China—Politics and government—20th century—Social aspects.
Classification: LCC DS775.7 .M34 2023 (print) | LCC DS775.7 (ebook) | DDC 951.05—dc23/eng/20221115
LC record available at https://lccn.loc.gov/2022051753
LC ebook record available at https://lccn.loc.gov/2022051754

In loving memory of Scott Manning, 1971–2020

Contents

Preface

In June 1958, my father disembarked from a German cargo ship onto a pier in Tianjin. Just twenty-one years old, Dad was backpacking his way across the South Pacific, Asia, and Europe, filing stories with Canadian newspapers about his experiences along the way. Of the more than two dozen countries through which Dad would pass, including Afghanistan and the Philippines, it was China that left the biggest impression. The sheer enormity of the country, its history, and the still new political project that was the People's Republic of China (PRC) captivated his imagination and upset many of his preconceptions about the world order and the place of women in it. One of my father's most enduring memories of his two-week visit was hearing a train whistle while standing on a railway platform. When he looked up, a young woman engineer waved and grinned down at him. As Dad would share with me much later, it had never occurred to his younger self that a woman could drive a train. Several of my father's photos from that brief trip appear on the book's cover and in chapter 8.

A little more than thirty years later, in August 1988, I arrived in Beijing to study Mandarin, knowing little of my dad's early travels or the impact that it had on his own studies. And yet my own postsecondary studies tracked a very similar route to his: intensive Mandarin training (Dad in Taipei, me in Beijing) while pursuing an undergraduate degree in Asian studies at the University of British Columbia. It was only on completion of our undergraduate degrees that our paths parted ways. After my father graduated, he did not speak Mandarin again until he spoke with me on the phone in Beijing. I, however, have spent nearly twenty-five years trying to understand that moment he landed in Tianjin.

In spring of 1958, Chairman Mao's call to make a Great Leap Forward (GLF) was being enthusiastically embraced by Chinese Communist Party (CCP) activists and leaders across the country. A movement designed to surpass the United Kingdom and the United States in steel production, the GLF mobilized the entire population, including women, to participate in collective agricultural and industrial projects, while socializing many forms of household labor. And yet by June, serious points of contention marked the project. This gendered conflict, and the familial politics which bound and shaped it, would have serious implications for China's rural populace. By 1960, the last year of the GLF, hundreds of millions would be suffering from malnutrition, and tens of million were dead or dying. The GLF famine would prove the deadliest famine the world has ever known.

While we know that women's labor, both inside and outside the household, made the GLF possible, to date there exists little scholarly record of the gendered politics behind the mobilization. This is as true of the political science scholarship that has focused on the struggles of elite men as it is of the feminist social histories, in many of which political struggles are curiously absent. In the vast majority of political science and historical treatments of the Maoist era, women become apparent as political actors only after the GLF: in the lead-up to and cataclysmic factional struggles that defined the Cultural Revolution. One cannot understand the train engineer's cheery wave to my dad, however, without seriously grappling with the gender and family politics that fueled the GLF and the famine that it produced.

Cai Chang, the head of the All China Women's Federation (ACWF), supported Mao's rise to power and would serve as one of his most fervent backers during the 1950s. As Mao's younger sister in the struggle, it was Cai Chang who would lead the charge to moderate the impact of the mobilization on rural families in 1958, even as she enthusiastically endorsed the GLF and the liberation of women, alongside her husband and economic czar, Li Fuchun. One year later the couple would prove central players in the reradicalization of the GLF, an effort that would directly exacerbate famine conditions developing across China.

This book takes family ties seriously as both a subject of and means of political struggle. The familial politics of Cai Chang, and several generations of women at the elite and grassroots of the CCP, cannot be reduced to factionalism nor to feminist attempts to escape the bounds of the family itself. Rather, family ties, and the women at their center, are the revolutionary story itself. Building on Pierre Bourdieu's concepts of field, capital, and kinship and more recent meditations on emotions and affect, this book theoretically accounts for a subject for whom ideology and family are themselves closely intertwined projects of the revolutionary state.

Family ties are affective, geopolitical enactments that profoundly shape the modern world, including the underpinnings of knowledge production. This is as true of Cai Chang's family ties as it is of mine. My dad's first exposure to the Chinese language was not to Mandarin but to Cantonese, in his family's kitchen. My father, like his mother before him, was raised in a home with cooks born in southern China. The settler colonialism that enabled the first generations of my white forebears to build wealth and amass political influence in British Columbia was intricately bound up with uneven trade regimes and racist laws of the nineteenth and twentieth centuries. And yet, in but one of the perfidious ways in which colonialism manifests, China and Chinese objects (art, jewelry, and yes, language) stood as a sign of wealth and power. My dad's Cold War travels and studies were shaped through this history, as were my studies and the origins of this book.

This book's interrogation of family ties can be traced back to my mother as well. In the autumn of 1988, at the same time I was learning to write characters and stumbling over simple phrases in Mandarin, my mother defended her doctoral dissertation in psychology at the California Institute of Integral Studies (formerly the California Institute of Asian Studies). The topic of the thesis? Sibling ties. As a single mother, my mum had struggled to support three teenagers on a small salary. It was only after completing her PhD and building a successful practice as a registered psychologist that her financial constraints eased. My early determination to pursue a PhD was, in part, an educational investment to prevent future scarcity. Although I now know that a PhD in no way secures financial stability, my family story told me that it did.

My mother's history intersects with twentieth-century expressions of Christian maternalisms as well. Long before having children, Mum started her graduate studies at Union Theological Seminary—one of the foremost American instigators of the social gospel. That a young white woman from the Canadian prairies ended up ministering to Black mothers in East Harlem in the early 1960s, as my mum did during her training, speaks to the righteous and racial certitude of social gospel maternalisms circulating in North America and in China at that historical moment. One of the central figures of this book, Li Dequan, widow of a man known as the Christian Warlord, developed a similar early passion for maternal reform through the social gospel. She would go on to lead one of the twentieth century's most successful efforts to reduce infant and maternal mortality as the PRC's first minister of health.

I start this preface and acknowledgments with my parents because they have been so key to this book's realization, and because our family ties illustrate dimensions of some of the geo-sociopolitical dynamics that this book endeavors to take seriously. My family story that a PhD could secure an economically viable future, and that story's eventual realization, was made possible in part by gendered enactments of cultural capital and maternal care too numerous to count. But there are other stories I could tell, stories in which both my parents, in different ways, have supported processes of truth, reconciliation, and justice. It is with their implicit and explicit teachings in mind that I have endeavored to pursue gender and racial justice inside and outside the university, and why I also begin my acknowledgments with the original peoples of the lands on which I have written this book. These lands include the unceded traditional territories of the Duwamish, the Ohlone, and the Kanien'kehá:ka peoples, and the traditional territories of the ləkʷəŋən peoples. I am grateful for the opportunity to live and work on these lands while cognizant that the work of truth and reconciliation, and all that it implies, is a lifelong commitment.

My gratitude also extends to the 163 people who agreed to share parts of their life stories with me. Their generosity and hospitality over the course of what in some cases was repeat visits was humbling. Many of the arguments that form the basis of this book are thanks to the willingness of interview participants to engage with and at times question my questions. Ultimately, I hope that this otherwise deeply uneven exercise in knowledge production will nonetheless contribute to a more fulsome understanding of the local and national struggles that so defined the first decade of the PRC and the lives of the women leaders at their center.

This book began in a seminar led by Susan Whiting in the spring of 1998. Indeed, it was not my dad who suggested I study women in the GLF but Susan, who was struck at the time by how little was understood about the gendered dynamics of the mobilization. I am grateful to Susan for pointing me in this direction and for providing me with the intensive early mentoring necessary to take on this ambitious and ultimately life-changing project. I consider myself lucky that Tani Barlow and Stevan Harrell also provided me with extensive feedback on some of the earliest drafts of this work. Tani's pathbreaking historical work and rigorous pedagogical methods have left an indelible imprint on my own scholarship and teaching. Stevan's insightful contributions to the book began only after I completed my first round of fieldwork. Joel Migdal's mentorship was also key. Joel's state-in-society methodology would serve as a critical foundation to this book's conception and realization. But it was Joel's attentive nurturing of my ideas and self-confidence that would prove most important. I am not sure I would have made it out of graduate school without him.

As a junior scholar, I could not have asked for more stimulating cross-disciplinary environments than those I experienced at the University of Washington and the Center for East Asian Studies at Stanford University. At the University of Washington, David Bachman, Nancy Hartsock, Steve Hanson, Christine DiStefano, Stephanie Burkhalter, Marilyn Zucker, Oscar Barrera Nunez, Ketty Loeb, Tamir Moustaffa, Patricia Woods, Ben Smith, Nicole Watts, Mary-Alice Pickert, Tom Lewis, Kenny Lawson, Niall O'Murcho, Isil Ozel, Senem Aslan, Diana Pallais, Judy Aks, Zhou Yingying, Cricket Keating, and Ki-young Shin all provided invaluable critical feedback and assistance at early stages of the book. I am similarly grateful for the community and individual support I received at Stanford, where Jean C. Oi, Matthew Sommer, Hill Gates, Melissa Brown, Kären Wigen, and Margaret Kuo were all significant and influential interlocutors. It was Hill, for example, who revolutionized how I undertook my second round of interviews in 2004, and it was Kären, who prompted me to investigate Total War as a way of further understanding the GLF.

Critical sources of financial funding were key at this early stage of the book as well. Specifically, funds provided by the Social Sciences and Humanities Research Council of Canada, the China-Canada Scholars Award, the University of Washington Graduate School Fritz Scholarship for International Exchange, the University of Washington Freeman Teaching Fellowship in Asian Studies, the University of Washington Huckabay Teaching Fellowship, and the Carrie Chapman Catt Prize for Research on Women and Politics were pivotal in the research and writing of this book.

The sponsorship of the history department of Peking University, secured through the China-Canada Scholars Award, was pivotal to the furtherment of this book. Given the increasingly precarious position of academics in the PRC, however, I have decided it safer not to include them in these acknowledgments. Unnamed are the dozens of colleagues, archivists, friends, and research assistants who engaged with my ideas, facilitated the development of my fieldwork, and commented on early drafts of my work. This book simply could not have materialized without their crucial support.

Since my return to Canada, work on this book was furthered with funding from the Fonds de recherche du Québec and with grants from Concordia University, my home institution since 2004. Concordia did not simply provide me with the financial resources to complete the book, however, but also the time to do so. Three sabbatical leaves (one full year, two half) and one semester of teaching release enabled me to at last complete my work on this book. The faith that Concordia placed in me as I slowly worked to finish the book while raising three children and pursuing additional academic, administrative, and political goals along the way is nothing short of remarkable. I will be forever grateful that the first two decades of my academic career was forged in an institution that enabled me and my growing family to thrive, and when we weren't thriving, to repair.

There are dozens of people who have generously given their time to provide feedback as this book slowly took shape over the past twenty years. Much of this feedback came at conferences and on drafts of the articles that I published over the first decade of the work on this book. I am grateful to the following journals for publishing articles that reflected some of my earliest thinking about the GLF: "Embodied Activisms: The Case of the Mu Guiying Brigade," *The China Quarterly* 204 (2010): 850–69, © 2010 School of Oriental and African Studies; "The Gendered Politics of Woman-Work," *Modern China* 32, no. 3 (2006): 349–84, © 2006 Sage Publications; "Making a Great Leap Forward? The Politics of Women's Liberation in Maoist China," *Gender and History* 18, no. 3 (2006): 574–93, © 2006 John Wiley & Sons; "Marxist Maternalism, Memory, and the Mobilization of Women in the Great Leap Forward," *China Review* 5, no. 1 (2005): 83–110, © 2005 Chinese University of Hong Kong. Many passages and arguments from these publications appear in the chapters that follow, even as the arc of my analysis, and the concepts that undergird it, move in new directions. I am also grateful to have had the opportunity to present early drafts of chapters 1 and 2 at the Canadian Political Science Association (2008), the Historical Society for Twentieth-Century China (2008), the International Gender Studies Conference (2009), and Wesleyan University (2009), and grateful for the opportunity to present early drafts of the book's introduction at McGill University (2015), at the American Political Science Association (2015), and at the University of Göttingen (2018). I would also like to thank the Department of Gender Studies at the University of Victoria for serving as my host while I completed the manuscript in 2021–22.

A number of colleagues and friends have made key interventions, whether in the form of advice, resources, and/or comments on papers, at various points over the more than twenty years I have worked on this book. To this end, I would like to thank Gail Hershatter, who gave me advice before I set out to do my first interviews in 2000, who engaged with my work at multiple conferences, and who commented on five chapters in 2015. I would like to thank Naihua Zhang, who generously photocopied and sent me *Zhongguo funü yundong wenxian ziliao huibian* (Collected documents of the Chinese women's movement), and whose dissertation has been an invaluable source of inspiration, knowledge, and insight throughout the work on this book. I would like to thank Dongxiao Liu, whose friendship and intellectual support was key before, during, and after graduate school. It was Dongxiao who first pointed me toward Theda Skocpol's work on maternalist state building in 2002, and it was Dongxiao who helped me to begin to see the "householder" as an important state subject in Maoist China in 2010. I would also like to thank Wang Zheng, who not only commented on early papers but provided me with multiple opportunities to present and publish my work over the past twenty years. And I would like to thank Kathy Harding, my friend, confidante, and editor, who worked over multiple drafts of the book introduction between 2009 and 2022, bringing it to the version it is now. It is because of Kathy that I finally found the courage to own my argument. Thank you.

I am deeply indebted to Delia Davin, Jennifer Guyver, Tina Johnson, Andre Schmid, Leander Schneider, Felix Wemheuer, and Xiaohong Xu, all of whom took the time to read the manuscript in its entirety and who provided me with invaluable feedback before I embarked upon my final round of revisions. There are dozens of additional people who have engaged with my ideas, and/or contributed to the completion of this book in a multiplicity of ways, including commenting on papers/chapters, providing resources and advice, and building the communities that have sustained my scholarship. To this end, I would like to thank Melinda Adams, Emily Andrew, Norman Apter, Barbara Arneil, Ceren Belge, Max Bergholz, Laurel Bossen, Jeremy Brown, Gillian Calder, Heath B.

Chamberlain, Timothy Cheek, Tina Mai Chen, Neil Diamant, Graham Dodds, Sarah Eaton, Elizabeth Elbourne, Harriet Evans, Deborah Gould, Vivienne Guo, Mary Alice Haddad, Nina Halpern, Marc des Jardins, Ellen Judd, Erik Kuhonta, Karen Kampwirth, Arang Keshavarzian, Michael Lipson, Elizabeth Littell-Lamb, Ching Kwan Lee, Freya McCamant, Mark Manning, Patrik Marier, Andrew Mertha, Lynette Ong, Maryjane Osa, David Ownby, Mireille Paquet, Laura Parisi, Hélène Piquet, Colette Plum, Amy Poteete, Annie Pullen Sansfaçon, Alison Rowley, Francesca Scala, Helen Schneider, Shaopeng Song, Julian Spencer-Churchill, Julia Strauss, Xiaoping Sun, Ralph Thaxton, Tuong H. Vu, Juan Wang, James Watson, Susanne Weigelin-Schwiedrzik, Genevieve Weynerowski, Joseph Wong, Yiching Wu, and Weiguo Zhang. To those that I have forgotten and do not appear on this list: I apologize. If you remind me, I hope to recognize and thank you for your contributions in another way.

I have had the good fortune to work with several generations of outstanding undergraduate and graduate students at Concordia, many of whom are now in the full throes of their own careers. Fang Chen spent several years seeking out archival documents, memoirs, biographies, and histories and then analyzing and annotating them on my behalf. Fang also coded interviews, undertook translations, and double-checked many of my own early translations. Simply put, this book could not have been realized without her. I also benefitted greatly from the research support of Félix Hébert, who helped me to prepare an early draft of the manuscript in 2014, and Jin Jin, who in 2015 worked tirelessly with the data set of interviewees to produce the numbers that now appear in chapter 4. In 2018 and 2020, Manon Laurent built comprehensive literature reviews of relevant research published in English and Chinese since the manuscript's original submission. If I have missed citing relevant publications (ever my worry), it is my responsibility alone. I would also like to thank Pan Yu, whose eleventh-hour research support proved vital to the completion of the GLF chapters, who reviewed the glossary, many of my translations, and citations for accuracy. I would also like to thank Jennifer Guyver, who cross-checked each bibliographic entry and built the index, and Gerald Crimp and Francesco MacAllister-Caruso for their editorial review. Finally, I would like to thank Bill Nelson for constructing the map that appears in the book.

It goes without saying that a publication of this length, and with this extensive a history, would not be seeing the light of day without the unwavering support of an extraordinary editorial team. Roger Malcom Haydon was an early champion of the book, providing key feedback on the introduction and then shepherding the manuscript through the review process. Roger also proved remarkably flexible, agreeing to my request to restructure the manuscript after I had signed the original contract, for example, and remarkably patient when work on the manuscript was delayed by my political activities in 2017, 2018, and 2019. Roger continued to make important contributions to the development of the manuscript up until his retirement in August 2020. Although I was more than a little heartbroken to see Roger go, Mahinder S. Kingra rapidly stepped into the breach. Over the past two years, Mahinder has been responsive, compassionate, and patient as I worked under pandemic conditions to produce the final version of the manuscript. I am also grateful to Mia Renaud's work on publicity, Karen Hwa's formatting guidance and copyediting, Jack Rummel's copyediting, and the entire editorial team for their efforts to see the manuscript through to production.

A book of this size and history, when overlapping with a growing family, also requires an extensive caregiving infrastructure. I was the beneficiary of several decades of feminist advocacy that enabled me to take three twelve-month paid parental leaves and that ensured subsidized, quality childcare after I returned to work. Studying, as I have, midcentury efforts to socialize housework in the PRC, I have never once taken for granted the advocacy necessary to produce these state- and institutionally funded policies. I have also not taken for granted a marital partnership that has been key to the flourishing of this book from the outset. Jason Ens postponed the completion of his own PhD twice so that he could accompany me on field work in 2000–2001 and support me at Stanford in 2003–4. Since the birth of our first child in 2005, Jason has also shared fully with me the joys and travails of raising three amazing kids (none of whom has ever known a time when I have not been working on this book). I am forever grateful to be a part of a loving partnership and all that it has enabled, including a pandemic reset when I needed to go home.

In the summer of 2021, Jason and I drove two of our children and twelve boxes of archives and books from Montreal to Victoria, British Columbia. Similar to many other families, COVID-19 had hit us hard. Moving back in with my mum and consolidating our household with renewed family and educational support seemed like the natural thing to do. For the past year, and as she has done so many times in the past, my mum took care of me and my kids, so that we could all recover and so that I could pursue this book to completion. Long conversations with my dad and many hours spent walking with cousins and old friends deeply enriched this time as well. It is thus the case that this preface ends where it started: with the family ties that made the work that became this book both desirable and possible.

Dad and Mum: I am so grateful for your support and all it has afforded. I love you.

Abbreviations

ACDWF	All China Democratic Women's Federation
ACFTU	All China Federation of Trade Unions
ACWF	All China Women's Federation
BDCW	Lily Xiao Hong Lee and A. D. Stefanowska, eds. 2003. *Biographical Dictionary of Chinese Women: The Twentieth Century 1912–2000.* Armonk, NY: M. E. Sharpe.
CC	CCP Central Committee
CCDYKK	ACWF, ed. 1988. *Cai Chang, Deng Yingchao, Kang Keqing: Funü jiefang wenti wenxuan* [Cai Chang, Deng Yingchao, Kang Keqing: Documents on issues regarding Chinese women's liberation]. Beijing: Renmin chubanshe.
CCP	Chinese Communist Party
CCWMC	Central Committee Women's Movement Committee
CLARA	Chinese Liberated Areas Relief Association
CMA	Chongqing Municipal Archives
CPPCC	Chinese People's Political Consultative Conference
CPRA	China People's Relief Administration
GCAWF	Gaoshan County Archives, Women's Federation
GLF	Great Leap Forward
GMD	Guomindang
GX	*Gaoshan xianzhi* [County gazateer of Gaoshan]. 1994. Shanghai: Shanghai shehui kexueyuan chubanshe.
HAPC	Higher-Stage Agricultural Producer Cooperative
HCAWF	Huoyue County Archives, Women's Federation
HX	*Huoyue xianzhi* [County gazateer of Huoyue]. 1993. Zhengzhou: Zhongzhou guji chubanshe.
LAPC	Lower-Stage Agricultural Producer Cooperative
LQW	Luo Qiong, ed. 2000. *Luo Qiong wenji* [The collected works of Luo Qiong]. Beijing: Zhongguo funü chubanshe.
MAT	Mutual Aid Team
MOH	Ministry of Health
MOJ	Ministry of Justice
PUMC	Peking Union Medical College

QJ   Luo Qiong, ed. 1997. *Qidi ji: Nüjie de jiechu qianbei* [An
                       enlightened collection: Outstanding women elders]. Bei-
                       jing: Zhongguo funü chubanshe.

TR   Jingu chuanqi zazhi [Stories of old and present times
                       magazine], ed. 2004. *Tiexue rouqing: Zhonggong shi dajie
                       shengsi chuanqi* [Blood and tenderness: The stories of the
                       life and death of ten elder sisters of the CCP]. Beijing:
                       Zhongguo funü chubanshe.

WCA   Wenhe County Archives

WCAWF   Wenhe County Archives, Women's Federation

WHDCC   Dong Bian, Cai Asong, and Chan Deshan, ed. 1992. *Women
                       de hao dajie Cai Chang* [Our good eldest sister Cai Chang].
                       Beijing: Zhongyang wenxian chubanshe.

WW   *Funü gongzuo* [Women-work].

WX   *Wenhe xianzhi* [County gazateer of Wenhe]. 1992. Zheng-
                       zhou: Zhongzhou guji chubanshe.

YMCA   Young Men's Christian Association

YWCA   Young Women's Christian Association

ZFWN   ACWF, ed. [1999] *Zhongguo funü wushi nian* [Fifty years
                       of Chinese women]. Beijing: Zhongguo funü chubanshe.
                       CD-ROM.

ZFYLZ (1927–1937)   Hu Lipei, ed. 1991. *Zhongguo funü yundong lishi ziliao
                       (1927–1937)* [Historical materials of the Chinese women's
                       movement]. Beijing: Zhongguo funü chubanshe.

ZFYLZ (1937–1945)   Wang Menglan, ed. 1991. *Zhongguo funü yundong lishi
                       ziliao (1937–1945)* [Historical materials of the Chinese
                       women's movement]. Beijing: Zhongguo funü chubanshe.

ZFYLZ (1945–1949)   Hu Lipei, ed. 1991.*Zhongguo funü yundong lishi ziliao
                       (1945–1949)* [Historical materials of the Chinese women's
                       movement]. Beijing: Zhongguo funü chubanshe.

ZFYWZH   Li Dongan, ed. 1988. *Zhongguo funü yundong wenxian zil-
                       iao huibian* [Collected documents of the Chinese women's
                       movement]. 2 vols. Beijing: Zhongguo funü chubanshe.

ZJSQ   Peng Peiyun, ed. 1997. *Zhongguo jihua shengyu quanshu*
                       [Encyclopedia of Chinese Family Planning]. Beijing: Zhong-
                       guo renkou chubanshe.

ZYW   ACWF, ed. 1996. *Zhang Yun wenji* [The Collected Works of
                       Zhang Yun]. Beijing: Zhongguo funü chubanshe.

Transliteration

This book uses the pinyin system of romanization with a glossary of Chinese characters appearing at the back of the book. In two cases I have referred to historical figures with the names by which they are most familiar, namely Sun Yat-sen and Chiang Kai-shek. The Wade Giles system of romanization also appears occasionally in the form of quotes, as written in the original source.

Weights and Measurements

jin	0.5 kilograms
liang	50 grams (before 1959: 31.25 grams)
mao qian	ten cents
mu	approximately one-sixth of an acre

Interview Citation

Throughout this book interviews are cited numerically, from 1 to 163, as shown in the table in appendix 2. An example of this is the source of the second epigraph in the introduction, Bao Qinglian, 160; details of this interview are given at item 160 in this list.

Major Historical Events

Chinese Revolution	1911
Founding of the Republic of China	1912
May Fourth Movement	1916–27
First United Front	1923–27
Jiangxi Soviet	1931–34
Long March	1934–35
Second United Front	1936–41
Sino-Japanese War	1937–45
Yan'an Rectification Movement	1942–45
Civil War	1946–49
Founding of the People's Republic of China	1949
Korean War	1950–53
1957 Anti-Rightist Movement	1957
Great Leap Forward	1958–60
Great Leap Famine	1959–61
Cultural Revolution	1966–76
Reform Era	1978–

MAP 1. China

THE PARTY FAMILY

INTRODUCTION
Family Ties as Political Attachments

> We are all women, all mothers, we all have the hearts of loving mothers, we all wish for the health of our children, socialism's next generation.
>
> —Luo Qiong quoting Cai Chang, "Cai dajie de jiaohui mingke xintou" (Elder sister Cai's teachings are engraved in my heart)

> In my life my feelings toward the Communist Party have run very deep [*ganqing shen*], and toward my mother have run very deep, and toward women-work have run very deep: in all the years I did women-work I didn't complain [*taoyan*]; women [can] make a great contribution to society [by] serving [*cihou*] the elderly, serving their mothers-in-law, [and] serving [their] children.
>
> —Bao Qinglian, 160, former commune leader

In 1949, the Chinese Communist Party (CCP) faced a staggering set of challenges. With the exception of a few short months between the end of the Second World War and the commencement of civil war, China had endured more than ten years of warfare. Hundreds of thousands of people had been displaced during the Japanese occupation, not all of whom had returned to their homes after 1945. Inflation was rampant, urban unemployment was high, and floods and droughts had taken a heavy toll on certain regions of the country. Famine also struck China over the winter of 1949 and 1950, with some seven million people in need of relief (Bian and Wu 2006, 692). The health and welfare of children was in especially dire straits: more than a million children in areas occupied by CCP forces required relief aid (or nearly 40 percent of the total number), with children in the provinces of Henan, Anhui, and Jiangsu suffering from anemia, malnutrition, and stomach ailments (Kang 1949 [1997], 24).

Given that much of the Chinese population was just emerging from decades of war, famine, and dislocation, it is no less than astounding that between 1949 and 1958 infant mortality declined by more than half: from two hundred deaths per thousand, to seventy deaths per thousand (MOH Lead Party Group 1958 [1997]), an achievement that Banister (1987, 82–83) attributes to an early focus on midwifery training, stable nutritional conditions for mothers, epidemic-control measures, and environmental sanitation. Equally astounding: transformative legal reforms enabled millions of women to successfully petition for divorce. And yet by 1960 these social policy achievements had been dramatically undermined, if not entirely reversed. Indeed, widespread overwork, disease, and starvation caused birth rates to plummet and gynecological injuries to skyrocket, and they produced a surge in the number of women and children subject to abuse, neglect, and trafficking. All told, as many as thirty to forty-five million people perished in the famine that swept the countryside between 1959 and 1962.[1]

What explains state capacity in processes of state formation and consolidation? In this book, I argue that family ties played a central role in the state's capacity to respond to crisis before and after the foundation of the People's Republic of China (PRC). And central to family ties were women as both subjects and leaders of reform. What I call political attachments, or the affective enactment of family ties in political struggle, shape how the state apparatus is imagined, constructed, and contested.

An approach to family ties as attachments focuses on the dynamic interaction between family and state in the context of fields. Following Ray (1999, 7) I define fields as "configurations of forces and as sites of struggle to maintain or transform those forces."[2] As a "meta-field" or "ensemble of fields" (Bourdieu and Wacquant 1992, 111–12), the state materializes through geopolitically uneven and historically specific struggles that are constantly subject to transformation.[3] Indeed, "struggles for domination take place in multiple arenas in which parts of the state are related not only to one another but each is a single force in a field of interacting, at times conflicting, social forces" (Migdal 2001, 100). As the state is both foundationally gendered and gendering (see Adams 2005; Connell 1990; and Pringle and Watson 1992) it also materializes doubly: as a form of infrastructural power, defined as "the capacity of the state actually to penetrate civil society, and to implement logistically political decisions throughout the realm" (Mann 1986, 113), and as a state effect, and that is, "the processes that make the state appear as an entity" (Krohn-Hansen and Nustad 2005, 14; see also, Mitchell 1991).[4] Attachments serve as relational circuitry that give rise to both enactments and their mutual constitution.

Read through a double vision, as I do in this book, the power of the state to extract and allocate resources, manage populations, and to control "a monopoly on the legitimate use of violence" (Weber 1946, 78) depends in no small part on the leadership and labor of women.[5] This is no less so during times of conflict and crisis, when displaced internal refugees, widespread malnutrition and disease, and high rates of maternal and infant mortality are perceived to threaten the viability of the state order. Seemingly removed from state efforts to tax and patrol, women leaders and citizens have nonetheless always played a key role in the consolidation of state projects and in the exercise of power these projects demand. As the relational underpinnings of the modern state, attachments and the women who often forge them are nothing short of the subject and constitution of statehood.

An approach to family ties as attachments considers two interacting processes: how families are constituted through policy regulations, scientific norms, and broader discourses and ideologies that shape ideas and practice, and how ideas and practice are simultaneously shaped through the enactment of family ties by political actors. By asking how political participants themselves construct notions of family and to what end, and how these constructions are challenged and shift over time in the context of fields, the very concept of the family itself becomes a key site to understand the gendered foundations of state power. Indeed, and as Adams (2005, 37) argues, "Family and gender are perennial and protean building blocks of political authority."

In this book, I define gender as "a set of repeated acts within a highly rigid regulatory frame that congeal over time to produce the appearance of substance, of a natural sort of being" (Butler 1990, 33). Such a definition problematizes the sex/gender distinction, refuses "to separate out 'gender' from the political and cultural intersections in which it is invariably produced and maintained" (3), and seeks to "understand how the category of "women" . . . is produced and restrained by the very structures of power through which emancipation is sought" (2).

Insofar as family ties are enacted through and in opposition to gender, these ties predispose political officials, movement actors, and broader publics to feelings that they may or may not always recognize or understand. Family ties are thus expressions of the circulation of "affect," or feelings, that are opaque to ourselves (Gould 2009, 20). Affect circulates between signifiers in an affective economy mediating the relationship between "the psychic and the social, and between the individual and the collective," in ways that "bind subjects together" (Ahmed 2004, 119).

Political attachments can thus be understood as family ties that congeal through the imperatives that hover just outside of consciousness. But family ties also congeal through the emotional highs and lows that political engagement produces and that become knowable to the self. In contrast with the "bodily, sensory, inarticulate, nonconscious experience" that is affect, an emotion is "one's personal expression of what one is feeling in a given moment, an expression that is structured by social convention, by culture" (Gould 2009, 20).[6] Terror, bereavement, relief, joy, desire, lust, devotion, betrayal, shame, fury, romantic love—all of these expressions, and many more, fuse ideological and personal commitment in time, as the CCP leadership itself recognized and sought to cultivate across many decades of revolutionary conflict.[7] In revolutionary China

(1900–1960), a period in which major economic, political, and social systems were being challenged, disrupted, and reshaped according to contending ideologies, political attachments were thus revolutionary attachments: attachments defined and enacted through an affective and emotional landscape of revolutionary struggle.[8]

An analysis of family ties as political attachments brings more fully into view the complex fabric of family ties that constitute the social movements, political networks, advocacy coalitions, and gendered forms of care work that are key to state formation and state capacity. In so doing, this framework builds on work by social movement scholars who explore how emotions (Hercus 1999; Jasper 1997; Robnett 1997) and culture (Polletta 2008) contour political mobilizations. Participating in movements can produce a sense of self-realization, or "emotional achievement" (Yang 2000, 594), that strongly unites people together (Perry 2002b) and spurs action in high-risk social movements (Goodwin and Pfaff 2001; Robnett 1997). But the mobilization of emotions can also lead to disaffection (Klatch 2004) and serve as a form of emotional suppression and inducement. What Hochschild (1983 [2012]) calls emotional labor, or a compensated public act that is directed by "rules of feeling" monitored by others (Hochschild 1975), can produce forms of social control. This approach thus also builds on the work of sociologists, anthropologists, historians, and political scientists, to explore how emotion management can foster compliance in state formation (Barnes 2018) and how emotion management, affect, and/or social ties can strengthen state power (Deng and O'Brien 2013; Hou 2020; Ong 2022; Read 2012; Yang 2015). In sum, an analysis of attachments can bring more closely into view what Strauss (2020, 4) calls the "hows" of state making: "What are the state's core agendas, how its political and administrative elites frame questions of strategy; how new capacity is generated, and how state-building programs and policies are implemented in practice."

In this book I argue that an extensive network of family ties underpinned the design and implementation of state building in the early PRC. What I call the Chongqing Coalition laid the foundations of major social policy reform in the 1940s, with elite participants, including Christian social gospel reformers, adopting high-profile positions in the new People's Republic of China (PRC) government in 1949. The Chongqing Coalition sought to realize nothing short of a new Chinese family in which father rule was severely diminished and in which mothers and fathers, wives and husbands, and sisters and brothers were mobilized to play equal but different roles in the radical restructuring of Chinese society. This "Marxist maternalist" form of equality made women responsible for "women-work" (*funü gongzuo*), or CCP tasks most commonly associated with women, children, and the family. Characterized by social policy reform focused on mothers and children, social policy delivery through the mother, and a leadership made up of women's policy networks, the world's first full-fledged "maternalist social policy regime" elevated motherhood to the status of a physiological, psychological, and spiritual mission.[9] The establishment of the All China Democratic Women's Federation (Quanguo minzhu funü lianhehui, hereafter ACDWF), or the PRC's mass women's organization, would serve as the hub of this work beginning in 1949.[10]

As the institutional embodiment of maternalism in post-1949 China, the ACDWF made the household more legible to the state through its efforts to reform family relations. This is not only because marriage registration, for example, provided the state with a new, albeit limited, capacity to count persons and households (Diamant 2001a), but also because of the attached enactment of women-work. Over the course of the 1950s, local women leaders managed knowledge of women's lives and the relationships that sustained them to increase the capacity of the state to rapidly improve maternal and infant health and transform rural marital practices.[11] The relational knowledge deployed by local women's heads, or the village leaders made responsible for women-work, however, simultaneously enabled the state to build its military, extract labor and grain, and enforce deprivation. The catastrophes of the late 1950s were thus made possible, in part, by the successes of just a few years earlier.

The catastrophes were also precipitated by Mao Zedong, the chairman of the CCP, and the people most devoted to him. This was true of Cai Chang, the chair of the Women's Federation, and her husband, state planner Li Fuchun, both of whom directly contributed to Mao's consolidation of power in the 1940s and to the development of the Great Leap Forward (GLF) (1958–60), Mao's massive movement to communize the countryside. This was also true of radical provincial leaders who sought to curry favor with the chairman and of the legions of grassroots leaders who did not personally know Mao but acted as if they did. Through the complex enactment of a "Mao Cult," which Leese (2011, 16) defines as a phenomenon of authoritarian political communication, these and other actors simultaneously made possible Mao's utopian dreams of a mobilized countryside and the catastrophes that followed.

My exploration of state power in the early PRC, and the attachments in which it was embedded, draws on more than twenty years of research and writing. As Swartz (2013, 29) argues, constructing a field of struggle requires digesting vast amounts of relevant historical material. To this end, I have conducted and analyzed interviews (2001, 2004, and 2006) in three counties in Henan, and in one county in Jiangsu, exploring the organizational and family dynamics among leaders and villagers within six villages as well as at multiple levels of party and state. All four county names are pseudonyms, as are the names of the individuals who were interviewed for this study (with the exception of Shi Jian, 110). Altogether 163 individuals participated in interviews, including 44 former Women's Federation leaders of whom at least 25 were local women's heads (plus at least two women's heads who later served in other positions).[12] In addition, I have analyzed Women's Federation documents from three county archives, from national archives, and from the internal journal of the Women's Federation, *Funü gongzuo* (Women-Work). Finally, I have collected and analyzed dozens of memoirs, biographies, and speeches of elite women CCP leaders, an archive which I read against canonical explanations of Chinese politics during the 1950s. A fuller discussion of research design and methods can be found both in appendix 3 and in the chapters that follow.

The approach to family ties as attachments that I develop in this book also draws on my critical auto-ethnographic work as a parent scholar activist in contemporary Canada (Manning et al. 2015; Manning 2017). Driven by my parenting experiences, I participated in the launch of social action research with caregivers of transgender children in 2011, was a founding board member of Canada's first nonprofit focused on transgender children and their families in 2013, and publicly advocated for the passage of federal and provincial laws to protect gender identity and gender expression in 2016 and 2017. I also spent 2018 and several months in 2019 running for public office. Throughout the course of this work, I have experienced moments in which my feminism collided with deep-rooted norms governing middle-class motherhood and the challenges of negotiating my parenting, advocacy, and candidacy in the context of complex family dynamics. I have also become increasingly aware of how much my political work, my research and writing on revolutionary China, and my own family history has been shaped by Canadian settler-colonialism and an abundance of professional, class, and racial privilege. Although the politics of midcentury struggles in China and contemporary Canada are distinct, they are nonetheless connected, informing and disrupting the stories I am ultimately able to tell.

If, as I argue, individuals are both shaped by and shape the field of struggle over family ties, the agency of revolutionary participation must be explained rather than assumed. Chapters 1 through 4 focus on crystallizing moments in which new collectivities gave meaning and direction to the transformations being sought. The resulting agentic forms produced through these collective, and at times traumatic, events would, in turn, make possible the state-building struggles discussed in part II.[13] By focusing on the relations, discourses, and practices informing agency (a state of activism) and the familial constellations producing and produced by political parties (the party family), the attached fabric underlying modern state capacity and failure comes into sharper relief.

States of Activism

How do we retain a view of the individual without reducing the individual to either a self-propelling agent or to an abstracted subject of social, economic, and historical forces?[14] This is by no means a new question. Indeed, Mao Zedong and Cai Chang weighed in on this question as they struggled to carve a way forward for China and Chinese women. But the fact that they did so, in part, in relationship with one another suggests that adhering to an analysis that locates agency in an autonomous actor may muddy the waters more than it clears them. It also risks depoliticizing the subject of study. Song (2015a) argues that while the current trend to "make an invisible subject visible" through focusing on individual agency has restored the richness of women's lives to center stage, it has also had the effect of derevolutionizing and depoliticizing Chinese women's history. Studying women's leadership through the lens of a state of activism is one way to recenter the political field in scholarship on gender.

A state of activism is composed of the relations, discourses, and practices that shape the field of struggle. As an expression of political engagement that is enacted intersectionally, or how "intersecting power relations influence social relations" (Collins and Bilge 2020, 2), relationality is key. Emerging through social capital, a state of activism enables a subject to act.[15] Indeed, both discrete and interlocking sources of oppression become thinkable not only through language but through the relations in which those sources of oppression take shape as sites of struggle. A state of activism thus assumes meaning and agency through the sociality that defines it, and through which it seeks to define.

Bourdieu (1986, 248) defines social capital as "the aggregate of the actual or potential resources which are linked to possession of a durable network of more or less institutionalized relationships of mutual acquaintance or recognition." Social movement scholars have long recognized the importance of social ties to social mobilization. Tarrow (2005, 104–5) argues, for example, that "the adoption of new forms of collective action often follows the segmented lines of interpersonal interaction among people who know one another and are parts of networks of trust." More recently, Ward (2016, 859) suggests that social ties "are best conceived of as conduits of processes affecting the likelihood individuals will support a movement, be motivated to participate, and/or actually participate." Following Kennelly (2009, 264, italics in original) I define relational agency as "the contingent and situated intersection between an individual's social position within a *field* of interactions, and the means by which the relationships within that field permit that individual to take actions that might otherwise be inconceivable—or, in other words, permit them to achieve a *habitus shift*." Habitus is like language; according to Bourdieu, it regulates the range of possible practices without actually selecting specific practices"; it is a kind of "improvisation within defined limits" (cited in Steinmetz 2011, 51). Social ties generally, and family ties specifically, open up new possibilities for the improvisational risk that accompanies social movement participation. In fields in which women have been prohibited from social and political spaces, these ties are crucial forms of access. Social ties are not only critical to the recruitment of women into revolutionary processes, however, but also a medium through which new forms of ideological commitment can take shape and unfold.[16]

A state of activism provides a legible analysis of the ills of society and a route for solving them: it materializes as a shared blueprint for social change. This blueprint may include an explicit political ideology, defined as "a coherent body of values, assumptions, principles and arguments which contains a view about the way in which historical development takes place, and includes both an assessment of the deficiencies of the past (and possibly the present) plus some guidance about what needs to be done in order to reach a more desirable state of affairs" (Gill 2011, 2). How ideology is understood and practiced, however, may change over time. One of the attractions of communist ideology for early adherents in China was its highly developed critique of the accumulation of global economic capital. While many of the founding members of the CCP, including Mao Zedong and Cai Chang, were educated elites, many later generations of the CCP were often illiterate or semiliterate, impoverished villagers. After the foundation of the PRC, the class and revolutionary background of one's parents, or even grandparents, increasingly became a measure of family pedigree. The advantages of economic and cultural capital, the latter of which Bourdieu (1980, 125) links to the appearance of an educational system, were thus inverted according to an ideological yardstick that in turn became the subject of revolutionary struggle.[17] In this instance, as in many others, the meaning of social capital as connected to economic capital, was field specific, and subject to transformation.

In addition to an explicit ideological program, a state of activism may also include less cohesive ideas and programs about how society should look and the paths necessary to get there. Scientific discourses, sociological theories, and nationalist narratives also inform the blueprints in the hands of activists. Stories also play a key role in sustaining or strengthening movement commitment (Polletta 1998, 430) and in linking problems and solutions to policymaking (Wong 2004, 20). Whether grounded in an explicit ideology or a looser set of norms and ideas, ontological blueprints connect adherents to the past, through founding stories of a movement, a party, and/or a nation, while simultaneously linking them to a possible future, or what Gould (2009, 119) calls the "horizon of political possibilities and imaginable futures."

Finally, blueprints provide guidance about how people should act, including specific protocols for actualizing agency. Emerging as they do through the circulation of affect, protocols may look profoundly different, depending on the field in which they are being enacted. Protocols may include individualized acts of agency, such as studying at school, cutting one's hair, taking a lover, and assuming a profession. But other "modes of being, responsibility, and effectivity" (Mahmood 2005, 14–15) may not look like individual agency at all. Maoist protocols designed to generate collective agency, for example, contained implicit and explicit critiques of the agency of the individual subject. Whether or not an activist was an impoverished rural laborer themselves, they could assume the standpoint of the poor peasant through engaging in repetitive practices of hard labor, self-criticism, and if literate, reading and rereading Mao's most important essays. As Reddy (2009, 312) argues, "Repetition of daily rituals and interactions in uniform spaces enhances the salience and self-evidence of crucial relationships, principles, and personal standards." In Mao's dynamic theory of the self, "right action" and "right thinking" are intimately interlinked.[18] An engaged, repetitive practice is not only a powerful representation of participation in a particular ethical order, therefore, but a process through which agency actually unfolds.[19]

In sum, a state of activism materializes through relationship(s) and in the form of desire to transform a social and/or political milieu: it is a temporal approach to social transformation that identifies a "problem" with a solution for its rectification that may or may not take shape through a highly articulated ideological program. Relational agency, or the interpersonal relationships that often constitute activism (Kennelly 2009), is by its definition dynamic: social, cultural, and economic capital, affective attachments, ideological practice, and political and religious rituals can, and often do, mediate how people see themselves and their role in struggle. But a state of activism is not always comprehensible. Indeed, insofar as a state of activism materializes through the circulation of affect, it produces imperatives that may remain obscure or hidden to even the most critical of revolutionaries.

In this book, I explore four primary states of activism that informed midcentury state formation: the New Woman, the Social Reformer, the Woman Warrior, and the Loyal Soldier. Neither discrete nor fixed, these states of activism overlapped, intersected, and were subject to mutual transformation. By limiting my discussion to four states of activism, however, I do not mean to suggest that this exploration is in any way exhaustive. The extraordinary regional, cultural, linguistic, institutional, and religious diversity that was revolutionary China informed the churn and whirl of state formation during the period under study. It is simply that these four states of activism appeared most frequently in the narratives of the grassroots leaders I interviewed and in the work of the elite leaders whom I have sought to understand. And what was important to these actors—how their revolutionary desire was ignited, expressed, and at times thwarted—is, in turn, key to understanding how they constituted and interfaced with state power during the 1940s and 1950s.

States of Activism in Revolutionary China

What was a liberated woman? What work should she carry out? And how should she undertake that work in relation to her family and the state? At the heart of these questions beat conflicting ideas about and critiques of patriarchy that had first emerged in early twentieth-century China and would continue to influence the development of political leadership and state policy up to, during, and long after the GLF.

In the late 1910s and early 1920s, many of the founders of the CCP viewed the patriarchal family structure, and its oppression of women, as an impediment to China's capacity to modernize (Wang 1999). Specifically, young communist adherents sharply criticized the Confucian ethical order of filial piety, which imperial and bureaucratic elites had carefully studied and worked to reproduce. In the eyes of young intellectuals, "father rule," or what Bourdieu (1977) would recognize as a form of official kinship, prevented women and youth from asserting their independent personhood (*duli renge*). This was certainly the case for Mao Zedong, who from a young age viewed himself in an antagonistic relationship with his own father (Snow 1938 [1978], 115–16).[20] In 1919, Mao Zedong publicly attacked the dominance of parental authority over the "free will" of youth when he penned several essays on the suicide of a young girl determined to evade an arranged marriage (Witke 1967).[21] One of many critiques of the patriarchal family published at that time, Mao Zedong's essay captured the ethos of the emerging May Fourth Movement (1916–27), which gave rise to ardent feminist critiques.[22] Ten years later, Mao (1927 [1959]) would write an even stronger critique of women's subjection to the authority of the husband as informed by his own developing application of Marxism to Chinese society.

It was during this flurry of new ideas, relationships, and possibilities that the New Woman state of activism first emerged. At this moment, agency was assumed to take shape external to the patriarchal family, and as a condition that was propelled forward and expressed by individual will, educational achievement, and professional contributions. Intense friendship and romantic love also defined this activism, as did a growing conviction that women should advocate for their rights and freedoms *as* women. The New Woman state of activism is most akin to a liberal feminist state of activism.

The antipatriarchal account that pervaded so much of the published work of intellectuals and activists during the May Fourth Movement would continue to inform the work of senior CCP leaders and bureaucrats after the foundation of the PRC in 1949. Drawing on the concept of "state feminism" that originated in studies of the institutionalization of feminism in state agencies in the West during the latter half of the twentieth century (see, for example, Stetson and Mazur 1995), Wang (2017, 8) argues that China's socialist state feminists "fought on multiple fronts—in their *formal* capacities as Communist Party members and state officials—toward an egalitarian vision of a socialist modern China premised on equality between men and women" (italics in original). Indeed, and as in the case of Australian feminist bureaucrats, or femocrats (Eisenstein 1996), PRC "inside agitators" (Wang 2017) would play key roles in the policymaking process.[23]

But the New Woman was not the only state of activism guiding the work of Women's Federation officials and bureaucrats. Overlapping and intersecting with the rise of the New Woman was the rise of the Social Reformer: a maternalist state of activism that prioritized the health and welfare of mothers and their children in the context of national crisis and recovery, state building, and international bridge building.

During the early twentieth century, maternalist ideologies "exalted women's capacity to mother and extended to society as a whole the values of care, nurturance, and morality" (Koven and Michel 1990, 1079).[24] Although political actors in revolutionary China did not use the term *maternalism*, organizations recognized today as maternalist dominated the social policy landscape prior to the establishment of the PRC. As argued by Hubbard (2018, 254), "Maternalism arose across the political spectrum in response to integrated political, social, and conceptual crises as both a theory for grounding woman and a praxis for redressing inequities." In its more conservative variants, maternalism sought to infuse private life with a woman's spiritual and psychological insights and therein rectify the moral weaknesses of the men entrusted to lead the nation. In its more progressive variants, maternalism sought to transform the welfare of mothers and their children by empowering women to serve as public officials themselves. In revolutionary China, many professional urbanites embraced the latter iteration. Indeed, the social policy innovations undertaken by the early PRC not only focused on mothers and their children, as did many reform efforts underway in other parts of the world at that time, but also went one step further by giving elite and local women leaders a mandate to achieve social transformation.

Maternalism also produced a specific emotional pedagogy or what Gould (2009, 34) defines as a "template for what and how to feel, in part by conferring on some feelings and modes of expression an axiomatic, natural quality and making other feeling states unintelligible within its terms and thus in a sense unfeelable and inexpressible." By representing and (unevenly) embodying the "hearts of loving mothers," as ACDWF chair Cai Chang called for in the quote that begins this chapter, elite women leaders brought a particular affective purpose to their mission of socialist transformation.[25] It is to this end that one of the world's first experiments in state feminism was enacted not only by women advocating as women per se, but also by women advocating as "mothers," "elder sisters," and at times, as "filial sons." By their very nature, maternalist and other emergent emotional pedagogies called women into the liberated socialist future through reworked expressions of filial piety, obligation, and mutual care, rather than through their elimination.

The maternalist commitments of commune leader Bao Qinglian, whose comments on women-work also open this introduction, were produced through a maternalist affective economy that first took shape well before Bao herself emerged as a local leader. But militant states of activism informed Bao's agency as well, giving rise, for example, to her leading a youth corps to Qinghai Province at the height of the GLF. Bao not only enacted the maternalist agency of the Social Reformer, therefore, but also that of the Woman Warrior, a filial state of activism made manifest through Maoist practices of nation building.

In revolutionary China, the Woman Warrior embodied an individuated state of activism that took expression, in part, through an emergent filial nationalism, a form of nationalism that Fong (2004, 632) characterizes as China deserving "the filial devotion of her children." Inspired by dynastic legends and revolutionary stories of women soldiers who left their families to take on the social responsibilities of men, national daughters could participate in a heroic ideal while keeping large parts of the prevailing gender order intact. Maoist thought would also come to inform this state of activism: over time, Woman-Warrior agency in revolutionary China was enacted through the Maoist concept of subjective initiative (*zhu guan nengdongxing*) in which an activist overcomes objective conditions through sheer force of will. Young activists who embodied this model were not necessarily interested in maternalist reform; indeed, some sought to eschew women-work altogether. However, idealized conceptions of the self as hero/heroine enabled some to challenge authority in order to protect vulnerable women and children who were, by definition, *not* revolutionary subjects.

The Loyal Soldier, by way of contrast, became a collective participant in revolutionary transformation through sublimating their individuality within violent class struggle. Male kin played an outsize role in the emergence and enactment of the Loyal Soldier. A familial attachment to Mao-as-leader, whether "real" or exegetical, was especially important in the embodiment and practice of the Loyal Soldier: Mao gave the orders, Loyal Soldiers executed them. For leaders whose activism was largely animated by this state of activism, the challenge was to discern Mao's true intentions through a dedicated study of his works, and through an ongoing commitment to mass struggle. It is this state of activism that would most profoundly inform Cai Chang's leadership.

Although Cai Chang attended all-girls schools, was raised by a feminist mother, and interacted with a large network of women activists, Cai did not embrace the feminism of the New Woman nor the maternalism of Social Reformer with the same sense of vision and urgency as did some of her comrades. Instead, time and again, Cai Chang materialized as the ultimate Loyal Soldier: attacking comrades and critiquing feminist advocacy in her effort to support Mao Zedong. Indeed, Cai Chang's revolutionary desire was largely mediated through her devotion to Chairman Mao, the closest friend of her martyred elder brother. Under Cai Chang, the marching orders for women-work were clear: lead production, promote family harmony, and institute household austerity. As I will show, however, not all those at the grassroots, also deeply loyal to Mao, would agree.

In sum, the official kinship of the early PRC reflected numerous emotional pedagogies, including a Maoist utopianism that centered the revolutionary sacrifice of family ties altogether. Although all of these enactments upended notions of father rule, none negated the family's role in producing gender relations. As Barlow (2004, 58–59) argues, "The Maoist interpretation of state and family made the body of women a field of the state, at the same time that it opened the state to inflection by kin categories." The revolutionary constitution of woman (*funü*), her work, and her relationship to her family was thus iterated differently, and with complex outcomes, in state-building projects of maternalist reform and Maoist mobilization.

Wilkinson (1999, 594) argues that in the early twentieth-century United States, "the maternalist episode offers a chance to move questions about agency inside the historical narrative, to ask how conventional notions about who might qualify as the agents (or the victims) of historical change themselves helped to shape the emergence of a political movement." By closely examining the role that different states of activism played in revolutionary China, new perspectives on patriarchy similarly come to light. Was the early PRC a "democratic patriarchy," as Stacey (1983) argues?[26] Not if one defines patriarchy as father rule, or even if one defines it as a modern form of fraternal rule (Pateman 1988; 1989). Although revolutionary practices continued to be shaped by the past, they were also subject to transformation through the revolutionary habitus, or the embodied and commonsense form of knowledge that coheres through iterative practice.[27] This is not to say that families were not hierarchically gendered, for they were, but that the emergence of the identity "women" as a modern sociological category (Riley 1988) profoundly shaped the political. In China, different strands of maternalism disrupted older forms of patrimonial and patriarchal power in no small part by "exalting women's capacity to mother" (Koven and Michel 1990, 1079) and by making women leaders responsible for projects of social reform and women's liberation. The coconstitutive and often conflictual rise of maternalist and revolutionary states of activism and the Chinese party family thus marked a sharp departure from earlier enactments of patrimonial and patriarchal rule, long thought to be at the heart of familial politics in China.

Kinship Ties in Movement

Studies of the family in politics have long been dominated by Max Weber's conceptualization of patrimonial and neopatrimonial power. Weber (1946, 297) defines patrimonial authority as deriving from the capacity of a ruler to confer privileges to individuals beyond those of his immediate kin and receive the loyalty of those individuals in turn. Patrimonialism is thus expressed through "predatory friendship," or personal networks made up of a wide retinue of patrons and clients, servants, and friends (Searle 1988).[28] Neopatrimonialism, in turn, is typically understood to "denote systems in which political relationships are mediated through, and maintained by, personal connections between leaders and subjects, or patrons and clients" (Pitcher, Moran, and Johnston 2009, 129–30).[29]

The neopatrimonial literature suggests that clientelist ties undermine ideological transformation and impede state-building projects. Defined as personal, dyadic relationships between individuals, clientelist ties are often conceptualized as a relationship between a patron and client, that can be face-to-face or brokered as part of a larger network of relationships (Hicken 2011, 291). Studies that explain the political behavior of grassroots and elite actors in Maoist China through clientelist (Nathan 1973; Oi 1989; Walder 1986; Zweig 1989) and neopatrimonial approaches (Lü 2000) argue that party and state institutional structures created incentives for actors to make use of highly personalistic forms of interaction, including familial ties. At the elite level of the CCP, vertically organized patron-client networks conspired for power as factions (Huang 2000; Nathan 1973).[30] At the grassroots, paternalistic expressions of power compelled compliance (Oi 1989; Walder 1986). Both expressions, in turn, weakened bureaucratic development, state capacity, and ideological transformation throughout the Maoist period, and especially during the GLF.

This book takes seriously these arguments, while simultaneously flipping them inside out. During the Maoist era generally, and the GLF specifically, clientelist and factional struggle played a decisive role in shaping the field of struggle. Factional struggle not only materialized as a means of political engagement, however, but also as a discourse about what was politically permissible. The CCP's doctrinal rule forbidding "factional struggle" (*paibie douzheng*) (Smith 2021) shaped CCP families and the form of political power that they could assume. Thus while members of the CCP were expected to establish long-lasting marital unions that supported the work of the new regime, participants in those unions carefully managed their representation so as not to "appear" as a faction. It is in this way that factions materialized as a "category of practice" (Brubaker and Cooper 2000) in which "ideology and dynamic processes of generating collective meaning" were paramount (Luo 2021, 3).[31] It is in this way, also, that CCP party families have been largely overlooked as an important arena in China's revolutionary struggle and state formation. Indeed, generations of scholars, working inside and outside of the PRC, have accepted the CCP's own discourse that as far as women were concerned, their absence at the highest level of the formal party structure precluded their involvement in the defining conflicts of the 1950s.[32] An examination of political families as party families, however, suggests a very different dynamic altogether.

The party family is a gendered site of kinship-based belonging, obligation, and conflict that is enacted in two distinct but intersecting ways.[33] First, the party family is a political network composed of family ties that give rise to, animate, and are embedded in party organizations and the wider field of political struggle. Following social network analysis, I define networks as linked nodes, in which "nodes typically refer to persons or organizations or states, while links represent some form of connection or flow between the nodes" (Ward, Stovel, and Sacks 2011, 246). Second, the party family manifests as a symbolic expression of a political party itself, in which individuals belong to a political family via party membership or close association. Both enactments are made possible by a complex interaction of codified and non-codified structures, or formal and informal institutions. In this book, I define institutions as "internal to sentient agents, serving both as structures (of thinking and acting) that constrain action and as constructs (of thinking and acting) created and changed by those actors" (Schmidt 2010, 14).[34]

Whereas most political studies of families primarily focus on dynastic succession, that is, how families transmit power across generations, this book seeks to widen the view by illuminating a multiplicity of kinship relations.[35] Constituted, in part, through conflict over gender, the party family materializes as a modern enactment deeply riven by the social changes to which it is simultaneously subject and which it seeks to transform.[36] The party family has thus emerged as a complex site of social and political transformation in often surprising ways. In the context of a revolutionary party, the transformative nature of contention is especially acute. As Tetreault (1992, 109) argues, when the family is "the locus of the socialization that produces cosmological beliefs and economic and political structures—and then becomes *part* of all of them—revolutionary transformation necessarily affects family life and women's roles as well as politics and the economy as a whole."

The party family is an expression of practical kinship, or the practices that often resonate with the official ethical order but nonetheless have their own sensibility (Bourdieu 1977, 33–43). Building further on Yan (2001, 226), who defines practical kinship as "flexible interpersonal relations negotiated by individual agents in response to social changes," I argue that the party family is historically specific and field enacted. The party family is also produced through regulatory regimes. As policy language, concepts, and categories shape ideas of how family should be, with time, the origins of policy can disappear from view, masking the historical struggles that established particular relations as normal, taken-for-granted practices.[37]

In revolutionary China, party family ties not only included ties among mothers, fathers, siblings, children, marital partners, and in-laws, and the relations of obligation that bound them together, but also relations of kinship constructed through struggle: revolutionary brothers, sworn sisters, the CCP as family, and the Women's Federation as *niangjia*, or "Mum's home." When party officials and activists make reference to and publicly practice family ties in relation to the policies and programs they are advocating, they also shape the field of struggle.[38] As Merkel-Hess (2016, 434) argues, the family lives of political figures can become part of a "unifying political story" also active in "courting and shaping public opinion." Indeed, the symbolic self-representation of family ties by movement actors and policy officials can be as important a locus of analysis as is the language and categories of the policies themselves: it is a means of further understanding the ways "in which the state mobilizes its citizens to demonstrate and embody its power" (Wedeen 1999, 19).[39] Party family ties have thus materialized as an important instantiation of what Ding (2022, 7) calls "performative governance" or "the state's deployment of visual, verbal, and gestural symbols of good governance for the audience of its citizens."[40]

Party families first materialized in China when the Guomindang (GMD) was established in the late nineteenth century. By the time the CCP was founded in 1921, CCP party families were already in formation; indeed, couples and siblings sought to join and build the young party together. In both parties, family ties took shape through and provided important access to *guanxi*, or "connections" (Gold, Guthrie, and Wank 2002, 3), that emerged as a consequence of shared native place and ethnicity or on the basis of common experiences, such as attending the same school, serving in the same military unit, or working in the same organization (Dittmer 1995, 12). Iterated practices in which relationships are "consciously produced, cultivated, and maintained over time" (Gold, Guthrie, and Wank 2002,

6), guanxi ties are based on an expectation of mutual reciprocity and obligation and often involve specific rituals based on the exchange of gifts.[41] In China, *renqing*, or the "system of ethics that guides and regulates one's behavior when dealing with others within one's guanxi network" (Yan 1996, 145), has been characterized by Yang (1994, 317) as a "feminine" relational ethics or "feminine" art (320), even as the political networks themselves were seemingly dominated by men.

For much of the twentieth century and into the present day, guanxi ties are frequently cultivated and exchanged in the context of male clientelist networks, or what Bjarnegärd (2013) describes as a form of homosocial capital. As Bjarnegärd (2013, 24) writes is the case elsewhere in Asia, Chinese expressions of homosocial capital are "predominantly accessible for other men as well as more valuable when built between men," relegating women to the margins of political power. In many contexts inside and outside China, moral codes regulating male-female interaction have made the establishment of relationships with non-kin relatives difficult for women activists and leaders.[42] Family ties have thus served as a key form of social capital that was necessary to realize access to mixed networks necessary for political success (see also Bjarnegärd 2013, 28). In the words of Stephan (2010, 538), women activists can "gain social capital from being able to show the full approval of their families and husbands."

As the original social network, the party family has offered a preexisting basis of solidarity in the context of uncertainty, rapid change, and danger. Similar to friendship ties, kinship ties are crucial in the formation and preservation of what Sageman (2004, 107–13, 139), writing about another context, calls a "small-world" network structure.[43] Although women's party activism is realized in the context of newsrooms, street demonstrations, classrooms, churches, and temples, it is also realized in the home: in the parlor and on the porch, in the kitchen and on the *kang*, the heated stone bed that served as the center of household interaction in central and northern rural China.

Several decades of comparative research shows that family ties have played a key role in the recruitment of urban and rural women into revolutionary activism and guerrilla warfare.[44] In Russia, some 37 percent of women Bolsheviks (or Bolshevichki) were introduced to revolutionary ideas by relatives who were already revolutionaries themselves (Clements 1997, 37). In El Salvador, preexisting family ties served as a basis of activism (Viterna 2013), with Kampwirth (2002, 62), finding that "family traditions of resistance," were especially influential: some 66 percent of her interviewees "mentioned the influence of relatives—parents, aunts, and uncles, grandparents, siblings—in the development of their political values or in the decision to join the revolutionary coalition." In the Huk rebellion in the Philippines, most women revolutionaries "acknowledged both the influence of kinship and friendship and their own principled motivations to explain why they joined" (Lanzona 2009, 69). And amongst the Liberation

Tigers of Tamil Eelam, Alison (2003) discusses women motivated to join the movement following the death of a brother or father who were already engaged in the struggle.

In the global history of social movement struggle, male leaders have repeatedly relied on wives or female relatives to undertake work they themselves would not or could not do. The "would not do" included both the management of domestic tasks and party housekeeping or managing the day-to-day business of a growing movement organization (Lanzona 2009, 69–70). The "could not do" included women bypassing norms of propriety that prevented men from recruiting women strangers directly, facilitating negotiations and brokering deals between otherwise estranged parties, and holding secrets. Indeed, because women are often perceived as nonviolent, they can assume strategic tasks with less risk of capture than their male counterparts.[45] To this end, male-dominated party organizations have often viewed women as a resource to develop political networks, with behind-the-scenes gift exchanges and social visits binding families together.

Within the CCP, interpersonal relationship management became essential to recruitment and to the ongoing process of political socialization and commitment. In an era of high-risk organizing when capture by the enemy meant certain death simply for being married to a senior organizer, one's fate necessarily hung in the balance with that of one's lover or spouse. At the same time, being tossed aside by one's spouse for a younger woman could mean a different kind of death: the rapid descent to political obscurity (Jin 1999, 141).

But just as male-dominated party organizations have made use of the emotional and physical labor of women members in ways that maintain more traditional forms of gender relations, they have also worked to challenge and upend male dominance inside and outside of China. Various expressions of "family feminism" (Fernea 2003; Stephan 2010), for example, have emerged globally in different times and places, with party families campaigning for expanded rights for women and serving as living symbols of women's emancipation.

Insofar as women leaders were made a central part of the Chinese revolutionary project, communist kinship profoundly transformed the practices that led to and maintained family ties within and outside of the CCP.[46] In the first three decades after the founding of the CCP, parent-child ties, sibling ties, and heterosexual-presenting couples played an important role in the emergence of the Chinese Communist Party and in the enactment of revolutionary state formation. Indeed, in early and midcentury China, the party family facilitated revolutionary recruitment and consolidation, intraparty diplomacy, and policy making, simultaneously embodying and instrumentalizing competing expressions of the revolutionary project.

Parent-Child Ties

The idea that young people should be devoted to their parents, including through the performance of ritual after a parent's death, played an important role in revolutionary China. In the words of Confucius, to be filial (*xiao*) was "to serve parents according to the rites when they are alive, bury them according to the rites when they die, and sacrifice to them according to the rites thereafter" (Kutcher 1999 [2009], 1). This perspective persisted. Just as Qing Dynasty officials performed rituals of devotion to their parents as a form of loyalty to the ruler (Kutcher 1999 [2009], 1), CCP officials expressed their devotion to communist martyrs and the mothers of communist martyrs through acts of ritual remembrance and other forms of filial sacrifice. At the same time, revolutionary enactments at the grassroots enacted an older form of practical kinship: mothers supporting daughters and women activists taking care of their parents as substitute sons.[47] In this context and so many others, revolutionary state building rearticulated new relations of familial obligation that felt both familiar and revolutionary all at once.

In the context of revolutionary China, mothers, and at times mothers-in-law, played a profound role in encouraging and supporting the political work of their daughters. Despite the enduring understanding that daughters were largely viewed as "other people's children" (or as belonging to their future husband's family), the closeness of the mother-daughter bond has a significant history. Indeed, Chinese daughters and mothers have persistently woven intricate patterns of mutual attachment and support.[48] It is thus not surprising that close mother-daughter ties featured prominently among the first generation of women CCP leaders and in the experiences of the rural women who feature in this study. Cai Chang attributes the fact that six members of her family became revolutionaries in no small part to the "influence of our wonderful mother," Ge Jianhao (Snow 1967, 243). A highly literate descendent of Zeng Guofan, a powerful Qing dynasty official who helped to defeat the nineteenth-century Taiping Rebellion, Ge Jianhao overcame the family's deteriorating financial situation by selling off valuables and by teaching school. She also committed to deepening her own political education by participating in the New People's Study Society founded by her son, Cai Hesen, and Mao Zedong. Inspired by the call of the May Fourth Movement, Ge Jianhao, Cai Chang, Cai Hesen, and Xiang Jingyu, Cai Hesen's wife, collectively traveled to France in late 1919 where they resided for the next four years as part of a work-study program. After their return to China, both Cai Chang and Cai Hesen relied on their mother to care for their children at key points of their political careers. Ge provided other forms of auxiliary support to the CCP as well, including making her girls' school the secret center of the

Communist Party in Changsha during the tumultuous years of the mid-1920s (Wiles 2003b).

The mother of Zheng Xiuwen, 163, a grassroots leader from Henan, was similarly "very enthusiastic" about supporting her daughter's work, staying with Zheng until the children were grown and married. They were very close (*you ganqing*): "Without my mother's support I couldn't have done my work." In fact, Zheng felt so indebted to her mother that she purchased a plaque that cost a thousand yuan "the day after she died," a filial act normally undertaken by sons or other powerful male relatives. The mother of grassroots leader Bao Qinglian, 160, not only helped her flee famine, but also aided her to escape from her prospective in-laws after she had been sold to them as a child bride.[49] When Bao became a women's head, her mother supported her work, cared for her children, and "never complained." Indeed, when other people gossiped about her work, her mother told her: "We are walking the upright road, don't worry about what people say." In the quote that begins this chapter, Bao's heartfelt expression of *ganqing* (abiding love/affection) seals the tie of mother and daughter in the process of state formation: the bond of "blood, unconditional support, and ultimate shelter" (Zhang 1996, 197) provided by Bao's niangjia, that is, her mother/Women's Federation/party.

Although fathers played a less prominent role than mothers in the emergence of the first generation of women CCP members, the phenomenon of fathers encouraging daughters to become politically active began to feature more prominently as the CCP shifted its base to the countryside. Indeed, the CCP sought to build its base by recruiting the family members of those already active in the Peasant's Union (Cai 1947 [1988], 130); as I will show, a minority of fathers and brothers not only recruited female relatives into the Peasant's Union, but also into the Youth League. At the same time, fathers who were not necessarily politically active themselves supported their daughters to attend school and assume positions of leadership in the new political order. The fathers of two activist cousins, Zhang Sumei, 20, and Hou Qiuyi, 132, who resided in contiguous villages in Henan during the earliest days of the People's Republic, for example, both encouraged their daughters' activism, including by taking up tasks their daughters might have otherwise assumed in the household.

Sibling Ties

Similar to mother-daughter ties, sibling ties have often been overlooked in fields in which official forms of patriarchal kinship prevail.[50] And yet, fraternal, sororal, and cross-gender sibling ties all played foundational roles in the constitution of the early Chinese Communist Party. The sibling relationship cultivated between Mao Zedong and Cai Chang can be first traced back to the brotherly friendship connecting Cai Hesen, Cai Chang's elder brother, and Mao Zedong (Cai 1992a). Both men played pivotal roles in Cai Chang's political formation and in her ongoing political commitments. Mao Zedong, in turn, relied upon Cai Chang for political support at key periods during his tenure as Chairman. This was not an anomaly, nor specific to the earliest years of the CCP. Zhang's (2014) research shows that in the 1950s, cross-gender sibling ties facilitated social mobility. My own research suggests a similar pattern, with elder brothers facilitating the entrance of younger sisters into CCP organizational life. Grassroots Jiangsu leader Fan Junxia, 83, for example, was strongly encouraged in her political work by her father and brother—both active village leaders. At the "advanced" age of twenty-nine, she chose to marry someone from within her own village—a decision that abrogated expectations of age and postnuptial residency. Similarly, the elder brother of grassroots Henan leader Ni Changqing, 161, himself a CCP member, encouraged Ni to quit school and participate in political work; he also defended Ni when she found herself the subject of familial ridicule and criticism. Ni, in turn, paved the way for her younger sisters, five (out of seven) of whom also became members of the CCP.

Significantly, and as was the case for Cai Chang and Mao Zedong, party family ties consolidated through enactments of symbolic siblinghood, or what Baker (1979) calls "non-kin as kin." Indeed, the idea that the CCP was itself a kind of "revolutionary family" was deeply ingrained in the parlance of the leadership. Of particular import to the construction of the CCP's revolutionary family was the usage of symbolic sororal ties, practices that have developed and maintained female intimacy beyond the natal and martial home. To name just one example, rural women workers formed sisterhood associations (*jiemei hui*), a form of mutual self-help based on native place ties, over the course of the 1920s, 1930s, and 1940s. By establishing night schools for sisterhoods, the Young Women's Christian Association (YWCA), and later the CCP, sought to shape the sisterhoods into a political identity (Honig 1986). Leaders of the Women's Federation would address members on sororal terms as well.

Symbolic cross-sex sibling ties also linked many party members into a web of kinship-based belonging. When Li Fuchun first met Cai Chang in France, for example, he addressed the woman who would later become his wife as "*dajie*" (elder sister), a title that became so ubiquitous within the CCP that it became another personal name for her (Huang 2004, 59). Whereas Cai Chang and Li Fuchun addressed Zhou Enlai as "premier," Zhou Enlai referred to the couple as "Elder Sister Cai" and "Elder Brother Fuchun." When Cai Chang met with Deng Yingchao in person, Cai referred to Deng as "little Chao," but in formal events she referred to Deng Yingchao as "Elder Sister Little Chao."[51] Wang Zheng argues that the usage of sororal terms avoided the pitfalls of labeling elite women CCP members the classed and dependent status of "wife" (*furen* or *taitai*), a subject position that elite women officials themselves rejected, while simultaneously acknowledging the senior rank of the women based on their lengthy revolutionary experience.[52] The practice of CCP male officials referring to one another as brothers, however, was much less common, perhaps to avoid the negative connotation of factionalism.[53]

Couple Ties

The activism of heterosexual-presenting couples within the CCP would also contribute to state-building before and after the foundation of the PRC, bridging the often otherwise gender-segregated operation of CCP power.[54] Gendered hierarchies were established within the CCP shortly after the party was founded. Indeed, marriage was not really a choice but rather an imperative, and for women it was "an unwritten requirement for advancement" (Gilmartin 1995, 108). But exceptions abounded. To paraphrase a response to Butler (2002) writing about a different context, kinship was not always already heterosexual. Relationships that might now be called queer also informed the field of struggle, including women CCP members who flouted strong prohibitions against same-sex relations (Diamant 2000, 193).[55] The fact that I did not come across examples of same-sex ties in my research likely says more about the limitations of the questions I asked, and did not ask, and what I as a researcher was able to perceive.[56]

In the earliest years of the CCP, an ethos of "sacred love," or the union of soul and body in "sacred love and marriage" (Pan 2015, 154; Sakamoto 2004, 351), prevailed. And yet, in party organizing, romantic unions rapidly became subject to a gendered division of labor in which women were made responsible for mobilizing other women, conducting party housekeeping, and at times, helping their husbands manage their own organizational files. The relationships themselves were often transitory and conflict ridden.[57] Xiang Jingyu and Cai Hesen, for example, were estranged at the time of their murder in the late 1920s, a development overlooked in the many hagiographic accounts of the CCP's first "model couple." Mao Zedong's marital and extramarital relations were similarly complicated. Mao's first "party wife," Yang Kaihui, was primarily preoccupied with raising the couple's three children during the 1920s.[58] Because of her association with Mao, however, she was executed after her capture by the GMD in 1930. In the meantime, Mao had already begun a relationship with the woman who would become his second party wife, He Zizhen. Assigned to be Mao's secretary when

FAMILY TIES AS POLITICAL ATTACHMENTS

she was only eighteen, He Zizhen endured tremendous hardship while the CCP was under relentless attack by the GMD in the 1930s, only to be divorced by Mao a few years later so that he could marry Jiang Qing, a young member of the CCP and former actress with whom he became infatuated in Yan'an.[59]

Organizations based on intimate networks, informality, and consensual decision making are not well suited "to take full advantage of a revolutionary crisis" (Goodwin and Pfaff 2001, 288), as senior CCP officials were discovering in the 1920s and 1930s.[60] Indeed, the hold of previous marital commitments, the fairly common practice of adultery, and the threat of political capture (in which one's spouse might betray the party and their beloved) created significant tensions within the early CCP.[61] By the time Mao married Jiang Qing, a new set of uncodified rules was guiding intimate party relationships within the CCP structure. In the late 1930s, CCP officials sought to place the needs of the organization before any romantic ideals or prior attachments of the participants themselves. These emerging practices included undertaking formal marriage proceedings with a fellow member of the CCP, rendering both men and women to the CCP's oversight when it came to love and marriage. According to Jin (1999, 140), "all marriages required party approval, and the party intervened whenever it concluded that a comrade's sex life would 'affect' his political career." In particular, the CCP leadership sought to consolidate itself as an organization by marrying its most active members and supporters to one another. Even the most senior party leaders were subject to the organization's active interventions, which included introducing and pressuring cadres to marry other prospective partners.

In this book, I focus on three forms of couples' activism in the 1940s and 1950s: clientelist, widowhood, and companionate. The clientelist relationship is the most scrutinized form of couples' activism discernable at the elite level of the CCP. When a wife's own illegitimate political status requires her to "borrow" a network from her husband who acts as her sponsor, the senior male official becomes patron to his wife (Bjarnegård 2013, 28). In the context of revolutionary China, some politically active wives served as a political secretaries (*mishu*) (Jin 1999, 149; Li and Pye 1992) to their husbands. In this "factional" activity, wives played key roles as part of their husbands informal network.[62] According to CCP lore, in the late 1930s senior party officials forbade Jiang Qing to participate in party politics because they deemed her an unsuitable candidate for Mao—a decision that would come back to haunt them during the onslaught of the Cultural Revolution, thirty years later.[63] But the factional politics that fueled the rise of Jiang Qing, as well as of other party families during the turbulent 1960s, has obscured the political role that widows and companionate couples played in Chinese state formation during the 1940s and 1950s.

In revolutionary China, the deployment of "widowhood" enacted another form of couples' activism. Widows and adult children of martyrs are particularly conspicuous as flag-bearers of parties in the postcolonial world. Not a few politicians have ascended to power in the wake of the death of a prominent relative in the party, including Violeta Chamorro, Benazir Bhutto, Indira Gandhi, Sonia Gandhi, and Aung San Suu Kyi.[64] Ramphele (1996) argues that the "the political widow embodies a desired social memory about the fallen hero and the nobility of the commitment he made to the struggle. A widow must demonstrate a worthiness to personify that social memory for the benefit of society."[65] In revolutionary China, Song Qingling, He Xiangning, and Li Dequan drew on the power latent in their dead husbands' legacies to advocate for maternalist policy change. As widow of Sun Yat-sen, the GMD leader and "father" of modern China, for example, Song Qingling would repeatedly broker deals between the warring GMD and CCP. As the widow of Feng Yuxiang, the "Christian Warlord," Health Minister Li Dequan would similarly mobilize her symbolic stature and dense network of family and personal ties to champion midwifery reform in the early 1950s.[66]

Political widowhood was closely related to a third form of couples' activism: the companionate marriage. Established on the basis of separate official portfolios, the companionate marriage maintained the importance of a woman official's bureaucratic and political autonomy even as spouses coordinated their work across their offices. In the early 1950s, for example, Deng Yingchao held the position of vice chair of the ACDWF, while her husband served as premier (among many other official positions both would hold). As senior officials, each of these leaders commanded separate offices with large staffs that they coordinated in order to achieve particular policy goals. The couple frequently traveled together and undertook joint investigations, shared information across their portfolios, and sometimes stood in for one another when the other was too busy or unwell to perform a particular official duty. The couple also projected themselves as living embodiments of the revolutionary project itself: equal, moral, and deeply devoted. Notably, Deng insisted that she be referred to by her own name rather than as "Madame Zhou," and after the founding of the PRC, refused to travel overseas as the premier's wife (although when protocol required it, she appeared at his side to greet visiting delegations) (Jin 1993, 2:581–88).[67] The fact that Zhou always had more authority than Deng, and that the couple was implicated in what Strauss (2002) describes as acts of paternalist terror and benevolence, does not diminish the impact of their work, nor the import of their self-representation; rather, it becomes central to the investigation itself. Indeed, hundreds of thousands of what I call party families served as a key hinge (Adams 2005, 15) in the construction of the post-1949 state, not despite their contradictions, but through them.

Cai Chang and Li Fuchun also participated in a companionate marriage. Despite a long history of close collaboration, the Cai-Li marriage was not as strong as the Deng-Zhou marriage. Cai Chang's mother encouraged the Cai-Li match when the three were studying in France, as a bid, perhaps, to extract Cai Chang from another less-desirable relationship (Zheng 1997, 138). Li Fuchun was also unfaithful to Cai Chang on several occasions, including in Yan'an; a transgression for which he was reprimanded by party authorities (Terrill 1984, 150).[68] Nonetheless, the couple, whose power imbalance was much less pronounced than that of Deng and Zhou, would have a profound impact on the development of the state. As I will show, the couple played a major role in the establishment of Mao's power in the early 1940s, and again in the two-year lead-up to and during the early months of the Great Leap Forward. Most important, the couple's unwavering devotion to the chairman dismantled the capacity of the Women's Federation to respond to the crisis of famine and injury in 1959, while reinforcing the very conditions that caused it.

Companionate marriages conveyed a certain measure of modernity: they modeled the equality and mutual support expected of men and women liberated from the vestiges of feudal thinking but in a way that always privileged the needs of the party.[69] Elite couples were thus upheld because their relationships did not interfere with their capacity to work on behalf of the CCP, and because they purportedly observed strict party discipline and did not reveal party or state secrets to one another (Fei 1998, 3; Cai 1992b, 190).[70] To this end, the CCP actively propagated an account of family ties in which a couple might support one another in their work but not form a "faction," or the basis of a faction, within the party structure. Although a full-scale hagiography did not begin until the reform era, popular perception of elite couples was already well ensconced among political elites in Yan'an. Indeed, one of the few Western journalists to have interviewed top CCP officials during the late 1930s and early 1940s, Helen Snow (1967, 233), once observed that "the prestige of the Communists in China derives to a high degree from some of the successful marriages its members have demonstrated, such as those of Cho En-lai and Teng Ying-ch'ao, and Ts'ai Chang and her husband."[71] It is important to note that while both couples were held up for public emulation, however, it was Zhou and Deng therefore who were primarily regarded as "the national model of the modern marriage" (Snow 1984, 272). According to Wilson (1984, 77), Zhou and Deng's marriage was to prove "one of the most successful, faithful, and durable marriages in Chinese public life."[72] The moral uprightness of the Deng-Zhou union served as a sharp rebuke to the perceived corruption of political families in the GMD and to GMD society wives, who were viewed to be in the shadow of their more powerful husbands.[73] The union also served as a very public rebuke to Mao's treatment of He Zizhen, and to the many other male party leaders who divorced older wives in favor of the younger, well-educated urbanites who flocked to Yan'an during the Anti-Japanese War in the late 1930s and 1940s.[74] To paraphrase Jasper (1997, 71), how the model couples lived their lives constituted an important "moral message."

Similar to the apex of the CCP in the 1940s and 1950s, companionate leadership couples emerged at lower levels of the political structure as well, with more than half of the former women's heads who participated in this study belonging to a companionate marriage.[75] Some husbands enthusiastically backed the work of their wives. Former women's head Miao Murong, 129, for example, relayed that without the support of her husband, she "couldn't have gotten anything done." But even if some husbands were supportive, the structure of companionate marriages nonetheless cohered to the gendered patterns of responsibility established at the CCP apex: husband as party secretary or head of the Peasant's Union, and wife in charge of women-work, with the wife expected to manage housework and childcare while remaining devoted to the cause of revolutionary struggle. This was the case with Yang Chunlan, 36, who was persuaded by both her husband, a county vice party secretary in Henan, and other county-level leaders to forgo a university education so that she could head up the county Women's Federation in 1956 and continue to care for their two young children. In this marriage, as in countless others, women were expected to serve as political handmaids in party consolidation and family life, regardless of the consequences for their collective and individual aspirations.

Although it is now well-recognized that family ties played a central role in the emergence of the modern political imagination (Adams 2005; Hunt 1992; Pateman 1988, 1989), it is less well understood how they continue to shape the political imagination today. Indeed, political families have rarely featured as a central subject of investigation in the study of the modern state.[76] Given the decisive role that family ties have played in the dissemination of a wide range of ideological agendas, this is a significant oversight. From prohibition to birth control, from gay rights to welfare, from abortion to the environment, family metaphors, policies, and ties have proven central to political struggle over the last century. The enactment of familial ties has served as one of the most potent vectors through which to imagine and practice visions of who "we" are and who "we" want to be, even as that enactment simultaneously naturalizes the family as a comfortably gendered terrain in which power relations and violence are so often concealed. An approach to family ties as attachments illuminates these processes, rather than washes over them. Throughout the twentieth century and up until today, the state's realization as an affective site of belonging has both enabled and impeded its simultaneous appearance as autonomous, objective, and immutable. Put another way, attached enactments are the heartbeat of state formation; they are what give the state its energy and form. It is the pulsation of these enactments, as both capacity and contention, that *The Party Family* seeks to explore.

Part I
STATES OF ACTIVISM

THE MAY FOURTH MOVEMENT

The liberation of women is the measure of society's liberation, [and] the happiness of children is the expression of society's progress.

—Deng Yingchao, "Report on the PRC's Marriage Law"

The effort a government puts into people's welfare is not only an accurate measure of its devotion to peace; it is also a reflection of its status among the nations of the world.

—Soong Ching Ling (Song Qingling), "Welfare Work and World Peace"

On October 1, 1949, Song Qingling stood side-by-side with Mao Zedong, Liu Shaoqi, Zhu De, and Zhou Enlai on the rostrum of Tiananmen Square to inaugurate the new People's Republic of China. As the widow of Sun Yat-sen, the leading revolutionary behind the toppling of the Qing Dynasty, Song Qingling's presence symbolized the new regime's desire to ground its legitimacy in the legacy of her late husband. But her presence also signaled another pressing preoccupation of the new regime: the desire to be recognized on the international stage as a civilized nation. Song Qingling's national and international advocacy work on behalf of Chinese women and children was being celebrated as an expression of China's arrival. Building on Towns (2010), who argues that women's suffrage became an internationally recognized marker of civilized status in the early twentieth century, I argue that the capacity of the nation to protect and uphold mothers and their children emerged as an equally important sign of a "standard of civilization." Song Qingling's presence that day at Tiananmen, reflected the maternalist dispositions of several key leaders at the apex of the CCP, who equated the well-being of Chinese mothers and their children as a sign of the well-being of China itself.

Until recently, the comparative study of social movements, social policy, and state building has largely treated maternalism as a late nineteenth- and early twentieth-century phenomenon or as a feature of regional protest politics.[1] Maternalist ideas, however, circulated across the globe, including in China (Hubbard 2018). In an era of high nationalism, anticolonial insurrection, global war, and civil war, the common quest to realize the "modern (national) woman" *as mothers* informed, and in some cases united, otherwise divergent ideological visions of the future. As part of a complex process of exchange, domestication, and reexportation (Haggis 1998; Dubois and Oliviero 2009), maternalist nationalist and state-building projects were undertaken in contexts as diverse as colonial India and Ireland (Thapar-Björkert and Ryan 2002), in the United States (Skocpol 1992) and the USSR (Hoffman 2011) during the 1920s, and in midcentury Chile, when politicians on the left and right spear-headed maternal health initiatives as part of their drive to win supporters (Baldez 2002; Thomas 2011).

Whether undertaken in China or elsewhere, maternalist interventions were not enacted without controversy—heated debates about marriage reform and access to abortion offer cases in point. But the source of the conflict focused on *who* should define motherhood, not whether motherhood should be subject to the national project at all. In China, leading women officials not only championed motherhood and children as causes, they also symbolized the causes they represented through their national and international personae. From the perspective of these elites, the physiological and spiritual uniqueness of women sprang from their innate capacity to mother; a capacity which, in turn, had important consequences for the welfare of the nation and for the nation's capacity to coexist in harmony with other nations (Rupp 1994; 1998). Maternalist internationalism, a diplomatic enactment of sororal and maternal solidarity that transpired through international organizations, conferences, and bilateral exchange, marked the PRC's foreign policy in the 1950s.[2] Song Qingling, recipient of the 1953 Stalin Peace Prize for her work on maternal and child well-being, would prove one of its most iconic standard-bearers.

Song Qingling first rose to public prominence during May Fourth, which is known both as a day when students gathered in Beijing to protest the signing of the Treaty of Versailles, and as a broader cultural movement. Central to the May Fourth Movement was the emergence of the New Woman, a liberal-humanist state of activism through which women assumed the right to participate in politics, to have an education, to pursue a profession, and to choose a romantic partner. The early writing, policy preferences, and political behavior of Song Qingling and Deng Yingchao were decisively shaped through New Woman activism in which independence from the family was a primary preoccupation. But their political work was simultaneously shaped by maternalist states of activism that proliferated during the May Fourth Movement as well. The proliferation of emergent May Fourth states of activism, and the personal and family ties in which they were embedded, would ultimately hold deep consequences for the leadership of both women and the new world that they sought to realize.

In this chapter, I argue that the maternalist articulations of the May Fourth era directly drew on, and contested, aspects of Pan-Asian maternalism and the maternalism embedded in Christian missionary work. May Fourth maternalisms were also strengthened by the state-building projects of the late Qing and early Republican governments, particularly in the formation of girls' schools, which many May Fourth activists attended. Although May Fourth activists and intellectuals rejected aspects of earlier, more conservative variants of maternalism, maternalist ideas nonetheless informed many progressive political articulations in the late 1910s and the 1920s, including suffragism, feminist continentalism, and social gospel organizing. Maternalism further strengthened under the First United Front (1924–27), a temporary collaboration between the GMD and newly formed CCP that was directed, in part, by the Soviet Union. In all cases, the shared personal encounters being forged among women of otherwise different political persuasions and the emergence of China's first party families, shaped the aspirational politics of the era. As the rebellious daughter of wealthy Methodists, the widow of the founder of the Republic, and a prominent figure in United Front work, Song Qingling's intergenerational ties to women and men inside and outside of the CCP further legitimized the New Woman and Social Reformer states of activism as central to state building in China.

The Rise of Maternalism

Chinese maternalism emerged during a period of profound international demographic anxiety. In the latter half of the nineteenth century, intensified international competition made governments focus on their "populations" in ways that they had not previously done. As Bock and Thane (1991, 11) note, "It seemed that nations needed fit work-forces, fit armies and fit mothers to rear them if they were to compete effectively in an increasingly internationalized market, for imperial domination and in war. Demographic issues became closely linked with national sentiment and discussed in terms of the 'national stock', the size and 'quality' of the 'race.'" The intrusion of foreign-controlled treaty ports and a series of humiliating military defeats pressed many Chinese intellectuals into a search for solutions to their nation's plight.

In the eyes of many late Qing reformers, Japan offered a powerful example of an Asian nation that was able to successfully compete with the West. The Japanese defeated the Chinese in the first Sino-Japanese War of 1895 and the Russians, a Western power, in 1905. Similar to other nations engaged in state building and renewal, Japan prioritized mass education, including the education of women. Meiji state builders argued that educated mothers would produce healthy, able, and patriotic offspring, thereby strengthening the Asian race. In turn, Chinese reformers justified the development of a new system of education for women through an articulation of Pan-Asian maternalism that was inspired by Japan and by the French and American ideal of republican motherhood (Judge 2008, 115). The emphasis on the mother was a significant departure from past practice: as Judge (2008, 108) argues "motherhood" rarely appeared in the classical canon, ancient and imperial.

Shimoda Utako (1854–1936), a Japanese educator and founder of the Practical Women's School for Chinese Women students in Japan, would prove to be one of the most influential voices in Pan-Asian maternalism. Shimoda argued that "educated wives and virtuous mothers" would strengthen Asian nations, who were in competition with the "white race" (Wang 1999, 126; Judge 2008, 110–15).[3] Drawing on the British eugenics movement and ancient Chinese female ethical principles, Shimoda's philosophy extolled the education of women as a means of transmitting patriotic values to their sons (Judge 2001, 772; Judge 2008). Here, science and nation became interwoven in the desire to catch up with and repel the colonial forces occupying East Asia.

In addition to Meiji reformers, Christian organizations shaped late Qing reform as well (Beahan 1976; Chin 2006; Hunter 1984; Kwok 1992). Christian missionaries opened the first girls' schools in the mid-nineteenth century to advance evangelism in China. Missionaries wanted educated Chinese Christian women to serve as helpmeets to their minister-husbands and positive role models for other Chinese women, and to become Bible women and teachers to further their evangelical aspirations (Kwok 1992, 16; Liu and Kelly 1996, 229).[4] Although the enrollment of girls in mission schools was initially slow, it increased dramatically toward the end of the nineteenth century when many Protestants came under the influence of the social gospel movement (Liu and Kelly 1996, 234; Hill 1996). Predicated on the idea that Christian evangelism could reconstruct society, the social gospel emphasized women's leadership both in the United States and abroad (Sasaki 2016). In China, an increasing number of single women missionaries became leaders of Christian social transformation projects.[5] As a consequence of these significant changes in focus and staffing, mission schools shifted their pedagogy toward a more liberal education model.[6] At the same time, Christian missionaries and practitioners began to address issues such as foot binding, concubinage, health care, and family reform, and Chinese women themselves began to play an increasingly active role in mission schools and organizations (Kwok 1992, 101). Despite their turn toward liberal education, Christian missionaries and practitioners, similar to the Pan-Asian maternalists, still sought to educate women and girls with the goal of improving their ability to mother (Chin 2003).

Song Qingling, the daughter of wealthy Methodist parents, attended the McTyeire School for Girls during the first decade of the twentieth century

(Liu 1988; Shang and Tang 1990). Founded by Southern Methodist missionaries, McTyeire's first administrators and educators ran the school in accordance with the belief that the "woman's sphere" of domesticity could transform society—an educational approach that was central to the Wesleyan tradition (Ross 1996, 212). Many of McTyeire's American educators were graduates of Wesleyan College for Women, which was a strong supporter of the "Gospel of Gentility" (211). Song Qingling and her sisters, Meiling and Ailing, pursued their undergraduate degrees at Wesleyan College, before returning to China and assuming influential roles in high-level political developments of the 1920s, 1930s, and 1940s.

Pan-Asian maternalism and Christian social reform offered the rationale and the blueprint from which early Chinese reformers began to develop new educational opportunities for women. Many women who were originally taught in Shimoda's school or in mission schools went on to work as educators and/or became nationalist activists, paving the way for a profound set of social changes (Hunter 1984; Judge 2001).[7] By 1917, around the same time that the May Fourth Movement began, there were 170,789 girls enrolled in government schools—more than triple the number enrolled in mission schools (Hunter 1984, 273). And many of the teachers, graduates of girls' schools themselves, were modeling a new, independent lifestyle for their students (Hunter 1984, 248–50). Because middle-school students attended sex-segregated institutions and often boarded at the county seat, new forms of subjectivity, such as the rise of the "girl student" (Wang 1999, 13–15), took shape alongside sororal identities and networks among educated girls and women.

The first meeting of the CCP took place in a girl's school in Shanghai, in July 1921 (Spence 1990, 322). As girls' schools did not attract the suspicion of the governing authorities, they provided cover for the fledgling organization. In this, and many other ways, the rapid expansion in the education of girls and women would have a tremendous impact on the development of the CCP and its earliest generation of women leaders.[8] As Gilmartin (1995, 99) argues, the provincially run middle and normal schools were "critical to the making of women political activists in the 1920s," in no small part through the forging of strong sororal, mother-daughter bonds, and intergenerational ties. Deng Yingchao, for example, became an activist at the age of fifteen while attending the First Tianjin Women's Normal School. Deng Yingchao's mother taught at some of the girls' schools that Deng herself attended (Jin 1993, 1:9–29), and Cai Chang's mother, Ge Jianhao, attended primary school alongside her children (Wiles 2003b, 174). Many other early CCP leaders, including Xiang Jingyu, Ding Ling, and Cai Chang, attended the progressive Zhounan Girls' Middle School in Changsha, Hunan. Although not all of these future CCP members and affiliates attended Zhounan at the same time, it is important to note how the school radicalized their understanding of politics at a key moment in their youth, while simultaneously generating new relational ties that would bind and shape future politics. Cai Chang, for example, introduced Xiang Jingyu to Mao Zedong and to Cai Hesen, Xiang's future husband, when Cai and Xiang were studying together at Zhounan (McElderry 2003, 579).

Almost as soon as young women began to embark on a path of public education they began to question the broader terms on which state builders had set out to educate them in the first place (Cong 2007, 53). For instance, after the 1911 revolution that overthrew the Qing government, Christian schools became a place in which students could discuss women's suffrage (Kwok 1992, 134). Moreover, many of the young women who studied at Shimoda's school in the first decade of twentieth century went on to embrace very different political positions than that of their Japanese mentor. Some, like the famous revolutionary martyr Qiu Jin, adopted men's dress and advocated for women to join in national revolution; others sought to participate in professional life. Ultimately, nearly all of Shimoda's former pupils would go on to reject the concept of "good wives and wise mothers" (Judge 2001; Chiang 2006).

By the commencement of the May Fourth Movement, a new generation of activists were rejecting marriage and motherhood altogether. This was particularly true of activists participating in anarchist organizations—including future party leaders Mao Zedong, Cai Hesen, and Cai Chang (Snow 1967, 236; Gilmartin 1995, 32–33)—as well as young women graduating from Christian colleges (Hunter 1984, 248–50).[9] Henrik Ibsen's *A Doll's House*, a play whose chief protagonist leaves her husband and children, was the focus of much discussion in the burgeoning youth press, as it resonated with educated youth struggling to gain control of their own lives (Wang 1999, 50). But while Republican notions of motherhood were discredited in more radical circles, other notions were almost immediately embraced. Indeed, many of the ideas in which earlier forms of maternalism were embedded, including eugenic explanations of society, persisted and intersected with emergent forms of maternalism being explored and debated during the May Fourth era.

The May Fourth Movement (1916–27)

Deng Yingchao emerged as an early and prominent student leader of May Fourth organizations in Tianjin, when German-held Chinese territories were handed over to Japan at the Paris Peace Conference. Given the fact that the Beijing government had declared its support for the allies in 1917 and sent some 96,000 Chinese laborers to the Western Front, the feelings of betrayal were palpable (Mitter

2004, 4–7). The small but violent demonstration that took place at Tiananmen Square on May 4, 1919, quickly bloomed into demonstrations and boycotts across China. The refusal of foreign powers to recognize the GMD government's claims as legitimate served as a kind of "moral shock" that drew many young people into the years of heightened activism that followed.[10] Deng Yingchao was no exception. In addition to working with others to establish the Tianjin Women's Patriotic Association, Deng Yingchao was active in the foundation of a number of prominent student organizations, including the Tianjin Students Union and the Awakening Society (Klein and Clark 1971, 2:839). In a cultural and political field very much dominated by men, her national reputation flowed, in no small part, from this student work—the union was among the most active of student organizations in the country—and from essays she penned in publications that she also helped to launch.[11] Combining her passion for patriotism and women's liberation, Deng Yingchao organized boycotts of Japanese goods, led student demonstrations, and gave fiery speeches. She also developed a reputation as a combative activist with little regard for her own safety during moments of direct confrontation with armed authorities. Indeed, Deng Yingchao sought to claim new public space for women by leading them in protest and through her efforts to free women from abusive domestic situations (Wong 2003, 132).

The emotional valence shared by May Fourth participants had long-term consequences for romantic relationships that were forged during this period. "The liberty to love" (Pan 2015, 151) was already gaining traction among young people when they took to the streets in late spring 1919. The drama, and dangers, of May Fourth protest would reinforce this romantic ideal, leading young people, including Deng Yingchao and Zhou Enlai, to view their budding relationship in the context of the collective euphoria of the moment.

It was just one month after the original student protest in Tiananmen Square that Deng first met Zhou Enlai. Six years her senior, Zhou was editing a Tianjin Student Union newspaper when he saw Deng speak out against the abuse Tianjin students had suffered when they had traveled to Beijing to petition the authorities. After making some inquiries, Zhou was introduced to Deng, and the two spent the early months of the May Fourth protests working side-by-side (Jin 1993, 1:30–57). When Zhou left to travel and work in Europe for nearly four years (1920–24), the two corresponded through mail. According to CCP lore, Zhou Enlai first declared his love to Deng Yingchao on a postcard with a picture of Rosa Luxemburg and Karl Liebknecht, a couple who became martyrs for the revolutionary cause: "In the future, [I] hope that the two of us can be like these two, and together ascend the guillotine" (Fei 1998, 58).[12]

After several years of separation, Deng and Zhou married in a brief ceremony in August 1925. By this time, both were members of the CCP and active in the increasing political mobilizations underway across China. An era of high excitement and expectation, young romance and danger, the May Fourth protests, and the larger cultural movement in which they were embedded, generated strong affective loyalties that would have important consequences for the CCP's revolutionary struggle and its aftermath.

First, May Fourth produced a powerful New Woman state of activism that informed many, albeit not all, of the CCP leaders and activists who came of age at this time. Deng Yinchao's own strongly held commitment to marital equality as a social ideal, for example, took shape at this historical juncture: a conception articulated through emerging understanding of women's rights, and as I will show, a heartfelt expression of sacred love. Similar to many other young women of the moment, Deng also adopted the physical presentation of a New Woman state of activism: cutting her hair short, for example, and wearing simple trousers and tunics. Deng Yingchao, in many ways, came to personify the New Woman state of activism, especially as it came to be enacted and remembered after the foundation of the People's Republic. In Deng Yingchao's March 1949 address to the first meeting of women representatives that would establish the ACDWF for example, she located the CCP's beginnings in May Fourth and depicted the Chinese women's movement as having been born during this revolutionary epoch (Deng 1949 [1988], 5–9). In Deng's narrative, the founding story of the Chinese women's movement is thus produced in direct relationship to the larger revolutionary project in which it was embedded.[13]

Second, Maoist and contemporary CCP discourse about the May Fourth Movement has also been embodied and retold through the relational nodes of the couples who shaped its work and its later meaning. This is evident in the characterization of the earliest days of the Deng and Zhou relationship by the official biographies and texts, cited above. It is also evident in the couple's correspondence as recounted and published after their death. In a 1959 letter recounted by Deng Yingchao's biographer, Zhou Enlai marked the passage of International Women's Day, with reference to the enduring linkages that would be maintained between the historical moment of their meeting and their ongoing project to liberate Chinese women (Jin 1993, 2:553–54).[14] Sentimental exchange was not necessarily true of all of their correspondence: indeed, one archivist who examined Deng and Zhou's letters suggests that the couple seldom focused on their personal relationship in their correspondence with one another (Fei 1998). Instead, he suggests, they primarily wrote about work. Nonetheless, endearments and an expressed longing to be reunited mark the very few of Deng Yingchao's letters to Zhou Enlai that have been made public (Zhou and Deng 1944; 1947; 1954 [1998], 24–27). The letters are thus expressions of revolutionary attachments as a form of statecraft. Deng and Zhou's idealized love has been used to shape the public meaning of May Fourth, just as much as May Fourth may well have given meaning to their marriage.

May Fourth is important to understanding the politics that followed for yet a third reason: the continuation and deepening of different expressions of maternalism in women's organizing. In 1950, when Deng Yingchao equated women's liberation with the happiness of children, as is evident in one of the quotes that begins this chapter, she was drawing on ideas that gathered strength during May Fourth. As I will show, the revolutionary attachments generated during this period played a key role in bridging generational, class, and organizational divides, shaping the politics of May Fourth, and thereby enshrining the relationship between a mother's love, women's liberation, and the well-being of the nation and the world.

Suffragism

Chinese suffragists took to the streets in 1912 in the wake of the establishment of the first GMD government. Informed, in part, by suffrage campaigns underway abroad, including in Japan, Europe, and the United States, they had "a repertoire of suffrage tactics and ideologies from which to choose" (Chin 2006, 503). Suffragists who sought the right to vote, hold office, and the constitutional recognition of equal rights, were not afraid to employ confrontational tactics to achieve their goals. The storming of the parliament in Nanjing in March 1912 by an armed group of women activists may well have been modeled on the tactics of the radical women's suffrage movement in England (Ono 1989, 84). Although the first movement collapsed within a little over a year and would remain a contested area of debate within elite circles, the ideals of suffragists were kept alive by a determined coalition of activists. As Edwards (2002; 2008) shows, coalitional activity focused on women's suffrage not only revived and expanded during the early 1920s but continued well into the 1930s. Ultimately, Chinese women won the right to the vote at the national level in 1936.

The first and second surge to achieve the vote, however, did not march totally in step with liberal feminism but contained and intersected with variations of maternalist feminism as well. While many Chinese suffragists asserted women's rights on the basis of independent personhood alone, some prominent suffragists made their claims on the basis of the superior virtue of women and/or mothers, or on the basis of independence and virtue combined. Indeed, Liu-Wang Liming (1897–1970), founder of the Shanghai Women's Suffrage Association in 1922 and chair of the first Women's National Assembly Promotion Association (WNAPA) meeting in 1924, argued that women were morally superior to men.[15] Educated in a Chinese mission school and at Northwestern University in Illinois,

Liu-Wang strongly believed that women contributed to society through the nurture of their children as well as through their efforts to sponsor social services, expand education, and improve child welfare.

To a certain degree, Liu-Wang's views reflected her participation in and leadership of the Chinese Women's Christian Temperance Union (WCTU). Indeed, a number of social gospel activists in the United States supported women's suffrage in order to improve social conditions for women and their children. However, the idea that women's rights activists should focus on protecting working mothers and providing child welfare, as Liu-Wang advocated, resonated with activists holding a wide range of political views. The Tianjin branch of the Women's National Assembly, which was founded by Deng Yingchao in 1924, for example, included the protection of mothers and children among its demands (Edwards 2002). Early CCP leaders, however, did not push for improved protections for women on the basis of women's virtue but on the basis of their understanding of women's physiological difference. This understanding was partially informed by an alternative strain of maternalism: continental feminism.

Continental Feminism

Barlow (1989, 23) argues that in the May Fourth era the "aim of liberating women was to free the repressed, biologically truthful individual trapped inside every filial daughter." The problem, she notes, was that many of the young (male) May Fourth scholars were not sure what a "new" liberated woman should look like. Scholar-activists, men and women, increasingly emphasized complementary social roles for the sexes as their answer to this puzzle. Working through new theories on human sexuality and evolution, as well as popular tracts on love and maternity, a number of May Fourth intellectuals came to view the sexes as equal, even if they were also physiologically different. Moreover, they concluded that these physiological differences implied different responsibilities for women and men and their relationship to the nation and to state-building efforts.[16]

An important development in the articulation of this new form of maternalist feminism was the translation and popularization of Ellen Key's writings in the *Ladies Journal* (*Funü zazhi*) during the early 1920s.[17] A prominent Swedish feminist who drew on the work of British sexologist Havelock Ellis to link motherhood and sexual fulfillment to individual freedom (Koven and Michel 1993, 15), Key argued that women should have access to birth control and thus the ability to choose to bear children or not. Key also tied sexual and emotional fulfillment in monogamous relationships to the well-being of the race and the advancement of civilization.[18]

Discord marked many encounters as Key emerged on the global scene. According to Tyrrell (1991, 67) Key did not ally with the WCTU, because of the "conventional conception of sexual morality that underlay the theme of purity in the Temperance movement." Both Key and Ellis were sharply critical of "aggressive" suffragist tactics and wary of the implications of the women's rights movement for societal development as a whole. Although Key's explicit rejection of campaigns for women's rights and communal childcare turned many away from her philosophy, her writings nonetheless influenced the development of social policy legislation and the rise of the Western welfare state (Koven and Michel 1993, 16–17). Her work also made an impression on the early leaders of the CCP.

Zhang Xichen, the editor of the *Ladies Journal*, the most prominent journal to focus on women's issues in the early 1920s, first took up Key's ideas and began to advocate for tempering appeals for women's rights with a recognition of the "sacredness of motherhood" (*shensheng de muxing*) (Wang 1999, 89). The concepts of sacred love and sacred motherhood as developed by Key and introduced by Zhang influenced an entire generation of activists, including many of those who became central to articulating the CCP's conception of women's liberation. Increasingly, ideas of independent personhood as well as new forms of social engineering were rearticulated in such a way as to help women to fulfill their maternal duty, or as Hubbard (2018, 253) argues, as a "shared yet inconsistently enacted capacity to nurture." At this moment, birth control, socialized housework, and daycare thus became the Chinese socialist answer to the question of how to free (biological) woman.

Echoes of Ellen Key's work can be detected early on among some of the most influential CCP leaders before and after they joined the party. In one of Deng Yingchao's early speeches as a May Fourth activist, for example, she draws on Ellen Key's work to advocate for independent personhood and loving marriages.[19] Cai Hesen and Xiang Jingyu, the most prominent CCP couple of the period, sought to practice their marriage as "sacred love."[20] Wang Huiwu, former May Fourth student activist and early communist organizer, linked the fulfillment of motherhood to birth control. In a 1922 article, Wang argued that birth control enhanced rather than detracted from women's maternal instincts by reducing the physiological and psychological pain associated with numerous births. Birth control also enabled a woman to enjoy nurturing her one or two children, and to lavish attention on them as, Wang suggested, one would "on a work of art" (Gilmartin 1995, 68). Based on her interviews with CCP activists from the 1920s, Gilmartin (1995, 113) argues that while they "looked forward to the day when a socialist state would relieve them of some of their responsibilities through the establishment of daycare centers and canteens, they adhered to the sanctity of *muxing* (maternal instincts) and thus failed to agitate for a re-division of household responsibilities with their husbands." As envisioned by these early activists, therefore, the socialization of housework was never intended to eliminate the mother's role in the family. Rather, it was intended to aid women in their natural obligation to mother. In the words of Chiang (2006, 537), "motherhood remained sacrosanct and non-negotiable."

Christian Social Reform

At the same time that Ellen Key's work was being popularized in the pages of the *Ladies Journal*, members of two Christian social reform organizations, the WCTU and the Young Women's Christian Association (YWCA), began to develop a more radical approach to social reform in China. Although the impact of Christian organizations on the CCP would remain limited until the 1930s, their activities in the early 1920s would help lay the groundwork for future reform and the recruitment of Christian women to nationalist and leftist causes.

As previously noted, Christians spearheaded the development of a new system of girls' education and led early campaigns to end foot binding and concubinage. Indeed, according to Kwok (1992, 2), Christian women were the first group of Chinese women to organize themselves in order to publicly address women's oppression. Despite their advocacy to improve social conditions for women, however, the majority of missionaries and Christian practitioners in China opposed women's rights activities. Hu Binxia (1888–1931), a prominent Christian intellectual who had studied in Japan and served as the first Chinese chairperson of the Chinese YWCA, for example, repudiated women's political activism while rejecting the notion of "good wives and wise mothers" at the same time (Chiang 2006, 526).[21] Indeed, Hu emphasized women's role in social reform over political change. In a related vein, missionary school students were discouraged from participating in May Fourth protests (Kwok 1996).[22] It is thus perhaps why Deng Yuzhi, a Christian graduate of Zhounan Girls' Middle School and future head of the YWCA's Labor Bureau, justified her participation in the May Fourth demonstrations as in accordance with "God's will to end exploitation" (Honig 1996, 249).

When Liu-Wang became general secretary of the Chinese WCTU in 1926, the International WCTU claimed a global following of more than a million people (Tyrrell 1991, 2). As an international organization, the WCTU sought to eradicate the consumption of alcohol worldwide, believing it to be one of the chief causes of social evil and broken families (Kwok 1992, 120–21). But it embedded this goal within a broader quest for women's liberation and social reform. According to Tyrrell (1991, 2), the WCTU "rivaled the achievements of the suffrage movement in the dissemination on an international level of the principles of women's emancipation." It was also the first mass organization among women devoted to social reform. As such, the WCTU functioned as a kind of "moral bureaucracy" that "purported to unite women in worldwide sisterhood" (Tyrrell 1991, 5, 38).

Chinese branches of the WCTU were first established in the late 1880s, just fourteen years after the founding of the WCTU in the United States by Frances Willard, its first president. Initially, the Chinese WCTU focused its campaigns on reducing alcohol consumption, opium usage, and cigarette smoking (Kwok 1992, 120–26). At this time membership was small, and the Chinese branches were largely run by Western women. Under the direction of Sarah Goodrich, general secretary in 1909, the WCTU reflected the growing influence of the social gospel movement in which missionaries were shifting their focus from saving "heathens" to regenerating "heathen" culture and society (Kwok 1992, 102). Indeed, Goodrich conceived of the WCTU as an organization of women "for the protection and betterment of their homes with the ultimate aim of abolishing those evils which blight Society, ruin homes and weaken the empire" (Kwok 1992, 121).

By the time the Chinese WCTU held its first national convention in 1922, it had broadened its mandate to include the promotion of (1) good life habits, (2) higher moral standards for men and women, (3) protection of motherhood, (4) child education and welfare, and (5) peace and goodwill among all peoples (Kwok 1992, 123). It had also expanded to include more than six thousand members and was active in eleven provinces. Perhaps most important, Chinese women had assumed leadership of the Chinese WCTU since 1911. Under the direction of Liu-Wang and Yuan Yuying, the Chinese WCTU became much more focused on the systemic origins of women's oppression, including poverty and illiteracy (Kwok 1996, 205). In Shanghai, where the WCTU was headquartered, for example, the WCTU established the Women's Vocational School, which trained women for new employment opportunities; the Shanghai Women's Apartment for single career women; and the Shanghai Settlement House—the only welfare institution for women in China (Wang 1999, 136–37).

But Liu-Wang did not just focus on the development of social welfare. She became one of China's most outspoken critics of sexual inequality during the 1920s and 1930s. Indeed, she not only continued to provide organizational leadership in the campaign for suffrage but also published an influential book, *The Chinese Women's Movement*, in 1934 and created a journal, the *Women's Voice*, to advance the goal of women's equality (Wang 1999; Edwards 2003). Both Liu-Wang's experience in the arena of social welfare and her ties to educated women elites would prove to be a significant asset to the CCP both during the Sino-Japanese War and its most active period of state building just prior to and after the foundation of the PRC.

Although the Chinese WCTU became more radical under the leadership of Liu-Wang, it was the Chinese YWCA that developed the most progressive and far-reaching practice of maternalist politics during the 1920s and 1930s. Similar to the WCTU, the World YWCA committed itself to extending the social gospel mission, and indeed, was inspired by the work of the WCTU and its first president (Tyrrell 1991, 3). Founded in England and the United States during the late nineteenth century, the YWCA drew on religious zeal to provide new social services to working-class women and women students (Kwok 1992, 126). After the first national committee of the YWCA was established in 1899 (Littell-Lamb 2010, 67), the Chinese YWCA worked primarily in cities, appealing to "a broad constituency, including students at mission and government schools, working class women employed in the cotton, silk, matches, and tobacco industries, as well as a new class of urban women, the wives of educators, businessmen, and government officials" (Kwok 1992, 126). While the Chinese YWCA employed a growing coterie of Chinese women professionals, they continued to be outnumbered by foreign staffers well into the 1920s (Littell-Lamb 2010, 71).

The Chinese YWCA worked on anti-opium and temperance campaigns. It also actively promoted physical education for women and girls. But its activities in urban welfare development and addressing industrial working conditions would produce its most lasting contribution.[23] According to Drucker (1979), the YWCA initially focused on educating school-age girls about the problems of the urban poor. Local YWCA chapters developed social services, including flood and famine relief, shelter for the homeless, child welfare stations, maternity clinics, and orphanages (Kwok 1992, 130). National student conferences were organized around the themes "Our Opportunity for Service," "Women and Society," and "Women and Social Change" (Kwok 1992, 129).

By the 1920s, both the WCTU and the YWCA were engaged in shaping an emerging maternalist internationalism. Specifically, they sought no less than to transform conditions for women and children under the banner of global sisterhood, peace, and social justice, and in partnership with their global counterparts.[24] Although their initial efforts to reform the employment conditions of women and children in Treaty Port factories failed, they did garner the attention of Xiang Jingyu (1895–1928), the CCP's most important spokesperson on questions of women's liberation during the 1920s.

The First United Front

Between 1923 and 1927, the CCP joined forces with the GMD, in what subsequently became known as the First United Front. Established by Sun Yat-sen in the wake of the overthrow of the Qing Dynasty in 1911, the GMD had faced great difficulties as a newly founded political party. Critically, Song Jiaoren, one of the most prominent elected officials of the GMD, was assassinated shortly after the GMD had won the largest share of seats in China's first parliament. In the years that followed, the CCP had to contend with the growth of regional warlords and the failure of the fledgling parliament to establish a working democracy. Encouraged by the Communist International (Comintern) to cooperate with the CCP, Sun Yat-sen saw an opportunity to strengthen political and military capabilities, solicit popular support, and reunify the country by engaging, most importantly, in a military campaign known as the Northern Expedition (1926–28).

Women CCP leaders played a pivotal role in developing the urban-based mass women's movement that supported the intraparty cooperation (Gilmartin 1995). Participants in this unprecedented social movement included activists from a wide range of student, worker, and women's rights organizations and groups, as well as the often overlapping and intersecting involvement of Christian-based women's organizations. Although the First United Front would ultimately collapse, it nonetheless paved the way for future maternalist cooperation.

More than any other figure, Xiang Jingyu was responsible for the development of a broad United Front among women activists (Gilmartin 1995). As the chief theorist on women's issues in the CCP during the early 1920s, Xiang Jingyu played a central role in developing a Chinese class analysis of gender oppression, highlighting in particular the plight of women workers. Similar to many other Communists of the day, including those she encountered during two years she spent working in France (1919–21), Xiang argued that one of the most severe limitations of women's rights feminism was its narrow focus on the concerns of bourgeois, elite women (Edwards 2002). But in this period of intense coalition activity, Xiang and the CCP leadership in general were willing to overlook the ideological shortcomings of women activists outside the party and to build bridges of shared concern.

Four months after her appointment to lead the Communist Women's Bureau in 1923, Xiang publicly changed her opinion about Christian social reform groups. Whereas she had previously criticized these organizations, and particularly the YWCA, as "a tool of foreign capitalism," she now publicly acknowledged the YWCA's commitment to social activism (Gilmartin 1995, 92). As Gilmartin notes, Xiang Jingyu's public endorsement of the YWCA was all the more remarkable given that a number of male Communist leaders were pursuing an anti-Christian agenda at the time.

Xiang Jingyu and Wang Huiwu, the first leader of the Communist Women's Bureau, were both admirers of Cheng Wanzhen, a YWCA staffer who worked hard to draw national and international attention to the conditions of women factory workers (Gilmartin 1995, 69, 92). Indeed, Wang invited Agatha Harrison, secretary of the YWCA, and Cheng Wanzhen to teach at the Communist-led Shanghai Pingmin Girls' School (Gilmartin 1995, 69). However, Xiang took her endorsement of Christian social welfare organizations and women's rights groups to a new level when she agreed to coordinate the Women's National Assembly Promotion Association (WNAPA) with Liu-Wang Liming, who chaired the first meeting.

The WNAPA, an umbrella group of women's organizations, sought to achieve women's suffrage as well as a host of other reforms focused on women, including equality of education and the protection of working mothers, in the National Assembly during late 1924 and 1925. Despite its failure five months after its start, the WNAPA bolstered the CCP's standing among urban women and led to a much greater involvement of women in the First United Front. Over the course of the First United Front, activists from across the political spectrum forged tighter links; key figures included Deng Yingchao, He Xiangning, Liu Qingyang, Song Qingling, Cai Chang, and Liu-Wang Liming—all future founders of the ACWF.

Song Qingling and He Xiangning's work during the latter period of the First United Front is particularly notable. Song had married Sun Yat-sen in Japan in 1914, when she replaced her sister Ailing as the famous revolutionary's personal secretary. Despite a significant gap in age, the initial opposition of Song's parents, and the fact that Sun had to divorce his first wife in order to marry Song, the two would enjoy ten years of intense romantic and political involvement. Song assisted Sun with his political work, taking particular responsibility for Sun's English correspondence, and participating in important meetings, including those that gave rise to the First United Front between the GMD and CCP (Epstein 1993, 99–113). Song and Sun's closest friends, He Xiangning and Liao Zhongkai, participated actively in many of those meetings as well.

He Xiangning and Liao Zhongkai were nascent revolutionaries studying in Japan when they met Sun Yat-sen in 1903. An extremely well-educated patriot, artist, and suffragette, He Xiangning was one of the first women to join Sun Yat-sen's revolutionary organization, the Tongmenghui. Unlike many of her other contemporaries who were beginning to reject the linkage between motherhood and patriotism, He Xiangning maintained strong maternalist dispositions, referring to women as "mothers to society" and "producers of civilization" (Edwards 2008, 46–47). Witnesses to the marriage between Sun Yat-sen and Song Qingling (Epstein 1993, 149), He Xiangning and Liao Zhongkai would actively support them in their love and politics. Indeed, when Song Qingling suffered from a miscarriage, caused, perhaps, by the stress of fleeing a violent insurgence (Lee 2003e, 467), He Xiangning helped her to reunite with Sun, from whom she had been separated during the uprising (Lee 2003b, 201). "The best and warmest of friends, personally and politically," (Epstein 1993, 149) the two women supported each other through the deaths of their husbands; Sun died from cancer in spring of 1925, and Liao was assassinated just a few months later. They also continued to rely on each other as they renewed and redoubled their political activism in the wake of the loss of their husbands, taking up government positions and playing leading roles in the mass mobilizations that played out across China between 1925 and 1927.

In January 1926, Song Qingling joined He Xiangning, Deng Yingchao, and Mao Zedong, among others, as a member of the Central Executive Committee of the GMD. Over the next eighteen months she would assume increasingly high-profile positions in the government, including serving as one of the thirteen members of GMD Political Bureau from January 1927. Song also served as minister of health and was the first head of the Red Cross of the Northern Expeditionary Army (Epstein 1993, 164, 181). He Xiangning also worked closely with Deng Yingchao and Cai Chang, both of whom served under He Xiangning in the Women's Committee of the Central Guangdong-Guangxi Area Committee of the Communist Party (Wiles 2003a, 22; Wong 2003, 133). Gilmartin (1995, 161–62) argues that He Xiangning was able to run a highly successful women's department through bridging the radical demands of younger activists, such as Deng Yingchao, with the nationalist—and I would add maternalist—concerns of older staff. Thus, alongside advocating for new legal codes to protect women, setting up night schools, and organizing mass rallies, He Xiangning also established an obstetrics hospital that provided services to more than ten thousand women during the year it was in operation (Meng 1991, 197–296).

Song Qingling's approach sought to strike a balance between women's liberation and nationalist mobilization. Similar to Deng Yingchao, for example, Song Qingling maintained a deep commitment to freeing young women, especially child brides, from the bonds of oppressive marriages (Shang and Tang 1990, 155). At the same time, Song Qingling maintained an emphasis on women's domestic roles. In a 1927 article she published, for example, Song encouraged women *not only* to serve as "good wives and wise mothers" in their own homes (*xiao jiating*), but *also* to serve as good revolutionary citizen-women in the larger home (*da jiating*) of the nation.[25]

Song Qingling was also becoming increasingly partial toward the Soviet Union, meeting with Soviet officials, including Stalin, when she traveled to the USSR for the first time in 1927. These ties, it should be noted, did not do much to undermine the maternalist dispositions of Song's childhood but may well have deepened them. Soviet policy elites were just as transfixed with questions of maternity and infant mortality as were their counterparts elsewhere (Hoffman

2011, 143–56). From the very founding of the USSR, efforts were made to demonstrate the superiority of the socialist system over the capitalist West by publicizing the care provided to women and children. In 1925, for example, Leon
Trotsky suggested collecting figures and comparing the mortality rates of women
and children in the capitalist West with those of the USSR (Trotsky 1925 [1973],
33, 45).[26] According to Leon Trotsky (1925 [1973], 45), "The most accurate way
of measuring our advance is by the practical measures which are being carried
out for the improvement of the position of mother and child." When Cai Chang
traveled to the Soviet Union in early 1925, she sought to learn about the Soviet
approach to women's liberation, paying particular attention to how the Soviets
reduced the household and childcare burdens of women. Cai Chang thus combined her studies at the Communist University of the Toilers of the East with
frequent visits to Soviet childcare centers during the approximately six months
she spent in the country (Su 1990, 40).

Deng Yingchao and Cai Chang also established a working relationship for
the first time during the mass uprisings of this period. Although the two had
never met previously, they had heard of one another and, according to Cai's biographer, immediately established a strong rapport (Su 1990, 224–25). As in the
Deng-Zhou relationship, the Deng-Cai relationship congealed on the basis of
revolutionary attachments: kinship ties that advanced the political work of the
moment through familial solidarity and the gendered protection it provided, but
also as a historiographic move to strengthen the project of party and state building through the warm feelings shared between two elder sisters. Later, when they
went underground in Shanghai, Deng and Cai lived with their mothers, and the
four women were able to pass themselves off as ordinary old friends meeting to
discuss poetry, art, and medicine while secretly undertaking work for the CCP
(Su 1990, 225). Cai Chang's daughter, born in 1924, referred to Deng Yingchao
as her "Love Mama" (Su 1990, 225). Interviews with a family relation of Cai and
with former ACWF colleagues, were adamant that the two women were close
(Interviewees 2–7). The many decades of revolutionary struggle, however, may
well have taken a toll on the friendship. Indeed, as I document in the coming
chapters, Deng Yingchao and Cai Chang championed different state projects at
different times; an outcome of health-related issues, perhaps, or a reflection of
distinct political priorities.

During the height of the mass mobilization in the mid-1920s, women joined
political organizations in unprecedented numbers. The Hubei Women's Association, for example, grew from eleven individuals in July 1925 to as many as seventy
thousand by July 1927 (Gilmartin 1995, 186). Political alliances crossing Marxist,
liberal, and Christian lines came to an abrupt end in 1927, however, when Chiang
Kai-shek, Sun Yat-sen's political heir and Song Qingling's future brother-in-law,

attacked the CCP and its radical allies in a surprise assault that became known as the White Terror.

In the months that followed, thousands of Chinese Communists, including Xiang Jingyu, were arrested and executed. The CCP scattered, and many remaining members either retreated underground or decamped to the countryside, beginning what would turn out to be a ten-year period of political exile. After a failed uprising in Hunan, the CCP attempted to rebuild through establishing bases in the mountainous region of Jiangxi Province. In 1934, facing the overwhelming military power of the GMD, the CCP broke through a military blockade and began the Long March, a six-thousand-mile trek that finally ended in the Shaanxi city of Yan'an.

The counterrevolutionary movement that drove the CCP underground geographically transformed the CCP's approach to women's liberation, temporarily breaking the coalition of progressive women's organizations and CCP women organizers. Maternalist politics did not die out with the end of the United Front, however. In fact, during the Nanjing Decade (1927–37) the GMD government actively facilitated the reemergence of a maternalist ideology not dissimilar to earlier explorations of republican motherhood. It is to this development and the CCP's complex relationship to maternalism as it deepened under wartime conditions that I turn to in the next two chapters.

Neither the origin of movement dispositions and goals can ever be fixed exactly in time and space. But at the very least we can trace out the contested intersections of the fields in which movement dispositions arise. The establishment of church and state-run schools for girls, the intense turmoil of the May Fourth mobilizations, the increasing influence of the Soviet Union, and the rise of women professionals worked to undermine one expression of maternalism only to replace it with other, far more radical visions of the relationship between motherhood, nation, and state. When the CCP leadership began actively to mobilize women in the early 1920s, these intersecting, and at times contradictory, strands of maternalist politics were already shaping some of the priorities and practices of the CCP. As I have shown, passionate debate about the role of women in the family during this early period never ceased. It is just that increasingly, the focus of debate centered on *how* women should mother, and with what forms of social support, rather than if they should mother at all.

But these histories were also deeply implicated in, and animated by, the relationships that gave rise to them in the first place. Indeed, the relational agency embedded in these projects, including the emergence and influence of mother-daughter ties and movement couples, was also key to how maternalism was understood and practiced: whether organizing meetings in schools or marching together in the streets, a new collectivity of shared sisterhood and romantic commitments would develop into life-long attachments. As such, the May Fourth Movement embedded maternalism in an affective circuit of relations that would continue to shape social policy reform in the decades to come. The stories that the CCP has told and retold about these attachments—sororal, fraternal, parent-child, and marital—would come to animate how the earliest years of the Chinese women's movement and the CCP would be remembered and practiced. Indeed, it is in exactly this enactment of "upright" family ties that Xiang Jingyu has been immortalized as "geming lao zumu," or paternal grandmother of the revolution (CCTV 2021), an emphasis that neatly elides Xiang's history of infidelity and subsequent loss of status in women's organizing just prior to her execution (see McElderry 2003, 579). The founding stories of the CCP thus brim with both omission and excess, grounding the revolutionary attachments of the May Fourth in an aspirational longing for a liberated future that are always, already tied to a familial past of sacrifice and redemption.

THE CHONGQING COALITION

> **When the victory over aggression is achieved, Chinese women will stand with the women of all countries, as those who have suffered so much more than even the men in the mad revel of fascism and war that has spread throughout the world, ready and willing to see that in the future all movement shall be forward, that the earth's present frightful testing-time shall be the last of its kind.**
>
> —Soong Ching Ling (Song Qingling), *The Chinese Women's Fight for Freedom*

> **The war . . . has undoubtedly hastened [the Chinese woman's] emergence and emancipation. It has fired her patriotism and given her scope for activities which were dreamt of but hitherto unrealized; it has given her opportunities to do her part as a member of society on an equal footing with her menfolk; it has given her the initiative to assume responsibilities hitherto discharged by men with long experience; and, finally, it has given her the means of self-expression as a creative force in helping to defeat the ravagers of her fatherland.**
>
> —Soong Chiang May-ling (Song Meiling), *This Is Our China*

In late 1937, Zhou Enlai paid a visit to the Wuhan home of Feng Yuxiang, the "Christian Warlord" and member of the GMD government, and his wife, Li Dequan, a prominent social gospel leader. Zhou had gone at the behest of his wife, Deng Yingchao, to see if he could convince Li Dequan to lead an initiative to aid orphans and children who were being victimized and displaced by the Japanese occupation (Jin 1993, 1:247–48). It was a critical moment in the war. Just a little over a year earlier, the CCP and GMD had forged a shaky Second United Front to combat the Japanese, who had occupied Northeastern China since 1931, and with whom full-scale war broke out in summer of 1937. Both governments were struggling to cope with extensive losses, including the impact of large internal refugee populations. Among these groups were children who had been orphaned or separated from their parents during the war.

Between 1938 and 1942, women worked across party lines to develop emergency relief for children displaced and injured by war and provide nascent forms of social services including collective childcare and child welfare facilities. Just as a mobilized response to a wartime crisis (Skocpol 1992) and party realignment (Baldez 2002; Beckwith 2000) enabled women's movements to play a prominent role in state building in other contexts, leading Chinese elites, including Christian social reformers, contributed to state building in the years leading up to the foundation of the PRC, and during the first few years after its establishment.

This chapter builds on the previous one to map the maternalist attachments that gave rise to the ACDWF and its central preoccupations and practices during the earliest years of the PRC.[1] In so doing, I lay stress on the historical legacies of social policy reform prior to the establishment of the PRC and the ongoing enactment of party families as symbolic agents of change and dynamically networked participants in state formation. In the late 1930s, elite women from across the ideological spectrum, including the famous Song sisters (Song Qingling, Song Meiling, and Song Ailing), Li Dequan, Deng Yingchao, and many others, set aside their differences to address the refugee crisis that was besetting the country (Ferlanti 2012; Guo 2019; Schneider 2012). As Guo (2019, 193) argues, elite women's networks in the war "manifested great diversity, flexibility, and resilience." Through their use of kinship ascriptions, party marriages, and the deft deployment of familial diplomacy, elite women consolidated cooperation among the warring parties. In this chapter I argue that foundational cross-party cooperation would, in turn, strengthen the maternalist state-building agenda of the new regime after its foundation in 1949, including the decision to make the ACDWF, and key women leaders, central to its articulation.[2]

Both the social policy achievements and the women's organizing of the early Maoist regime have been understood, in part, as building on the CCP's close cooperation with the Soviet Union.[3] Many senior CCP and CCP-affiliated women leaders, including Cai Chang, Deng Yingchao, Song Qingling, and Li Dequan spent significant amounts of time in the Soviet Union and were influenced by the Soviet approach to childcare, infant health, and women's programming.[4] In addition, the Soviets made important contributions to the restructuring of the Chinese medical system in the 1950s as well as to facilitating specific programs, such as epidemic reduction drives (see, for example, Fu 1953). When one views social policy reform from the perspective of women's leadership, however, China's post-1949 reforms more closely resembled American social policy reform in the 1920s, when women professionals advocated for and established the embryo of what Theda Skocpol (1992) has called the world's first maternalist welfare state. The programs that stemmed from the Sheppard-Towner Act, the first American piece of federal social welfare legislation, were largely led by women professionals. The various bureaucratic offices of the Sheppard-Towner programs (and its earlier iteration as a Children's Bureau) focused on providing social benefits and services to mothers and their children and was justified by its protection of American families, and more specifically, the universalization of mother love (Skocpol 1992, 522–26). Although the Sheppard-Towner Act would be short-lived, it would nonetheless lay the basis for future welfare reform in the United States. It would also be mired in a racial and class politics of exclusion, as argued by subsequent historians (see, for example, Ladd-Taylor 1994).

In China, women officials built on their friendship and professional and family ties to interlock mass organizations, party, and state in a new policy apparatus: a maternalist social policy regime. The similarities between the United States and China were not coincidental: indeed, the transnational social gospel networks focused on the professional feminization of education and medicine in the 1910s and 1920s emerged, in part, through what Sasaki (2016, 88–92) describes as the "Gospel of Americanism." But other geopolitical factors shaped the contours of maternalist state building in China as well. Starting in the late 1930s, the war with Japan not only elevated the importance of the health and welfare of mothers and their children as a subject of state building, but also centered the leadership of women officials in the efforts to realize these objectives. In 1949, the ACDWF subsumed the WCTU, YWCA, and CCP women's organizations within its hierarchy, establishing itself as China's new moral bureaucracy on the national and international stage. As with the earlier American experiment in maternalist state-building, the Women's Federation, and the maternalist social policy regime in which it was embedded, would have a profoundly complicated legacy.

The Sino-Japanese War and the Rise of the Chongqing Coalition

Mao Zedong once likened his relationship with his mother to a kind of "united front" opposed to the household patriarch, Mao's father. Indeed, Mao's mother sought to prevent open attacks and overt displays of emotion, which, she said, was not the Chinese way (Snow 1938 [1978], 115–16). In the realm of revolutionary Chinese politics, Song Qingling assumed a similar role to that of Mao's mother. Although Song was deeply sympathetic to the left-leaning cause of the Communists from an early juncture, when necessary, she endeavored to bring the CCP and GMD together and "keep the peace" for the benefit of the nation as a whole.

As previously discussed, Song Qingling participated in many of the early meetings that established the First United Front and assumed increasingly high-profile roles in the GMD government in the wake of her husband's death. By the late 1930s, Song Qingling was known by school children as the "mother of the nation" (Epstein 1993, 364). The behind-the-scenes work of Song and many other women complemented and, at times, enabled the more high-profile public cooperation of party officials and their families. Similar to the spouses of diplomats, these informal power brokers provided the kind of social cohesion necessary to soften interaction and thus make possible what might otherwise be difficult-to-achieve outcomes.[5] Contact between the wives and sisters of "leading men" can thus facilitate a conduit between two political parties or factions when a formal overture is not possible, making the otherwise impossible, possible.

Song Qingling also played a decisive role in the establishment of the Second United Front. On December 12, 1936, Chiang Kai-shek, president of the Republic of China and Song Qingling's brother-in-law, was kidnapped by members of his own government in a bid to convince him to abandon his fight with the Communists and focus, instead, on deterring the Japanese. During the height of the crisis, which subsequently became known as the "Xi'an Incident," Song Qingling reportedly facilitated a deal between Joseph Stalin, the CCP, and the GMD, in what Spence (1990, 423) calls "some of the most complex and delicate negotiations in China's modern history."[6] Song Qingling had personally met Stalin when she traveled to the Soviet Union after the collapse of the First United Front in 1927. She is also said to have subsequently joined the Communist International Party in 1930 (Fang and Zhou 2008, 139). Although Song Qingling remained politically at odds with her sister, Song Meiling, and brother-in-law, Chiang Kai-shek, she reportedly delivered Stalin's message to the CCP, instructing them to spare Chiang's life so that the GMD might join forces with the Communists to fight the Japanese instead (Epstein 1993, 316–19). She also delivered substantial sums of money from Stalin to the CCP leadership in support of realizing Stalin's goal of establishing a new united front (Pantsov and Levine 2013, 311). In the immediate aftermath of the crisis, Song Qingling, He Xiangning, and Feng Yuxiang, among thirteen progressive figures, attended a session of the GMD's Central Executive Committee to begin to establish the process of reuniting the country. At the meeting, Song Qingling urged for reconciliation, even as she railed against "politicians . . . who underestimate the power of the Chinese people" (Epstein 1993, 320–21; Liu 1988, 329).

There is plenty of evidence, at both the grassroots and elite levels of the CCP, that party family brokerage was often motivated by the quest for family advancement. But behind-the-scenes maneuvering during moments of intense political struggle has not always been motivated by nepotistic goals alone. As in the case of the Xi'an Incident, Song Qingling's familial interventions were intended to advance the cause of left-leaning patriotic movements in China rather than to establish power for the Song-Chiang family, as her brother-in-law and sister might have well preferred. Ultimately, the success of the Second United Front, and the policy legacies it engendered, owed much to elite cross-party mobilization of women that emerged on the basis of party family diplomacy in early 1938.

Dominated by members of high society, party officials, and prominent public intellectuals, the elite-level organizing that emerged during the Second United Front was an important forerunner of issue networks focused on women's rights that emerged later in the century in other parts of the world. Htun (2003, 5) defines an issue network as an elite coalition of lawyers, feminist activists, doctors, legislators and state officials who endeavor to bring about policy change. Members of issue networks are linked by an "interest in a particular policy area, not collective identity, occupational category, place of residence, shared values, or ideological orientation (though members of issue networks may share these things)" (Htun 2003, 15). Thus, while issue networks may grow out of social movements, their goals are more specific, and include members from both state and society.

Members of the network that emerged first in Wuhan, and then reconsolidated in Chongqing, included some of the day's most outspoken proponents of women's rights in China. They were able to take advantage of a moment of party realignment to save the country by advancing women's status. Indeed, and similar to the signing of the Versailles Peace Treaty in 1919, the Japanese invasion in late 1937 constituted a kind of "moral shock" to national elites across the ideological spectrum, many of whom viewed Japanese atrocities with a deep sense of outrage. Mobilized by nationalist sentiment and united through family, friendship, and professional networks, many elite women set aside previous animosities to work together in an unprecedented moment of cooperation (Guo 2019). Li Dequan, future minister of health (MOH) in the PRC, played a critical role in the realization of this effort.

On the face of it, Li Dequan (1896–1972) seems to have been an unusual choice of ally for the CCP. Hailing from a family that had been Christian for three generations, Li's father was a Protestant minister and Li herself was educated by Christian missionaries and attended the Christian women's college that would later become Yanjing University. Li's first jobs, moreover, were very much in keeping with the social gospel mission: during the late 1910s and early 1920s Li taught at a girls' school, worked as a pastor's assistant in a Congregational church, and served as secretary general of the Beijing YWCA (Klein and Clark 1971, 1:531–34; Merkel-Hess 2016, 435; Zhao 2003a, 302).

After Li and Feng married in 1924, Li Dequan gave birth to five children while simultaneously caring for at least three of Feng's children from his previous marriage (Zhao 2003a, 302). It has been suggested that Feng converted to Christianity shortly after the 1911 revolution. Whether or not he did so for reasons of political calculation is unclear (Sheridan 1966, 52–54). Feng Yuxiang nonetheless made religious indoctrination an important part of the education he provided for his troops. Sheridan (1966, 122) estimates that approximately half of Feng's troops had been baptized as Christians in 1924.

Feng and Li sought to present their companionate union as both replete with affection and equality (Merkel-Hess 2016, 437), with a shared enthusiasm for social reform. An early feminist, Feng ran a girl's school for the family members of his officers, which included instruction in the "Bible, ethics, arithmetic, hygiene, and various aspects of domesticity, including the delivery of children" (Sheridan 1966, 122 and 175). Feng also outlawed sex work and foot-binding in the areas he controlled (Merkel-Hess 2016, 436; Shao 1984, 43). Li Dequan herself opened a midwifery school in Kaifeng, Henan, in 1927 or 1928 and played a strong leadership role in the province's anti–foot binding movement at that time (Johnson 2011, 160n40; Shao 1984, 20–21).

Similar to Deng Yuzhi of the YWCA, Li brought a leftist vision to maternalist reform. Li Dequan was politically active during the May Fourth Movement, organizing participation in demonstrations in her capacity as chair of the Xiehe Women's College Student Association (Huang 1997, 124). When Li married Feng in 1924, both were already developing leftist sympathies; it is thus difficult to know who influenced whom (Sheridan 1966, 130). The couple met Vladimir Lenin's widow, Nadezdha Krupskaya, and possibly Stalin when they traveled to the Soviet Union in 1926 (Li and Zhang 2007, 280).[7] Back in China, Li Dequan was rumored to have worked through her "back channels of wifely connections" to advance leftist causes (Merkel-Hess 2016, 439). Together, Li and Feng established fifteen schools for the children of local peasants (Zhao 2003a, 302), and over the course of the 1930s, became increasingly active within communist circles. Li would later sit as executive director of the Chongqing Sino-Soviet Cultural Association (Klein and Clark 1971, 1:531–34). Although Feng continued to hold high-level positions within the GMD, assuming the office of vice chairman of the Military Affairs Commission on the eve of the war with Japan (Sheridan 1966, 274), for example, Mao Zedong and the CCP viewed Feng Yuxiang as a potential ally. It is exactly in this light that Mao Zedong wrote to Feng Yuxiang in late 1936, beseeching him to bring a halt to the civil war and fight the Japanese (Mao 1936 [1992], 460–61).

Deng Yingchao actively encouraged Li Dequan's involvement in a United Front effort to protect children's welfare because of Li's leftist leanings *and* her high profile in GMD circles (Jin 1993, 1:248). At the time Deng Yingchao and Zhou Enlai approached Li Dequan, Li was serving as one of the nine founding members of the Women's Advisory Council of the New Life Movement (Merkell-Hess 2016, 442). Launched by Song Meiling in 1934, the New Life Movement blended Confucianism and Christianity in an attempt to "civilize" the Chinese people through the promotion of personal virtue. Feng Yuxiang had already gained the trust of Chiang Kai-shek, Song Meiling's husband, when Li Dequan had offered to accompany Song Meiling to Xi'an at the height of the Xi'an Incident (Jia 2012, 18). But while the couple was deeply embedded within the highest echelon of the GMD, they were nonetheless making clear overtures to the CCP. Deng Yingchao impressed Li Dequan and Guomindang officers, for example, when invited by Li Dequan to speak before the Women's Academic Council in August 1937 (Jin 1993, 1:226–28). Li was thus in a key position to assist the CCP to establish closer ties with the GMD during these crucial early days of the United Front. But Li Dequan was not the only prominent figure to aid in these efforts.

In addition to Li Dequan, high-profile Shanghai lawyer Shi Liang and the famous feminist intellectual Shen Zijiu also played significant roles in uniting the GMD and CCP to fight the Japanese and forge new social policies focused on women and children. MacKinnon (2001, 127) argues that Shi Liang was the "spark plug behind Wuhan's relief work, especially in caring for women and children," crediting Shi with mobilizing the politically divided Song sisters and focusing public attention on refugee relief.[8] Shen Zijiu, an experienced journalist and editor, founded the journal *Women's Life* (*Funü shenghuo*) in 1935 (Wang 1999, 202).[9] In 1938, Shen Zijiu and Shi Liang often hosted editorial meetings for *Women's Life* at their homes, meetings that included future ACDWF leaders including Liu Qingyang, Cao Mengjun, and Deng Yingchao. Shen Zijiu was also present when Li Dequan successfully persuaded Song Meiling to become head of the WACW (Jin 1993, 1:248; Luo 1989 [2000], 218). Deng Yuzhi and Liu-Wang Liming were involved as well: Deng Yingchao and Zhou Enlai personally recruited Deng Yuzhi to participate in the CCP-organized resistance movement during this time (Honig 1996, 259; see also, Jin 1993, 1:263), and Liu-Wang Liming joined her close friend Shi Liang (Edwards 2008, 202) in cross-party women's organizing in Chongqing in 1939 (Guo 2019, 170).

Although the United Front itself was never ideologically coherent, the efforts of high-profile women supporting war efforts within the United Front— including Li Dequan, Shi Liang, Shen Zijiu, Deng Yingchao, He Xiangning, Xu Guangping, Liu-Wang Liming, Cao Mengjun, and Song Qingling—were remarkably successful. As Guo (2019, 46) argues of the more general mobilization of elite women networks during this period, they "facilitated communication and cooperation among different political sides at the beginning of the war." Their success was especially evident under the auspices of the Wartime Association for Children's Welfare (WACW, Zhanshi ertong baoyu hui).

The WACW was formally established in March 1938. The first group established on the basis of the Second United Front (Jin 1993, 1:249; Li and Zhang 2007, 290), WACW activities were embedded within the much larger effort to organize women across party lines in wartime mobilization. Headed by Song Meiling and staffed by an executive leadership of GMD-affiliated and nationalist intellectuals and society wives, left-leaning Christians, and Communists, the association was largely responsible for mobilizing state and society to build and subsidize wartime children's homes and childcare. Leading intellectuals such as Shi Liang and Shen Zijiu had been publicly campaigning on behalf of refugees and refugee children since the beginning of 1938.[10] With the founding of the WACW, they and others were able to draw on a wide range of resources, including newly established women's wartime associations, donations from elite Chinese at home and abroad, and a high-profile leadership. The importance of this work was not simply material. As Barnes (2018, 89) argues, the highly public efforts of women elites, including Song Meiling and He Xiangning, modeled a form of emotional labor intrinsic to state-sponsored caregiving. It is a pattern of maternalist governance that would later become embedded in the work of the ACDWF as well.

The WACW was set up to transport children from occupied areas to safety as well as to provide care for and education to refugee children once they had arrived. Over the course of the war, the WACW established some sixty-one children's homes (Plum 2006, 71). The WACW also played a significant role in relocating orphanages and childcare centers when the GMD abandoned Wuhan for Chongqing in the fall of 1938. More than fifteen thousand children were evacuated from wartime orphanages in Wuhan in a total of twenty-eight groups (Plum 2006, 77). At least one prominent future ACDWF leader, Cao Mengjun, led some of these rescue operations (Jin 1993, 1:251; Plum 2006, 75–76).[11]

By mid-1938, close to 15 percent of 430,000 war refugees were being provided with shelter (MacKinnon 2001, 129). More than forty state-supported childcare centers were established in southwestern China (MacKinnon 2001, 130) and some 220,000 war orphans were housed in children's homes in both GMD- and CCP-controlled regions (Plum 2006, 11–12).[12] Ultimately, approximately half of those in need were assisted in some way by relief efforts (MacKinnon 2001, 127).

The roster of officials affiliated with the WACW was impressive. In addition to Song Meiling, who served as chair of the association, and Li Dequan, who served as vice chair, the board included some of the most powerful national political leaders of the day, including Chiang Kai-shek, Feng Yuxiang, Song Ziwen (brother to sisters Ailing, Meiling, and Qingling, also known as T.V. Soong), Zhou Enlai, and other senior male CCP leaders, including Zhu De, Peng Dehuai, and Ye Jianying. Despite the ideological differences among those associated with the work, there was a clear shared commitment to the welfare of children as a means of upholding the future of China. As Plum (2011, 189) observes, orphans became symbols of the continuation and revitalization of the *minzu*, or the Chinese race. Deng

Yingchao herself argued as much in an essay published in the *New China Daily* (*Xinhua ribao*) in the spring of 1938: "Childcare is a great undertaking. It is not only necessary to save and educate children, but also to cultivate a strong spirit (within) children (as they) will become the masters of building a new China" (cited in Jin 1993, 1:250). Inscriptions that senior CCP leaders prepared in recognition of the founding of the WACW reflect this emphasis as well, including: "Long live the children [*ertong wansui!*]" by Mao Zedong, and "Protect the next generation [*baoyou houdai*]" by Zhu De (Wang, Liu, and Chang 2002, 316).

WACW also built directly on Song Meiling's previous leadership of the New Life Movement. Similar to the Late Qing reformers, GMD state builders sought to make mothers central to the remaking of the nation. To this end, the GMD revived the term *good wives, wise mothers*, launching an "education by mothers' movement" (*mujiao yundong*), in which women were made responsible for the moral direction of the nation through scientific childrearing (Guo 2019, 99; Schneider 2011). Song Meiling's goal to mobilize educated, professional women to modernize housekeeping and to civilize families through the science of hygienic principles and childcare rapidly expanded and deepened during the war with Japan (Ferlanti 2012; Schneider 2012).

Yanjing University, a Christian institution, was one of the first to establish a home economics department in China, with an explicit focus on home management (*jiating guanli*) (Schneider 2011, 120). While the original intention had been to train women to be better homemakers and teachers, by the mid-1930s Yanjing's home economics curriculum was focused on the skills necessary for women to become professionals outside the home (Schneider 2011, 124–25). During the war, preexisting emphases on childrearing and nutrition took on greater import, with students experimenting in ways to create economical and nutritious meals under wartime conditions (Schneider 2011, 138). At the same time, the GMD sought to expand their social service administration, with particular emphasis placed on collecting data about children's health and development and increased training in domestic management (Schneider 2011, 157, 169). Ferlanti (2012, 188) argues that New Life efforts to mobilize women civil servants to fundraise, promote frugality and outreach, and engage in the urgent demands of relief work "prevented the disintegration of society and administrative institutions under the impact of the war in the first phase of the conflict."[13]

During the same period, the GMD government also oversaw a major expansion of public health services, including the immunization of children, sanitation campaigns, and a rapid expansion of nurses and midwives (Barnes 2018). These were extraordinary developments given that prior to the war the state had played a much more limited role in the provision of social welfare. These accomplishments were also highly gendered. According to Barnes (2018, 53), the physical and emotional work undertaken by women on the frontlines of healthcare played an unprecedented role in connecting people's homes and bodies to the state. As such, it would prove to be an important node in a much longer process of state formation. As argued by MacKinnon (2001, 127), wartime relief aid and public health work "laid the foundation for the comprehensive social-welfare and health programs that were later instituted in the PRC and ROC." Wartime relief aid and public health work would similarly lay important foundations for post-1949 women-work as well.

The Emergence of Marxist Maternalist Equality

It should be noted that for all of the early and effective collaboration that took place during the Second United Front, progressive women leaders sought to differentiate their vision of women, and women's organizing, from that of the New Life Movement under Song Meiling's direction. In one of Deng Yingchao's (1937 [1991]) first published essays after the full-scale invasion by the Japanese, she argued that the war had caused a change in the status of women; specifically, that the disruption had freed women from the feudal bondage (*fengjian de shufu*) of kitchen and home. This was a statement that unequivocally equated housework with oppression and was thus at odds with GMD efforts to remake the household in service of wartime work at that same moment. In May 1938, at a cross-party gathering of women elites in Lushan, while Deng Yingchao and Meng Qingshu endorsed the New Life Movement, they nonetheless emphasized the needs of women workers, advocating for reproductive health protections and the urgent work of eliminating violence against women and children, including the abandonment of baby girls and foot binding (Deng and Meng 1938 [1991], 44–53). In the earliest months of the Second United Front, Deng Yingchao also insisted on the importance of representing and speaking for the most oppressed (Deng 1938 [1991], 77) and advocating for a Marxist-Leninist view of liberation, which could not be separated from the "liberation of humankind as a whole" (1939 [1991], 164). By staking these claims, Deng Yingchao seemingly sought to replace a subjectivity for women defined exclusively through the home, or through a professional life geared toward the improvement of the family and household, with the possibility of a liberated laboring woman subject (*laodong funü*). Just as important, Deng Yingchao laid out a vision of a national organizational structure through which to mobilize women. Deng proposed that a Women's National Salvation Association, should build and expand on preexisting organizations to link women at every level of the polity: village, county, and province, and implicate women from all walks of life, regardless of party status, religion, profession, or class. Although Song Mingling's preference prevailed, and the organizers opted to build on the New Life structure to mobilize women professionals, it is notable that Deng Yingchao was already identifying the basic organizational shape of the ACDWF, as it would be established a decade later.

The fact is, progressive elite women had long been outraged by the revival of term *good wives, wise mothers* under the New Life Movement. One debate featured prominently in *Women's Life* during the mid-1930s. Another, much more focused critique was published in the *New China Daily*. In these outlets and other high-profile publications, left-leaning women, including Shen Zijiu, editor of *Women's Life*, upheld revolutionary struggle as the path for women's liberation (Luo 1989 [2000], 213; Ren 1989, 226–29). Song Qingling (1942 [1953]) made these arguments overseas as well.

At the same time, other leading public figures continued to struggle for the realization of women's rights and suffrage in the context of wartime. Liu-Wang Liming and Shi Liang, for example, actively campaigned on behalf of women's suffrage after both women became councilors on the People's Political Council (*Guomin canzhenghui*), a semidemocratic, multiparty forum (Edwards 2008). Li Dequan, in her writings on the wartime mobilization of women, insisted on the importance of women's intrinsic personhood and the necessity of raising women's consciousness (Li 1943 [1991]). And Song Qingling (1939 [1991], 245–46), writing from Hong Kong, fiercely critiqued fascism's toll in Italy and Germany. Fascism, Song argued, was squeezing women out of opportunities for economic independence and reducing women to raising "cannon fodder machines." She contrasted this example, and other examples of women's oppression in Japan, with the role of China's wartime women, some of whom were fighting on the front lines, and others who were caring for wartime orphans and the wounded.

While progressive elites openly advocated for women's rights and sought to free women from many of their traditional domestic duties, however, they by no means rejected all notions of sex difference. Indeed, outspoken feminists ranging from Liu-Wang Liming, who never relinquished her views on the role of mothers in the home, to more hardline communists, stressed the importance of women's responsibilities vis-à-vis family life. For example, in 1936, Luo Qiong (1936 [2000], 143–44), one of the CCP's most prominent women-work theorists, refuted the "good wife, wise mother" slogan in an essay in *Women's Life*. In an otherwise critical piece that made a mockery of the so-called biological and ethical basis of wifehood and motherhood, Luo nonetheless suggested that women "should" (*yinggai*) become wives and mothers, arguing that she was not opposing the "biological characteristics of women" (*shengli shang de texing*), but rather opposing the "unreasonable social system" (*bu heli de shehui zhidu*). At the 1938 Lushan meetings, Deng Yingchao and Meng Qingshu (1938 [1991], 45) reinforced a maternalist vision of nationally purposed professionals, when they called for the mobilization of childcare workers, women teachers, and women doctors, as well as "new model mothers" (*mofan de muqin*) and "model caregivers (or) Chinese Nightingales" (*mofan de kanhu, zhongguo de nan ding ge'er*), in rear support work for the war. Despite enduring and important ideological differences between the two parties, both the GMD and CCP nonetheless shared a commitment to motherhood specifically, and maternalist reform, generally, as a means to save the nation and reconstruct the country (Hubbard 2018).

In 1942, Deng Yingchao and Zhou Enlai waded into the "good wives, wise mothers" debate, publishing separate critiques in the *New China Daily*. Deng's article, published in April of that year, was the more progressive of the two, unequivocally insisting that both fathers and mothers had an equal responsibility to care for their children (Deng 1942 [1987], 182–86). Indeed, although Deng Yingchao asserted that mothers were "suited" (*shiyi xing*) to the work of parenting, she nonetheless placed parenting into a larger context of a shared and collective project, which required the liberation of women. In an essay published five months later, Zhou Enlai presented a slightly different perspective on motherhood. While Zhou also insisted that both parents should share the responsibility of raising their children, he simultaneously asserted that women had unavoidable natural responsibilities (*tianzhi*).[14] In particular, he argued that maternal duty (*muzhi*) is crucial to the well-being of society and the nation. In advocating this concept of "maternal duty," Zhou, like earlier women party activists, did not think that if housework were socialized, women would no longer have a special obligation to motherhood. To the contrary, even if a public day care system were perfect, he wrote, children would still require their mother (Zhou 1942 [1991], 611). To this end, Zhou Enlai not only repeatedly refers to the duty of motherhood, but also to *muxing*, or the maternal instinct. Zhou Enlai was also at great pains to differentiate the subjectivity of womanhood under capitalism and socialism: whereas *nüzi* are women without access to a supportive social structure (legal and economic), *funü* have the social support necessary to fulfill their duty to mother, whether alone or in partnership with a husband. In accordance with Zhou Enlai's rendering, the CCP liberated subject, funü, should be glorified and supported on the basis of their particular gendered contributions to the well-being of society.

Of the two visions of motherhood, it is Zhou's that prevailed, encapsulating, I would argue, the ethos of "Marxist maternalist equality" that was emerging within the CCP at that historical moment. Marxist maternalist equality combined Engelsian and May Fourth principles of sexual equality with a concern for protecting reproductive health and maintaining the family at the center of the national project. This vision diverged from Engel's vision of women's liberation in several ways. Whereas Engels deemed that women's participation in economic production and the provision of collectivized housework was sufficient to realize women's equality, the CCP leadership insisted that more support was required. Women required special consideration and assistance because they had suffered more than men under feudal patriarchy. This assistance included consciousness raising, for example, so that women could overcome their inherent sense of inferiority, as well as legal redress for past injustices. Women were different from men, the evolving CCP doctrine determined, not just because of historical injustice but also because of the natural physiological characteristics of the two sexes. To this end, women were encouraged to fulfill their physiological and spiritual destiny through motherhood and the cultivation of the democratic socialist family.[15] While men were simultaneously expected to share in the division of household chores, it was made clear that the primary responsibility for the well-being of the family—including cooking, making clothes, economizing, cleaning, and minding children—was that of women.

Zhou Enlai's essay was published shortly after the alliance between the GMD and the CCP had shattered and in the context of the first major rectification of CCP women's organizing. Led by Mao Zedong and Cai Chang, the Rectification Movement critiqued past practices of the women's movement, including rights-based advocacy, in favor of mobilizing a broad mass of women in support of the war effort. In an era of increasing hardship, including tightening Japanese blockades and the cessation of GMD subsidies, Mao Zedong and Cai Chang argued that rural women could ensure the survival of their families through their ability to produce and to economize. Protecting "rural women's interests" meant understanding their physiological and emotional limitations and honouring the familial duties that they were bound to uphold. While Zhou's careful attention to the glorious duties of motherhood can be read as a critical response to his wife's more progressive vision, it can also be read as an important part of the CCP story that was simultaneously playing out in CCP-occupied base areas in the early 1940s. As I discuss in the next chapter, the goal of this rectification was not the liberation of an individuated rights-based subject nor the liberation of a collective revolutionary subject, but the realization of a new, more dignified status for the rural woman in the context of her household, neighbourhood, and family fields: the household manager.

The Maternalist Social Policy Regime

After a long and bloody civil war, progressive elites found themselves in 1949 with a newfound capacity to undertake social reform on a scale that few of its participants had previously imagined was possible. With the support of the infra-structure of the preexisting bureaucracy, a powerful party apparatus, and the establishment of a new mass organization, the ACDWF, elite progressive reform-ers were suddenly able to systematically tackle the worst "ills" of a war-ridden nation: sex work, addiction, extreme poverty, disease, sexual inequality, and social decay. Indeed, with the formal establishment of the ACDWF the maternal-ist ideal that women should participate as leaders in the governance of home and nation as funü became institutionalized on a wide scale for the first time. The differing physiological and spiritual capacities of women not only positioned women as the "natural" caretakers of children but also as the "natural" leaders of social policy reform, a priority for the most powerful CCP officials who viewed the well-being of women and children as a sign of the civilizational status of the nation as a whole.

Neither the establishment of the ACDWF nor the larger social policy regime in which it was embedded, however, were predetermined outcomes in early Mao-ist state building. The fact is, not one woman held a seat on the Politburo, the Commanding Heights of the new regime in the 1950s, an outcome that, in the case of Deng Yingchao, stemmed directly from Zhou Enlai's fear of how such appointments would be perceived within the upper echelons of the CCP.[16] Time and again, Zhou Enlai forbid Deng Yingchao from assuming a more powerful role than that which she would have otherwise assumed. In 1982, Deng Yingchao spoke with "infinite emotion" (wuxian ganqing) about this history of exclusion to nephews and nieces:

> In the early days of liberation, they [renjia] wanted me to join the gov-ernment affairs committee, [but] your uncle didn't agree; when the Women's Federation was restored, they again asked me to join, but he still disagreed and argued with them; when it was time to fix wages, elder sister Cai Chang was given a level three, and I was allocated level five, [but] when [the matter] came to him, I was assigned a level six. When it was time to [celebrate] the tenth anniversary of the National Day and he saw that I was to be on the list to be on the podium, he crossed it out again, because I was his wife. Now I am the vice chair of the National People's Congress, a member of the Politburo, and secre-tary of the Disciplinary Committee, tasks all assigned by the Party. But if your uncle was still here, there is no way he would have let me take these posts. (Guo 2004, 97)[17]

"The larger picture," was likely twofold: a fear that the couple would be regarded as constituting a faction, or the basis of the faction, and a fear that the couple would be perceived to profit from their higher offices as a family.

In this instance, the gender norms of practical kinship prioritized Zhou Enlai's political status and power over that of his wife; an excruciating irony given Deng Yingchao's status as the PRC's most prominent feminist.

Rather than appointing women to the Politburo and other positions of direct influence within the CCP and new government structure, the leading men of the CCP deliberately established institutional mechanisms through which women officials could advocate for social reform and women's rights through other channels. While this approach perpetuated the marginalization of women's issues within the highest echelons of party and state, it nonetheless legitimized and formalized preexisting family and friendship ties as part of the fabric of the new bureaucracy.

In the lead-up to the formal establishment of the PRC, Mao, Liu Shaoqi, and Zhou Enlai appointed senior women leaders to multiple, concurrent posts through careful management of the *nomenklatura*, the name list of the most senior official appointments in the new regime, and from which women officials themselves could actively fight for maternalist policy reform. These "interlocking positions" (Zhang 1996, 193), or "interlocking directorates" (Lieberthal 1995, 212), enabled senior women officials to achieve rapid and significant progress in their effort to remake the social policy landscape. It is in this way that a wartime mobilization evolved from an issue network, made up of state and society actors across the political spectrum, into a full-fledged state-based "advocacy coalition" that Sabatier (1988, 139) defines as "people from a variety of positions (elected and agency officials, interest group leaders, researchers) who share a particular belief system—i.e. basic values, causal assumptions, and problem perceptions— who show a non-trivial degree of coordinated activity over time." What scholars recognize as a form of "policy entrepreneurship" (Kingdon 2003, 179–83; Mertha 2009) was actually baked into the design of the new state.

Nested within a larger matrix of bureaucracies and informal ties, the Chongqing Coalition drew its strength from the larger maternalist social policy regime in which it was embedded, and which it sought to expand. Focused on social provisions and regulations, the maternalist social policy regime was composed of an interconnected and fragmented system of authority that included offices of the CCP, local and national governments, and mass organizations.[18] In many ways, the maternalist social policy regime reflected the system of power in which it was embedded: what Lieberthal (1992) identifies as a fragmented form of authoritarianism that operated through a horizontal and vertical system of accountability, in which individual officials reported to several masters while being forced to seek compromises with bureaucratic units operating at the same level. Although negotiating this complex grid often made decision making and policy implementation a challenging and protracted process (Lieberthal and

Oksenberg 1988, 24; Lampton 1992), it also enabled leaders occupying multiple offices within party, government, and mass organizations to leverage their positions to "carry out the functions of the state despite the separate responsibilities and tasks of the organizations" (Bachman 1991, 35).

In the new government, a number of senior cross-sectoral appointments were made on the basis of an attached logic. Indeed, the CCP leadership deliberately drew on preexisting informal ties, including those forged through elite party families, to focus policy attention and praxis. The maternalist social policy regime thus emerged as an early example of what Evans (1995, 12) calls "embedded autonomy" or "bureaucracies embedded in a concrete set of social ties that binds the state to society and provides institutionalized channels for the continued negotiation and renegotiation of goals and policies." The appointment of He Xiangning and her son Liao Chengzhi as director and vice director of the Overseas Chinese Bureau, for example, centered their revolutionary contributions and sacrifice, foreign contacts, and national networks, in the development of the PRC's relationship with Chinese communities outside of China. After Japan's invasion of China, He Xiangning had relocated to Hong Kong and worked alongside Song Qingling to raise funds among the overseas Chinese community (Lee 2003b, 203). He Xiangning's daughter, Liao Mengxing (Cynthia Liao), who worked as Song Qingling's assistant during the war (Snow 1967, 101) and whose husband had sacrificed his own life to save Zhou Enlai (Phatanothai with Peck 1994), was simultaneously made head of the Foreign Affairs Department of the Women's Federation. As Evans (1995, 49) argues, "Internal networks are crucial to the bureaucracy's coherence." In the case of the early PRC, deeply embedded ties among key members of government, strengthened institutional efficiency, enhanced the symbolic legitimacy of the new regime, and reinforced the state as a site of familial care and belonging.[19]

Operating at the heart of this bureaucratic system of fragmented authority was the ACDWF: the key institutional embodiment of the PRC gender order during the first years of the PRC. Work on the ACDWF began shortly after Mao Zedong issued instructions in October 1948 (Mao 1948 [1991], 289). A committee led by Cai Chang (chair), Deng Yingchao (vice chair), Li Dequan (vice chair), and Xu Guangping (vice chair), was struck in January 1949, and by April seven national women's organizations, including the WCTU and YWCA, were formally organized under the mass umbrella organization of the ACDWF.[20] The niangjia of Chinese women, or "Mum's home," was thus in place six months before the PRC was established.

In 1949, no less than one-third of the ACDWF Permanent Standing Committee appointments were former participants in the wartime mobilizations of the previous decades, including Deng Yingchao, Li Dequan, Shen Zijiu, Cao

Mengjun, Liu-Wang Li Ming, and Deng Yuzhi.[21] With these and other ACDWF officials holding concurrent official posts in government departments and party organizations, the realization of large-scale maternalist social policy reform suddenly became possible in a way that had never before been imaginable. Song Qingling and He Xiangning both served as honorary chair of the ACDWF while holding other governmental positions: Song Qingling as vice president of the Central People's Government and He Xiangning as head of the Overseas Chinese Affairs Bureau. Deng Yingchao, Li Dequan, Xu Guangping, and Shi Liang all served as members of the Standing Committee of the Chinese People's Political Consultative Conference (CPPCC); and Cai Chang, Deng Yingchao, and Xu Guangping all became members of the Standing Committee of the National People's Congress when it was first convened in 1954.

Among the most prominent cross-appointments included, Shen Zijiu, who concurrently served as editor-in-chief of the journal *Xin Zhongguo funü* (New Chinese Women) and Li Dequan, who served as minister of health. Although Shi Liang, minister of justice, was not appointed to the Permanent Standing Committee of the ACDWF in 1949, she was promoted to vice chair of the ACDWF in 1953—an appointment that coincided with a large-scale mobilization to promote the 1950 Marriage Law.

The predominance of interlocking positions held by women officials led to two mutually reinforcing practices in the development and implementation of maternalist social policy during the early 1950s. First, multiple official appointments enabled senior women officials to build consensus and then concentrate the organizational resources of different bureaucratic sectors on a particular objective, a form of bureaucratic management known as *xitong*.[22] Second, the multiple appointments enabled officials to achieve several objectives in one campaign. As I will show, the multiple concurrent appointments held by both Li Dequan and Shi Liang increased their effectiveness to tackle midwifery reform and marriage reform.

Over the course of the early 1950s, the ACDWF played two intersecting roles in state building: enhancing the PRC's international status and serving as a hub through which major social policy reform could be realized. One of the very first international meetings hosted by the newly established government in late 1949 was the International Asian Women's Conference, attended by 165 participants from fourteen different countries (Ren 1989, 305–6). A central focus was the common problems of women and to "work out a programme of action for their social economic rights and peace" (Keith 1949, 2–3). By immediately organizing an international meeting about and for women, the new regime was sending an important signal to the rest of the world: the PRC was not only meeting the standards of civilization, it was leading them.

Wartime leaders also served as international representatives of the new regime, including Liu-Wang Liming and Deng Yuzhi. Liu-Wang Liming attended the International Asian Women's Conference held in Beijing in 1954 and led a delegation to West Germany to attend the WCTU Congress, a meeting at which she was elected vice president of the WCTU (Edwards 2003, 376).[23] The ACDWF Leading Party Group viewed Deng Yuzhi, head of the Chinese YWCA, as an asset to help build the PRC's reputation overseas; suggesting in a 1953 report, for example, that the CCP should publish some of her writings (ACWF 1953).[24]

Song Qingling also brought standing to the new regime as a senior ambassador of maternalist internationalism. Song had spent much of the early 1940s fundraising overseas on behalf of the war effort to fight Japan, including the effort to support orphanages (Shang and Tang 1990, 429). After the foundation of the PRC, Song oversaw the management of the China Welfare Institute, which focused on maternal and child health. The Child Welfare Institute also published the English-language periodical, *China Reconstructs*, a venue in which Song "linked the welfare of women and children to the arena of foreign affairs" (Johnson, Littell-Lamb, and Manning 2018).

Next to Song Qingling, it was Li Dequan who emerged as one of the PRC's most influential representatives overseas. Indeed, Li Dequan would represent the ACDWF and MOH on multiple occasions, including in 1955 when she led a delegation of twenty-two to attend the World Mothers' Congress in Switzerland (Li and Zhang 2007; Li 1955). Appointed head of the Chinese Red Cross, Li Dequan engaged in a number of sensitive negotiations on behalf of the PRC (Merkel-Hess 2016, 448–49), including overseeing the repatriation of 417 Japanese war criminals to Japan (Cathcart and Nash 2009, 95). Between 1949 and 1962, Li Dequan made some forty-two separate trips abroad to twenty-four countries (Klein and Clark 1971, 1:533–34).

At first glance, the ACDWF's role in policy formation seems to have been determined by the CCP. Indeed, the relationship between the CCP and the ACDWF would prove central to the operation and continuation of the federation, with the CCP leadership setting the parameters on the federation's top priorities and processes. It was Liu Shaoqi, for example, who instructed the Central Committee's Women's Movement Committee (Zhonggong Zhongyang funü yundong weiyuanhui, hereafter CCWMC) and the ACDWF to make marriage reform, midwifery reform, and childcare its first priorities (Luo 1998b [2000], 23). But Women's Federation officials were also proactive participants in the policy formation process. As a "conveyor belt," the ACDWF was expected to solicit feedback from women, make recommendations to the central party apparatus, and thereafter implement new policy measures at local levels.[25] Initially designed as an umbrella group for a diverse set of women's organizations, the ACDWF was composed of committees at every level of government, from the province down to the township level. These committees maintained close horizontal connections with the local government and party; indeed, funds for Women's Federation activities came from local government. Significantly, however, the committees also responded to and implemented directives that came from the ACDWF. Organizational autonomy in this context thus meant the ability of women's organizations to realize Marxist maternalist objectives in cooperation with, albeit independently from, local authorities.

The CCWMC, however, also played a key role in policy development. Indeed, the committee was expected to maintain cohesiveness between the CCP and women-work, a point Mao Zedong drove home in November of 1952 as the ACDWF leadership prepared for a spring campaign on the new Marriage Law. When Deng Yingchao reported to Mao that the CCP committee was unavailable for meetings and thus not living up to its word, Mao urged Deng Yingchao and the other members of the CCWMC to be both active and reciprocal in their dealings with the CCP, advising senior women leaders to strengthen their relationship with the CCP through providing more material on their work, pushing for a rapid response, and by being willing to give and receive criticism (*yi song, er cui, san piping*). Mao urged them to be nothing less than forceful with the CCP: "If they won't see you, you can wait outside their office, cursing; wait there until they have to see you" (Jin 1993, 2:490–91). In her discussion of Mao's instructions, Kang Keqing (1977 [1988], 432) interprets Mao to mean that the Women's Federation leadership could criticize the CCP leadership when it was warranted, while urging the senior women leaders to advocate for their work through the CCP organizational structure.[26] As I show in chapters 4 and 5, Deng Yingchao would prove particularly adept at managing this art.

The highly impactful role the ACDWF played as a vehicle of social policy reform flowed from the built-in "connectedness" and determination of its senior leadership. The official appointments that enabled the Chongqing Coalition to establish the maternalist social policy regime, however, were not a sufficient basis from which to launch and deepen social policy reform. Indeed, given both external and internal resistance to the work of the Women's Federation, senior Women's Federation officials developed additional methods of advocacy.

Wang (2005) describes the strategies of contention, negotiation, and compromise leveraged by senior Women's Federation officials as a form of "insider agitation." Senior ACDWF officials drew careful attention to the official pronouncements and policy statements of senior party leaders as a means of legitimating their work and as a means of maintaining the legitimacy of the Women's Federation itself. Optics were extremely important: when senior men officials, including Mao Zedong, Liu Shaoqi, Deng Xiaoping, Zhou Enlai, Peng Dehuai, and Zhu De attended high-profile

Women's Federation events, as they did on a regular basis throughout the 1950s, or spoke out on particular issues related to women-work, as they did from time to time, they signaled to the rest of the CCP the importance of the work of the federation and that it had the full support of the most powerful male officials in the CCP. Senior male officials could also legitimate the organization in times of crisis. When several senior men officials argued against establishing a Women's Federation because the USSR did not have an equivalent (the Soviets disbanded the Zhendotel in 1930), for example, it was Liu Shaoqi who actively defended its importance (Luo 1998b [2000], 19).

Senior Women's Federation officials were also adept at "waving the flag to oppose the flag."[27] What Wang (2017, 18–19) has called a "politics of concealment" enabled senior Women's Federation officials to camouflage their agenda through the usage of dominant party language. These practices, in turn, bolstered the position of key ACDWF leaders within the party apparatus, a strategy that has continued into the Reform Era (see, Liu 2006; Jiang and Zhou 2021).[28] The representation of the Women's Federation made visible in the post-Mao publication of memoirs, biographies, and select archival sources, for example, is further evidence of a strategy of historical legitimation that continues until this day.

Finally, the informal ties that key Women's Federation leaders maintained with senior male officials at the apex of the CCP would prove crucial as well. As Oksenberg (1974, 29–30) notes, informal communications in the Maoist Chinese bureaucracy were just as important, if not more important, than formal communications. Lampton (1992, 56–57) similarly observes that "old friends" and relatives were critical in bureaucratic bargaining in China, with marriage patterns playing a particularly important role in establishing lines of influence and obligation. Senior women officials thus drew on their guanxi ties to senior men officials as "crucial channels of access to the male-dominated center" (Wang 2017, 70). The role of personal ties generally, and party families ties in particular, however, shaped the work of the ACDWF in ways that went well beyond strategic access. Indeed, the revolutionary attachments underlying the new regime embedded the ACDWF within a matrix of loyalty and fervor that would also define the priorities of the organization in complex ways.

By the time the PRC was founded in 1949, the senior CCP leadership had spent decades living, working, and socializing with one another. In addition to the most high-profile companionate marriages, other longstanding personal ties facilitated the work of the maternalist social policy regime. Deng Yingchao and Zhou Enlai lived next door to Deng Xiaoping and his new wife in the late 1920s (Vogel 2011, 26), for example, just one of many shared intimacies that created the basis for mutual trust and cooperation. Deng Yingchao and Zhou Enlai had similarly worked with Liu Shaoqi for years. Although Zhou and Liu were at times rivals (Wilson 1984), Deng Yingchao and Zhou Enlai maintained good relations with Liu and his wife, Wang Guangmei, and attended their wedding (Jin 1993, 1:431). After the foundation of the PRC, many of the families of the most powerful CCP leaders lived in Zhongnanhai, a former part of the imperial city, or in nearby compounds. Birthdays and other moments of shared celebrations reinforced the connectedness of the leaders and their shared histories.[29] This was particularly the case for Cai Chang and Mao Zedong. As a "member" of Mao Zedong's natal family, Cai Chang took care of family matters for the chairman and frequently visited Mao's residence to attend celebrations and weddings, eat dinner, and listen to Mao recite new poems (Li 1997, 51).[30] As I will begin to discuss in the next chapter, it was a relationship that would have a powerful impact on the development of women-work and the mission of the Women's Federation.

During the late 1930s, densely networked party families altered the course of the war by cementing the Second United Front and, in so doing, laid much of the groundwork for social policy reform that would be taken up in the PRC. The elite women leaders who participated in these families helped to realize the conditions that made party realignment possible and, in so doing, established conditions for the more active participation of women in formal politics. Nonetheless, they were still very much subject to the conditions of history. They were agents, yes, but agents struggling to strengthen the Chinese nation in a time of war through improving the welfare of mothers and their children. The rationale driving many of these women, therefore, was not only based on the concept of independent personhood (duli renge) but also a highly relational concept of woman-as-mother of the nation.

Koven and Michel (1990, 1085) describe maternalism as "extraordinarily protean," as an ideology "capable of drawing together unlikely and often transitory coalitions between people who appeared to speak a common language but had opposing political commitments and views of women." This was no less the case in the forging of Chinese maternalism (Hubbard 2018). Indeed, the extraordinarily protean nature of Chinese maternalism is evident in the two quotes that begin this chapter. Whereas Song Meiling, the key figure behind the conservative New Life Movement, refers to women's emancipation, Song Qingling's comments reflect an almost apocalyptic maternalism in which women were exhorted to struggle against the scourge of fascism and war to forever end "the earth's frightful testing time." Although the quotes reflect the foreign audience for which they were intended, I would argue that they are also a testament to the way in which maternalism was continually circulated and reinvoked in midcentury China, in no small part through the enduring influence of social gospel Christianity.

Just as pre-1949 patterns of labor mobilization impacted labor relations within the PRC (Perry 1994), and the wartime expansion of social services played a role in the development of health work after 1949 (Barnes 2018; MacKinnon 2001, 132; Mitter and Schneider 2012; Plum 2006, 17; Yip 2001, 184), pre-1949 women's mobilizations and networks shaped the discursive and organizational features of Maoist-era social policy reform and the state institutions that undergird it. Social gospel efforts to eradicate drug and alcohol abuse, wipe out sex work, and transform mothers into hygienic and frugal household managers would be magnified tenfold after the establishment of the PRC and supported by an army of women professionals who had previously trained in education, the domestic sciences, social work, and medicine. From the perspective of senior Chinese Communist women officials, the expansion of these programs was an enactment of a national duty that first emerged during early state building and activism, and that crystallized into policy and practice with the onslaught of the world war.

The most powerful leaders of the ACDWF were decidedly *not* social gospel reformers. But they and the CCP male leaders most concerned with social reform, including Mao Zedong, Liu Shaoqi, and Zhou Enlai, believed that mothers and their children required the state's protection. As argued by Caldwell (1986, 210) commenting about China and other low-mortality countries, these societies "took it for granted that their political and social energies should be devoted to these goals."

Significantly, and in contrast with many other world leaders at that moment, the senior CCP leadership also believed that women-as-mothers had an historic role to play in the shaping of the new polity. To this end, the importance senior male leaders attached to women's leadership cannot be understated: women were viewed as best suited to undertake the serious work of social policy reform and were strategically cross-appointed as leaders in government, party, and mass organizations to enable them to do just that. In contrast with the factional model, which has suggested that bureaucracy serves as a trellis on which personal ties develop (Nathan 1973), the process here was reversed: informal ties served as the foundation of bureaucracy. Indeed, it was through the deliberate formalization of an issue network into a legitimate advocacy coalition that the Chongqing Coalition became key to the social policy apparatus of the early PRC.

By 1949, maternalist thought was so deeply ingrained that leading CCP officials no longer identified some of its complex early origins. In Deng Yingchao's talks commemorating the promulgation of the PRC's new constitution in 1954, for example, she explicitly linked "sex equality" with the "moral and good social practices" of respecting mothers and caring for children (Jin 1993, 2:506–7), an emphasis that would resonate loudly with the language of the New Life Movement and an earlier generation of American social reformers.[31] And yet, Deng

Yingchao's complex enactment of social reform, and the progressive and party family politics in which it was entangled, suggest at the very least an ongoing ambivalence regarding the relationship between women's liberation and the family. As I will show, this tension would become particularly acute in her work on the 1950 Marriage Law.

Liu Shaoqi's active defense of the ACDWF points to some of the additional challenges that senior women officials faced in their "institutional quest for legitimacy" (Mackay 2014, 556). As I argue in the chapters that follow, important divisions not only marked the collective leadership of the ACDWF, but also the complex states of activism that marked women-work at all levels of the new regime. Conflict, not cooperation, shaped the priorities of the ACDWF, including deep disagreement over the Marriage Law, the regulation of pregnancy and birth, and policies governing the rural household. The fact that some of these same women and men officials were simultaneously committed to maternalist reform and Maoist ideology and praxis, only served to compound the conflicts and complexities in the workings of the maternalist social policy regime. This is not only because of the violence inherent in maternalist reform, a dimension I discuss more deeply in part II, but also because maternalist reform refracted through at least two distinct, albeit overlapping, Maoist expressions of revolutionary agency. It is to these states of activism that I turn next.

THE LONG MARCH TO YAN'AN

I simply don't know how to be a woman [so] I can't do women-work
[Wo genben bu hui zuo nüren, wo bu neng zuo funü gongzuo].

—Demobilized soldier, 1939, cited in Zhu Chengxia, "A Year of Women-Work in
Dabieshan"

Many women cadres of intellectual backgrounds in leading
organizations for women-work only know what they have learned
about "freedom of marriage," "economic independence," [and]
opposing "the oppression of the four-year-olds, etc. . . ." [They] never
think about where to start based upon actual conditions.

—Cai Chang, "Welcoming the New Direction in Women-Work"

Kang Keqing was just fourteen when she resolved to become a soldier.[1] Born
into a destitute family, the illiterate teenager had been raised by foster parents.
When Kang heard rumors that the Northern Expedition was recruiting women
to join their forces, she prepared to join them. Although the expedition never
passed by Kang Keqing's Jiangxi village, Kang was quickly drawn into revolutionary politics: Kang's foster father served as chair of the Peasant Union, and Kang
herself became the township director of the Women's Association and a member
of the Chinese Communist Youth League, a feeder organization established in
1920 to help young people study communism. Kang finally realized her dream of
becoming a soldier when she joined the Red Army at the age of seventeen (Kang
1993, 1–31). Over the course of a decade, Kang survived the GMD's hunt for
Communists, the CCP's withdrawal from the Jiangxi Soviet, and the devastating
losses of the Long March. Kang also married Zhu De—one of the party's most
powerful military commanders and a man some sixteen years her senior—at the
age of eighteen.

Kang was reportedly a sharpshooter and successfully led troops in battle,
although her primary tasks within the army involved propaganda work and par-
tisan organizing (Kang 1993; Snow 1972, 211–18). In her 1937 interview with
Helen Snow (1939 [1977]), Kang Keqing expressed fierce pride for having been
only one of two women to command troops. As Snow (1939 [1977], 187) notes,
Kang was not interested in feminism but rather in "equal rights for command

over men for equal fighting ability."[2] When Snow tried to get Kang to speak about "the women's problem," Kang bristled at the American reporter's line of questioning: "I don't care much about the women's problem; I always work with men, not women" (Snow 1939 [1977], 188)."

In order to begin to unravel the puzzles of post-1949 social policy reform, including its rapid successes and brutal catastrophes, it is important to look beyond the legacies, founding stories, and kinship ties that flourished in GMD-controlled cities and consider, as well, the revolutionary politics that animated the mobilizations of the rural hinterlands. As discussed thus far, the complex reconfigurations of gender during the first decades of the twentieth century were driven by a determination to transform "woman" into a site of national rejuvenation. The circulation of New Woman and Social Reform states of activism enabled new generations of elite Chinese women to reimagine their futures as educated students, citizens, professionals, and party officials, dedicating themselves to enlightening women so that women might improve the welfare of present and future generations of Chinese children as well. Rooted largely in a physiological, psychological, and spiritual understanding of womanhood (women-who-become-mothers), maternalist states of activism became central to Republican-era state building and the Maoist era that followed. But maternalism was not the only vision of emancipation available to young Chinese women in revolutionary China.

This chapter focuses on the rise of Woman Warrior and Loyal Soldier states of activism, as they manifested in the context of the CCP's revolutionary struggle. The sacrifices made by women on the Long March, and in the revolution more generally, served to reinforce and transform the heroic model of the Woman Warrior that predated the CCP. The Woman Warrior willingly sacrificed herself for national revolution, while upholding, or even as an enactment of, filial attachment. The Woman Warrior also advocated for women, children, and the family ties they represented, even if only grudgingly. In the late 1930s and early 1940s, revolutionary struggle and the increasing dominance of Maoist thought, however, would embed wartime suffering and idealized notions of sacrifice in ways that would simultaneously marginalize the mother-child tie. As a system of ideas, Maoist thought was by and large disinterested in physiological gender difference and state building; rather, Mao, and the militants who followed him, sought to subject bodies, minds, and social spaces to violent processes of revolutionary transformation. The intense contradictions embedded in Maoist thought and in Mao's work would only continue to proliferate. Indeed, at the same moment Maoist thought was being enshrined within the CCP, Mao Zedong and Cai Chang sought to make the rural woman householder and her family ties central to wartime mobilization and state building.

Cai Chang's harsh rectification of the Chinese communist women's movement would serve as an early enactment of the Loyal Soldier, a revolutionary subject single-mindedly following Mao, the man, regardless of the consequences for those in their charge. As I will show, the founding stories, practices, and goals of Maoist revolutionary struggle would reverberate with important and divisive consequences in the activism of many women leaders, both elite and grassroots, during the 1950s.

The Woman Warrior and Revolutionary Resistance

Han Chinese folklore is replete with biographies, poems, operas, and mythical tales about women who leave home to become monks (*chu jia*) and heroic men (*da zhuang*) through their brave deeds and achievements. There are stories of Buddhist women becoming men due to their high spiritual achievement (Crane 2004; 2011), and many more that involve women acting, dressing, and fighting as men, or "Women Warriors" in which they socially transition into men (Dong 2011; Edwards 1994). Some of the most famous include Mu Guiying, a woman general from the Northern Song Dynasty, and Hua Mulan, a young woman who disguised herself as a male soldier to fight on behalf of her ailing father, from the Northern and Southern dynasties era.

In Chinese folklore, a Woman Warrior is a woman who leaves her family to undertake adventure or better the welfare of the family, often in the guise of a man (Dong 2011; Judge 2008).[3] Qiu Jin, who was executed trying to overthrow the Manchu Dynasty in 1907, is perhaps the most famous of the twentieth-century Chinese Women Warriors.[4] Although Qiu Jin drew on the stories of Hua Mulan and Knight-Errants as inspiration from a young age, it was not until her mid-twenties that she left her husband and promptly embarked on an extraordinarily radical life course for the times. Among other acts, Qiu Jin spent the next four years founding a school for girls, studying in Japan, and participating in revolutionary activism, including becoming one of the first members of Sun Yat-sen's Revolutionary Alliance (Tongmenghui) (Gilmartin 1995, 228). She also frequently attired herself in Western men's clothing, practiced fencing and boxing, and rode horseback. However, despite her interest in women's issues, she was not an advocate of women's rights as an end in itself but rather as an expression of revolutionary (Witke 1970, 55–62) and filial (Ying 2009) desire. Indeed, according to Ying (2009), Qiu Jin constructed herself as a public figure in no small part through her self-presentation as a son in mourning.

The mythologization of Qiu Jin as a revolutionary martyr and the ongoing glorification of Mulan presented another vision of revolutionary participation in which women could emerge as activists and soldiers free from what many perceived to be the negative associations of domestic life. As Crane (2011), drawing on Barlow (1994b), argues, the flexibility of Chinese cosmology—in which *yin* and *yang* do not produce sexes but rather generate forces in relation to one another—means that, when a woman leaves home, she also abandons the relations that domesticate her as a woman. Women escaped from Confucian expectations by becoming *zhangfu* (husband or man) or *da zhangfu* (heroic man): "A woman who acts like a man does not expand the idea of what a woman can be, but is rather reclassified to suit her new behavior as a man" (Crane 2011, 196). Moreover, and according to Wang (1999, 350), these "modern Mulans perceived that their self-interest could best be served through the struggle for the national interest."

Stories about Hua Mulan and Qiu Jin, which the CCP knew would help participants make sense of and contribute to the revolutionary project, figured strongly in twentieth-century revolutionary struggle. Similar to guerrilla mobilizations in El Salvador, the CCP made "*emotional appeals* about 'how people like you' should act given *historical moments* like this" (Viterna 2013, 111; italics in original). Several of the earliest CCP members, including Liu Qingyang (Gilmartin 1995, 225) and Xiang Jingyu (McElderry 1986, 96), framed their activism in the 1920s on the Hua Mulan model. Deng Yingchao also drew on the Hua Mulan's legacy in her own early revolutionary activism when she and other women students raised money for a girls' school by holding operas based on Hua Mulan's life (Jin 1993, 1:32–33). It was a model of political engagement that would continue to animate revolutionary states of activism well into the 1960s.

New revolutionary models emerged during the Civil War with the GMD (1945–49) as well. Fifteen-year-old Liu Hulan, for example, became immortalized after she was killed by the GMD while working for the CCP. Liu had run away from home at the age of thirteen to train to become a woman cadre and subsequently took on women-work, becoming the secretary of the Women's Rescue League in her natal village. Lore has it that her work was so outstanding that the Fifth District Party Committee made an exception to its normal age requirements by granting her a "rear-guard" membership at the age of fourteen (normally one had to be at least eighteen). When the GMD caught Liu Hulan and taunted her about her upcoming execution, she reportedly shouted, "Cowards don't belong to the Chinese Communist Party!" (*pa si bu dang gong chan dang*). After her death, the CCP granted her official membership status, and Mao Zedong's remarks that Liu Hulan had "lived in greatness, and died in glory" contributed to her immortalization (Bai 1988, 183).

The life and legacy of Liu Hulan would become an important touchstone among some of the former women's activists I interviewed in Henan. While Wenhe grassroots leaders Yuan Jinyu, 158, and Tang Li, 159, were inspired by the sacrifice of Liu Hulan, for example, Bao Qinglian, 160, identified Liu Hulan and the "Elder Sisters" of the Long March as her primary role models. It is in this way and many others that Woman Warrior stories of sacrifice and endurance would come to be retold and enacted among successive generations of the CCP.

Revolutionary Stories: Mothers on the Move

Between the years 1929 and 1935, the CCP was on the military defensive. GMD troops and their warlord allies attacked the Red Army, both from the ground and the sky, in an almost unceasing barrage. The CCP itself responded by developing and practicing a new form of guerrilla warfare, relying closely on the support of rural villagers. The few rural women who were recruited into the CCP at this time were often trained in Marxist doctrine and were expected to support the Communist troops. While some also received training in women-work, the protection of mothers and children was the last thing on their minds. On the Long March (1934–35), when the CCP retreated from Jiangxi to a new base in Yan'an, most women tried to ignore, postpone, or avoid pregnancy altogether.[5]

In October 1934, the Communist forces began to withdraw from the Jiangxi Soviet. With the CCP overwhelmed by GMD forces, which had effectively encircled and blockaded the Soviet, the CCP leadership launched a massive evacuation involving tens of thousands of troops. Over the next 370 days, the communist forces would traverse nearly six thousand miles before finally arriving in Yan'an, a small city in the province of Shaanxi.[6] Mythologized and canonized as the most heroic feat of the CCP's early history (Saich 2021, 93), the Long March and the Yan'an years that followed would prove pivotal to the emergence of an egalitarian impulse in Chinese women's organizing for the coming decades. Similar to their male comrades, women forged rivers, traversed mountains in blizzards, and endured routine bombardments by the enemy. The heroic feats of women on the Long March—and their revolutionary experiences in the years that followed—had important implications for activism after 1949. Retold in books, operas, and through training regimes, these founding stories decisively shaped the emergence of the Woman Warrior and Loyal Soldier as agentic models of revolutionary change.

Kang's dismissal of the "women's problem" in her interview with Helen Snow, was deeply connected to a pervasive view within the CCP that women could undermine the path to military victory. According to Zhu De, Kang Keqing's husband:

> Many women are very anxious to join the Red Army but we can't take them in. The main problem is one of discipline. Then, too, the Red Army is so mobile that they cannot keep up with such fast marching as our maneuvering requires in fighting, nor carry the necessary burden easily, and also they get sick more often than men, as the life is extremely hard. However, their fighting spirit is good, and they would make good soldiers for any ordinary army. There have been many brave women in the partisan groups. (Snow 1939 [1977], 174)[7]

The reference to "discipline" here is key: Zhu De not only feared that romantic relationships would undermine the strength of the troops but that they would lead to unwanted pregnancies and the arrival of children, which would in turn slow down the progress of the army. It is for this reason that only a small number of women were allowed to participate in the Long March, primarily the most senior women officials within the CCP—almost all of whom were married to male leaders themselves.

In fact, many of the most senior women leaders within or closely affiliated with the CCP had already foregone motherhood themselves: Song Qingling suffered a miscarriage while escaping an armed attack in 1922—a crisis that is believed to have prevented future pregnancies (Epstein 1993, 94–98). Five years later, Deng Yingchao's newborn did not survive a three-day period of labor. Forced to flee from the GMD immediately after giving birth, Deng's womb "never recovered" and she was not able to bear any more children (Gao 2007, 48).[8] Cai Chang's childbearing and child-rearing was also impacted. In the wake of a failed attempt to procure an abortion in France (Huang 2004, 47), Cai Chang left her daughter, Li Tete, with her mother. Li Tete would only live with her parents for a total of three years, residing in the Soviet Union from 1939 to 1952. But even when Cai Chang was in Moscow, she spent little time with Li, telling her daughter that she couldn't show her affection because she was busy "driving the Japanese aggressors out of China" (Su 1990, 113; Wiles 2003a, 24).

The women who did not forego motherhood, including Mao's second wife, He Zizhen, endured extraordinary tribulations. In her 1937 interview with Snow (1939 [1977], 189), Kang Keqing explained why having women with children on the Long March took such a toll:

> Most of the troubles of the women with the Red Army are the babies they are always having. This is bad for their revolutionary work, and many of them are sick from the strain. Mao Tsê-tung's wife now has

her fifth baby here in Yen-an. Hsiao K'eh's wife nearly died in childbirth during the Long March, when her boy was born in the grasslands. We call him the "Grasslands Baby." Ho Lung's wife has just sent her year-old little girl to Sian to live with a family there.

What is important about Kang Keqing's words is not just how they framed a particular attitude at a particular historical moment, but how they came to frame the revolutionary experience itself. He Zizhen, Mao's second wife, gave birth to five children before the age of twenty-eight, all the while enduring the extreme conditions of a perilous wartime retreat (Wiles 2003c, 207).[9] During the 1930s, He Zizhen entrusted several of her newborn infants to the care of others, and left one in an abandoned hut. From He's perspective, there was little choice: either she would continue with the Red Army or stay behind and risk capture, torture, and certain execution, which had been the fate of Yang Kaihui, Mao's wife before her.

By 1939, He Zizhen and Mao's relationship had fallen apart. The story of that dissolution and He Zizhen's fate in exile would continue to circulate within elite circles of the CCP for years to come. And it was a particularly awful fate: He Zizhen was committed to a Soviet psychiatric hospital when she refused to allow her daughter to board at a full-time daycare after she had nearly died of pneumonia. Indeed, she was so distraught after having lost a newborn shortly after arriving in the USSR that she did not want to let her daughter out of her sight (Lee and Wiles 1999, 127–33; Wei 2004, 24–26; Wang 1997, 51–62).[10] The "moral" of the founding story of Mao Zedong and He Zizhen was clear: CCP cadres could only have children and develop attachments to them at their own peril. Not surprisingly, Kang Keqing never had children herself.

Biographical information about Kang Keqing, Cai Chang, and Deng Yingchao appeared in early glowing accounts of the Chinese revolution penned by Americans Edgar and Helen Snow, *Red Star Over China* (1938 [1978]) and *Inside Red China* (1939 [1977]). Both books were translated into Chinese and were read widely by Chinese intellectuals, some of whom made the trek to Yan'an on the basis of the books' contents (Spakowski 2005, 153). Both were also assigned reading at the university in Yan'an (Snow 1984, 232). Shi Jian, 110, former head of the Jiangsu Women's Federation, for example, was deeply influenced by *Red Star Over China*, which had been retitled as "Journey to the West" (*Xixing Manji*) to avoid creating trouble with the GMD:

> This book had a lot of women who were a generation older, like Elder Sister Cai and Elder Sister Deng. At that time, I had just finished school and was eighteen years old. I really envied these women who were the same generation as our mothers who had already become so progressive. They were our models. We all felt that we eighteen-year-olds were not doing

enough. Having seen their situation in the Red Army . . . it made an even larger impression on us. So, all the way along our whole country has felt very respectful toward these elder sisters, and they loved me very much.

Shi Jian herself postponed having children until after hostilities with Japan ceased. She was twenty-five years old when she married and thus considered an "old maid." But it was not just that women postponed having children or gave up or abandoned their infants; sometimes, they murdered them. Revolutionary infanticide by mothers who sought to protect fellow guerillas from detection would reverberate throughout the polity in the years to come. Indeed, what some women saw as temporary measures necessary to "maintain army and Party discipline," other women took as the revolutionary standard after military engagements had ended. In the mid-1950s, former local Jiangsu Youth League director Tian Min, 85, recalled how a County Women's Federation director drew on her experience of revolutionary infanticide as a model to approach the dual demands of work and parenting:

> [She] told me: "Even though you have children now, you should work as hard and carefully as you did [before]. You should keep your enthusiasm at work. Your children should not affect your work." She also offered an example from her own [life]. She said, "I threw my son into a mountain ditch for work, for the revolution. If [I] hadn't thrown him, the child would have cried [and] the enemy would have thrown bombs and discovered [our] location, thus influencing the entire troops. So [I] just had to reluctantly toss [my] child out. You can't think that because [you] have children [you] can forgo work." She was doing ideological work on me.

"Ideological work," or *sixiang gongzuo*, was a central concept in Maoist thought. Influenced by the Long March and the rectification campaign in Yan'an (Schram 1974; Meisner 1986), Maoist thought waxed and waned in importance relative to specific policy ideas. Over the course of the 1940s, 1950s, 1960s, and beyond, however, the CCP nonetheless consistently deployed "ideological work" in the creation of revolutionary subjects committed to Mao and Maoist enactments of national and local leadership.

Maoist Thought

Karl Marx (1978, 608) famously dismissed peasants (*nongmin*) as having the revolutionary potential of a "sack of potatoes"—a sentiment that would be mirrored in the early Chinese Communist movement. By way of contrast, Mao Zedong sought to harness the revolutionary potential of peasants, including that of rural women whom he identified as even more oppressed than male peasants. In his early musings on peasant revolution, for example, Mao (1927 [1959]) argued that rural women were not only dominated by political, clan, and religious authority, they were also subject to the authority of their husbands. As Tina Mai Chen (2011, 58) suggests, both "woman" and "peasant" materialized in Maoist thought as "the most recent instantiation of a historically situated emerging consciousness." Appearing as both "vanguard elements through which the future will be realized" and as "the dying vestiges of a past oppression," the simultaneity of these multiple iterations of oppression/liberation as they existed in reference to each other (T. M. Chen 2011, 58) reinscribed practices of domination within Maoist discourse and practice. For while Mao argued in 1927 that "leadership by poor peasants is absolutely necessary," and that "without poor peasants there would be no revolution," it is also true that Mao and the CCP leadership would continue to regard Chinese peasants as "backward" subjects that required the enlightened leadership of the CCP to emancipate and modernize them (Cohen 1993). Moreover, if not mobilized properly, peasants, especially women peasants, could turn reactionary. Mao may well have viewed the "country woman" (*nongcun funü*) as a potential threat to the revolution and to the project of socialist construction in the countryside. In 1955, for example, Mao drew on the image of the foot-bound woman "tottering along" to attack what he felt was his comrades' conservative approach to collectivization (Chang 1975, 15). Mao and others in the CCP leadership may have feared the "natural conservatism" of older, rural women and their corrosive influence on their kin and communities.

During the late 1920s, 1930s, and 1940s, the CCP leadership sought to achieve a delicate balancing act: liberate the country woman from the feudal, patriarchal fetters which limited her, and by extension, limited the capacity of China's revolutionary transformation, without alienating her male kin, and her larger community, in the process. When Peng Pai organized a Peasant Movement Training Institute in Guangdong in the mid-1920s, for example, he bypassed recruiting dedicated feminists in favor of a small number of rural women activists in the organization (Gilmartin 1995, 167–73). In 1927, the CCP Committee of Hunan made clear that family problems, including divorce, marriage, and domestic abuse, was not to get in the way of a husband's revolutionary work (Hunan Sheng weitonggao 1927 [1991]). After the retreat of the CCP to the countryside in the late 1920s, the CCP conducted various experiments in mobilizing rural women in Jiangxi, where the CCP established Soviet base areas. But women's rights activists quickly came under fire. Arguing that middle-class women were blithely wreaking havoc on the lives of the rural women masses through their romantic ideas about women's liberation, for example, one county party organization directed that all independent women's organizations, such as the Soviet Women's Reading Collective, be disbanded (Yong Xin Xianwei, 1931 [1991], 157–60).

For much of the 1930s, ruptured communication among CCP organizing efforts in different parts of China led to a diverse array of approaches to the mobilization of rural women (Spakowski 2005, 142). With the onset of the Long March and the scattering of armies, the CCP devoted little attention to figuring out how it should best incorporate rural women into its national struggle of liberation. Women's organizing was often ignored, given lip-service, or even discarded by all except for the few women placed in charge of the women's committee for a particular province or region. The limited organizing among women that did take place was directed by women cadres hailing from a variety of backgrounds, many of whom had different understandings of the project of women's liberation.

To be sure, neither the CCP leadership nor Mao retreated completely from a commitment to women's liberation during this period. For example, Mao personally signed a new Marriage Act protecting the rights of women and children in the Jiangxi Soviets (Kang 1977 [1988], 433).[11] He also insisted that rural investigations include a focus on women and children (Kang 1977 [1988]). Indeed, Mao's own investigations in late 1933 detailed the social and political conditions of both women and children. He not only examined marriage freedom and advocated for the elimination of domestic violence, for example, but also stressed the importance of reducing the physical abuse of children (Mao 1933 [1995], 584–622). Mao was also prone to lecture those around him on the subject of women's oppression, including Kang Keqing at their first meeting. When Kang Keqing criticized her birth mother for giving her up and her foster mother for beating her, Mao explained to Kang that all three women—birth mother, foster mother, and Kang—had been subject to the weight of thousands of years of Chinese feudalism (Kang 1977 [1988], 433). At the opening of the Chinese Women's University in 1939, Mao also criticized the sexism of some of his comrades: "Not everyone supports our founding the Women's University. In particular, the "stubborn elements" do not support it. They are opposed to those students who are coming to Yan'an to study, [and] do not want women to realize a thorough emancipation" (Mao 1939 [1991], 149–50). And yet, in this speech, and in other commentary, Mao Zedong reinscribed "woman" as a revolutionary subject in need of liberation, if not always as an agent directly engaged in revolutionary transformation herself.

In Maoist thought, agency is realized through collective struggle; a violent process in which both self and class are subject to mutual transformation. As a system of ideas laid out by Mao Zedong in his most important essays and speeches, Maoist thought combines Marxist class analysis with a Promethean vision of man's ability to overcome all natural and material conditions. In a departure from Marx and Engels, who argued that, while individuals make history, they did not do so under conditions of their own choosing, Mao argued that people do not have to wait for economic conditions to be sufficiently mature to make revolution; rather, he insisted that men could change their material conditions if they had sufficient desire to do so. Mao's emphasis on revolutionary will was not totally new. Lenin, for example, had made use of it to a certain degree in the Russian revolution (Schram 1974, 71). However, Mao went far beyond Lenin in his belief that communism could be willed into being on the basis of ideas and effort. According to Meisner (1986, 41), "For Mao, the essential factor in determining the course of history was conscious human activity, and the most important ingredients for revolution were how men thought and their willingness to engage in revolutionary action." The ultimate goal was liberation (*jiefang*) from class, feudal, patriarchal, and religious (superstition) oppression.

Maoist thought prompted no less than the emergence of a new ethical order in revolutionary China. Unending struggle, heroic sacrifice, self-denial, diligence, and courage became the virtues necessary to remold the world (Meisner 1986, 34–35). Once an individual adopted a new revolutionary position, Mao believed, he could transform his objective material conditions such as his class essence or even the natural world itself. Emotion plays a key role in this process: as Perry (2002b, 119–20) argues, Mao (1942 [1996], 1122–32) underlined the importance of emotion in a pivotal speech delivered in May 1942:

> In this respect I can say a word about my own experience in the transformation of my feelings. . . . I could wear the clothes of other intellectuals because I thought they were clean, but I did not want to wear the clothes of the workers, peasants, or soldiers because I felt they were dirty. After the revolution when I joined the workers, peasants, and soldiers, I gradually came to know them thoroughly, and they too gradually came to know me. At that time, and only then, did I basically outgrow those bourgeois and petty-bourgeois sentiments which the bourgeois school had taught me. At that time I compared the unreconstructed intellectuals with the workers, peasants, and soldiers, and felt that the intellectuals not only were in spirit unclean in many places, but their bodies too were unclean. The cleanest ones still were the workers and peasants—even taking into account that their hands were black and their feet covered with cow dung, they were still cleaner than the bourgeoisie, big and small. This then is what is meant by *outgrowing one's sentiments and changing from one class to another*. If our intellectual literature would make their own works welcomed by the masses, they *must transform*

and completely reconstruct their own thoughts and feelings. Otherwise, no work will be successful or effective. [italics are Perry's]

These transformative struggles were not easily realized, however. Rather, they were inherently violent and required constant vigilance. Indeed, Mao perceived nature as "an enemy against whom one 'declares war' in order to wrest from her the food necessary for survival and the resources necessary for economic and military power" (Schram 1974, 100). He also argued that new adherents to Marxist thought could become subject to ideological backsliding and thus required constant reeducation.

The key to developing and maintaining the virtues that composed a revolutionary will was exposure to political training and struggle, often through political mobilization. A mobilization campaign was "a government sponsored effort to storm and eventually overwhelm strong but vulnerable barriers to the progress of socialism through intensive mass mobilization of active personal commitment" (Bennett 1976, 18). Over the course of Mao's leadership of the CCP, he repeatedly drew on political mobilizations not only as means to achieving a material end (for example, increased productivity or victory over the enemy) but also as a means to transform the individual consciousness of both men and women.

Unlike the family-focused state-building objectives of the Social Reformer, the Maoist activist was largely devoid of familial attachments or, at least, acted as if she were. The Maoist activist was an autonomous agent capable of contributing directly to the task of socialist construction through her miraculous feats—whether in the fields or on the factory floor. A total believer in Maoist teachings, she sought to serve as a catalyst for mobilizing the masses and to submit herself willingly to the needs of her organization, be it the Youth League or the CCP itself (Chan 1985, 6–7). Moreover, it was the process of physically engaging in mobilizations and other forms of collective work that enabled the activist to assume a socialist (utopian) subjectivity that was, ultimately, devoid of maternalist content. This process involved applying subjective initiative to overcome obstacles and assume a super(hu)man status. According to Mao,

> Men are not slaves of objective reality. Provided only that men's consciousness be in conformity with the objective laws of the development of things, the subjective activity of the popular masses can manifest itself in full measure, overcome all difficulties, create the necessary conditions, and carry forward the revolution. In this sense, the subjective creates the objective.[12]

One had *fanshen*'ed, or freed oneself, when one had physically and ideologically turned oneself over. In the words of Chen (2003, 274): "The liberated female body, similar to that of other heroic bodies of the Maoist period, was driven by a will that refused to allow the body to succumb to physical discomfort. This perseverance reportedly enabled historical progress as the woman liberated herself from historical, familial and economic oppression through physical reconstitution and relocation of the body." In effect, a heroic body was a militarized body. When women cadres in Yan'an donned military attire and changed their names (Spakowski 2005, 154), they were enacting a Maoist vision of revolutionary freedom. But while Maoist liberation gave rise to the possibility of a martial and class-based agency, CCP discourse and practice in Yan'an simultaneously invoked "woman," funü, as a failed revolutionary subject, and women-work as a revolutionary backwater.

Women-Work and the Destiny of Backwardness

Almost all of the prominent women leaders who survived the Long March took up women-work in the late 1930s and early 1940s.[13] The problem was that CCP discourse and praxis continually delegitimized women and women-work. Xiang Jingyu, for example, struggled against her own marginalization within the party in the early 1920s. According to Cai Hesen, Xiang's husband, Xiang was always uncomfortable being associated with women-work, feeling that she had been delegated to women-work because women were not seen as capable as men comrades. Thus Xiang, arguably the most important leader of the early communist women's movement, felt stymied from achieving greater political aspirations by her gender, and the (woman-)work it determined (Gilmartin 1995; McElderry 1986; Wang 1999). By the time the CCP arrived in Yan'an, the denigration of women's leadership and women-work had only become further embedded within the CCP. Base area reports from the 1930s and 1940s show that resistance to women-work, by both men and women cadres, remained a powerful drag on the ability of the CCP to establish and maintain a presence among women in rural areas. According to a 1939 document from the CCWMC, for example, the most important shortcoming of women cadres and of women intellectuals was their tendency to discriminate against women-work, including a tendency to look down on laboring women.[14] Women cadres complained about their women-work assignments on the basis that there was nothing to it (Ou 1947 [1991], 128), and that they were built for more hardy responsibilities than miscellaneous preoccupations of women-work; indeed, some despised it (Zhu 1939 [1991], 214, 225).[15] One demobilized soldier denied having the ontological knowledge necessary to "be" a woman, as is evident in the first quote that begins this chapter.

Discrimination against women and women-work was rife within the CCP. In Yan'an, the subjectivity of "woman" had become what Goffman (1963) calls a "spoiled identity"; indeed, to be a woman was to locate oneself outside the revolutionary project. When Mao's political rival, Wang Ming (Chen Shaoyu) was made president of the Women's University after losing his bid for the CCP's leadership, for example, the goal was nothing short of humiliation (Gao 2018, 281). According to some former Yan'anites, "People thought it was a very clever way to be insulting and generous at the same time" (Apter and Saich 1994, 173).

It was not just that women were considered inadequate revolutionaries themselves (although some clearly felt that way); it was more that for many members of the CCP, women-work itself was by and large preoccupied with "trivial matters" and was, therefore, unimportant. Wang Shiwei, a prominent Yan'an intellectual who was imprisoned and later executed for criticizing inequality within the CCP reveals the pervasiveness of this belief in his famous essay, "Wild Lilies." Wang argues that the party's leadership in Yan'an had grown too complacent and self-indulgent, not paying enough attention to the details of party life. He writes, "The so-called small things theory is linked with this. A criticizes B. B tells A he shouldn't waste his time on 'small things.' Some 'great masters' even say: 'Damn it! It's bad enough with the women comrades, now the men are spending all their time on trivia too!'" (Wang 1942 [1996], 1107).

In 1939, when Deng Yingchao (1939 [1991], 164–75) spoke to students enrolled at the Women's University, she decried those in the CCP who were treating women-work as a "joke" (*kaiwanxiao de*). Speaking with the collective voice of Marxist-Leninism, she called-out male chauvinism, and in so doing, linked the liberation of men to that of women:

> We believe that the correct attitude should not be influenced by the contempt for women in Chinese society. On the contrary, if we want to struggle, we should fully express our vanguard posture and shoulder the great task of women's liberation. We believe that it is a most glorious task that [should be approached] with pride. At the same time, this is not just the case for women, but also for men comrades; as long as they seek their own liberation and national liberation, they should work hard for women's liberation.

Additional problems, however, abounded. An uneven sex ratio, conservative sexual mores, and the demands on married women to assume responsibility for household chores, also exacerbated the pressure experienced by women cadres. In Yan'an, there was only one woman for every eighteen men (Apter and Saich 1994, 365). While strict rules governed the kinds of relations allowed between women and men (Huang 2019), not a few CCP leaders developed sexual liaisons and/or marriages with young women students who had arrived in Yan'an after the Long March. These liaisons shocked the male soldiers because they considered the free relationships between men and women as very wrong (Apter and Saich 1994, 166). These liaisons were also frowned on by the highest women officials (Snow 1972, 253; Terrill 1984).

Ding Ling became the most vocal critic of the sexual double standards rife within the CCP. In her essay, "Thoughts on March Eighth," Ding Ling argued that women cadres often married and had children in Yan'an so that they could avoid becoming the subject of gossip. Once women leaders began to have children, however, they were either criticized for trying to avoid their home responsibilities by hiring nannies and seeking abortions or for becoming "backward" as a result of staying home with their children.[16] Women's association with the "trivial" work of raising children, Ding Ling tried to point out, resulted from the impossible expectations placed on women:

> Before marrying, they were inspired by the desire to soar in the heavenly heights and lead a life of bitter struggle. They got married partly because of physiological necessity and partly as a response to sweet talk about "mutual help." Thereupon they are forced to toil away and become "Noras returned home." Afraid of being thought "backward," those who are a bit more daring rush around begging nurseries to take their children. They ask for abortions and risk punishment and even death by secretly swallowing potions to produce abortions. But the answer comes back: "Isn't giving birth to children also work? You're just after an easy life; you want to be in the limelight. After all, what indispensable political work have you performed? Since you are so frightened of having children and are not willing to take responsibility once you have had them, why did you get married in the first place? No one forced you to." Under these conditions, it is impossible for women to escape this destiny of backwardness. (Ding 1942 [1989], 318–19)

The shock for women who bore and raised children in Yan'an was great. Zeng Zhi, a veteran of the Long March and wife of senior party leader Tao Zhu, for example, found herself struggling to take care of their first child in Yan'an alone, much in the way that was described by Ding Ling. Despite the fact that Zeng Zhi had suffered a catastrophic postpartum hemorrhage, Tao Zhu rarely spent time with Zeng Zhi and their newborn, nor did he assume responsibility for any of the physically demanding chores such as fetching water from afar. Tao's neglect enraged her, especially when he spent his one day off with Li Fuchun, Chen Yun, and others, partying until late. When Zeng Zhi finally confronted Tao Zhu, he smashed a teapot and the two fought. Eventually, she resigned herself to the fact that older party men like Tao Zhu were not capable of overcoming their latent male chauvinism (Zeng 2011, 253–54).[17]

Instead of addressing the growing gendered disparities of revolutionary life in Yan'an and other base areas, however, Mao sought to enshrine them. Specifically, Mao sought to realize the relational capacity of rural women to educate and mobilize family members in service of the war effort. When Mao addressed the Women's University in 1939, for example, he did not simply highlight the "thorough emancipation of women" as a goal in and of itself, but rather as a means of mobilizing family members. Mao argued, "Educating children, encouraging husbands, educating the masses, all of this must go through women; it is only when women are mobilized that all of the Chinese people will be mobilized, this is without question" (Mao 1939 [1991], 149–50). It was not until 1942, however, that an attached wartime mobilization at last became possible. Led by Cai Chang and Mao Zedong, the first mass rectification of the CCP women's movement brought women-work fully under the leadership of the CCP in a total war vision of national liberation.

The Rectification of the Women's Movement

Helen Snow (1984, 276) once described Cai Chang as Mao's "best woman friend." Cai Chang's periods of greatest political activity in the 1940s and 1950s coincided with those of Mao's: during the 1942–43 Rectification Movement in Yan'an and 1956–60, both periods when Jiang Qing, Mao's third wife, was banished from politics, as was discussed in the Introduction. In an emerging political culture that required close family ties to help "seal the deal," especially when it came to establishing a new direction in women-work, Mao needed a trusted female relative with whom he could collaborate closely. The younger sister of Mao's martyred friend, the wife of one of his closest comrades, and one of the few high-ranking women leaders in the CCP, was the natural person for the job.

Cai Chang's friendship with Mao Zedong began early when Mao occasionally lectured at her girls' school. At this time, Mao provided Cai Chang with individual tutoring, and she followed his published work carefully. But it was the close relationship between Mao and Cai Chang's elder brother Cai Hesen that would shape Cai Chang's political formation most profoundly (Cai 1992a, 219–20). In an interview undertaken by Helen Snow in 1937, Cai Chang describes her growing respect for and allegiance to both young men:

> At this time [mid-nineteen's] my brother, Ho-sheng [sic], five years older than I, entered the First Normal School of Changsha, where he became a good friend of Mao Tse-tung [sic]. By 1918 when my brother

had entered the Higher Normal School, we were already influenced by the "new thought," though this was a little before the May Fourth Movement. The two organized the New People's Study Society. My brother and I were good friends and I was the only girl permitted to join this society. Though my brother did not talk much to me on political questions, I learned a great deal from listening to conversations and participating in the society's activities.

I admired Mao Tse-tung and my brother and wished I could study with them, but I had to earn money to support the family so it was necessary to continue my teaching. Mao Tse-tung was a diligent student and very brilliant and far-sighted. He was advanced in his ideas even then. (Snow 1967, 235)

Once the Cai family moved to France, Cai Hesen focused more intently on Cai Chang's political education, passing on to his younger sister works written by Marx and encouraging her to participate in the French worker movements underway at that time (Su 1990, 33–38). By the time Cai Chang returned to China and began to participate in the great uprising of 1925, her political loyalties were firmly sealed. When Mao and Cai Hesen advocated for peasant revolution in the aftermath of the 1927 bloodbath, for example, a position unpopular within the CCP at the time, Cai resolutely supported the two men (Su 1990, 217). In the wake of the murder of Xiang Jingyu and Cai Hesen, Cai Chang placed all of her political fealty on Mao Zedong, her remaining "elder brother" and first political tutor in the struggle (Su 1990, 83). Cai Chang, in turn, was one of only a very few who "had a substantial influence on Mao" (Huang 2000, 124n66). According to Cai's biographer, Su (1990, 82–83, 215–20), whenever either one of them called on the other for assistance, support was immediately forthcoming. Cai Chang's leadership of the rectification of the Chinese women's movement emerged directly out of this relationship of trust and commitment.

When Cai Chang became party secretary of the CCWMC in June 1941, she replaced Wang Ming (Chen Shaoyu), a returned student from the Soviet Union who was, briefly, a chief contender for the ideological leadership of the CCP (Gao 2018, 282).[18] At the approximately same time, Cai Chang's husband, Li Fuchun, replaced Wang Ming as the leading official of the Yan'an Women's University (Apter and Saich 1994, 239). Li Fuchun simultaneously served as one of a small group of Mao loyalists composing the Central General Study Committee, which was responsible for implementing the Rectification Movement.

Mao Zedong first began to lay the groundwork for the CCP's Rectification Movement (*zhengfeng yundong*) in the spring of 1941 with a series of speeches, directives, and conferences (Teiwes 1993, 54). Over the course of the larger movement, established party cadres, new recruits, and soldiers undertook inten-sive efforts to study Marxist ideology and Mao Zedong's own emerging corpus of work. Participants at all levels of the party were expected to engage in acts of "self-criticism," subjecting themselves and others to a process that would focus their understanding of how best to apply Marxism to the challenge of war and revolution in the Chinese context. Employed as a tool for establishing unity out of heterodoxy and division, the Rectification Movement enabled Mao to posi-tion himself as the "personification of the heroic struggle in the anti-Japanese national resistance" (Selden 1995, 159) and became a form of "exegetical bond-ing" (Apter and Saich 1994, 264).[19]

Much ink has been spilled analyzing the, at times violent, role that Kang Sheng played in executing the Rectification Movement on Mao's behalf (Apter and Saich 1994; Gao 2018; Huang 2000). Whereas Kang Sheng "was a crazy dog," however, Li Fuchun served as a key conduit of information in Mao's decision making (Huang 2000, 124). In Gao's (2018) detailed analysis of the Rectification Movement, he describes Li Fuchun as one of "Mao's few intimates in Yan'an" (263), "Mao's long-time confederate" (549), and "completely loyal to Mao" (413). Indeed, Gao (2018, 333) argues that Li Fuchun was "one of the cadres on whom Mao relied the most," and that he became, "almost as powerful as Kang Sheng" at this key juncture.

Mao and Li Fuchun had a long history. Similar to his wife, Li Fuchun originally hailed from Hunan and attended school with Mao Zedong and Cai Hesen. Dur-ing and after Li Fuchun's sojourn in France, he became increasingly politically active under the leadership of his wife's older brother and Mao's close friend, Cai Hesen. On the Long March, Li served as a political officer in Mao's First Front Army, and in Yan'an, he served as head of the Central Committee's Organization Department from 1935 to 1937, among other positions (Klein and Clark 1971, 1:494–495). During the Rectification Movement, both Li Fuchun and Cai Chang worked together in the Organization Department (Gao 2018, 258).

Replacing Wang Ming with both Cai Chang and Li Fuchun was thus par-ticularly strategic: although Mao Zedong had already defeated Wang politically by June 1941, Wang Ming "was still useful to Mao as a strawman to be attacked as Mao moved to justify his becoming the sole voice interpreting the Chinese revolution" (Apter and Saich 1994, 59). By placing two of his most Loyal Soldiers in multiple overlapping roles, Mao simultaneously strengthened his capacity to secure his dominance of the CCP while launching the CCP's first substantive revision of women-work.

Just a few months after assuming her position as party secretary of the CCWMC, Cai Chang took up the call to attack Wang Ming through a scathing critique of his leadership of the CCP women's movement. Specifically, Cai Chang accused Wang Ming of falling prey to objectivism, for cavalierly advocating slogans such as "sexual equality [*nannü pingdeng*]," "marriage freedom [*hunyin ziyou*]," and "oppose the four oppressions [*fandui si zhong yapo*]," without taking the time to investigate and understand the real-life circumstances of the rural women they were supposed to lead.[20] In her criticisms, Cai Chang painted a picture of Wang Ming as a theoretician with his head in the clouds; someone whose single-minded advocacy of women's liberation was producing theoretical chaos and a blind and strident implementation of a superficial "equality" at the grassroots (Su 1990, 118–19; Luo 1992, 49).[21]

Cai Chang's critique of Wang Ming in December 1941 did not simply reinforce Mao's emerging dominance in the CCP, but it also positioned Mao and Cai to undertake the most consequential revision of women-work in the CCP since the party's origins in 1921. Following an enlarged Politburo meeting in September 1941, during which time the CCP began to criticize policies associated with Wang Ming and returned students from the USSR, Cai Chang threw herself into remaking the Chinese Communist women's movement (Ou 1983).

Cai Chang began by inviting Mao to give a talk to the Women's Life Investigative Unit, in which he gave very explicit instructions as to how grassroots investigations should be conducted, emphasizing the importance of learning about the real conditions of the peasants, and not just what they were imagined to be (Kang 1977 [1988], 431; Su 1990, 118–19). While the investigative unit conducted research in the Yan'an countryside, Cai Chang convened more than a dozen meetings of the CCWMC and met with senior men party members as a means of gathering information and assessing the way forward (Su 1990, 118–19; Luo 1992, 48–49). One of Cai Chang's (1943 [1991], 650) central arguments was that women's leadership in the base areas included educated women elites who had little understanding of or contact with the daily struggles of rural women. To this end, Cai Chang famously attacked Ding Ling shortly after the publication of "Thoughts on March 8th" and led investigations of other women leaders who returned to Yan'an after working in Guomindang-controlled areas (Johnson 1983, 74–75; Ou 1983, 43).[22] According to Zeng Zhi (1992, 29) who was also serving on the CCWMC during this period, Cai Chang encouraged a frank exchange of opinions, a "democratic" approach that exposed the two different strands about women's organizing that were currently emerging in the party. Gao (2018, 552–53) argues, however, that the CCWMC, took an "ultra-left stance," attacking a teenager, for example, who was believed to have been a secret agent (Gao 2018, 552–53).[23] Ou Mengjue (1983, 43), a member of the Rectification Committee of the CCWMC, insinuates that Cai Chang subjected comrades to unfair criticism and interrogation, a role that Ou says, Cai Chang never forgot, and which she later sought to correct.

While Cai Chang targeted the organizing methods and goals of Chinese Communist leaders, however, she refrained from critiquing the cross-party wartime work under way in Chongqing and other GMD-controlled parts of China at the same time. Indeed, in a speech published on the same day as Ding Ling's "Thoughts on March 8th," Cai Chang (1942 [1988], 76–79) argued that war-time women's organizing should be inclusive, incorporating all women over the age of fifteen, regardless of class, party, ethnicity, occupation, and religion. She also urged CCP leaders to learn to "humbly listen to the opinions of people outside the Party, and [adopt] an attitude and style [necessary] to work with them." Cai Chang's goal was to make it easier for more women from a variety of circumstances and beliefs to participate in the mobilization against the Japanese, and not to impose ideologically pure methods on elite allies and rural populations not yet ready, or able, to become frontline activists or members of the CCP themselves. To this end, Cai Chang defended women CCP members for wearing "fancy clothing" when working in areas controlled by the Guomindang (Cai Ming, 5; Gao Jian, 6; Li Lan, 7). Later, when Civil War broke out between the Communists and the GMD, Cai Chang (1947b [1988], 104–5) publicly praised the contributions of a number of left-leaning women, including Liu-Wang Liming, Li Dequan, Song Qingling, and He Xiangning, among other non-CCP elites, for their efforts to unite women against GMD violence.

The rectification of the Chinese Communist women's movement enabled Cai Chang and Mao to place rural women-work directly in support of the war effort as an auxiliary force. In February 1943, the CCP Central Committee officially promulgated the "1943 Resolution" in which household production and austerity were made the main focus of CCP rural women's organizing. Cai Chang led the writing of the original draft with Mao Zedong making numerous additions and revisions, including changing the title and placing far greater stress on the role of rural women in production than was evident in the original version (Ren 1989, 209–10). After Cai Chang presented the final version to the Central Committee it was passed in February 1943 (Luo 1992, 49).[24] Cai subsequently invited Mao to write an eight-character couplet for the *Liberation Daily's* commemoration of March 8. Mao Zedong wrote: "Go deeply into the masses, don't speak empty words" (Su 1990, 120).

By making the rural householder into an auxiliary force supporting the war effort, the resolution was offering its own version of total war mobilization underway in Chongqing and other parts of the world at that historical moment. Total war mobilized citizens as part of a wartime social system, according to a gender-specific division of labor (Ryūichi 1998, 137, 142). In nations on opposing sides of the conflict, total war mobilized mothers as household managers, in which "the family dinner became a weapon of war, and the kitchen a woman's battlefront"

(Bentley 1998, 5). Oko Mumeo, a housewives' crusader in wartime Japan, for example, built on her prewar work on consumption to call for housewives, to "live within their means and to regulate consumption in line with national policies" (Ryūichi 1998, 146). Writing in the United States at the same moment, Margaret Culkin Banning (1942, 177), stressed that while women had a role to play in civilian defense works, "the first task of every American mother is the adequate training and discipline of her household." Banning further argued that mothers should make "national consumption, national nutrition, and national morale" into "arms of total war" (Banning 1942, 232). Cai Chang's contribution at this historical moment was not simply to transplant the total war model underway in the United States, Japan, and in GMD-occupied China onto the rural household, however, but rather to transform total war into a context in which, for example, many households did not have access to stand-alone kitchens, much less heat, running water, or the guarantee of a regular food supply. Following the promulgation of the resolution, Cai Chang (1943 [1991], 650–54) published a longer piece in the *Liberation Daily* (*Jiefang ribao*) in which she outlined a mobilization that would make rural women responsible for a range of activities, including weaving, raising pigs and silkworms, planting, cooking, and housework as well as for maintaining household austerity. As I will show, Cai Chang would subsequently revive this rural model of total war in the mid-1950s.

Having successfully reoriented the focus of CCP-led women-work into a "home front" plank of the war, the rectification of the CCP women's movement seemingly had a final target: addressing the problem of women leaders resisting the mantle of women-work. Peng Dehuai, a senior commanding officer during the Long March and in the war against Japan, took up this task with vigor.[25] On numerous occasions, Peng (1941 [1991]; 1943a [1991]; and 1943b [1991]), not only criticized independent women's organizing but also criticized women leaders who did not want to undertake women-work at all. In a short article published just prior to the onset of the Rectification Movement, Peng argued that women-work was an important part of the revolutionary struggle, what he called the "revolutionary family." At the same time, Peng insisted that women-work was the natural responsibility of women, thus placing the onus for this particular kind of revolutionary work on the shoulders of women. He wrote,

> Whether one's viewpoint is far from politics, whether it is from the interests of war, everyone must place the women's movement into an important position. Whoever considers himself a part of the revolutionary family and looks down on or discriminates against the women's movement indulges in empty talk and are good-for-nothing revolutionaries. Unfortunately, we see a lot of people like this, even some

women comrades who are themselves unwilling to do women-work. I think participating in women-work is women's natural responsibility. If women don't do women-work, then who are we supposed to get to do it? Although women's liberation cannot be separated from class struggle and the liberation of national minorities, they also cannot be mixed up together. "The liberation of women and the liberation of women workers should be the business of women and women workers." This famous sentence by Lenin was directed toward those women who look down on or ignore women-work. (Peng 1941 [1991], 495)

The increasing centrality of Maoist thought in the Communist movement, and the CCP's subsequent attempts to crack down on "independent feminist organizing," I would suggest, is related to the general resistance to women-work among women cadres that Peng identifies and criticizes in this article. In Peng's work on the subject, as well as in the writing and speeches of other senior party officials, the problem of independent feminist organizing is often linked to the problem of women-work being ignored altogether. CCP leaders systematically identified independent feminist organizing as a "rightist" deviation and the disbanding and ignoring of women-work activities as a "leftist" deviation. The repeated emergence of "leftist" organizing tendencies, flowed directly from the Maoist emotional pedagogy permeating military and CCP organizations. Indeed, the continuous effort by CCP leaders to legitimate women-work as "revolutionary" is just one indication of how "un-revolutionary" women-work was deemed during this period. When Zhu De later admonished a group of women leaders in 1948 for refusing to undertake women-work, for example, he made exactly this equation:

> Women revolutionaries must first set an example of serving the women masses. No matter what their position all women leaders should pay attention to mobilize the women masses, to guide them. Of course, women-work is not only the responsibility of women comrades, men comrades must also [perform this work]. But the liberation of women must primarily rely on women diligently struggling themselves. But many women comrades are not willing to perform women-work because of their position or [lack of] interest. This kind of attitude is not correct. Revolutionary cadres should not only seek their own progress, but also take responsibility for aiding those more backwards than them progress. There are also some men cadres who look down on women-work. Some of them think that doing something for women isn't worth anything. This way of thinking is also incorrect. (Zhu 1948 [1991], 277)

What Zhu De failed to see was that the attribute of "backwardness" did not always convince women cadres that they should leap to the aid of their more oppressed sisters. In fact, the very idea of "backwardness" sent many running in the opposite direction. The persistent belief that women-work "wasn't worth anything" haunted CCP women's organizing to such a degree that some sought to disassociate themselves from women-work altogether. "Backwards" country women represented exactly what revolutionary women leaders were trying so desperately to overcome: ignorance, conservatism, and the physiological weight of thousands of years of oppression. Unlike revolutionary Maoism, the tasks associated with women-work did not promise an escape from this backwardness. Rather, in the eyes of some, women-work required them to give up the escape from backwardness that they had achieved for themselves through heroic sacrifice and revolutionary triumph.

When Zhu De reminded women cadres of their "natural" responsibilities to undertake women-work, his remarks were likely directed at one woman in particular: his wife. In what would prove one of the greatest ironies of the post-1949 era, Kang Keqing, renowned base area soldier and senior official in her own right, was made a vice chair of the ACDWF and placed in charge of children's welfare programs shortly after Zhu De's speech. Kang's "conversion" to maternalism did not come easily. Kang admits to having felt uncomfortable (*bu tai anxin de qingxu*) when first assigned to duties involving women-work. Cai Chang consequently urged Kang not to ignore the liberation of millions of women and that she should think beyond her own interests; "there is so much work to do," said Cai Chang, "if women comrades aren't willing to do women-work, whom do we get to do it?" (Kang 1993, 13). But Kang's reluctance persisted, and in the winter of 1947–48 she formally attempted to resign from the Central Committee's Women's Council at Xibaipo in Hubei Province. Her reasoning? She did not have enough experience with women-work. Moreover, Kang argued that she would be far more effective serving in the institutional environment she knew and loved best: the Red Army (Kang 1993, 374).

According to Kang Keqing (1993, 373–74), it was Zhu De's speech and the persistent work of her comrades that changed her mind. Zhang Qinqiu and Yang Zhihua, for example, tempered their efforts to persuade Kang Keqing with praise for her contributions. Drawing on the language of maternalism, they urged: "[If we] don't solve the problems regarding children, the problems of women and other related matters won't be solvable [either]; and child welfare is an important part of the cause of construction." Deng Yingchao, however, was less patient: "The Central Committee chooses the membership of the Women's Central Committee, [I] hope you will give up this kind of thinking." Facing a united front composed of some of the most senior women in the CCP and her husband, Kang

Keqing had no choice but to relinquish her dream of remaining in the army and accept a leading role in women-work in its stead.

Kang Keqing's struggle to become and remain a soldier freed from the restraints of motherhood and women-work, I would argue, is reflective of the revolutionary field in which her activism materialized: a party family in which male authority loomed large, first with her foster father and later with her husband, Zhu De, and revolutionary norms that disqualified motherhood and women-work from a liberated future. But Kang Keqing's lack of enthusiasm for motherhood was also shared by other CCP leaders, not all of whom were survivors of the Long March. Indeed, the trials and tribulations of the first generations of revolutionary women, retold in text and trainings, would constitute and reconstitute militant states of activism through which later generations of women activists sought to disassociate themselves from what they considered the "trivial" preoccupations of childbirth, childrearing, and household management. Ironically, some of the very women charged with implementing maternalist policies not only refused to identify as women and mothers but also looked down on women's organizing as a waste of revolutionary resources.

By the 1940s, it had become clear that there were two major fault lines within CCP women's organizing in base areas: a militant orientation, emerging out of the Woman-Warrior tradition and Maoist theory and practice, in which leaders such as Kang Keqing struggled to be recognized as comrades undifferentiated from their male counterparts, and a feminist orientation, that centered women's liberation in the context of communist struggle. While both orientations were valued, Mao Zedong and Cai Chang deployed the Rectification Movement to craft a centralized and unified approach to rural women's organizing that delimited the perceived extremes of both, while reformulating women-work as a central plank in a Total War strategy to achieve national victory. The fact that Mao Zedong personally revised drafts of the 1943 Resolution that set the parameters of base-area women-work indicates the degree to which he regarded its import. Also significant is the proactive role that Cai Chang played alongside her husband to implement the Rectification Movement, a movement Apter and Saich (1994, 264) describe as a "strange mixture of non-kin familialism and ruthlessness."[26] In this effort, Cai Chang and Li Fuchun sealed their loyalty to Mao, laying the stage for the companionship advocacy that would follow.

Cai Chang's determination to rectify grassroots women's organizing in Communist-held base areas, however, did not inure her to the importance of the United Front work underway in Chongqing. In many ways, these were parallel activities, with Deng Yingchao serving as the primary link between the two. Indeed, and similar to many other Chinese Communist leaders stationed in

"white," or GMD-controlled areas, Deng Yingchao returned to Yan'an to participate in the Rectification Movement. As previously noted, and as will become
increasingly evident in the chapters to come, Deng Yingchao would always prove
a much more vocal advocate for women's rights than Cai Chang. However, this
advocacy should not obscure Deng Yingchao's willingness to strong-arm women
officials into roles that they did not wish to play. Deng Yingchao's stern talk
to Kang Keqing in the winter of 1947–48, for example, would foreshadow her
damning critique of the wives of diplomats seeking to serve independently from
the offices of their husbands not quite ten years later (Jin 1993, 2:581–89).

Ultimately, Cai Chang's attachment to Mao Zedong, Deng Yingchao's feminist advocacy, and Kang Keqing's martial yearnings would foreground, and in
important ways shape, the origin and content of rural women's organizing in
Henan and Jiangsu during the late 1940s and early 1950s. Both Cai Chang and
her husband were low-key but nonetheless central participants in the rise and
endurance of the Mao cult in the 1940s and 1950s. As I will show, a commitment
to Mao and his teachings continued to hold great meaning among some former
grassroots women activists and leaders I interviewed in the early aughts, their
passion for him enlivening their understanding of their role in the revolutionary
project and socialist construction long past his death. At the same time, however,
Cai Chang's efforts to proscribe independent women's organizing during the
1940s nonetheless contributed to a political climate in which familial relations
decisively shaped the possibilities for and enactment of rural women's activism.
Indeed, Kang Keqing's reluctant journey from teenage activist to hardened soldier to child welfare advocate and spokesperson, I argue, would foreshadow the
trials of young rural women recruited by emerging party families. Unlike Kang
Keqing, however, grassroots women would not be subject to personal pressure
from the senior party and federation leadership. The complicated encounters
between a revolutionary Maoist party structure and maternalist reform in rural
China would thus produce profoundly different trajectories than that of Kang
Keqing's own tale.

LAND REFORM

Doesn't Party work include women-work?

—Deng Yingchao, "The Party Has to Strengthen Its Guidance, While Women Cadres Have to Be Self-Critical"

My personality is like a boy's personality. I am not like women comrades.

—Tian Min, 85

I'll tell you: everyone wants to be someone! Whether an important or minor position, [a women's leader] is still a cadre. People always say: "Whether it's a prestigious or minor position, it is better to be an official than a seller of tree leaves."

—Zhang Sumei, 20

Ding Xueqin, 64, was appointed head of her local Peasant Association (*nongmin hui*) in the spring of 1950. Similar to Kang Keqing some twenty-five years earlier, Ding Xueqin was just a teenager when she was recruited and trained by a local CCP work team that had arrived in her remote mountainous village. As a member of an impoverished family of six, the "poorest family in the village," Ding Xueqin helped her widowed mother survive by weaving cloth to sell. Despite her family's deep poverty, however, Ding Xueqin's mother was strongly opposed to her eldest daughter joining forces with the communists. The first time she returned home chattering excitedly about the execution of local landlords at a struggle meeting, her mother retorted: "And what will you do when they cut off *your* head?"

When Ding Xueqin recounted her recruitment into local political work, it was the third time we had sat down together. As the commune cadre responsible for women-work during the Great Leap Forward, Ding Xueqin had trained and led many village women's heads, including several I interviewed. Deeply committed to the memory of Mao Zedong, Ding Xueqin's recollections of her earliest days as an activist reflected both the excitement and grave uncertainty of those times and the much improved, yet still straitened, circumstances of her current life. The many local stories of corrupt officials that abounded at the time of our discussions contributed to some bitterness. "Socialist nostalgia" (O'Brien and Li 1999; Rofel 1999) thus likely played a role in Ding's recollections, but, as I discuss in chapter 9, her remarks on the past were nonetheless shot through with ambivalence and loss as well.

The risks attached to participation in communist activism in the 1940s and early 1950s were high. Over the decade prior to the arrival of the work team in Ding Xueqin's village, the county had endured occupation by the Japanese and repeat battles between the CCP and the GMD. Perhaps most terrifying for Ding Xueqin's mother was the possibility that the GMD might return.[1] Just two years earlier, the CCP had established a temporary foothold in a small part of the county. For a few short months, the CCP mobilized poor villagers to identify the wealthier landholders in their communities for struggle sessions. When the CCP abruptly retreated in the face of a GMD attack, however, many of the CCP's newest local recruits faced torture and execution.[2] It was not until 1949 that local CCP members began to openly organize. In the meantime, the CCP would continue to track down, capture, and kill some four thousand "bandits"—the CCP's name for the GMD and anyone resisting CCP rule—and confiscate their weapons (WX 1992, 77–79).[3]

It took three months of coaxing by CCP organizers before Ding Xueqin herself dared to speak in public. But once she did, she faced another immediate obstacle: how to know what to say. Similar to the vast majority of other rural young women of the era, Ding was illiterate. In order to cope, Ding Xueqin memorized the instructions of the work team so that she could then repeat them back to villagers at night. Commuting to higher-level meetings would prove another challenge: with only grass shoes to protect her feet, Ding Xueqin walked four days to attend her first county meeting. Despite these obstacles, Ding Xueqin was quickly promoted and transferred out of her village. Over the course of the 1950s she was able to teach herself to read, and by the time of the GLF, she was appointed head of women-work for an entire commune. But Ding did not undertake this work alone. While Ding Xueqin's husband, a commune official, was not around much, Ding Xueqin's mother supported her daughter's tenure as leader, through caring for her grandchildren.

This chapter explores land reform as a fulcrum for political recruitment and agency during the waning days of the civil war and the earliest months of the new PRC, or the time that was often referred to as "liberation" (jiefang) by the individuals I interviewed. In 1948, Deng Yingchao led the CCP to pivot from approaching women as country householders, to making women's liberation a central part of the land reform movement. The end of the brutal Japanese occupation and an increasing optimism that the CCP would triumph over the GMD produced a new and more promising opportunity to advance the rights of rural women—an opportunity which Deng Yingchao grasped and sought to mold. With the direct support of Liu Shaoqi and Zhou Enlai, Deng Yingchao used her powers of persuasion to not only convince the top brass to realize new land and marital rights for rural women, but also to include rural women in the land reform movement as leaders. It is thanks, in part, to Deng Yingchao that a much more visible, autonomous, and revolutionary role than that of "household manager" was made possible for rural women during this transformative moment.

The chapter also explores the affective dimensions of land reform in Henan and Jiangsu. As I show was the case in the county of Wenhe, visiting teams and local party organizations cultivated kinship relations with local women while training them to analyze and speak about their collective past as the oppressed victims of patriarchal landlords. This was a process of politicization markedly different from what was experienced by the young women leaders active during the May Fourth Movement. Whereas many of the first generation of communist women leaders and their left-leaning allies were politicized through girls' schools, the vast majority of grassroots activists had received little to no formal educational training. Instead, they became politicized in their homes, through the persuasive efforts of visiting "elder sisters" and in mass consciousness-raising sessions where they learned to articulate a class-based analysis about their painful and impoverished pasts.

They also were politicized by family members. The chapter analyzes the early activism of two cousins as the CCP sought to consolidate itself in the county of Huoyue. Although there were many ways in which Maoist state building undermined women's equality by reinforcing local parochialism, the capacity of women to become and remain local leaders was nonetheless dependent on the strong support of family members. For these two cousins, and many other early grassroots leaders, revolutionary agency was predicated on, and enmeshed within, familial circuits of obligation and belonging. As I will show, the states of activism produced through early encounters with visiting work teams and local party organizations were not, therefore, the liberation of the New Woman or Social Reformer but rather the liberation of kinship-inflected revolutionary agents.

Located in southern Jiangsu, the periurban county of Gaoshan had a much longer history of women's organizing than did rural Wenhe or Huoyue. And yet, former Gaoshan Youth League activist and women's representative, Tian Min, was indifferent if not hostile to women-work. Politicized through the Youth League, Tian Min far preferred her work with young people, and facing an abusive mother-in-law, fantasized about running away and joining the army. As I show beginning in this chapter, and continuing in part II, Tian Min would come to embody a Woman Warrior state of activism in which she sought to shed familial attachments and the gendered burdens of women-work, while remaining filial to her parents and protecting the vulnerable women and children in her charge. It would prove a heavy burden to carry.

Centering Women-Work in Land Reform: Policy Openings and Attached Advocacy

The early recruitment of young women such as Ding into local leadership was made possible, in no small part, by Deng Yingchao's unrelenting advocacy for the rights of rural women in land reform.[4] In spring of 1947, after successfully evacuating the children of prominent CCP leaders from Yan'an with Kang Keqing, Deng Yingchao began an immediate assessment of the fast moving and uneven experiment with land reform underway in CCP-occupied areas. Developing a multifaceted, intensive, and tactical approach, Deng championed the inclusion of women leaders and women-work, as a central plank of the land reform process. Over the course of many months, Deng Yingchao convened dozens of meetings with local officials, dispatched members of the CCWMC to undertake local investigations, and herself spent three months leading a working group "squatting in place" (*dundian*) as a visiting cadre in Fuping County, Hebei. In doing so, I would argue, Deng Yingchao was following Mao's dictate, from 1941: "If you have not investigated, you have no right to speak" (*meiyou diaocha jiu meiyou fayan quan*) (Huang 2005, 172).

She also advocated relentlessly with members of the Central Committee at major land reform meetings, using all of her political capital to call out sexism in the ranks, and to ensure that the final land reform documents issued by the CCP leadership would attend to the specific challenges rural women faced as a consequence of the patriarchal family structure, heavy household burdens, and an indifferent or hostile base of male CCP cadres. Over the course of the winter of 1947 and 1948, the CCWMC made five recommendations to the Central Committee, all of which were adopted.[5] On December 20, 1948, the Central Committee approved a detailed document that would serve as the guiding source for rural women-work moving forward. The instructions, which Mao Zedong personally revised line by line (Kang 1977 [1988], 435), stressed the importance of women in production and the protection of women's special interests, as a central part of revolutionary work (Mao 1948 [1991], 289). Ultimately, it was under Deng Yingchao's leadership that the CCWMC was able to push for and achieve the right of women to own their own land (Luo 1993, 237).

Deng Yingchao was attuned to the importance of fostering political openings and then leaping on them when the time was ripe, an approach consistent with Kingdon's (2003, 122–31) description of policy entrepreneurs in the West. Indeed, Deng Yingchao was a master at surveying the political scene and adjusting her strategy accordingly. A year earlier, Liu Shaoqi had advised Deng Yingchao that the Women's Committee could gain the support (*cheng*) of the Central Committee to unite rural women-work and the peasant movement by strengthening their back (*yao*) (Luo 1993, 237–38). Deng Yingchao's deliberate, methodical approach, which she sought to pass on to other women cadres, was to gain that support not with a full-frontal assault, but rather by soliciting input while waiting for conditions to sufficiently mature, and to effectively plant the seeds so that the CCP leadership could see that the approach she was suggesting would ultimately strengthen the land reform movement as a whole (Deng 1948 [1988], 148; Wang 2017, 46–47). This is an approach that Deng Yingchao would also take to the writing and passage of the 1950 Marriage Law, discussed in chapter 6.

Deng Yingchao's victory is all the more remarkable given that neither Kang Keqing nor Cai Chang fully embraced Deng Yingchao's incisive critique of feudal patriarchy, and the party work such a critique required, at this historical moment. Indeed, it was in 1948 that Zhu De and Deng Yingchao refused Kang Keqing's petition to exit women-work and return to military life. It was also during this moment, and the work on the new marriage legislation that followed, that the ideological differences between Deng Yingchao and Cai Chang would become increasingly apparent. Although Cai Chang contributed to advancing women-work in land reform, she did so without the feminist urgency of Deng Yingchao. Whereas Cai Chang (1947 [1988], 126) labeled politically suspect young women joining the land reform movement as whores (*poxie*), for example, Deng Yingchao critiqued party officials for their indiscriminate use of the same term (Wang, Zhou, and Liu 2007).[6] In this moment, and in others, Deng Yingchao would prove herself a daughter of May Fourth in ways that Cai Chang never would be.

Ultimately, Liu Shaoqi was true to his word, emphasizing the importance of women-work at a land reform conference in September 1948 (Jin 1993, 1:399). Deng Yingchao also received the public support of additional senior CCP officials, including Zhu De (1948 [1991]), whose adult son had worked alongside Deng Yingchao during her investigation in Fuping County, and Zhou Enlai, Deng Yingchao's husband. Although Zhou Enlai was working in a separate region at that time, he supported her efforts to realize a stronger position for rural women in land reform. When Deng Yingchao sought Zhou's advice after encountering challenges carrying out land reform in Fuping, Hebei, in 1948, for example, Zhou responded with two lengthy letters of instructions (Zhou and

Deng 1944; 1947; 1954 [1998]).[7] In 1948, Zhou Enlai himself admonished local leaders for not including women in land reform: "How can [one] discriminate against women? Our mothers are women. From here on in if someone is discriminating against women, you can tell them: if you discriminate against women, you are discriminating against your mother!" (Liu 1984).

The revolutionary attachments that enabled Deng Yingchao to champion and realize rights-based claims for women-work were thus a central part of the land reform story. Built into this moment was a latticework of ganqing, enduring, affective relations of belonging and obligation that connected, shaped, and disrupted the enactment of the revolutionary family. It was not only Zhu De's son who played a part in Deng Yingchao's efforts, for example, but the children of Liu Shaoqi and Mao Zedong as well. Indeed, among the sixty children that Deng Yingchao and Kang Keqing evacuated from Yan'an just weeks before Deng Yingchao began her advocacy were two of Liu Shaoqi's children and Mao Zedong's six-year-old daughter (Jin 1993, 1:392). This is not to say that Liu Shaoqi and Mao Zedong would have been in anyway beholden to Deng Yingchao for her efforts to keep their children safe, but rather to note that this otherwise invisible work in the march to revolutionary victory shored up trust, loyalty, and the maternalist gender order, making it more possible for Deng Yingchao to push forward with her agenda. Indeed, and as is evident in Zhou Enlai's conflation of womanhood and motherhood, a maternalist affective economy continued to shape the possibilities for reform in the acquisition of land and family rights. The politics of land reform would be similarly subjected to a complex array of revolutionary attachments and their contradictory enactment in the counties of Wenhe, Huoyue, and Gaoshan.

Learning to Speak, Learning to Kill

A rural region marked by hilly terrain and steep ravines, Wenhe County is located in western Henan, not far from the border of neighboring Shaanxi Province. In the late 1940s and early 1950s, some of the region's poorer residents dwelled in caves, chambers dug into the sides of cliffs and fashioned with doors and windows. The dwellings made for precarious living, however, as they were prone to collapse, especially during the rainy season. Many villagers survived at subsistence levels: men folk sowed what they could, including wheat, corn, legumes, peanuts, and/or tobacco. Cotton was also cultivated for export to Tianjin and Shanghai before and after the foundation of the PRC (WX 1992, 382–85). Over the course of Ding's childhood several calamitous natural disasters struck the region, including flooding and droughts. And violence was endemic: the Japanese and GMD fought pitch battles in Wenhe, only to be followed by battles between the GMD and CCP during the civil war (*WX* 1992, 75–76, 319–27).

Land reform officially began in Wenhe in December 1949, although the movement would not begin countywide for another full year. As elsewhere, land reform work teams sought to consolidate the CCP's local power through documenting and categorizing households according to wealth and means of livelihood, recruiting the most impoverished villagers into the Peasant Association and isolating those perceived to have the greatest stakehold in the previous regime (Ruf 1998, 77–86). Although class assignments were supposed to be based on strict criteria of evaluation, the variability of local conditions and the diverging views of the assessors produced a great deal of unevenness in the demarcation of familial class status in the new order.[8] In Wenhe, visiting work teams determined that local landlords and rich peasants, while only compromising some 5.35 percent of the population, occupied some 41 percent of the arable land. By the end of the land reform movement, those who had been classified as poor peasants and peasants-for-hire were allocated 78.7 percent of the land, and those classified as middle peasants were allocated 21.3 percent (*WX* 1992, 205)

Being classified as a "poor peasant" produced new forms of social capital under the new regime, including the possibility of community leadership. And, indeed, land reform work teams typically identified young, economically impoverished, and oppressed villagers as future leaders for two reasons. First, the oppressed-turned-leaders could serve as living bridges between the injustice of the old society and the promise of the new socialist reality; and second, the party leadership believed that the most economically "backward" villagers often had the most advanced farming skills because they had had to labor for their survival prior to 1949.[9] The recruitment of women activists on this front was no different: by 1964, 90 percent of commune and county Women's Federation officials in Wenhe originally hailed from poor peasant backgrounds.[10]

During the land reform movement, local women's organizing itself could only take place in the context of peasant associations (Cai 1947a [1988]).[11] With the formal establishment of the ACDWF in 1949, county-level women's organizations became possible for the first time on a national scale. But even so, visiting work teams, the Youth League, and the party itself became the primary route by which rural women were recruited and incorporated into activism. Work teams generally included women dundian cadres, or visiting cadres, charged with the task of mobilizing local women and identifying potential women activists and leaders. In Hershatter's (2011, 72–77) study of visiting cadres in neighboring Shaanxi, many had at least a middle school education and had received a brief training course in Marxist-Leninism, the works of Mao, and the history of Chinese women.[12] Strongly committed to liberating women through mobilizing them to work in the fields, these outsiders were expected to recruit and train young village women to take up local positions of leadership. Shaanxi visiting cadres billeted in the homes of locals established close and, in some cases, familial-like ties with village women. Indeed, many went out of their way to help women with their housework, and they often joined them for lengthy chats on the family kang. As one former visiting cadre remarked, "The main thing was to establish a close relationship. Some old ladies wanted to make me their goddaughter. That's how good our relationship was. I didn't do it for fear of being criticized for establishing private relationships . . . I would help around the house, even emptying the chamber pots for the old ladies. I would act as a sister to the young wives. I called the older people 'mama' and 'grandma,' and the young wives 'elder sister-in-law'" (Hershatter 2011, 75–76). A former Wenhe village and district women's head, Yuan Jinyu, 158, established similar bonds with the people with whom she boarded: "I had the key when the house owner was not home. The masses regarded me as their own family." By winning over at least some highly suspicious older women, visiting cadres were able to forge an early affective connection between the center of the home and the CCP's state-building project.

The capacity of the visiting cadres to establish viable grassroots women's organizations was, however, limited (Hershatter 2011, 313n34). In Wenhe, this organizational weakness was apparent during land reform, when community suspicion of women's participation in public meetings was extremely high, and when misunderstanding and variable methods for organizing women marked the women-work underway. Also troubling women-work was the tendency of some overzealous and impatient cadres to beat, tie up, and hang people.[13] A little over three years later, however, the Wenhe Women's Federation was still struggling to meet the needs of the moment. Some county-level women cadres were not active, others were ideologically confused and depressed (*sixiang kumen*),[14] and many village-level women's organizations were not fully functioning.[15] The challenges faced by grassroots women's organizations was not only due to the temporary nature of the visits by external cadres but also to the limited parameters of women-work, the gendered norms under which they operated, and the initial resistance of women themselves.

Visiting work teams strove to walk a fine line as they engaged with local women. On the one hand, they sought to mobilize women to participate in public events, including the land reform movement. This involved convincing women to think of themselves as existing independently from their familial relationships, as liberated selves realized through productive labor and political mobilizations. On the other hand, work teams simultaneously sought to police the boundaries of the family not only because they wanted to avoid alienating members of the community at large but also because of their own understanding of what constituted virtuous conduct. Land reform had long been plagued by sexist assumptions about the women who became active participants in the process, with contradictory signals coming from the very top of the CCP. As Johnson (1983, 131) argues, "Women cadres were vulnerable to accusations against their moral character simply because they were engaged in new public social roles long considered unsuitable for decent women."

A Wenhe Women's Federation description of local resistance to the mobilization of women illustrates this tension well:

> Because women had suffered from thousands of years under feudalism they believed they should be at home and that they weren't capable of doing anything except housework. These women thought that "outside" work was for men, and women weren't to participate in labor. The women themselves also expressed misgivings [*gu lu*], and the naïve ones refused to have contact with the women cadres, lest they be conscripted as women soldiers. For example, every time we cadres go into a village, they all ask questions such as: "How were you able to leave home?" "How far is your home from here?" "Did your family allow you to come here?" The few who wanted to have contact with the women cadres encountered restrictions from the traditional family, and so also weren't willing to come out. Often it was the unvirtuous [*bu zhengpai*] women who were most willing to come out. Because of [their own] marital trouble, they would introduce an element of scandal/impurity into the organization, and raise alarm and misapprehension among the older women and young men, who feared that [the women] would want to divorce or become corrupt [*xue huai*].[16]

The report highlights "feudalism" as the primary impediment to mobilizing rural women outside of the home, a stock analysis of the CCP then and now. Indeed, and as discussed in the previous chapter, Mao's country woman—the conservative, ignorant, and superstitious homemaker—looms large in the team's description of the resistance the team encountered. But it is also evident that misconceptions about the CCP's plans for local communities prevailed as well. The fact that some women feared being conscripted as soldiers suggests that rumors were circulating about what, at that point, was still an alien organization in their midst. Most interesting, perhaps, are the questions posed to the women team members. They suggest a deep suspicion within the community that women whose families "let them" leave their homes might not be morally upright themselves. Instead of directly countering the assumptions inherent in these questions, however, the work team reinforced them with their final observations that the women who did dare to come out were unvirtuous.

The report went on to note that one local woman leader, "General Broken-Shoe" as the villagers called her, was purged from her post for sexual indiscretions.[17] Villagers referred to young women's representatives and women's heads as "bai mao nü" (white haired girl) or "shan ye" (wild).[18] Tang Li, 159, for example, a former Wenhe women's head, first heard the term *white haired girl* during land reform when "some women's families didn't want them to become cadres because they were worried that they would become wild, and run away with some men with whom they had had affairs." In this instance, and in many others, visiting work teams and party leaders rearticulated and mobilized community norms of sexual shame as a means of policing the very women they were trying to recruit as a new generation of local leaders.

Given the concomitant risks of physical and social death, many of the CCP's earliest recruits in areas newly "liberated" did not choose to become activists at all, much less activists on women's issues.[19] Instead, the CCP had to persuade individuals to think of themselves and their social world in an entirely new way (Gao Xiaoxian 2006; Hershatter 2011; Ruf 1998). Yuan Jinyu, 158, a former Wenhe women's head, describes her own reluctant journey into activism as follows:

> The Peasants' Association was established after Liberation. A woman called X, who was a middle school student when I was in school, was in the Work Team here. The first women's meeting was held, and the militia was holding guns. I was called to attend the meeting, but I was so scared that I began to cry, and didn't want to go. Finally, I went to the meeting. [Another woman] knew me, so she got the women to elect me as the women's representative. Afterward when I went to the district meeting, drums and gongs were beating boisterously. The [villagers] had me ride on a draught animal and sent me to the meeting. I went to a district meeting twice, and then came back to lecture to the women in the village.

Yuan's narrative of the process that swept her into activism is almost evacuated of her own individual will. It was the leaders (a visiting cadre and a local cadre) who convinced her to attend the meeting and who put her forward as a candidate for election. And it was the villagers who propelled her forward to the district meeting on a draught animal, a symbol of her newly elevated status but also a sign, perhaps, of her continued reluctance to participate in these revolutionary events. It was not until Yuan returned to her village that her new collective agency became apparent in the form of the lectures she delivered to the women of her village.

During the early 1950s, hundreds of thousands of women learned a new vocabulary of terms and restructured their understanding of community power and their own place within it on the basis of these new terms.[20] Learning "how to speak" was thus a key part of the process of recruitment during land reform: it enabled individuals to see that their fate was no longer subject to the whims of ancestors, landlords, or a deity, but rather that they could overturn (*fanshen*) their historical oppression and shape their future under the leadership of the Chinese Communist Party. Speech acts, and particularly the public testimonials of "speaking bitterness," would play a powerful role in the formation of local activist subjectivity (Hershatter 2011; Ruf 1998). Women, including new activist recruits, were often encouraged to describe the cruelty that they had experienced as young child-brides or as abused servants, experiences that were reread as products of the patriarchal and feudal system of the "old society." Whether standing before a small community gathering or a mass rally of ten thousand people, the women who participated in acts of speaking bitterness were visible and audible symbols of the arrival of a new order in which even the most oppressed could have a voice.

Speaking bitterness was a highly charged practice of emotion management: many women sobbed on stage, and others became so angry that they had to be physically restrained (Hershatter 2011, 79). But emotion management also includes processes that are not always readily apprehended (Goodwin and Pfaff 2001, 284; Gould 2009). As Perry (2002b, 114) argues, "A distinctive facet of human feelings is their ambivalence and malleability; the genius of the CCP approach lay in its capacity to appreciate and capitalize on this fundamental reality." Acts of speaking bitterness contributed to the constitution of a new emotional habitus, which "structures what members feel and how they emote" (Gould 2009, 34). According to Gould (2009, 28), emergent emotional pedagogies, "'make sense' of affective states and authorize selected feelings and actions while downplaying and even invalidating others." In the context of the land reform struggle, one of the emotions that poor peasants were expected to eradicate was pity—in particular, pity for the suffering of landlords. To this end, several Wenhe villagers were criticized for not being resolute enough in their standpoint when they provided food to a landlord who had not eaten for several days; while other Wenhe women, including one militia member, were praised for their willingness to support the execution of local landlords and for participating in the capture and murder of bandits.[21] Tang Li, 159, personally participated in the execution of a landlord. As she recalls, she and other representatives of the Peasant Association made this decision in secret and carried it out the next day: "All of my family thought that the CCP was good because it liberated us."

The CCP, in fact, discouraged spontaneous executions. A Central Committee "Directive on the Land Question" issued in 1946 stipulated that "we should accede to the people's demands for the execution of those collaborators and public enemies who have committed heinous crimes by sentencing them to death after trial by the courts. Apart from this, however, we should generally enforce a policy of leniency and refrain from executing people or beating them to death" (Liu 1946 [1984], 375). But clearly these were very difficult processes to control and persecution of "landlords" often materialized as nothing more than vigilante justice. Deng Zihui, the army's head of propaganda, recognized the "settling of accounts with bullies" as an especially big problem in Henan (Wou 1994, 383).

By participating in controlled and sometimes uncontrolled acts of speech and violence in settings of mass mobilization, the newly recruited activists and villagers were given a means of collectively managing their fear while expressing new collective forms of revolutionary emotions including rage and celebration.[22] Strauss's (2002, 95) observations of the urban mobilizations of the Campaign to Suppress Counterrevolutionaries that took place in the early 1950s are equally apt here: the highly public campaign "simultaneously crushed the individuals concerned, served as a warning for those of their ilk, and struck fear into the hearts of their sympathizers while soliciting the chorus-like participation of that most amorphous of groups, 'the masses,' in heavily staged political theatre."

Through publicly parading, criticizing, and in some cases, executing the worst offenders during the height of the land reform movement, the CCP leadership believed it could convince farmers that a new era had arrived and, indeed, that there was no going back. But while some newly minted activists were able to serve as role models in the fields and public meetings and thus meet the party's expectations, others failed dramatically. The archives, official publications, and my interview transcripts are filled with stories of failed and aborted women's leadership in rural localities during the earliest years of the People's Republic.[23] Between 1951 and 1953, party membership among women in Huoyue actually *declined* by 18 percent (from 361 to 295), while party membership among men *increased* by nearly 10 percent (from 1,770 to 1,958) (*HX* 1993, 278).[24] By 1953, men party members in Huoyue outnumbered women party members nearly seven to one.

The low numbers of women activists can be explained, in part, by the intense familial, community, and party surveillance to which early women activists were particularly subject. The strong objection of in-laws largely featured in the low numbers and attrition of women activists, with some family members resorting to violence and even murder to prevent their female relatives from participating in political activities.[25]

In many parts of China, patrilocal marriage systematically undermined the continuation of activism over the medium to long term. Moving to the village of one's husband often entailed leaving behind carefully forged political connections and thus curtailing opportunities for political activism.[26] Although marriage of individuals from the same village were rare and generally considered a sign of weakness on the part of the husband, it is remarkable that at least one-third of the twenty-two women activists I interviewed in Wenhe, Huoyue, and Gaoshan, and for whom I have data, married within their natal village. Moreover, many others maintained important connections with their natal family after leaving home.[27] The activism of eleven of the former women's heads I interviewed was supported by members of their natal families (out of seventeen) and the activism of twenty Women's Federation cadres was supported by their natal families (out twenty-eight).

Hao Lianfen, 131, who stayed within her natal village after her marriage, was strongly supported by both her parents: "If I didn't take my child to a meeting, my father would carry [the child] across several brigades so that [I] could feed him. At that time there was no powder milk. If I was absent, then [he] would find someone else to nurse the child, [and] if I was around, I would do it." In post-1949 northern China, mother-daughter ties were especially strengthened through frequent visits (Judd 1989) and gift exchanges that bound several generations together (Yan 1996). But suffering and revolution bound mothers and daughters together in unexpected ways as well. Sun Qinqin's, 162, mother aided her to escape from famine and from the fate of being a child-bride and would later care for her daughter's first two children. Sun Qinqin, 162; Bao Qinglian, 160; and Zheng Xiu Wen, 163, all expressed deep gratitude to their mothers for supporting their activism. In some cases, sympathetic mothers-in-law provided essential help with children and household tasks as well. Peng Xiufen's, 32, mother-in-law supported her because she "loved her dearly." He Jinxiu, 31, another Huoyue women's head, explained that her mother-in-law's support for her work was rooted in the political changes that had transpired after the founding of the People's Republic. Her mother-in-law had been widowed at a very young age and suffered greatly. After having liberated herself and gaining enough to eat and drink, she was "very active" and "willing to do anything," including minding her grandchildren.[28] There were other stories as well: Yuan Jinyu's, 158, mother, for example, accompanied her as she traversed the countryside after her baby was born: "It was snowing, and I was walking in front while my mother, (with) bound feet, followed behind. I carried the baby while my mother carried the baby's things." Some politically minded mothers, however, were more interested in undertaking women-work themselves, than caring for the children of their grown daughters. Former women's head Rong Litang, 116, resented the fact that her mother also became a women's head and thus did not have time to care for her grandchildren.

Natal and marital families not only provided key household and emotional support, but political support as well. No less than half of the women leaders

I interviewed had relatives who were active in the CCP or connected organizations prior to their emergence into activism.[29] As noted in the introduction, Cai Chang encouraged this practice. The Wenhe Women's Federation encouraged local CCP and Youth League leaders to convince their wives to participate in grassroots organizations, as well.[30]

Many of the male relatives who encouraged, recruited, and cultivated young women leaders were early CCP members, former soldiers in the People's Liberation Army, or members of the Youth League or local peasants' association—a finding reflective of the local histories of violence and instability in Wenhe, Huoyue, and Gaoshan. The CCP's policy to target the female relatives of already-active male leaders dated back to the foundation of the CCP when the lovers of prominent CCP leaders were assigned to head up women's programming in the new party structure. But it would continue as the CCP sought to build its grassroots organization in the Chinese countryside before, during, and after the foundation of the PRC as well. In addition to fathers and brothers, politically active in-laws and husbands also played a decisive role in the emergence of women activists and in the capacity of these women to continue and deepen into their work as grassroots leaders. This pattern was particularly evident in the activism of two cousins in Huoyue County, Henan.

The Local Party Family

Huoyue, located to the south of Henan's provincial capital, was indelibly marked by the waves of violence that rolled through the region in the 1930s, 1940s, and early 1950s. In 1938, Feng Yuxiang traveled to Huoyue, recruiting some eight thousand volunteers to fight the Japanese (*HX* 1993, 24). In 1941 more than ten thousand Japanese soldiers invaded the county (*HX* 1993, 25); villagers hid in underground tunnels to escape the soldiers who arrived in the area with guns and dogs (Hou Qiuyi, 132). During the civil war, the struggle to control Huoyue was also fierce: indeed, it took nearly eighteen months of fighting before the CCP was able to pacify local resistance to its rule. In 1948 there were 54 battles in which 178 bandits were captured, 34 were injured, and 46 were killed. In one battle, for example, five district governments were attacked, and more than twenty CCP workers were killed (*HX* 1993, 282–83). Once the civil conflict ceased, hardened war veterans broke the power of local landlord families: between the spring of 1949 and February 1950 some 1,025 local tyrants (landlords) and 195 bandit chiefs were struggled against through land reform (*HX* 1993, 283). The hearts of the worst offenders were cut out with scythes after they were publicly executed (Hou Qiuyi, 132).

Prior to the establishment of the PRC, the Huoyue population was primarily engaged in agricultural work, cultivating wheat, cotton, corn, millet, Chinese sorghum, and sesame (*HX* 1993, 101–6). Similar to Wenhe, Huoyue was also prone to natural disasters, including flooding and drought. In 1949, with only 14 women CCP members out of a total of 221 (approximately 6 percent) (*HX* 1993, 278), the CCP needed the support of poor rural women and their families; in Xicun, that support was built through family ties.

In Huoyue I sought to conduct interviews in two villages: one that had a history of strong *jiazu* (clans), Xicun, and one that did not. Based on the scholarship of the time, I expected that family-dominated local CCP organizations would inhibit and constrain women's activism and knowledge of women's liberation. According to the analysis of this earlier generation of scholarship, Maoist policies and institutions reinforced conservatism among male peasants and village-level male cadres by allowing new collective structures to organize on the basis of preexisting kinship groups (Andors 1983; Diamond 1975; Parish and Whyte 1978). Collectivization reinforced kinship structures not only among villagers but among local party leaders as well, a factor that served to increase the power of "traditional" forms of familial authority over villages (Domenach 1995; Friedman et al. 1991).[31] According to Lü (2000, 24), resistance to the revolutionary force of the CCP

> arose mainly from the paradox that the regime created for itself, namely, a structure that reinforces traditional ways rather than sustaining new norms, and from the precariousness of revolutionary values that cannot successfully transcend, transform, and, more important, maintain even the regime's own rank and file as loyal and dependable agents.[32]

Conservative practices among grassroots party organizations thus increased the traditional social structure of rural life and undermined the ideological agenda of the CCP (Lü 2000; Shue 1988; Zweig 1989).

Peasant conservatism, scholars argue, especially hampered the spread of ideas of sexual equality. Specifically, they suggest that during the 1940s and 1950s, conservative male peasants and leaders raised such a furor over incipient women's rights campaigns that the CCP leadership reversed course and downplayed any discussion of sexual equality (Johnson 1983; Stacey 1983; Stranahan 1983). Although passage of the 1950 Marriage Law temporarily reversed this trend, Johnson (1983) argues that the subsequent outcry by male peasants and rural male cadres dissipated the strength of the law and the effort put into its implementation. Ultimately, the continuation of strong family units at the base of rural life served to strengthen parochialism and patriarchy in the Chinese countryside (Diamond 1975; Friedman et al. 1991; Shue 1988). It was only during the GLF, when a climate of fear drove leaders to political zealotry, that the traditional family temporarily shattered. Indeed, according to Stacey (1983, 247), the GLF violated the unarticulated "patriarchal pact" among China's male peasants, male grassroots cadres, and the male-dominated CCP.

As I will show in subsequent chapters, local party families did constrain local women's organizing. But they also enabled it. What rapidly became apparent as I began to interview in the village of Xicun and in surrounding hamlets that did not have a history of strong clans was that local party organizations and families often proved central to the recruitment and the political formation of local women activists and leaders. Rather than subverting the state-building agenda of the CCP, however, local women cadres embedded in party families strengthened the state's capacity to transform the conditions in which women gave birth, forged their families, and upheld the rural economy.

In Xicun, Zhang Sumei's, 20, natal family were early enthusiasts of the Communist reforms. Growing up in a six- or seven-room house, Zhang Sumei's natal family was assigned the status of upper-middle peasants though, according to Zhang Sumei, they were really "bankrupt landlords."[33] Zhang Sumei's father insisted that his daughter attend school during a literacy campaign and her mother's brother, a work team leader, encouraged her to become a cadre. Zhang Sumei joined the Youth League as a teenager, served as a model cotton planter and production leader, and rose to become the women's head in her village a year before she married. According to Zhang Sumei, it was because her father was so enthusiastic (*jiji*) that the leadership appointed her women's head, and it was because of her work as a women's head that she ended up marrying into another party family, also assigned the status of upper-middle peasant. Indeed, Zhang Sumei's future mother-in-law was so impressed by Zhang Sumei's beautiful speeches as women's head that she urged her son, away at school, to marry Zhang Sumei. In the early 1950s, Zhang Sumei's brother-in-law, then village party secretary, trained both Zhang Sumei and her husband to be women's head and accountant.

Zhang Sumei's cousin, Hou Qiuyi, 132, who lived in a neighboring village, also emerged as an activist during land reform with the strong support of a politically active natal family behind her. Hou Qiuyi secretly began to participate in meetings shortly after the arrival of the Communists, spying on local landlords from treetops. She was also chosen to "speak bitterness" prior to the execution of landlords, sometimes before crowds that were, she said, as large as ten thousand people. Her own enthusiasm and strong familial support resulted in rapid entry to the Youth League in 1950 and early praise by local authorities. When the local party committee wanted to send Hou Qiuyi for further training to become a government cadre, however, her father objected: "If you leave it is the same as becoming someone else's daughter-in-law—you become theirs. You are too young. There are some tasks you just can't do now, people will pick on you about stuff. You could be killed like Liu Hulan."

As discussed in the previous chapter, Liu Hulan was immortalized by Mao Zedong after she was executed by the GMD at the age of fifteen. While the Shanxi revolutionary served as a role model to many young women, in this case, the life and death of Liu Hulan was interpreted as a path best not followed.[34]

In contrast with Zhang Sumei's natal family, Hou Qiuyi's family was absolutely destitute when the CCP arrived. Her family was so poor, she recounted, that they had to grow their crops on grave lands. Her uncle sold salt and her father worked as a bonded laborer, planting and harvesting for others. Prior to becoming a cadre, she was always hungry. Even after 1949, she said, they were reduced to preparing meals from tree bark, collecting wild vegetables, and borrowing grain from others. Despite selling nearly everything they had, they nearly starved to death. After she began her work with the CCP, however, things changed. Some forty-four years later, Hou Qiuyi spoke with intricate detail about the bountiful meals she and other cadres were served at district-level meetings, and the real sense of motivation they provided:

> The first time I went to a county meeting you don't know how well the leaders treated us. The tables were laden with food. In the morning I got up and had water to wash my face, tooth brush water was prepared in front of me. Lunch was hotpot and the meat was flavorful [sweet and salty]. Meat was cooked with sugar and then with salt. We were treated well. It was like this for several years at the county meetings and even combs for your hair were prepared in the places we stayed. We had meat and steamed bread. So how could we not work well? We worked very well because of that.

Having a politically active daughter or daughter-in-law could bring particular advantages. Indeed, early enthusiasm for a daughter, wife, sister, and even daughter-in-law to become an activist was often based on the perceived status and benefits that the family could accrue through their collective participation in the new political order. Of course, the stakes were high, and the future was unknown. But the fact that Hou Qiuyi's father drew on the logic of "marrying out" to persuade her to forgo advancement at higher levels suggests he was gambling that the family as a whole might begin to reverse its fortunes through the local leadership prospects of his daughter. Similarly, Zhang Sumei's future mother-in-law courted her on the basis of her leadership potential; a gambit made, no doubt, to help cement her son's future power at the local level as well.

Zhang Sumei herself noted the (familial) benefits of leadership, in one of the quotations that begins this chapter.

Leader Zhang's natal and marital families did not just subvert social custom by encouraging her activism but also by arranging for her to marry someone from her natal village. The fact that Zhang stayed meant that she was able to maintain the political connections she had already established. In the words of Zhang, "If you don't have background, who is going to take you on [as a cadre]? It is all done by references, it is all done by introduction." In rare circumstances, however, powerful natal party families could provide the support necessary for women's activists to continue their work after "marrying out" to their husband's village. This was the case for Huoyue women's head Liu Yuezhen, 10, who came from a politically active natal family, including an older brother who was a cadre at the township. In the face of strong opposition from her marital family, Liu's natal family and the village party secretary who recruited her supported her and enabled her to continue as a leader for more than two decades.

While the families of both Zhang and her husband benefitted from their union, the companionate relationship shared by Zhang and her husband, however, was much more than a straightforward enactment of parochial familial advancement. Rather it also reflected romantic attachment, mutual regard, and a self-conscious recognition of an emergent, if hierarchically embedded, expression of sexual equality. A widow of several years by the time we first met, Zhang Sumei stressed the closeness and equality that characterized her relationship with her husband: "We were always together. The women in the village would laugh at me, saying: 'You can't tear [yourself] away from him, and he can't [tear himself away] from you.' We knew what was what, he respected me and I respected him."

This mutual respect extended to their work life as well:

> He had no [problem] with [my work], he supported me. If we had to attend a meeting, we went together. We never quarreled about [my work], we were destined to marry. [He] never said: "You are out of control with your work, [I] forbid you to work." Never! If he went to town to attend a model meeting, we attended the meeting [together], [where] the prize was a cow. I also went if he went to attend the People's Congress meetings. . . . He was an understanding [person]. He never got angry and criticized me because I spoke with other men, never. As long as my thinking was pure, I never feared [anything].[35]

Similar to many other companionate couples, Zhang and her husband enjoyed a separate, but not-quite-equal status within the CCP. Alongside the shared affection, the playful teasing, and joint work life, it is clear that Zhang was subject to expectations that her husband was not. The relationship between Zhang and her husband was animated by mutual respect, yes, but a respect that was qualified on the basis of a communist morality in which Zhang had to police her own "thinking" or be accused, by her husband or others, of not being *zhengpai* (upright). The appearance of uprightness was critically important in Xicun: the first women's head had likely only served in her position for a few months before being dismissed for having had a "serious moral problem" (*zuofeng bu hao*). While zuofeng can also mean work style—and, indeed, Zhang Sumei, mentioned that the woman constantly held meetings—"illicit sexual relations" (*nan nü cuowu*) were implicated as well. Nearby, Miao Murong, 129, also a former women's head, shared the story of a comrade who was dismissed for having an affair with the party secretary. Whether or not the rumors and accusations were true matters less than the way that they shaped local activist practices: in this context, supportive husbands could establish and shore up the propriety of women's activism. Of course, the activism and leadership of men did not similarly require the attached affirmation of their wives.[36]

Zhang Sumei's position as women's head was also much less powerful than that of her husband, who was the village accountant, and to whom she had to submit requests for funding. She was also subject to his orders. On one occasion during the GLF, for example, Zhang Sumei's husband instructed his wife to join a work team on a site away from the brigade. As soon as she arrived, however, she was told to return to the brigade. According to Zhang Sumei, the site team leaders recognized what her husband did not: her young children needed her more at home than did the team at the site.

Although Zhang Sumei had become politically active before her husband and indeed encouraged him to become a leader, she was plagued by self-doubt as a leader. Similar to so many other former women leaders that I interviewed, Zhang Sumei repeatedly stressed her illiteracy as evidence of her lack of ability. Zhang Sumei could not read or write. Given that over 95 percent of the Huoyue population was illiterate or semiliterate in 1949 (*HX* 1993, 4), this was not surprising.[37] She compared herself unfavorably to her mother-in-law, who she says learned how to read in a literacy training class, and to her husband, who had a primary school education: "I learned from my husband. If you are illiterate, you are really obedient. I just led people to work, [that] is all."

Zhang Sumei's critical self-assessment flowed, in part, from having to manage much of the household work, with little time left to study. Zhang's mother-in-law, only in her early forties, helped out with chores, including making meals and sewing clothing for the children: "No matter how late I came back, she always had a meal ready." But Zhang Sumei also noted that her mother-in-law abdicated responsibility for the big decisions: "As soon as I [joined the household] she said she would no longer be in charge and threw everything on my shoulders." It is clear that Zhang continued to be responsible for much of the household work for her marital and natal family, including twisting hemp into cloth, sewing clothes, and making the soles of shoes, work that she undertook at meetings, and at home while the rest of the family slept.

The familial attachments that gave rise to and shaped the contours of Hou Qiuyi's marriage were even more fraught than those of Zhang's. Hou Qiuyi had already been politically active for two years when she married her husband, a former soldier and full-time cadre who would go on to hold leadership positions at the district level and above during his several decades in office.[38] A local CCP leader served as their matchmaker:

> My husband and I were at the same meeting for several days. One night a leader asked both of us to have a chat and then introduced us to each other. The leader said: "I'll handle it. You must marry a person from the poor peasant class, you can't marry someone from the landlord class, that is the fundamental issue. You are doing class struggle every day now so you can't marry their people, you have to listen to Chairman Mao so what do you think?" So, I said I had to go back to discuss this with my parents. Without my parents' permission I couldn't do this, but a man could decide for himself. I didn't say yes right away. And I always had meetings so every time the leader saw me, he asked me about my marriage.

In the case of Hou Qiuyi and her future husband, it is clear the CCP was not a neutral arbiter of two equal parties. Whereas "a man could decide for himself," about whom to marry, Hou Qiuyi felt obligated to consult her parents on the matter. Hou Qiuyi was also pressured to comply with the introduction, a practice that Deng Yingchao (1942 [1985], 6) had vigorously opposed a decade earlier when she argued that marriages should not be based on "politics alone." But at the founding of the PRC, and for many years to come, the CCP continued to play matchmaker, prioritizing the political backgrounds of potential spouses as a way to strengthen the party, and, in some instances, as a reward to low-ranking male cadres for their revolutionary service. Former Meihua County teacher and CCP member, Sun Qinqin, for example, was punished (*chufen*) for refusing to marry a party secretary. Former Wenhe women's head, Tang Li, 159, however, did not feel she could refuse. Tang was still grieving the loss of her husband when she was pressured by county-level officials to marry a former soldier who had joined the revolution in 1927 and sacrificed much for his country: "Cadres in the county and commune said to me that I had a good heart so I should take care of [the former soldier's] five children. Nobody was taking care of those children when he went to work. They were in school and the youngest one was just this tall, very pitiable. I cried, and later I agreed. When he went to work, I took care of those five children. [I] went to meetings during the day and came home to cook at night."

The extensive household responsibilities that Tang Li managed while simultaneously serving as a local leader were not atypical. Of the twenty-six women's heads for whom I have a record, four had at least one child, and fifteen had two or more, over the course of the 1950s. Hou Qiuyi herself was responsible for feeding and clothing her new family of nine—a family as impoverished as her natal family had been.[39] The family had many debts and Hou was often reduced to foraging for wild plants to feed her new relatives. Given heavy household responsibilities, she was unable to attend literacy classes. In the meantime, her husband was away receiving the political training that Hou had wanted for herself but was dissuaded from pursuing by her father.

If that was not enough, however, Hou was subject to a tough political inspection after her marriage to ensure that she would remain faithful and committed to the CCP. She felt that she had already been tested in 1951 when she was first asked to join the CCP as an "advanced activist." But then, after the party insisted that she marry, the organization tested her again. She was furious that she had to wait another four years before she could finally join the CCP. The political necessity to marry, therefore, would simultaneously prove a political liability.

Over the course of her tenure as a local activist and leader, Hou Qiuyi served in various positions including as a small group leader in the Peasant's Association, a member of the Youth League, Youth League branch secretary, women's head, and vice party secretary of the village. She spoke with pride about her work as a cadre, especially once she assumed the position of vice party secretary. It was challenging to gain the trust and respect of the other leaders, but she proved herself capable, she said, through her hard work and dedication. Like Zhang Sumei, however, she nonetheless remained subject to the authority of her husband's leadership at a moment when public displays of "special treatment" might be viewed as politically suspect. She recounted one story about the first time she was pregnant and went into labor: "I was at a brigade meeting when I said I wasn't feeling well. I said I wanted to go home but my husband wouldn't agree. I said: '[If] you don't agree [to let me go home] I won't be able to stand it.' I gave birth the next morning at breakfast time."

The emergence of Zhang Sumei and Hou Qiuyi as local activists and leaders must be understood, in part, through the party families to which they belonged. Whether up on stage before thousands of people, or setting an example in the first collective fields, Zhang and Hou emerged as central players in the rapid transformation of power in their communities, in no small part because of the support they received from their natal and marital families. But, denied opportunities for advancement, burdened with heavy housework, and obliged to follow the orders

of husbands with greater authority, they were equally subject to these transformations as well. Party families thus created a context in which women activists
could be read as revolutionary agents free from "feudal patriarchal oppression"
even as they were subject to party surveillance and struggled with household
responsibilities from which their spouses were largely excused.

Some of these complex formations are evident in Hou Qiuyi's words when
I inquired about the community's response to her earliest days organizing:

> People would talk behind my back, not to my face. The landlord said,
> "Hey, look at that woman who has become a cadre, [she is] shaking
> [her] butt [*pigu niu li*], on a Yangko [*Yangge*] troupe, [she] doesn't know
> that it is shameful [*xiu*]. When it came time to hold meetings, he was
> hauled up onto the stage and scared silly. He was terrified of being hit,
> and so he didn't dare say anything again. The lower and middle peas-
> ants were in solidarity. He knew if he said that so and so had a big butt
> and was flirting with a Yangko dance, that he would be hauled up and
> struggled against in the meeting. His body would go limp [*su le*]. So he
> didn't dare to say anything. Women and men are different. The division
> of labor is different. You do whatever the branch secretary tells you to
> do. And after we returned [we] summarized our work, [and discussed]
> who did well, and who didn't do well. And [we] praised who did well,
> and then criticized [those] who didn't do well.[40]

Shame featured frequently in the recollections that Hou Qiuyi shared with
me.[41] Here, Hou Qiuyi inverted prerevolutionary power relations and reassigned
the landlord, limp and terrified, as a (feminized) subject of shame. Revolutionary
lower and middle peasants, of which Hou Qiuyi was one, were now in charge.
But in almost the same breath, Hou Qiuyi went on to assert that "women and
men are different" and that they "do different work" and that her goal was to "do
whatever the party secretary tells you to do." In this narrative, it is the lower and
middle classes, and the branch secretary, as their leader, who embody revolutionary agency. Women's difference, and the work associated with it, is thus accepted
as just one part of the larger revolutionary struggle, even as this acknowledgement of difference also contained its shadow: the quiet talk of villagers and some
cadres, about women leaders. It is in this way, among many others, that "women
in different guises and social positions haunted the very formation of peasant as
a category" (Chen 2011, 73).

When I interviewed Hou, she had been widowed for two years, and was residing in her courtyard home with one of her sons and his family. She was also
financially aiding grandchildren to pursue university studies, albeit on a meagre
pension. She was bitter that she was not receiving the compensation that she

deserved given her many years of service, the level of leadership she had attained, and in light of the rampant corruption of the moment: "Joining the Party [then, in 1955] is not like today when you have to buy your way in." Rather, "when you joined the Party," she said, "you took an oath to arduously struggle [*jianku fen-dou*]." Over the course of two days of intensive and lengthy interviewing, Hou Qiuyi repeatedly drew on Maoist slogans to define her leadership. She also consistently centered Mao Zedong: after his death (in 1976) and the communes were broken up, she said, she became deeply discouraged (*xieqi*).

Hou Qiuyi's leadership was also forged in the context of formal party organizations that were linked to a longer revolutionary past. Indeed, Hou Qiuyi located Huoyue's local leadership within a revolutionary narrative, sharing that the county-level women's head and district women's head had survived the Long March, and that "generally speaking male cadres in that era participated on the Long March."[42] While neither Hou nor her cousin participated in the Long March nor as part of the local militias who fought the Japanese and the GMD, the fact that they were recruited and trained by men who were war veterans profoundly shaped how they perceived themselves as activists and leaders and how they perceived the work with which they were entrusted. Indeed, the violent class struggle of land reform became the basis through which local activism was constituted as a force of history. As I will show in the chapters that follow, Hou Qiuyi and Zhang Sumei would implement select regulations and policies of the maternalist social policy regime through ideological instruction, community shame, and at times, the threat of violence. At the same time, they would submit their own bodies and, in some cases, the bodies of the women they were mobilizing to the demands of a Maoist work ethic of total physical sacrifice: an ethic modeled by male leaders who insisted, for example, that their wives attend a meeting while enduring labor contractions. In these ways and many others, state formation in Xicun and in its neighboring hamlets, would transpire not despite family ties but through them.

The Youth League

Former women's head and Youth League activist Tian Min, 85, witnessed the ritual act of speaking bitterness at a large women's federation gathering in Gaoshan, Jiangsu, in 1952:

> A woman stood on the stage giving a speech. We sat below with our notebooks all crying. She didn't cry a tear herself. She had been abused by her in-laws—[they] made her eat pig food and even burnt her. At

that first meeting we were all invited to watch a movie [and the woman] sat in front of me. We were watching a war film. She became so frightened that she hid underneath her chair. I myself was a child bride. By comparison, my mother-in-law was pretty good to me.

Public acts of speaking bitterness would prove as important to the rise of women's activism in Jiangsu as they were in Henan. In Tian Min's account, the woman on the stage is doubly imagined as a heroic figure (for being stoic and not crying like her audience) and a feudal subject to be pitied (for enduring worse abuse than the narrator, a child-bride turned activist herself). By encouraging former child-brides and abused wives to see that economic and familial oppression was a remnant of the "old society," both the activist and her agency were made possible. As in Wenhe and Huoyue, speaking bitterness provided a means of recognizing and naming abuse and transforming victimization into a new form of ethical empowerment.

I spoke with Tian Min at length in 2001 and 2004. Both times we met in the home in which she had been living with her husband and mother-in-law since 1997—a three-story building with spacious finished rooms and several Karaoke stations. Tian's four children were all financially successful: her son was the head of a factory, one daughter was the head of an opera troupe, and yet another was a member of the CCP. Tian had also spent a great deal of time reading about China's revolutionary past, including a biography of Mao written by his granddaughter. But while Tian's later life was opulent in comparison with that of Zhang Sumei and Hou Qiuyi, Tian's adolescence had been wretched.

Before she became a child-bride, Tian Min had been living with her parents in Kunming, the capital of Yunnan province. She was just beginning third grade when her schoolwork was interrupted violently by the Japanese invasion. Tian Min's parents arranged for her to be married at the age of fourteen into a family thousands of miles away, in part, it would seem, because they thought she would be provided with an education. A colleague of Tian Min's father, Tian Min's future father-in-law, transported Tian Min to Gaoshan from Kunming in July 1947. After Tian Min arrived in her new home, however, she immediately became subject to the abuse of her in-laws. According to Tian Min, her mother-in-law refused to feed her properly and Tian suffered from severe malnutrition as a consequence. Tian Min's in-laws also betrayed their promise to educate her.

Between the ages of fourteen and seventeen, Tian Min worked alongside her fiancé's grandmother in the family fields. They primarily grew rice and wheat, as well as mulberry trees on the side in order to raise silkworms. In the meantime, and not unlike other young men of the region, her fiancé left, in 1949, to work in Shanghai. Residing close to three major cities, many Gaoshan residents straddled urban and rural forms of employment; Tian Min's fiancé subsequently worked as a full-time factory employee making pens. Tian's mother-in-law, however, would not let Tian Min herself take advantage of an opportunity to work in a textile mill in Shanghai, because all the people working in textile mills were "bad."

In the winter of 1948–49, Tian Min began her first foray into activism by serving as an underground courier for the local CCP. Tian officially became an activist after land reform when she joined the Youth League in 1950. In 1952, she became the women's head, in 1953 the Youth League secretary, and in 1954, she joined the CCP.

Local women's organizing was not totally without precedence in the area: in the 1940s, a Gaoshan women's organization undertaking literacy work boasted a membership of 18,043 (GX 1994, 633); in striking contrast to widespread illiteracy in Wenhe and Huoyue, the Gaoshan population was 66 percent literate by 1928 (GX 1994, 182).

In addition, nearby Shanghai and Nanjing had long histories of active women's organizations, including the YWCA, which had mobilized women workers during the 1930s and 1940s (Honig 1986; Lu and Miao 2000, 19–21). But prior to Tian Min's activism with the CCP, she had had no contact with locally based women's organizations. As far as Tian Min was concerned, she far preferred her work with the Youth League.

> When I was doing Youth League work, I told the leader that I liked doing Youth League work. Because the Youth League was made up of young people, it was very lively. Women-work was very hard to do, women comrades were very idle and lacked discipline. I said I didn't want to be the women's head. The leader wanted me to do it. It was funny when [I] went to the district to attend meetings. The two meetings were held simultaneously. . . . When I was asked which meeting [I would] attend, I said that I'd attend the Youth League branch secretary meeting. I didn't attend the meetings of the women's heads. But I still had to do the work, [I] still had to complete the work.

Tian Min remarked that women were not as progressive as the youth, that they were "ideologically lazy." As Tian Min's quote at the beginning of this chapter illustrates, she did not feel herself to be like women comrades. Were Tian Min given a choice, she would have far preferred Youth League work over serving as a women's representative.

The Chinese Communist Youth League had a long history in China's revolutionary struggle. Established in 1920 to help young people study communism, the Youth League served as a feeder organization into the party in which young activists could prove themselves worthy of party membership and, in the interim, serve as support for the implementation of particular party policies.[43] Although limited to young people between the ages of fifteen and twenty-five, and thus subject to a built-in process of turnover, the Youth League grew from 1.3 million in 1949 to 25 million in 1959.[44] Whereas the peasants association declined rapidly in importance after land reform, the Chinese Communist Youth League would play an increasingly important role in recruiting, training, and supporting the activism of young women over the course of the 1950s.

Tian Min was not alone in her preference for Youth League work. In Gaoshan, a county Women's Federation investigation found that those most unwilling to become women's heads included women cadres who had previously been active in the Youth League or had been responsible for some aspect of a cooperative's finances or production.[45] Many of these women leaders thought that women were "backward," that there was no glory in women-work, and that they would much rather be involved with the Youth League while they were young and energetic. Some went so far as to declare that they would rather give up the cause altogether and go home than do women-work. In Tian Min's case, she thought of running away to join the army, as other young women were doing at that time. Indeed, in Huaiyin Prefecture, 1,455 women cadres enlisted, and in nearby Nanjing, one-third of the students who were signing up for military service in 1950 were women (Lu and Miao 2000, 123). According to Tian Min:

> In 1952 I went to X village for militia training. A relative living next door told my mother-in-law that if they continued to abuse me [then] I would join the army. In fact, I wanted to become a woman soldier. At that time, they were accepting women soldiers to go to X. Later [they] did not accept women soldiers and so I didn't go. . . . During the militia training, my mother-in-law gave me fifty cents. If [my relative] hadn't said that to my mother-in-law, then my mother-in-law would never have given me that fifty cents. [But] she would never prevent me from working such as attending meetings and working. She left in 1951.

Although Tian Min's range of options was limited, so were the options of her mother-in-law. Thus, while Tian's mother-in-law was able to prevent her from taking a job in Shanghai, she knew that she might not have been able to stop her daughter-in-law from joining the army if that is what Tian Min wanted. Since her arrival in the household at the age of fourteen, Tian Min told me, she had refused to address her grandmother and mother in-law with the terms *taipo* and *gupo*, monikers of respect, as was socially expected at the time. She also refused to listen to their commands because "wasn't I a person just like them [*wo bushi he tamen yiyang shi ren, a*]?" Tian was thus insisting on an individuated subjectivity for herself in ways that would sharply contrast with a Loyal Soldier state of activism, evident in the early activism of Hou Qiuyi. That is not to say women activists in Wenhe and Huoyue did not also see their work through the prism of the Woman Warrior, for, indeed, some did. Former Wenhe women's head Tang Li, 159, for example, attempted to sign up for the army but failed the test. Young Wenhe activists asked: "If the government is raising women's rights, why can't women join the army?"[46] When Tian Min contemplated exiting her familial obligations and taking up the time-honored tradition of the Woman Warrior, therefore, she was reflecting a desire in the wider revolutionary discourse and affective economy also salient in Wenhe and Huoyue. I discuss the complex reasons why Tian Min did not flee and join the army in chapter 6.

As Ruf (1998, 88) argues, "Land reform represented a major watershed on the local landscape, fundamentally altering conceptions of time and space and transforming the ways rural farmers conceived of their relationships to the land as well as to each other." Insofar as many of the struggles inherent in land reform focused on the subject of women, the attached processes by which women became activists, and the work they strove to undertake, were deeply salient in the enactment of local state formation.

Deng Yingchao knew this. Her struggles to ensure that women were eligible to receive land and to advocate for women's activism and leadership in land reform would decisively shape the local state of the early PRC. Without Deng Yingchao's deliberate interventions, sixteen-year-old Ding's abrupt transition into local leadership might never have been thought possible, much less put into practice.

Transitioning from the relative safety of the kang to the exposure of the podium, however, was a huge risk for young women. As Deng Yingchao also recognized, many activists were scorned and ridiculed by members of their community for "running around outside" and speaking with male strangers. In Wenhe, Huoyue, and Gaoshan young women activists found themselves underestimated because of their young age; at worst, they were shunned for perceived impropriety. Many simultaneously struggled to perform under conditions of a patrilocal marriage system, illiteracy, heavy household burdens, and poor compensation—all factors which impacted the retention and advancement of women leaders. The capacity of young women to become and remain leaders thus often depended on and reflected the support of close family.

The emergent party leadership in Xicun and its neighboring hamlets established itself on the basis the party family. Both Hou Qiuyi and her cousin, Zhang Sumei, came into leadership through their participation in political networks dominated by male family members. Although the cousins emerged as activists independently of their husbands, they would not access the same leadership opportunities as their spouses, and indeed, would find that their party marriages made them subject in new ways to the authority of the CCP and the authority of their husbands. This was true, even as Zhang Sumei identified clear (familial) benefits to local leadership, and even as companionate activism reflected new expressions of equality. Hou Qiuyi's reflections on her leadership were shaped through a historic process of ongoing class struggle. A former women's head and vice party secretary whose local leadership spanned more than three decades, Hou Qiuyi was far more committed in memory to the leadership of the CCP and Mao Zedong than was her cousin, Zhang Sumei, whose leadership, as I discuss in chapter 9, would be cut short in 1959.

Tian came to leadership without the support, or constraints, of a party family: her parents lived thousands of miles away, and her mother-in-law subjected her to unrelenting emotional and physical abuse. For Tian, it was the Youth League that would prove pivotal in the formation of her political subjectivity. Whereas Hou Qiuyi's agency was animated by the Loyal Soldier, Tian's agency would more closely reflect that of the Woman Warrior. As I will show, Tian would continue to prefer her work with the Youth League over women-work, even as she sought to adhere to the mandates of the emerging maternalist regime and even as she sought to fulfill her filial duties to her parents. When necessary, she would even defy party orders.

Rather than generating a collective understanding of a new socialist ideal of womanhood, therefore, the drive to recruit and mobilize young activists created deep fissures within activists and between the activists and their communities. Indeed, the challenges of attracting and retaining "a cadre of state agents that will be loyal *and* competent, willing *and* able to implement state directives and programs" (Strauss 2020, 34; italics in original) would prove much more complicated when it came to local women's leadership. At the same time that activists were expected to be "upright" and "virtuous" subjects, they had to show that their political orientation was not captured by the "miscellaneous" occupations of women-work; they had to daily demonstrate that their primary commitment was to socialist construction, not to a collectivity of "women" or even to their own family.

These were huge challenges. As I will show, the few women who did manage to assume and maintain positions of local leadership for any period often ended up embodying a kaleidoscope of states of activism that refracted the deep contradictions evident in the theory and practice of Maoism and an emergent maternalist social policy regime. In effect, many local women's heads expressed their activism as party militants by which they sought to embody a total devotion to political work while simultaneously executing maternalist policies that would serve as the basis of the new familial order. Local fears that women would be conscripted as soldiers was thus not entirely unfounded. It is just that the war in which they served would unfold in home communities and households rather than on the front lines of a foreign land.

Part II

STATE CAPACITY AND CONTENTION

MATERNAL BODIES

In the eyes of our women, the most urgent and important responsibility is the work [involved in] caring for the welfare of children.

—Kang Keqing, "Thoughts on Child Welfare Work"

We must satisfactorily protect and bring up new-born babies according to the Constitution's provision that "mothers and children shall be protected by the State." If we fail to do so, then we are really immoral and violating the fundamental function of public health work.

—Li Dequan, "Birth Control and Planned Families"

[Women] were liberated. Chairman Mao called for huge production. Socialism needed successors. [Women] were taken care of.

—Ma Meiying, 41

One of Tian Min's first tasks as a young activist in the new PRC was to recruit men to join the army. After entering the war on the Korean Peninsula in October 1950, the PRC needed the support of a new generation of soldiers to fight the "American imperialists."[1] Coming on the recent heels of victory over the Japanese and the GMD, the recruitment drives replicated mobilizations of the recent past, as is evident in the confusion from one woman in Wenhe: "You say you are all against Japan all of the time. Japan is so far away from us, so why are we against others?"[2] It also elicited deep resistance. Tian Min, 85, for example, spent two weeks recovering after she was attacked by a mother for trying to convince her to send her son to fight in Korea: "Parents weren't willing for their children to suffer the difficulties of military [life]."[3] But the Korean War mobilization was nonetheless effective in soliciting the participation of millions of women in demonstrations, fundraising, and yes, the recruitment of brothers, sons, and husbands, at a gestational moment in the PRC. Indeed, In the Huaiyin region of Jiangsu, more than forty thousand women sent their husbands and sons to join the army (Lu and Miao 2000, 123).[4] The enthusiastic support of young women, some of whom themselves sought to sign up to fight, including Tian Min, and 2,700 women students from nearby Nanjing (Lu and Miao 2000, 123), suggests that the national call for heroic sacrifice was heeded by women beyond the confines of the household as well.

The maternalist social policy regime, and the elite and grassroots ties that undergirded it, took shape in the context of violent conflict with an occupying power. This chapter, and the four that follow, consider the consequences of implementing maternalist reform in a countryside that had been devastated by war and was, for all intents and purposes, still at war during the formative first years of the PRC. The state's capacity to simultaneously wage war, reduce malnutrition, minimize disease, and extract resources depended on a systemic, multipronged, and coordinated effort across party, mass, and government organizations. It also depended heavily on the physical and emotional labor of grassroots women activists and leaders, and the local ties in which they were embedded.

In the early 1950s, a densely woven relational fabric underpinned the capacity of the state to both recognize and respond to crisis. Dong Biwu, an elder CCP statesman who had worked closely with key leaders of the Chongqing Coalition since the war with Japan, would oversee the earliest efforts to address malnutrition, disease, and displacement.[5] With the expulsion of international aid agencies from China, however, the new state required a high-level of infrastructural power to achieve its goals. Li Dequan, the PRC's first minister of health, would prove key to the success of this effort.

The widow of the Christian Warlord, Feng Yuxiang, Li Dequan has long been dismissed as a mere figurehead in post-1949 China (Lampton 1977). But as is evident in her leadership in the Chongqing Coalition, Li Dequan was no mere figurehead. Over the course of the 1950s, Li Dequan played a pivotal role in the development of public health, particularly in the domain of midwifery reform and birth control. Drawing on her stature as a prominent widow and social reformer, her concomitant leadership position within the ACDWF, and her ties to other members of the Chongqing Coalition, Li Dequan successfully circumnavigated a conservative and male-dominated Ministry of Health (MOH) to spotlight women's health. As a consequence of Li's insider agitation, the national program of midwifery reform produced one of the most dramatic improvements in maternal and infant health care of the twentieth century.

The grassroots health-care reform movement developed under Li established mechanisms to advance additional interventions, including dissemination of birth control and legalization and provision of abortions. Building on pre-1949 efforts to "fight starvation with contraception" (David 2018, 52), a small coterie of women physicians supported policy work to incorporate births into the economic plan. In this effort, senior CCP officials, including Deng Yingchao, Zhou Enlai, Deng Xiaoping, and Liu Shaoqi, not only had to overcome the conservative reservations of senior male physicians, but also other leading CCP members who were pushing pronatalist policies similar to those of the USSR. The contentious nature of this process, including emergent disagreements over the status of abortion in the PRC, delayed the deregulation of abortion until 1957. As I will argue in chapter 8, Li Dequan would oversee a combined push to expand birth control and midwifery during the earliest months of the GLF.

The rapid expansion of new forms of reproductive health care alongside other social reforms in the 1950s was neither complete, however, nor benign. There were important linkages between the roll out of vaccination programs, for example, and efforts to fight biological warfare during the Korean War (see, for example, Brazelton 2019); the latter in which Li Dequan would also play an important role. The maternalist social-policy regime enacted a complex and at times contradictory form of what Chen (2014), drawing on Foucault, calls "biopower," and what is described by Goldstein (1998, 177), as a "new ideological and political order of a controlling and at times repressive state management." Overlapping and intersecting campaigns to reform birth, marriage, and household, and the state project in which they were embedded, operated through a eugenic logic of social reform. Translated literally, eugenics (*youshengxue*) is the study of optimal birth (Barnes 2018, 187). Although eugenic ideology was subject to critique before and after the foundation of the PRC, the core concept, defined as "the science or technology of human betterment through the application of genetic laws designed so that the dominated could measure up to Civilizational standards" (Chung 2002, 3), would permeate efforts to regulate the bodies of women and the households women managed.[6] Song Qingling's early writing in *China Reconstructs*, for example, legitimized China's engagement in the Korean War as a means of protecting children from future conflict: "Mothers today need to send their children to the front so that mothers tomorrow won't have to" (Goldstein 1998, 173). The post-1949 military recruitment drives were one manifestation of an emerging regime that viewed women and their offspring through the needs of the state, in a relational project of civilizational advancement.

The effort to achieve multiple policy goals through the household also built directly on the experience, practices, and relationships that had been established under the previous GMD government. As was argued in 1944 by Yang Chongrui (Marian Yang), a physician who played an important role in the development of midwifery reform and birth control before and after the foundation of the PRC, and her colleague Wang Shijin:

> Improving mothers' and children's health can be the way inside the homes of the people whom we wish to touch with other health measures. For example, the work that is involved in educational propaganda, moral cultivation, and other health work, such as epidemic prevention

and environmental hygiene, can be brought before the people smoothly and effectively by mothers' and children's health workers who have earned the housewives' trust. (Barnes 2018, 187)[7]

The establishment of the PRC enabled a previously unimaginable expansion of coordinated care, connectivity, and control. To this end, midwifery reform "opened the door to state intervention in family and personal life through ongoing vaccination and health campaigns" (Fang 2017, 438), thereby realizing the dreams of wartime reformers to educate and reform housewives on a national scale (Barnes 2018; Hubbard 2018). Even as midwifery reform and other public health interventions improved health outcomes in the counties of Huoyue, Wenhe, and Gaoshan, they would simultaneously render women's bodies and their closest family members increasingly subject to state oversight and intervention.

At the center of these processes was the local women's head. In addition to supporting the early work of land reform, women's heads would be tasked with a number of overlapping duties that variously included military recruitment, collective field work, birthing babies, marital reform, and curtailing household consumption. In so doing, they cultivated attached methods of implementation, including methods that relied on an intimate knowledge of the bodies and the relationships of the women in their charge. As the pressures of collective agricultural work intensified in the mid-1950s, young women's heads would increasingly struggle to comply with new health regulations designed to protect the reproductive bodies of female field laborers. But not all saw women's bodies in need of health protections, either. From the outset, militant states of activism would also shape the local implementation of the maternalist social policy regime. Ultimately, the mobilization of maternalism and militancy would prove to be a deadly combination.

"Let No One Die of Hunger"

At the First National People's Welfare Congress in April 1950, existing welfare and relief organizations were amalgamated under a new umbrella: the Chinese People's Relief Administration (CPRA). Song Qingling served as chair of the CPRA, with Dong Biwu, Wu Yunfu, and Li Dequan serving as its most active administrators.[8] Wu Yunfu, who had become active in the Communist movement in the early 1930s, worked alongside Li Dequan in the Chinese Red Cross Society in the 1950s, ascending to vice president in 1961 (Klein and Clark 1971, 966–67). Whereas Wu Yunfu probably played the most important role in day-to-day relief operations (Klein and Clark 1971, 2:878, 966), Dong Biwu was responsible for setting the national guidelines of the new organization.[9]

Dong Biwu had forged strong ties with leading figures both within and outside of the CCP, including with Deng Yingchao, Zhou Enlai, Song Qingling, and Li Dequan, during some of the most searing moments of the CCP's revolutionary struggle.[10] As one of the founding members of the CCP, Dong had served with Song Qingling on the Branch Committee of the Guomindang Political Bureau in Wuhan in 1927 (Epstein 1993, 164). During the Long March, Dong led the unit that cared for Deng Yingchao, who was suffering from tuberculosis, and Mao's wife He Zizhen, who was pregnant. In his role as one of the chief Communist representatives in Chongqing during the Sino-Japanese War, Dong had also worked with Deng Yingchao, Liu-Wang Liming, and Shi Liang on the CPCCC.[11] During the civil war, Dong Biwu worked as one of Zhou Enlai's top aides (Klein and Clark 1971, 2:878).

During the latter half of the 1940s, Dong Biwu chaired the Chinese Liberated Areas Relief Association (CLARA), an organization that worked closely with Song Qingling's China Welfare Foundation. CLARA channeled relief supplies donated by the United Nations, the Red Cross, and other groups to the Communist base areas. After the foundation of the PRC, Dong Biwu and Li Dequan worked together and with a variety of private and public organizations, including the Chinese Red Cross in which Li Dequan played a senior leadership role after 1949 (Bian and Wu 2006; Li and Zhang 2007, 330). In this work they were also aided by YWCA leader Deng Yuzhi: in 1950 Deng served as an executive member of the CPRA, and an executive member of the Chinese Red Cross (Lee 2003a, 136).

In 1949–50, with seven million people lacking food, clothing, and shelter, the need for relief was intense (Bian and Wu 2006, 688). Guided by Mao Zedong's instructions that "no one should die of hunger" (*buxu e si yige ren*), the senior leadership, including Liu Shaoqi, Zhu De, and Zhou Enlai, closely followed the reports being issued at the grassroots. Chen Yun, a senior economic czar, was subsequently made responsible for dispatching hundreds of millions of catties of grain to the affected areas, while Dong Biwu was made vice minister responsible for the rescue work, pressuring local governments to report on and respond to the crisis (689–91). Work on disease prevention simultaneously rolled out: according to Kang Keqing (1952 [1997], 69–73), hundreds of millions of children were vaccinated against a range of diseases during the first three years of the PRC, including more than one million children for tuberculosis. In 1950, more than fifty-seven million people were vaccinated for smallpox (Li 1952, 19). With the aid of the USSR, the PRC also battled and overcame an outbreak of pneumonic plague (Bian and Wu 2016, 687; Li 1952, 16), with nearly six million inoculations (Li 1952).[12]

But a concentrated and multisector focus on emergency relief would only last for the first two years of the CCP's administrative tenure. In the meantime, efforts were already underway to transform the economic and political conditions that the Communists believed gave rise to the need for relief aid, in the first place. To this end, the CCP sought to sideline, reform, and replace preexisting private charitable organizations, especially charitable organizations tainted with imperialism, with state organizations (Wang, Liu, and Chang 2002). Early on, the CCP signaled that it would no longer welcome the active participation of overseas charities in Chinese relief work and sought to cut all ties to foreign Christian aid missions in particular ("The People's Relief Administration of China" 1952).[13] At the same time, the CCP focused on transforming welfare work by organizing urbanites into work units (*danwei*) where they would perform "productive work." According to this rational, if the country could attain full employment, individuals would no longer require aid (state or otherwise) and emergency relief would be rendered obsolete. The urban unemployed, including beggars, pickpockets, and the homeless, were thus shuffled into reeducation seminars and trained for new forms of employment.[14] Reformers would especially target two populations in the early reeducation campaigns: sex workers and housewives.[15] In early Maoist China, the work unit, local residence committees, and local Women's Federation organizations provided varying forms of social assistance to urban residents, with housewives playing a prominent role in social service delivery on behalf of the latter two organizations, in particular.[16]

In the countryside, the CCP undertook land reform as the initial means of securing a basic livelihood for farmers. Although many farmers immediately benefited from the reform, however, malnutrition would continue to persist and new burdens were placed on the shoulders of women householders. For despite the fact that women were entitled to land, and thus to a source of revenue independent from their relations, in reality land reform and the experiments with collectivization that followed would reinforce the family unit and the responsibility of women to maintain it. As the decade unfolded, the CCP began to increasingly rely on women, as activists, farmers, and householders, to play the chief role in maintaining basic family welfare in the countryside, a policy choice that would intersect with and build on Li Dequan's work in midwifery reform and contraception.

Midwifery Reform

During the 1950s, the MOH was a male-dominated and research-oriented organization—a legacy of its pre-1949 past. As Lampton (1977) shows, the MOH was led largely by a relatively educated and professionalized elite group of individuals; all of the original vice ministers of the MOH had received their medical training in the West or in one of China's missionary hospitals.[17] But while Lampton (1977, 23) is correct that vice ministers may have controlled much of the initial decision making that transpired within the MOH during the early 1950s, his analysis overlooks another legacy of the social gospel for the development and practice of medicine in China: midwifery reform.[18] The PRC's first minister of health, Li Dequan, "a pillar of Protestant morality" (Snow 1967, 86), not only spearheaded the massive effort to treat and prevent the spread of infectious diseases but also provided the leadership that led to a dramatic decline in maternal and infant mortality. Similar to other Chongqing reformers, Li drew on her multiple offices and worked across a broad range of personal contacts to achieve one of the most remarkable public health success stories of the twentieth century.

When Li Dequan was appointed as the new minister of health in 1949 she was widely respected in many circles. Although her husband had been the more high-profile figure (she was referred to as Madame Feng Yuxiang in international venues), Li had built a positive reputation both abroad and at home as a highly effective administrator of relief services during and after the anti-Japanese War. In Zhou Enlai's address at the opening of the Chinese Women's University in 1939, for example, he praised Li's "tremendous contribution" to the WACW and the consequent rescue and care of tens of thousands of children (Zhou 1939 [1991], 151). For the remainder of the war with Japan and during the civil war, Li Dequan continued to organize activities with many of the same women from the early days of the wartime mobilization, including Shi Liang, Liu Qingyang, Cao Mengjun, and Liu-Wang Liming (Li and Zhang 2007, 294). She also provided important leadership to the Women's Friendship Association and the Sino-Soviet Cultural Association and held special tea salons in which she gave talks on the importance of women's rights. Among those who attended were Deng Yingchao and Dong Biwu (Li and Zhang 2007, 295). In October 1946, Li Dequan would represent Deng Yingchao at the World Congress of Women in New York, just months before her husband would perish in a shipboard fire (Zhao 2003a, 302–3).

Li and other reformers did not just seek to inoculate individuals against the worst diseases that plagued China's cities and rural areas. Similar to their Guomindang counterparts and base area health workers, they also sought to transform the conditions in which people lived through the creation of a new, more hygienic China (Rogaski 2004). The changes that Li and her colleagues sought for women were ambitious, vast, and in many ways, straight out of the social gospel play book. Resources, however, were scant. As of 1949 the country was home to 10,000–20,000 trained doctors (Lampton 1977, 14) and only 1,740 obstetricians and gynecologists, 15,700 midwives, and 44,000 midwives assistants (Lim 1959, 375). Given that a mere 1 percent of total government expenditure in the PRC was allocated to health care (Lampton 1977, 25), new approaches were needed.[19] In public health generally, and maternal health, specifically, Li Dequan sought to meet this challenge through the development of a grassroots approach to medicine.

During the earliest years of the PRC, Li Dequan vocally called for expanded health-care delivery in the countryside, a view not shared by all at that time (Li and Zhang 2007, 318–19). Under Li Dequan's leadership, the MOH instituted guidelines to foster capacity in the development of grassroots health stations, one strategy of which included training rural schoolteachers and Youth League members to serve as local health workers. She also actively supported the establishment of rural health model counties in the countryside of Hubei and Jiangsu (Li and Zhang 2007, 319) and championed epidemic prevention (Li and Li 2015; Xun 2020). When Zhou Enlai initiated the 1952 Patriotic Health Movement, Li undertook investigations and pushed the MOH to realize the campaign's goals of eliminating the "four pests": flies, mosquitos, mice and rats, and bedbugs (Li and Zhang 2007, 316–17; Liu 1995, 153–54).[20] At a moment when the Western-oriented MOH was largely focusing on high-level medicine, Li Dequan was laying the groundwork for a new national program in disease prevention (Xun 2020, 52–53). She was also prioritizing women's health: "Don't forget about women and children," Li Dequan constantly reminded deputy ministers and medical directors (Li and Zhang 2007, 327).

When Li assumed her post, efforts were already underway to study and address maternal and infant health outcomes in the northeast, north, and northwest of China. Kang Keqing, who was at this time emerging as a public champion for the welfare of women and children, reported on the high rates of maternal and infant death: one two-year study conducted in sixteen villages of northwest Liberated Areas found that 1,852 of 4,053 infants (or 45.6 percent) had died, most from umbilical tetanus (Kang 1949 [1997], 24).[21] In June 1949, northern base areas responded by training some 23,000 midwives (ACWF 1950 [1999]). In addition to establishing mobile medical teams and propagating scientific knowledge of health care and childcare, base area governments increased the number of facilities available to treat rural patients in need of care (Kang 1949 [1997], 25). Li Dequan thus was equipped with key findings to build on in her determination to mobilize retrained midwives as a key resource in rural public health.

But Li Dequan herself had a great deal of experience and contacts to bring to the table, including having opened a midwifery school several decades earlier (Johnson 2011, 160). One of Li's first acts after assuming her post as minister of health in late 1949 was to convince her former classmate, Yang Chongrui, an obstetrician, to leave her post at the World Health Organization (Wang 2003, 613) and return to China to aid in the restructuring of medical services in the new People's Republic (Li and Zhang 2007, 327). Given Yang's influential role in developing and expanding midwifery reform and advocating for contraception under the GMD, this was a huge coup for the new regime. Yang Chongrui's return also had the highest backing possible; indeed, it was none other than Mao Zedong and Zhou Enlai who issued the official invitation that Li Dequan then extended to Yang (Wang 2003, 613).

As the former director of the first National Midwifery School established in 1929, Yang Chongrui had been the most visible and influential advocate for midwifery and birth control reform under the GMD. As Johnson (2011, 105–14) shows, Yang Chongrui was personally responsible for the establishment of midwifery as a recognized profession in China, at a time when Americans were promoting physician-assisted hospital births, and at a time when Chinese nurses themselves were advocating for the right of their profession to oversee the birth process. Yang Chongrui had also served with Li Dequan on the Guomindang National Midwifery Board in the early 1930s to develop training, curricula, and oversee the registration of midwives (Johnson 2011, 133) and had participated in the meetings that led to the establishment of the WACW, during the war with Japan (Lei Jieqiong 1990, 2). Perhaps most notably, over the course of 1943 and 1944, Yang Chongrui led efforts in the city of Chengdu to invest in maternal and infant health. As a consequence, Chengdu experienced a precipitous drop in maternal deaths: from fifteen per thousand to three per thousand (Zhang 2013, 154). Under the GMD, Yang had "assisted the transformation of childbirth in China from a family affair into a state affair" (David 2018, 47). In her new role as director of the Women's and Infants' Section of the MOH, Yang was in a prime position to shape the education of hundreds of thousands of grassroots midwives (Lei Zhifang 1990, 18), as part of the PRC's new state-building project.

The willingness to incorporate the knowledge of old-style midwives into the training programs nonetheless marked an important shift from the work that Yang Chongrui and Li Dequan had undertaken during the late 1920s and 1930s. The National Midwifery Board of the 1930s, on which both Li Dequan and Yang Chongrui had sat, made it illegal for old-style midwives to practice unless they had undergone extensive retraining and obtained a license, a policy that essentially excluded old-style midwives from the newly regulated birth environment (Johnson 2011, 151–53). Indeed, past medical elites had vilified old-style midwives for being "unsanitary, dangerous, backward, and *uncontrollable*" (Johnson 2011, 150, emphasis in original). But with close to 90 percent of "old-style midwives" providing birthing support in parts of the country (Li 2014), Li and Yang chose to work with the women who were already on the ground. By incorporating the actual skills of old-style midwives into the training programs and encouraging adaptation based on locally available materials, Li and Yang relocated modern health-care delivery from the hospital room to the kang.[22]

Li Dequan's success in midwifery reform also built on her ability to connect the work of the ACDWF with the MOH (Li and Zhang 2007, 328) to propel a rapid transformation in basic childbirth services.[23] According to Kang Keqing (1993, 387–88), Li served as the linchpin guiding the cooperation between local health departments, which were responsible for providing technical service and guidelines, and the local women's federations, which were responsible for mobilizing, organizing, and educating women.[24] A Women's Federation official spoke directly to the coordination underway in 1952 when she argued that

> Women's Federation cadres at all levels [but] particularly at lower levels, must learn common knowledge [regarding] maternal and infant health and *become propagandists and assistants of the MOH*. All levels of the Women's Federation should have a plan to train a large number of midwives and transform [the skills of] old midwives. [All levels] should immediately organize these trained midwives and enhance [their] political thinking. (Zhang 1953 [1996], 133–34, emphasis mine)

In Huoyue, where the rate of infant mortality was as high as 50 percent in 1949, coordination between the local Women's Federation and health authorities marked the implementation of midwifery reform.[25] Indeed, midwifery training was undertaken jointly by the Huoyue Women's Federation and the Sanitation and Hygiene Department. By 1958, the county would boast 473 midwives trained in the new method of childbirth (*HX* 1993, 392), including Hou Qiuyi, 132, who was among the first to receive training in new birth practices. And by 1963, ten years after the trainings had first begun, some 3,755 individuals had been trained (*HX* 1993, 392). Over the same period, Huoyue County undertook significant efforts in public inoculation. Between 1950 and 1966, Huoyue County administered a total of 2,372,593 inoculations to treat smallpox, typhoid fever, and a number of other contagious diseases, which may well have contributed to increasing the life expectancy of infants and children as well.[26]

In Wenhe, midwifery reform was also an early priority. By 1954, 49 midwives had undergone training and some 13 birthing clinics were established.[27] By 1959, 115 maternity clinics were established and consolidated, opening up a total of 533 birthing beds (*WX* 1992, 824).

But challenges remained. One of the primary constraints impeding a full incorporation of midwifery reform was the desire of many women to keep birthing under the care of family members and traditional midwives (Fang 2017, 438; Goldstein 1998, 166). As Johnson (2011, 101) argues, "The primary function of the old-style midwives was ritualistic, not medical, and focused on introducing

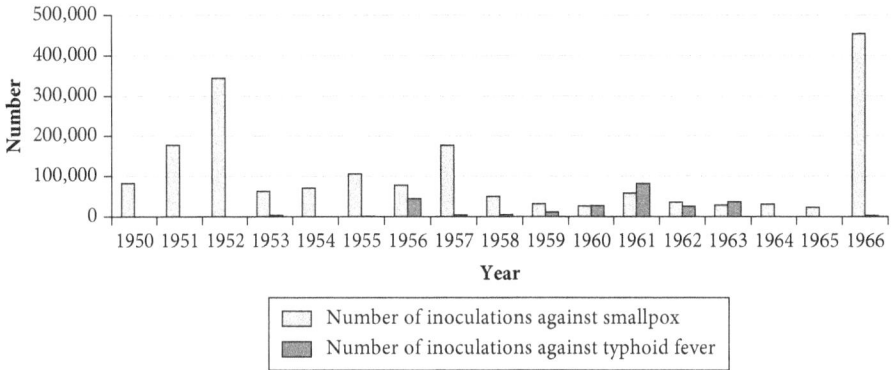

FIGURE 1. Number of inoculations against smallpox and typhoid fever, given in the thousands, in Huoyue County (1950–66). *Source: HX* 1993, 394.

the new child into its family and the wider community." Women-work cadres "brought to political activity the power/knowledge of sanitation, physiology, and scientific midwifery" (Barlow 2004, 58–59) in ways that incorporated this science into a local field of meanings and relationships (Hershatter 2011, 166–70, 178–81).[28] Both menstruation and childbirth were regarded as "polluting and unmentionable" in rural Shaanxi, for example (Hershatter 2011, 157). It was these beliefs, and the associated norms of sexual propriety that governed them, that led former Wenhe women's head Yan Shuqun, 43, to refuse the assistance of a male midwife trained in new methods.

Yan Shuqun first received a brief training course in midwifery when she was sixteen and still living in her natal village. A member of the Youth League, Yan lost her mother when she was just three years old and with no one to mind her she ran around "wild." After relocating to her husband's village upon marriage, she became a party member and spent two years working outside of the village in a factory and on a water reservoir construction project during the GLF. When she returned to the brigade she was assigned to the role of women's head. One of the most stressful tasks, she told me during our first interview in 2001, was establishing social welfare services—including a birthing station:

> I didn't like being criticized by the leaders when I didn't have every-
> thing set up. When I did get the clinic established, no one wanted to
> use the facility. The villagers said that I was only a twenty-something
> girl with no kids herself—how could they trust me when I had no
> experience? They preferred to go to the old women. After a short
> time, the clinic was disbanded. The commune went on to emphasize
> something else.[29]

The difficulties Yan faced setting up expanded welfare facilities was a common problem during the GLF, which I will discuss further in chapter 9. Here, however, I want to address the challenge that women's heads and other medically certified individuals faced when they sought to radically alter the conditions under which birth could take place. Indeed, it was not just villagers who rejected new style birth support; local leaders could also exhibit reluctance, including Yan who refused the services of the newly appointed male midwife when she delivered her first child in 1962:

> In the old society the old women would deliver the babies in the village, there were no midwives, and the infant mortality rate was high. There were newborn corpses everywhere, the majority of whom died after just seven days. When my first child was born, the brigade had a male midwife and I first thought to get him to deliver the baby. [But] when some others from around here had him deliver [their baby], the old women of the village cursed them and said vile things. I was so pitiful, no matter how much I suffered, I did not dare to have him deliver the baby. The old women who delivered [the baby] not only were not sterile but placed the scissors under the sheet on the kang. Back then all of the kangs were made of dirt and weren't at all hygienic. After the baby was born, they took the knife off of the kang to cut the umbilical cord. It became infected. After six or seven days, [the baby] became ill and I ran down to X village for Chinese medicine to give to her. An old man blew the medicine into the baby's mouth but it was no use.

A few days after her infant died another woman from her village delivered her child under the care of the male midwife at the hospital; the baby grew up to adulthood: "I shouldn't have listened to what other people said or didn't say, I should have broken with convention and asked [the male midwife] to do the delivery."

It is evident that more than ten years after the establishment of the PRC, and during a moment in which midwifery reform had emerged as a local priority, not all expectant mothers were turning to midwifery services for help; in this case, not even the women's head responsible for establishing the services availed herself of them. That Yan chose not to apply this care to the delivery of her first child can be attributed, in no small part, to the fact that the midwife was a man. Male midwives were relatively rare and for good reason: convention dictated that nonkin men should not participate in anything so intimate as the birth of a child. Although it would have behooved Yan to be a role model in using the services of the male midwife, doing so would have subject her to a relentless barrage of criticism from her neighbors. As a young female leader, Yan was already sexually suspect in the eyes of many of her community; no wonder she felt torn and ultimately chose to deliver with the assistance of a midwife who had not been trained, for example, to sterilize equipment. But it was not just Yan who avoided the aid of newly trained midwives, male or otherwise. Fang Huayun, 51, a team leader from Yan's brigade, acknowledged that when a family member was available to assist with a birth, they did not call anyone from outside (*jiu bu jiao wairen*).[30] Similarly, and despite receiving twenty days of obstetrical training in 1959, Yan only assisted at the births of family members, including at the births of infants born to her sister-in-law, older sister, and younger sister. The one task she was not able to perform, she said, was administering shots.

These narrated experiences suggest that local and CCP norms may have slowed the implementation of midwifery reform, but that they did not prevent it. By 1956 the nearly 500,000 newly trained attendants (Li and Li 2015, 62) were increasing the survival rates of newborn infants and their mothers. The Nanyang region in southern Henan, for example, reported a 90 percent drop in the condition of umbilical tetanus between 1951 and 1952 (Shao 1984, 104). As of 1951, national rates of infant mortality due to umbilical tetanus had decreased

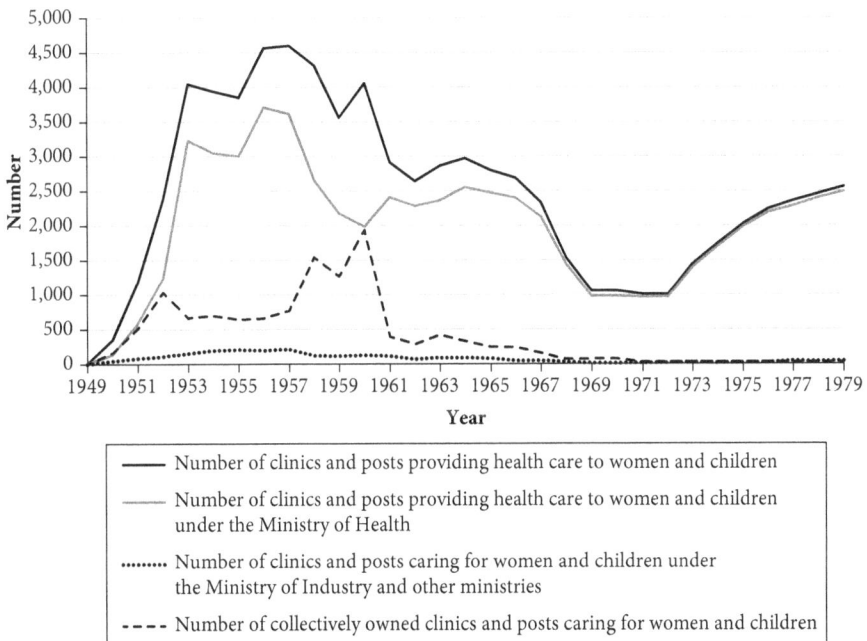

FIGURE 2. List of clinics and stations caring for women and children, categorized by their administrative affiliations, from 1949 to 1979. *Source:* Zhonghua quanguo funü lianhehui funü yanjiusuo 1991, 479.

to 7.2 percent and by 1954 the figure was even lower: 0.54 percent (Kang 1993, 388).[31] Maternal deaths from puerperal fever had also plummeted (Kang 1993, 388). Li Dequan would later give credit to the Women's Federation, without whom, she argued, the rapid achievements in women's and children's health would not have been possible (Li and Li 2015, 63).

Early Birth Planning

The rapid strides that Li Dequan, her colleagues, and grassroots attendants realized in improving life expectancy created pressure elsewhere: that is, the need to feed the babies, children, and adults whose health had been protected through the intensive public health interventions of the early 1950s (Liu Shaoqi 1954 [1997], 146–47). As the CCP prepared to roll out the First Five Year Plan, Deng Xiaoping simultaneously administered the PRC's first census, hoping to obtain a better grasp of the challenges that lay ahead. The results only reinforced what he and other economic planners already suspected: high birth rates and low death rates had increased China's population by nearly 54 million people between 1949 and 1953 (Deng, Ma and Wu 1986, 2:231).

Thus, in 1953, Zhou Enlai raised a troubling question: how does one plan for rapid population growth? It was, he noted, a "big burden" (Zhou 1953 [1997], 133).[32] As White (2006) argues, in the early 1950s, planners sought new ways to ease the increasing demand being placed on the food supply; these concerns dovetailed with the contraception advocacy efforts of a number of key CCP women officials, namely Deng Yingchao. But there were other key players pushing for birth control liberalization as well, including Li Dequan and a small coterie of women physicians from within MOH. It is in this way that planners, women officials, and women physicians joined forces to liberalize birth control access and create a new basis for population control: birth planning.

Deng Yingchao was first to step into the ring. According to the official record, Deng Xiaoping acknowledged the need for birth control advocacy only after Deng Yingchao submitted a report written by women requesting increased access in April 1953 (Shi 1988, 120n1).[33] Four months later, Deng Xiaoping introduced the first formal discussions of birth control liberalization when he delivered a report on the topic to the ACDWF and instructed the MOH to retract restrictions on importing contraception and to begin advocating birth control (Shi 1988, 116). The inclusion of the ACDWF in the first discussions focused on reforming access, I suggest, was no accident. The economic planners needed women officials to be intimately involved in birth control for the same reason they believed they needed them to lead other aspects of the maternalist social policy regime: birth control was women-work. Women officials, as the physiological and spiritual "mothers" of social policy reform, were best suited to advocate for and legitimize this issue in much the same way they had done with midwifery reform.

Opposition to birth control within the CCP had long been linked to the belief that once socialism was instituted, the challenge of population growth would be resolved (Gilmartin 1995, 57–59; Gilmartin 2003, 535). A belief shaped in part by the European socialist parties of the 1920s, pronatalism became only more entrenched within the CCP when the Soviets tightly regulated access to contraception and abortion in the postwar Soviet Union.[34] While Mao Zedong did not directly address birth control during the early 1950s himself, his passing comments about the need for a large population further dampened interest in the liberalization of birth control (White 2006, 19–20). But there was an additional factor that stymied liberalization: resistance from within the MOH itself. The most powerful physicians in the MOH, men who were by and large trained through missionary institutions, were dead set against liberalization (White 2006, 22). Indeed, they were responsible for writing the initial regulations that imposed severe restrictions on access to contraception, abortion, and sterilization (White 2006, 22–23).[35]

Unlike many of their male colleagues, however, senior women officials and physicians within the MOH and the CCP had been advocating for access to birth control for years. Yang Chongrui, for example, director of the Women's and Infants' Section of the MOH (1949–57), had been China's most outspoken advocate for birth control since the 1920s. Yang Chongrui invited the famous birth control advocate, Margaret Sanger, to come to China (Wright 2009, 123). She also opened one of China's first birth control consulting services in 1932 (Wang Bing 2003, 612). While Yang's advocacy work was motivated primarily by a desire to decrease the physical, financial, and emotional burden of numerous pregnancies and children that so many women faced, she was also compelled by eugenics arguments that saw birth control as a means to create a healthier and more manageable Chinese population (Barnes 2018, 187).

The revolution was long, and as was discussed in previous chapters, many women Communists struggled to fulfill their revolutionary work while managing pregnancies and the needs of small children, a challenge that their male comrades and partners did not share nor always appreciate. When Zhou Enlai discovered that Deng Yingchao had an abortion in late 1925, for example, he exploded in fury, outraged that she killed their child as if it were a piece of "private property" (Jin 1993, 1:106–7). By the early 1950s, many women Communists had struggled through multiple pregnancies, abortions, and miscarriages, or ministered to others who had. It is in this context that Zhao Xian, one-time chair of the Shanghai Women's Federation, told Wang Zheng (2005, 542) that she and other women leaders refused to call on women to follow the Soviet Union and be glorious mothers (*muqin yingxiong*). But while Zhou Enlai was ready to liberalize access to birth control in the 1950s, many of his comrades and the physicians controlling the MOH were not. Both outside and inside the MOH, dissent was vocal, with some arguing that "more children, equals greater happiness," that the PRC should follow in the Soviet Union's footsteps by advocating "glorious mothers," and that birth control was unethical (Luo 1998b [2000], 26–27; MOH Lead Party Group 1954 [1997], 1–2). As a consequence, the CCP leadership received letters opposing liberalization throughout 1954 (Shi 1988, 117). Given the strength of resistance within the CCP and the MOH, a skillful approach was thus devised; one that combined the influence of Zhou Enlai's office with the contacts, experience, and commitment of the Chongqing Coalition.

For his part, Zhou Enlai undertook an investigation of the living conditions of workers, comparing the outcomes for households with many children to those for households with few. He then passed on these findings to cadres in the MOH (Deng, Ma, and Wu 1986, 2:231–32). In May 1954, Deng Yingchao wrote a letter to Deng Xiaoping requesting that the MOH help cadres resolve their birth control needs (Deng Yingchao 1954 [1997], 146). Her impeccable timing may have stemmed from her marital relationship with Zhou Enlai and from her working relationship with Deng Xiaoping who was also serving on the Standing Committee of the CPPCC at that time.[36] She reported that the need for birth control was widespread, noting that the CCP, government, MOH, Worker's Union, and the ACDWF had received numerous letters from women workers requesting that restrictions on access to birth control be lifted. Deng Xiaoping's short response to Deng Yingchao's letter was unequivocal: birth control was absolutely needed. Deng Xiaoping then instructed Xi Zhongxun, vice premier and father to future paramount leader of the PRC, Xi Jinping, to approach the MOH, which, he noted, had been "less than enthusiastic," and to try and come up with effective measures to address the issue (Deng Xiaoping 1954 [1997], 146). In this effort, they had at least one important ally: Li Dequan, the minister of health.

As previously discussed, Li Dequan's power within the MOH itself was limited; neither a physician nor a member of the CCP, she also had the decided disadvantage of being preoccupied with issues that many of her medically trained male colleagues viewed as of less importance: namely, public health, midwifery reform, and the health and welfare of women and children more generally. Thus, even though she ostensibly had the most seniority, she was unable to single-handedly force the MOH to change its guidelines on contraception. But Li was a proactive inside agitator. Specifically, she undertook research with and carried out discussions about contraception with Ma Yinchu and Shao Lizi, two of the leading intellectuals advocating for birth control at that time (Kang 1997, 122;

see also Liu 1995, 154). According to Kang Keqing (1997, 122), Li Dequan "really cared about birth planning, [and she] endorsed the population theory of Ma Yinchu." In September 1954, Shao Lizi advocated that regulations regarding birth control and abortion be relaxed (Shi 1988, 118), generating a furor (MOH Party Group 1955 [1999]).[37] In July of 1955, Ma Yinchu gave a speech at the National People's Congress about the fundamental contradiction between the high rate of population growth and economic growth, in part based on a study he conducted in Zhejiang in 1954 (Shi 1988, 120–21).[38] Given the contentious nature of Ma and Shao's views at the time, Li Dequan's collaboration with and endorsement of these men was no small matter.

Just as important, Li Dequan, Deng Yingchao, and Zhou Enlai were also able to activate the experience and influence of China's two leading women obstetricians, Yang Chongrui and Lin Qiaozhi (also known as Lim Kha-ti), to make their case (Zhang 2005, 226). When given the chance, Yang and Lin became actively involved in discussions to liberalize PRC birth control policies that transpired over the second half of 1954 and into 1955. Lin Qiaozhi, Yang Chongrui, and Ma Yinchu all participated in a series of meetings on birth control that Liu Shaoqi organized during this period (Zhang 2005, 277; Wright 2009).[39]

The fact that Lin Qiaozhi served as Deng Yingchao's personal physician, may also have facilitated her participation in this process. Lin, a devout Christian, had become sympathetic to the CCP and its post-1949 state-building mission as a consequence of its early efforts to close down brothels; indeed, Lin, like many other social gospel reformers, viewed sex work as "filthy" (*wuhui*) (Zhang 2005, 211).[40] Lin Qiaozhi subsequently became close with Zhou Enlai and Deng Yingchao after treating Deng in the early 1950s (Zhang 2005, 212–15). Kang Keqing was also deeply impressed by Lin Qiaozhi after Kang became one of her patients as well (Zhang 2005, 212–16). Over the course of the 1950s, Lin Qiaozhi served as vice chair of the Chinese Medical Association, deputy director of the Chinese Academy of Medical Sciences, and was elected a representative of the National People's Congress (Wright 2009, 127). She also published in English periodicals intended for overseas consumption, including in *China Reconstructs* and in medical journals (see, for example, Lim 1953; 1959).

It was in the wake of the roundtables that a decision finally came down. On December 27, 1954, Liu Shaoqi announced that the CCP was endorsing birth control (Liu 1954 [1997], 146–47). Toward the end of his speech, Liu Shaoqi instructed the ACDWF that it was the federation's job to educate peasants that they could now use contraceptives. Interestingly, Liu explicitly forbade a rural campaign on the issue; an indication, perhaps, that some had been pushing for this approach. But advocacy continued, nonetheless. The chief editor of *Women of New China (Xin Zhongguo funü)*, Shen Zijiu, for example, made the decision to print stories about birth control before any others were willing to do so (Dong 1991, 162–63). And Li Dequan became the most visible woman official to defend the new regulations, justifying them on the basis of women's welfare and the needs of socialist construction itself (Li 1957 [1965], 295–99). Finally, Cai Chang also took up the mantle: endorsing birth control in a 1956 speech to a gathering of the most powerful party officials at the Eighth National Congress of the CCP (Cai 1956 [1988], 295).

But there remained more specific controversies as well. Indeed, despite the new openness to birth control in general, tight regulations on abortion made that procedure almost inaccessible.[41] Resistance likely stemmed from several fronts. Ma Yinchu, for example was strongly opposed (*jianjue fandui*) to abortion (Shi 1988, 130) as a method to pursue birth planning, as were a number of physicians, including Yang Chongrui and Lin Qiaozhi (Lei 1990, 18; Zhang 2005, 275). Based on her Christianity and her view that abortions posed health risks for women, Lin refused to administer abortions to women even when they pleaded with her to do so. Lin and other leading obstetricians were consequently furious that doctors were not consulted prior to the announcement by the MOH, on May 15, 1957, that abortion was being deregulated. Lin Qiaozhi even went so far as to express her consternation to the *People's Daily (Renmin ribao)*. Chief among Lin's complaints included the lack of beds and equipment necessary to undertake the procedure, and the health toll that abortions would have on women. Both Lin Qiaozhi and Hu Jingfu, a researcher at the Chinese People's Liberation Army Academy of Medical Sciences, were furious (see also, also Zhang 2005, 276–81). Hu explicitly blamed "the leadership" (*lingdao ren*) of the MOH for "disrespecting and distrusting the opinion of scientific experts" (*People's Daily*, May 26, 1957, 2nd ed). In so doing, the two physicians may well have been taking a direct swipe at Li Dequan's lack of medical credentials or, more likely, at the MOH Lead Party Group that would have made the final decision to fully deregulate. Either way, it was a bold move.

The decision to deregulate abortion was also made despite the expressed concerns of the CCWMC, which as late as 1955 was still advocating that both abortion and sterilization include strict protocol oversight. The CCWMC noted in its instructions to lower levels of the federation that "abortion not only influences the health of women and their infants, but is dangerous to the point where it can threaten women's lives. Tubal ligation causes permanent infertility and is not a carefully considered action, so we do not advocate that" (ACWF 1955b [1999]). In a supplemental document that accompanied the CCWMC's instructions, the MOH Lead Party Group (1955 [1999]) laid down a strict set of criteria under which abortions and tubal ligations would be permitted. While medical reasons and reasons of study and work could be considered for the termination of a pregnancy, all abortions required multiple levels of approval including an application signed by husband and wife, a medical certification by a doctor, and approvals obtained from the director of the medical department and the hospital.

The views of the CCWMC and obstetricians may have continued to hold some sway, even after Li Dequan delivered a formal address to the CPPCC signaling that all restrictions regarding abortion and tubal ligation were to be removed (Li 1957 [1965], 295–99; Shi 1988, 127–28). In Li's speech, published in the *People's Daily* two months before doctors received official notice of the protocol change, she stated:

> All personnel concerned with women's and children's health services and midwives' work should henceforth make the decision whether to perform the operation mainly on the basis of the wish of the individuals, and limitations on its discretion would be abolished. But this does not signify the promotion of induced abortion, which we are compelled to carry out in certain circumstances. Induced abortion is not only harmful to a woman's health, work and studies, but also cannot achieve the purpose of birth control. (Li 1957 [1965], 298)[42]

Li Dequan's argument that abortion should not be used as birth control, was echoed by Lin Qiaozhi two months later when she spoke to the *People's Daily*. In her words: "The solution to the problem of overpopulation is to promote contraception, not abortion" (*People's Daily* May 26, 1957, 2nd ed). As I discuss in the conclusion, this was a position that would entirely give way in the decades of birth planning that followed.

Motherhood and Reproductive Health at the Grassroots

In an early speech delivered just months after the establishment of the PRC, Li Dequan stressed the relationship between China's health-care conditions and its productive capacities (Li and Li 2015, 60). Promoting public health was a goal in its own right, but as more and more of the rural population were mobilized to participate in collective field work and industrial and environmental projects, public health was increasingly linked to economic development. It is thus not surprising that as women engaged in collective work outside of their households, the maternalist social policy regime moved from a limited focus on birth and contraception to a more holistic approach that targeted rural women throughout their reproductive cycle. One elderly Wenhe woman seemingly summed up this rationale when I asked about her experiences during the 1950s, in a quote that begins this chapter.

In December 1956, Cao Guanqun, ACDWF party general secretary, praised the Sichuan Women's Federation for assigning menstruating, pregnant, and lactating women work that was light, dry, and close by (Cao 1957 [1988], 273). This practice became known as the "three transfers," a phrase taken up as a slogan by county-level federation leaders beginning in the early months of 1957.[43] Federation and party officials also advocated that women *zuo yuezi*, or sit the month out, after giving birth. Specifically, they advocated that women avoid physical exertion (i.e., that they not perform housework, work in the fields, cook, or look after older children) in the month following childbirth.

Several of the injunctions regarding women's health, including avoiding drinking or being exposed to cold water while menstruating or pregnant, reflected long-standing scientific cosmologies that were being codified at that time (Evans 1997, 146–51). The requirement to assign women to "dry" work, for example, addressed the belief that women's reproductive organs can become injured through exposure to cold water when pregnant or menstruating. Similarly, the practice of "sitting the month out" is another example of a custom that predated the establishment of the PRC but that was subsequently incorporated into the scientific discourse of the maternalist social policy regime. As with the implementation of midwifery reform, the implementation of menstruation regulations was challenging: many women did not want to openly discuss their menstrual cycles with their leaders. Not surprisingly, compliance was uneven, with some women feeling too "shy" to have their cycles on display for others to see and thus deciding to carry on regardless of whether or not they were menstruating.

When Yan Shuqun, 43, for example, sought to implement the "three transfers" on a work construction site during the Great Leap Forward, many women were reluctant to share information about their menstrual cycles with her: "The bottom was covered with weeds and was wet. Whoever had their period could request to take a break. There were some who lied and [so I] used various methods to counter this. [I relied on] a woman's bedmates to tell me whose period had started, and so who not to [assign to work] in the water, to work up higher where it was dryer."

Another Wenhe woman team leader relied on the women themselves to tell her or the woman's head: "Women would stay behind after the village meetings to talk. The women would say if they had any difficulties, for example, were menstruating and couldn't work for three days and wanted to request leave. The women would speak with the women's head and the women's head would speak with me. I wouldn't call her out to work" (Fang Huayun, 51). And still others employed the use of a menstruation board so they could keep track of the menstruation cycles of the women they were organizing to work in the fields.

Protecting the reproductive body, as outlined in the "three transfers," was, however, constantly disrupted by two factors: a blatant disregard of the three transfers by local leaders, and the militant states of activism of women leaders themselves. Guidelines for protecting women's health were often ignored either because local leaders would not permit a work transfer, or if they did, because they would provide less compensation for lighter and dry work thus eliminating much needed remuneration for women who were trying to feed themselves and their families. One former Wenhe women's head, for example, recalled her inability to receive a transfer to dry work despite her ill health and, it should be noted, despite her status as a local leader:

> At the commune meetings we were always being told to pay attention to women's health but [the leaders] below didn't pay attention. My health was really bad that year, I was sick, my period wouldn't stop flowing. Every day I lost a lot of blood. At that time I was sent to X river to sift for metals. I said, I'm sick, wait until I'm better and then I'll go. The cadres were no good and insisted that I go. I didn't go. The next day I went to the commune and said I'd like to be assigned to the marketing coop where they were currently hiring. But they wanted me to go to the river. That kind of thing needs people with good health. I was sick and they still wanted me to go. (Liang Jinfeng, 57)

Certainly the decision to ignore the three transfers was often a response to the tremendous political pressure of the era. To that end, Oi argues, that local team leaders often engaged in a kind of ideological performativity. Specifically, she argues that they strove to *biaoxian*, or maintain, "the façade of compliance by exhibiting at all times correct 'manifestation of attitude'" (1989, 16). But when it came to women-work, ideological compliance was not always just for show. Indeed, Maoist states of activism were often at work as well.

I first caught a glimpse of militant mobilization practices when I interviewed leader Liu Yuezhen, 10 in 2001, a former women's head in Huoyue. When queried whether anyone asked to be excused from work because of menstruation, she replied that such women were "afraid of hard work." Moreover, she repeatedly denied the existence of health-care policies for women—an assertion that stands in stark contrast to the response of her brigade party secretary Zhao Kaitai, 8, who recited the three transfers to me when I asked him the same question. In 2004, when I asked Liu if she worked in cold water while menstruating she explained further:

> Some people insisted on not going in, but that didn't fly. You had to get in cold water when digging ditches, no matter what, even when you had your period. You were working, you couldn't just say you had your period and then quit could you?

[What if you were pregnant?]

If you were pregnant, you would have to talk to the brigade leader (for a leave); if he did not agree, then you might get some lighter work. Sometimes, they would not take any consideration and there was no lighter work, then you had to do the job, (there was) no way out.

Leader Liu Yuezhen's, 10, earlier comment that "some people were afraid of hard work" insinuated that those who asked for leave because of menstruation were lazy, while her later comments suggested a more pragmatic outlook. In 2001, Women's Head Zhang Sumei, 20, similarly criticized women who wanted to get out of hard labor for health reasons as not "upright." In 2004, Zhang's more elaborate response acknowledges that she was expected to make allowances:

What about when your period came, did you go in the water?

Back then we did all sorts of work, and no one ever said: "My period came today and so I won't work." No one said that.

[No one?]

No one. I'll just tell you how it was. People were stupid in the past, not like people today, [when] they say they don't feel well, they just don't work. Back then [people] only cared about working. Back then people were really miserable. Nowadays people use menstruation pads, in the past women used cloth.

[Could women do lighter work when menstruating or pregnant?]

If they had too much (blood), more than before, they would say something. If they said something about it, they would be allowed to stay at home; if they did not say anything, they would go work just like the others, but I did not know that. If they told me, I would let them go. If anything came up, I would let them stay at home, [I] never drove anyone to the corner. Do as you like. I always treated people that way.

But this grudging allowance to "do as you like" is not consistent with the duty of the women's head to protect, nor is it consistent with the memories of Zhang's neighbors and her cousin who were adamant that Zhang drove people to perform hard labor regardless of their reproductive states.[44] In the earlier interviews, both Liu and Zhang condemned those who contravened the more important ethos of the 1950s, which was to contribute to socialist construction regardless of one's bodily condition. This is despite the fact that Zhang herself had received some early obstetrical training and thus would have had additional exposure to maternalist reform.

In fact, Zhang's relationship to her own pregnant body suggests that maternalist regulations had little relevance for her personally:

> When I was just about to give birth I cut several hundred *jin* of sweet potato slices and spread them on the ground. I was thinking then that I couldn't keep going [but] if I gave birth, [I] wouldn't be able to go pick them up in someone else's field. That's the rule. (So) I picked them up and brought them back. [That] evening, my baby was born after dinner.
>
> [So when you were pregnant you were still working in the fields?]
>
> Yes, it was just like [carrying] something outside my body. I am of small stature [laughs] but I still worked, [I] did not try to save energy. You are both young girls, I'll tell you, I didn't want to have that many [children]. I gave birth to six, and had two miscarriages. [I] deliberately carried a basket. What would I do with that many children? If [I] could just get tired enough that [I would miscarry and] there'd be no problem! [But I] didn't succeed. I'm just very strong! [laughs] During my month of confinement [I] ate millet. I gave birth to six: one boy, five girls.[45]

Zhang thus did not implement maternalist protections for others or for herself. Indeed, the modeling provided by women's activists and leaders themselves often ran counter to ideas about the vulnerability of the reproductive body. When former women's head Lin Xiaohong, 73, first became a cooperative leader in Gaoshan, for example, she was so worried that she could not convince the older male villagers that she could do the work that she planted more than forty mu herself and then obsessively checked on the fields with a flashlight at night. She also ceased menstruating.[46] Another former women's head, Tang Xiuying, 37, continued to work in the fields until she was close to term with her third daughter, only returning home when the commune party secretary insisted that she stop working. Others simply "didn't care." When I asked Tang Li, 159, if she worked in water when menstruating she replied, "Yes, I wasn't afraid of anything. Some people told me not to wash clothes and not to walk in the water, but I still did and it was all right. Sometimes I didn't menstruate for a few months, [but] I didn't care, and after a while it started again."

By the mid-1950s the inconsistent understanding and application of protections at the grassroots generated a brewing crisis in reproductive health, undermining some of the public health achievements of just a few years earlier. As I will show in subsequent chapters, this was a crisis that would only intensify with the launch of the GLF.

In the early 1950s, the PRC achieved what few other developmental states had been able to achieve prior: and that is, dramatically reduce maternal and infant mortality. Thanks to the committed and strategic engagement of Li Dequan, the networks in which she was embedded, and a growing grassroots infrastructure of women birth attendants, the new regime was able to systematically transform health outcomes in just a few short years. These findings upend more than six decades of political science scholarship, none of which have recognized Li's leadership nor the singular importance of her achievements. Indeed, Li has long been dismissed as nothing more than a figurehead; a widow whose primary source of power died with her husband. A closer examination leads to the opposite conclusion: Li was a highly effective administrator who played a key role in building a functioning primary health-care system. Indeed, Li's effectiveness stemmed from multiple sources, including her stature as mother of the nation, an extensive background in midwifery reform and grassroots health-care delivery, numerous personal ties to senior CCP officials and innovative physicians, and multiple concomitant bureaucratic appointments. In the arena of maternal health reforms, PRC state capacity effectively built on and through the strength of Li's personal and institutional attachments, just as it built on and through the preexisting familial and village attachments of women's heads and birth attendants. Maoist state power emerged because of the affective enactment of personal ties, not despite them.

Political scientists have missed Li not only because of who she was but also, perhaps, because of the kind of work that she prioritized: the bloody, and at times violent, work of birthing babies. Yan's grief, forty years after the death of her newborn, shines a spotlight on the stakes at play for the millions of women desperate for their newborns to survive birth and its aftermath. The fact that Yan could have received the support of a trained midwife, but chose not to, sheds further light on complexly interacting local and CCP norms and practices as they shaped maternalist reform on the ground.

Of course, not all women wanted babies. As Zhang's discussion of her later pregnancies make clear, she sought to self-induce miscarriage through her manual labor. Zhang's antipathy to unwanted pregnancy was by no means new: Chinese women Communists and social gospel reformers had been calling for the liberalization of birth control for years before Liu Shaoqi finally gave the okay in the mid-1950s. Rising fears about China's rapidly growing population led state planners to make a sharp turn and embrace contraception as a tool in economic management (White 2006). But the state planners could not overcome the opposition of conservative male physicians and senior officials alone. In this instance, as in others to follow, the advocacy of connected women officials and physicians temporarily overcame bureaucratic deadlock.

Ultimately, the maternalist social policy regime played a central role in strengthening state capacity to manage its population. In the 1950s, this success enabled a minority of women to control whether they became pregnant and, if they did, the conditions under which they birthed. The deeply uneven implementation of maternalist reform, however, always had a darker side: that is, a simultaneous strengthening of the state's capacity to subject women's bodies and households to the project of socialist construction, whether to wage war, plan births, or manage family ties. As I will show next, the implementation of the 1950 Marriage Law would further strengthen the capacity of the state to surveil and manage the socialist family.

FILIAL BRIDES

> Prior to the introduction of the Marriage Law, getting married was like "closing your eyes and jumping into hell": In the past women were the lowest of the low, [just like] noodles didn't count as food, women didn't count as people. Women were like a broken-down cart [*po che*]. [You] could beat and curse them whenever you felt like it. [You] had to beat them at least once every three days.
>
> —Hou Qiuyi, 132

> After the promulgation of the Marriage Law, the men and women who were oppressed by the feudal marriage system gained their freedom and filed for divorce. They were able to leave their less than ideal spouse [*bu ruyi de pei'ou*] and search anew for a beloved partner [*chongxin xunzhao xin'ai de duixiang*].
>
> —Deng Yingchao, "Report on the PRC's Marriage Law"

As a woman's head in the earliest days of the PRC, Hou Qiuyi was responsible for implementing the 1950 Marriage Law, legislation that signaled the start of a new era in family life, and which included the right to single party petition divorce. The impact was almost immediate. Indeed, statistics compiled from civil court proceedings show that between 1951 and 1954 the number of divorces totaled 2,785,702 (Bachman 2006, 939). By 1953 the annual number of divorces recorded reached a peak of 940,369, nearly six times the 197,060 divorces granted in 1950. Given that some 58 percent to 92 percent of the marriage dispute and divorce cases were brought forward by women (Deng 1950 [1988], 172–73), a trend that continued after the law's 1950 promulgation (Tang 2011), this was an extraordinary outcome. And yet, in 1954, the year following CCP instructions to suppress divorces, the number of divorce cases was already rapidly declining: from 940,369 in 1953 to 597,933 in 1954 (Bachman 2006, 939).

Over the past two decades, scholars studying the implementation of the law have celebrated the agency of rural women who creatively made use of the new legislation and legal environment to their personal benefit (Diamant 2000; Huang 2005; Cong 2016). Diamant's (2000) detailed archival study of marriage reform in the early years of the PRC argues that rural women were able to bypass the pressure of local mediators by petitioning for divorce at the county level, concluding that while "there was little direct legal penetration into villages, the Marriage Law campaign itself created an atmosphere of fear and provided new institutions a rough legal framework, and opportunities for women to seek redress" (Diamant 2000, 169–70). These, and other forms of resistance, decreased the "reach" of the local state (Diamant 2001b), while empowering peasants to seek out higher-level political institutions to obtain justice (Diamant 2000, 279).

While the creative circumnavigation of the state was well in evidence in the 1950s, the mobilization of the Marriage Law nonetheless strengthened state power, to surprising effect. As Glosser (2003) argues, the CCP was able to control many aspects of post-1949 life due to its successful appropriation and implementation of the Republican-era discourse of family reform.[1] In this chapter I argue that the state's capacity to alter family life was not only built through the ideological groundwork laid by reformers during this earlier period (Glosser 2003, 195), but also through the attachments that reformers, and a new generation of grassroots women cadres, brought to their work. The collapse in divorce rates following the rapid surge of the first three years of the 1950s, I argue, was due in no small part to the intimately enacted gatekeeping of women's heads. Indeed, women's heads, arguably the least powerful of state actors in the new PRC, increased state capacity to suppress divorces by directly monitoring and shaping family life in the village. Hou Qiuyi, for example, did not view divorce as a solution to domestic violence. Rather, Hou made it her mission to deter divorce among the families in her charge. In her words, obtaining a divorce was nothing short of "shameful."

This chapter discusses the contested elite politics behind the drafting and passage of the 1950 Marriage Law, and its implementation in the counties of Huoyue, Wenhe, and Gaoshan. Building on Johnson (1983) who documents the tireless work of reformers to transform the Chinese family in the early PRC, this chapter argues that key members of the Chongqing Coalition, reformers that Altehenger (2018, 46–49) describes as "hidden legal innovators," sought to free women from abusive conjugal relationships and poverty, as an expression of maternalist state building.[2] That senior officials were able to achieve one-party petition divorce was due, in part, to their familial ties; an attached assertion of a New Woman state of activism had marked the work of the coalition from its outset. Nonetheless, the actual implementation of one-party petition divorce would quickly falter, demonstrating the limited power of the Chongqing Coalition to achieve its goals when faced with widespread elite and grassroots opposition to a controversial policy issue.

Key members of the Chongqing Coalition were nonetheless able to creatively respond in the face of a violent backlash to the Marriage Law. Specifically, Shi Liang, minister of justice, sought to work around local male officials by strengthening the collaboration between the ACDWF and the Ministry of Justice (MOJ).

Unlike midwifery reform, however, coordination activated through the maternalist social policy regime backfired. Below, I show how expectations of mediation shifted from a thoughtful exchange among equals to an exercise in which divorce-seeking women were subject to intensive "persuasion" by local women's heads to remain in their marriages, an outcome I argue that contributed to the collapse in divorces obtained. Indeed, once the CCP prioritized collectivization over marriage reform, local women's heads made it a point of pride to deter divorce. With the exception of the early 1960s, divorce rates remained low until the late 1970s.

The local suppression of divorce, and the larger discourse of family harmony in which it was embedded, would significantly shape how women's liberation was understood and enacted. Focusing on the recollections of a retired Gaoshan Youth League director, I also examine the complex negotiations involved in carving out a liberated identity in the context of enduring commitments of filial obligation, highly stringent revolutionary mores, and the changing terrain of Marriage Law implementation. Despite a desire to run away and join the army, Tian Min did not do so. Nor did she divorce her husband as her mother urged her to do; instead, she resigned herself to being a "good" daughter to her parents by remaining with her marital family. Tian Min's decision to adhere to gendered, filial practices that were themselves contested by her parents, speaks to the affective power of these attachments and their complex enactment during a moment of rapid social and political change. Tian Min's decision also speaks to the conflicted understanding of and commitment to women-work by women's heads themselves as they contended with the increasing demands of the ACDWF and the CCP at the rural grassroots.

Writing the Law

During the pre-1949 experiments with land reform, Deng Yingchao had quickly determined that marriage reform was an urgent necessity. In Deng's eyes, feudal marital practices could not be eliminated through land ownership and the participation in production alone. Rather, they must be resolved through a "conscious, gradual establishment" of marital freedom (*hunyin ziyou*) (Luo 1993, 236). Deng Yingchao's views were subsequently reflected in Liu Shaoqi's final drafting of the National Land Conference in September 1947 when he endorsed marriage freedom as important work for the CCP (Jin 1993, 1:399).

Deng Yingchao had actively worked on expanding women's legislative rights since the early 1920s. During the Anti-Japanese War, she had joined forces with Shi Liang, Liu-Wang Liming, He Xiangning, Song Qingling, Li Dequan, and other members of the Chongqing Coalition to agitate for the improvement of women's constitutional rights (Edwards 2008, 214–25). Moreover, she spoke out strongly in support of the importance of women's legal and political rights in 1943 (Deng 1943 [1988], 80–81), the same moment that the topic of women's rights was being sidelined in Yan'an. In this text, as in others that would follow, Deng establishes women's liberation an important measure of political progress overall. Deng Yingchao's efforts to draft the 1950 Marriage Law thus built on years of advocacy and coalition building.

Work on marriage reform began in October 1948 when Liu Shaoqi formally assigned the CCWMC with the task of drafting a new Marriage Law. A strong advocate of women's rights and the role of women's leadership in socialist construction, Liu Shaoqi stipulated that the new law should reflect the basic principle of the Jiangxi Soviet's Marriage Decree, originally signed by Mao Zedong in 1931 (Wang, Zhou, and Liu 2007). Whereas courts in the base areas had discouraged divorce (Cong 2016; Johnson 1983; Stranahan 1983, 34), the earlier Jiangxi Decree established "freedom as the principle of marriage" (*yi ziyou wei yuanze*) (Cong 2016, 144). By directly instructing the CCWMC to consult the Jiangxi-era document, Liu Shaoqi was making clear his support for a more progressive divorce law. At the same time, however, he was also clear that the women leaders of the CCWMC were to undertake research in base areas, and to discuss, compare, and synthesize their findings. Once again, Deng Yingchao approached her advocacy through a careful mobilization of research, persuasion, and personal ties.

The marriage drafting group was composed of seven leading women officials: Shuai Mengqi, Kang Keqing, Yang Zhihua, Li Peizhi, Luo Qiong, Wang Ruqi, and Deng Yingchao (Jin 1993, 2:457; Wang, Zhou, and Liu 2007). With the exception of Kang Keqing, all of the committee members were well-educated and deeply influenced by the May Fourth Movement (Cong 2016, 248). Several members brought personal experience to the table as well: Yang Zhihua, for example, had divorced and remarried in the 1920s (Gilmartin 1995, 102–3). Given that only one member of the drafting group, Wang Ruqi, was actually a lawyer, however, undertaking the writing of the draft law proved a formidable challenge.[3] There were significant disagreements as well.

Over a period of several months, the group met seven or eight times, sitting on a kang and exchanging views, with Wang taking notes and revising each subsequent draft. According to Luo Qiong (1993, 236–38), the biggest source of disagreement was a Jiangxi-era clause that permitted one-party petition divorce. The group debated openly about the merits of not restraining access to divorce, with several members arguing that it would produce instability and reactionary responses in the countryside by hurting some peasants' interests. Others worried that some male cadres would use "marriage freedom" as an excuse to abandon their rural wives or that it might influence morale in the military.[4] Still others were concerned about the way that the marriage law had been used to oppress women. In some places, for example, women were being labeled as "broken shoes" (sex workers, *po xie*) as an excuse to deprive them of their right to land (Wang, Zhou, and Liu 2007).[5]

From the outset, Deng Yingchao understood that objections from senior party members and grassroots cadres were a serious threat to the promise of legislative reform. Worried that grassroots cadres with an insufficient understanding of marital rights might negatively impact the implementation of the law, Deng knew the law had to be strong enough to curtail their execution of local power. Deng Yingchao's contributions to the draft group discussion suggest that she feared that unless the new law included recognition of one-party divorce petitions, rural women would never be able to realize their new rights (Wang, Zhou, and Liu 2007).

Despite Deng Yingchao's strong advocacy, however, one-party petition divorce remained highly contentious as the first draft moved into consultation. In Deng's meetings with the MOJ, the Youth League, the Organizational Department, and the ACDWF beginning in November 1949, only one individual (from the Organizational Department) supported her position on one-party petition divorce (Jin 1993 2:457). Deng thus not only faced opposition from senior men leaders but also continued to face questions from the senior ranks of the Women's Federation itself. In a meeting with the CCWMC in early January 1950, Deng Yingchao continued to advocate her position, arguing that requiring both parties to agree to a divorce was against the interests of the many women who had been forced into marriages they did not want. By not allowing one-party divorce petition, she continued, the law would increase the number of tragedies, including suicides and murders occurring in base areas where only two-party petitions were allowed (460). She also directly addressed the concerns of the older women cadres by arguing that women who found themselves in the position of being divorced by their husbands should seek solace in their work and develop greater inner strength (458–59).

By the end of January 1950, however, it became clear that the consultation process was at an impasse. Given the number of bureaucratic units involved and the need to build consensus, the complex process to draft the law became hamstrung, an outcome that is consistent with Lampton's (1992) description of bureaucratic bargaining in Maoist and reform China.[6] Over the previous two months, several drafts had undergone numerous revisions, including the addition of a stipulation that one-party petition could only proceed after a couple had undergone formal mediation led by the district government and MOJ. Deng Yingchao now needed more support, and so she turned directly to the CCP leaders who had charged her with the task to undertake marriage reform in the first place. To this end, Deng Yingchao forwarded the fifth draft of the Law to Mao Zedong, Liu Shaoqi, Zhu De, Ren Bishi, Zhou Enlai, and Wang Ming, with a personal letter attached in late January 1950.[7] Her letter summarized the conflict, noted her own disagreement with aspects of the draft, and included materials reflecting both sides of the debate, suggesting that at that point those opposing one-party petition outnumbered those in its favor. Some kind of intervention was necessary, she wrote, if the process was to continue to move forward (Wang, Zhou, and Liu 2007). Within a few days, Deng had her response: one party-petition was to be included in the Marriage Law.

Deng's direct request, and the rapid affirmative response she received in her favor, momentarily released the consultation process from the "matrix muddle" (Lieberthal 1995, 169) that had so often befuddled legislative and bureaucratic processes of consultation in the PRC. Deng 's unique revolutionary status in the CCP and her marital relationship with Zhou enabled her to drive forward what Luo Qiong (1998b [2000], 24) calls Liu Shaoqi's agenda to realize "true sexual equality" (*shixing zhen zheng nannû pingdeng*), which Deng had long been advocating, but which clearly was meeting with fierce opposition from within the ranks of the military, government, party, and from within the Women's Federation itself. Following this decision, another three months of intensive consultation and revision took place under the direction of Dong Biwu, who was appointed as acting premier while Zhou Enlai was in the Soviet Union (Bian and Wu 2006, 711–12), and under the leadership of Mao Zedong who led discussions on revisions on two occasions as well (Gu 2013, 23). Cai Chang also assisted the Legislative Affairs Committee to complete the draft of the Marriage Law (Li 1992, 77). In total, major points were revised thirty to forty times and minor points were revised ten to twenty times before the final draft was signed into law by Mao Zedong on April 30 and officially promulgated on May 1, 1950 (Wang, Zhou, and Liu 2007). The final version nonetheless included an important caveat: women married to men in the military or to men who were veterans, could not unilaterally petition for divorce. On this issue, Liu Shaoqi capitulated to the military's desire to maintain morale among its rank and file (Luo 1998b [2000], 25).[8]

Early Implementation

By passing the 1950 Marriage Law, Chongqing reformers sought to replace the patriarchal family with a small family (*xiao jiating*) headed by a heterosexual couple in a monogamous union (Glosser 2003). In the new family system, marriage was to be established on the basis of *ganqing* (affection) and equality, and freely chosen by participants who were of legal age (twenty for men, eighteen for women). The power of the patriarch and/or mother-in-law in these newly constituted and smaller family arrangements was expected to diminish, thus overturning past practices in which elders of extended kinship networks oversaw the management and distribution of property, marital unions, and day-to-day oversight of the household. Practices of polygamy, polyandry, child betrothals, and interference in the marriage of widows (previously taboo in many places) were explicitly forbidden. The new Marriage Law also contained eugenic features, prohibiting marriage in cases in which a partner was deemed sexual impotent or suffering from venereal disease, and in instances when a couple shared blood lines. All new marriages were required to be registered with the People's government of the district or township. As Chen (2014) argues, the new law seemingly provided the basis for liberation, while simultaneously positioning socialist bodies to meet the needs of the new regime. The implementation of the law at the grassroots as recounted by Hou Qiuyi brings this tension into sharp relief.

From the perspective of former Huoyue women's head and party secretary Hou Qiuyi, the passage of the Marriage Law was game changing: prior to the law, women were bought and sold as child brides and concubines, subject to the violence of mothers-in-law and husbands, and lacked any right to speak out on their own behalf. As Hou Qiuyi also acknowledged, wartime and famine conditions had limited the options of many parents. Some parents subjected their daughters to arranged marriages in order to protect them from sexual assault and capture. The raging battles between the GMD and the CCP in Wenhe, for example, prompted the parents of Yuan Jinyu, 158, to arrange her marriage at age twelve to a boy who was then sixteen. Gu Xiulan, 42, a former production brigade leader, fled from famine in the Luoyang region with her older brother and sister-in-law. After being separated from her family, she ended up settling in Wenhe as a child bride, married at the age of fourteen to a man twelve years her senior.

According to Hou Qiuyi, women who hailed from impoverished families had been particularly subject to abuse from local powerholders:

> I had a cousin who was good looking. She caught the eye of one of the members of the clan and was kidnapped and made into a concubine. Three years later, when the 8th Route Army arrived they captured both of them (her cousin and cousin's husband) and killed them. But it wasn't her fault that she was forced to be a concubine! The daughter of the *Baozhang* [however] was a bad woman and slept around.[9] People said "Poor women are virtuous and the wealthier ones sleep around" [*tiandixia pao de shi zhenjie nü, xiulou shang xiu de shi yang han jing*]. So

all of us cadres were cautious about this. During land reform, we forced
the concubines to re-marry and the first wives stay with the household.
The concubines were all daughters of poor households, they were pretty,
and [therefore had been] kidnapped.

Hou Qiuyi's cousin was captured and executed by the Eighth Route Army, probably in the heat of battle and perhaps before the Marriage Law was promulgated. As is evident here, not all CCP activists and leaders were operating from
the same playbook. Whereas the conquering soldiers of the Eighth Route Army
viewed Hou's cousin as an oppressor, Hou viewed her cousin as victim of feudal
practices. In Hou's description it was the landlord's wife, a sexually promiscuous
woman compromised by wealth, who cadres needed to guard against. Hou's conflation of class and virtue reflected and reinforced the emerging socialist morality
intersecting with local norms at the grassroots.

The chaotic implementation of family reform in the months before, during,
and after the promulgation of the Marriage Law was not unique to Huoyue. Antic-
ipating that the law would meet challenges during its implementation, Zhou Enlai
formed a committee to guide the implementation process four months before
the law was finalized.[10] Chaired by Shen Junru, an influential male jurist and
wartime ally of Shi Liang, the vice chairs included Liu Jingfan, Peng Zemin, and
Xiao Hua, plus two Chongqing reformers, Deng Yingchao and Shi Liang, and one
of the elders of maternalist reform, He Xiangning (Bian and Wu 2006, 711–12).
Beginning in April 1950, several implementation meetings were convened, with
Li Dequan overseeing one large gathering of more than twenty units on April 20
(Yang 1991, 19). The following month, Deng Yingchao sought to explain the rea-
soning behind the Marriage Law and mollify its critics both at upper and lower
levels of the party, in an address given before an enlarged cadre meeting held by the
Zhangjiakou Municipal Party Committee and Municipal People's Government.
In her talk, Deng (1950 [1988], 169–85) emphasized the highly consultative process that produced the legislation. The law, she noted, had been subject to several
iterations of review and revision and was ultimately approved by none other than
Mao Zedong. She also distinguished the new law from GMD family law—which,
she stated, was superficial and ineffective—while at the same time justifying the
greater latitude for divorce that existed in the 1950 law than was available in the
Soviet Union's current legal structure—where, she noted, women had already
made great strides in achieving equality (1950 [1988], 171). Most important, she
tried to assuage fears that the Marriage Law was causing "social chaos" by arguing
that, in fact, it was the lack of freedom to marry and divorce that was creating the
current rash of divorces; the increase in divorces, she stressed, was only a temporary phenomenon (Deng 1950 [1988], 174; see also Johnson 1983, 118).

While the Marriage Law was publicized in major media outlets, including in *Women of New China* (Zhang 1996, 160–61), grassroots cadres initially received little preparation or concrete instruction as to how to implement the law most effectively (Johnson 1983, 101). Given these complexities, it was not always clear how to best proceed, and many newly minted leaders did their best to cobble together their own strategies for implementation.[11]

One response was to organize show trials at which abusive husbands could be paraded and criticized—and sometimes even executed.[12] The Henan Women's Federation, for example, submitted the names of more than twenty men to be executed in the second half of 1951 for having murdered women (Shao 1984, 103). Some Wenhe cadres took a similar approach, suggesting that marriage campaigns should be carried out like the large political campaigns in which the guilty were arrested, sentenced, or killed and thereby set a bad example for others.[13] But absent clear directives, educating abusers and the communities from which they hailed was not always a straightforward matter. Wenhe village head, Qiu Mingli, 63, for example, found herself improvising a response when a woman who had been violently beaten by her husband came to her for help in 1952. After Qiu ordered the husband's arrest, however, the woman denied that her husband had beaten her and said that she fell and hit her head. Initially stumped as to how to deal with the situation, Qiu held a huge meeting to criticize the man, and then threw him into jail for a couple of days. If she hadn't intervened, Qiu said, the woman would not have been liberated.

The sheer pervasiveness of domestic violence rendered it a seemingly intractable problem, especially given that male leaders themselves could be as violent with their wives as they were with the former landlords, enemy soldiers, and bandits in their jurisdictions. Well before the establishment of the PRC, CCP officials had great difficulty persuading male grassroots party leaders to desist from "feudal" and "patriarchal" practices, especially given the long-standing assumption that husbands were entitled to physically abuse their wives.[14] In his early commentary on the Marriage Law, Wang Ming suggested that "the actual number of divorces would have been higher had it not been for the impeding forces of tradition, domination by the clan, fear of the neighborhood, and even the influence of minor government officials who prevented women from divorcing their husbands and took the side of the husbands against the wives" (Meijer 1971, 102). Many women said: "If you want to divorce, you must pass three [tests]: the husband [test], the mother-in-law [test], and the cadre [test]; the cadre [test] is the most difficult" (Zhang 2010, 38).

One of the gravest risks of implementing the Marriage Law was that it empowered women to resist familial abuse, and in so doing, generated the ire of in-laws and spouses, many of whom viewed marital ties as a form of familial investment and status. As Wang Ming and other senior officials quickly discovered, women were murdered and committing suicide at an unprecedented rate, often under the noses of indifferent local leaders. The Henan Women's Federation, for example, reported that 672 women in six special districts had either committed suicide or were killed over a six-month period (Shao 1984, 103). There were similar cases reported in Wenhe (WCAWF n.d.). Investigative reports from the Central-South region of China carried out by the Military Government Council, the Party Bureau, and the Women's Federation revealed findings even more shocking: more than ten thousand women had died due to murder or suicide (Gu 2013, 27–28; Johnson 1983, 132). More recently, it has been suggested that, between the law's promulgation until the end of 1952, as many as seventy thousand to eighty thousand women died or were killed as a consequence of the law's implementation (Tang 2011, 134).

Contributing to the violence was the CCP leadership's decision to prioritize the implementation of land reform over promotion of the Marriage Law for the first three years after the law's passage (Johnson 1983). But Zhou Enlai did not fully relinquish the reins. Rather, he and other reform minded CCP officials took steps to reinforce the hand of the Chongqing Coalition. First, he widened the scope of ongoing investigations, giving Shi Liang, minister of justice, the authority to send out countrywide inspection teams (Johnson 1983, 130).[15] Second, his office criticized grassroots cadres who were themselves either ignoring the new law or were directly interfering with the law's implementation (Central People's Government Administrative Council 1951 [1988], 2:121). And third, he appointed Chongqing reformers and other allies to key government positions as a bid, I would argue, to strengthen their hand.[16]

In the meantime, officials within the Women's Federation continued to call for a new campaign to implement the Marriage Law (Johnson 1983, 135–37). After months of insider agitation, a decision was thus taken to organize a campaign for one month in the spring of 1953. Johnson (1983, 139) argues that unlike the first campaign, which had lacked preparation and competed with land reform, the second was "more extensive, more coordinated, better directed and better prepared for." It also had the concerted backing and direct oversight of key members of the Chongqing Coalition, including Deng Yingchao, Shi Liang, Liu Qingyang, and He Xiangning, who were appointed to the National Committee for the Thorough Implementation of the Marriage Law (Johnson 1983, 139).[17] These three women, plus Cao Mengjun, also a Chongqing reformer, and Shen Junru, served on a committee to implement the mobilization established in February as well (Yang 1991, 55).

It is at this point that Shi Liang, minister of justice and a high-level official of the ACDWF, became a critical player. One of the first women to graduate from the Shanghai Law College in the 1920s, Shi Liang worked with the National Salvation Association and cultivated a close, personal relationship with the three Song sisters: Song Meiling, Song Ailing, and Song Qingling during the Anti-Japanese War.[18] When Shanghai fell to the communists in 1949, Shi was elected to executive committees of both the ACDWF and the CPPCC. Shortly after the establishment of the People's Republic, Shi Liang was appointed minister of justice (Lee 2003d, 453).

During the discussions of the Marriage Law that transpired, Shi Liang grounded her support of single-petition divorce on the basis of her legal experience: "Because of my lengthy personal experience trying cases on behalf of women, I knew that in the context of loveless marriages, Chinese women suffered greatly. I thus advocated that women had the right to a one-party petition for divorce" (Shi 1987, 76). Shi Liang is also said to have frequently quoted Song Qingling: "Now that [the nation] is liberated, women's status has gone through a great change. However, because of the influence of several thousand years of feudal system and feudal thinking, more must be done to raise women's status, you must [draw on] the law to emphasize the protection of women and children's interests" (Luo and Zuo 1997, 115–16).[19]

In addition to leading investigations, Shi Liang's work on the Marriage Law had already taken a myriad of forms, including explaining the concept of mediation as well as advocating strategies to remedy problems associated with the law in articles published in leading party organs. She also sought to charge women leaders with implementation. One of her recommendations, for example, was to make women judges responsible for divorce courts (Luo and Zuo 1997, 116). Through her cross-appointment with the Women's Federation, Shi Liang was able to coordinate work at the grassroots, including deploying women's federation cadres to educate district cadres to correctly understand the new marriage policies. In September 1950, women cadres were charged with educating people about the marriage law, mediating family conflict, and serving as jurors in marriage cases, which the federation and Supreme People's Court formalized with the promulgation of a joint notice (Yang 1991, 24). While actual divorce cases were to be handled at district or municipal courts, this was a last step in the process. The MOJ thus relied heavily on the labor of lower-level women's federation cadres to propagate and implement the law.

It was no coincidence that Shi Liang was also promoted to vice chair of the ACDWF in 1953, the same year the ACDWF planned and launched its biggest mobilization of the law. Zhang Yun, responsible for propaganda work for the ACDWF, was promoted to vice chair as well. Zhang Yun's writing in *Women of New China* in early 1953 suggest that she was deeply concerned about the lack of understanding of the law among grassroots cadres, including women who did not understand why the law was necessary, during preparations for the month-long mobilization in the spring (see, for example, Zhang 1953 [1996], 136). But Zhang Yun, a senior member of both the ACDWF party group and CCWMC, served as a key interlocutor between the ACDWF and CCP. As such, her writing also reflected division about the Marriage Law within the CCP, as well.

The timing of the appointments indicates that, at the very least, Zhou Enlai was initially behind the campaign, even as many in the CCP, perhaps the majority, were against it. A contributing factor to the confusing and at times violent responses to the law at the grassroots level was the division within the central leadership, which became even more acute as the campaign was put into motion (Johnson 1983, 101). Between late 1952 and February 1953 the Central Committee issued two directives (December 26 and February 19) and the Government Administrative Council issued another (February 1) on the planned March campaign to implement the law. The directives became weaker with each modification, sending mixed signals about how seriously the campaign should be taken (Johnson 1983, 141). Signed by Zhou Enlai, the final directive was a significant retreat from earlier instructions. Indeed, Zhou emphasized the need for patience in the slow, painstaking work of marital reform, work in which improving marital ties should be emphasized, and in which divorce was to be permitted (*pizhun*) only in the most egregious cases (Zhou 1953 [1988], 2:153–55). Zhang Yun's (1953 [1996], 136–39) instructions to women cadres in January 1953 anticipated this shift. Specifically, she stipulated that advocacy of marriage freedom was to be limited to the unmarried; for the married, advocacy would focus on establish household unity and happiness through the resolution of conflict. To this end, cadres were not to mention the ban on arranged marriages among those already married; instead, they were directed to help couples strengthen their already-existing relationship. Deng Yingchao seemingly received the message as well. Whereas, in 1950, Deng Yingchao had argued that men and women should be able to leave their "less than ideal" partners and seek out new love interests (Deng 1950 [1988], 174), by April 1953, Deng (1953 [1988]) was praising families (couples, and mothers and daughters-in-law) who had improved their relations through mediation.

Insider agitation, nonetheless, continued. In November 1953, the CCWMC sent a detailed report to Mao Zedong and the Central Committee describing "serious problems" with violence, murder, and suicide across the country, requesting support to organize and dispatch investigative teams (ACWF 1953 [1999]). But the CCP leadership had other plans: a deepening and broadening of collectivization across the countryside, a development I discuss in chapter 7. Concerned that a new Marriage Law mobilization would prove a distraction, the Central Committee vetoed the ACDWF's campaign (CC 1953 [1999]).[20] When

Women of New China explored the cause of suicides in 1954 and during the first months of 1955, it thus placed editorial emphasis on strengthening the self in relationship to the socialist project (Dong 1991, 161–62).[21] Even Shen Zijiu, former Chongqing Coalition veteran and editor of the ACDWF flagship journal, could go no further.

Mediating Marriage

Instead of supporting the efforts of women to leave unhappy and violent marriages, women's heads enacted attached forms of mediation to keep women within them. The emphasis on mediation was, in fact, built into the structure of the law.[22] Before proceeding to the courts, prospective divorce petitioners were required to undergo a round of mediation with a mediator appointed from within the village, often the local women's head or another cadre. In establishing this framework for formal mediation, the law's architects were not just responding to the more conservative voices in the CCP, but also building on experiments with mediation undertaken during the early 1940s (Huang 2005; Lubman 1967, 1286, 1306). In the context of the 1950 Marriage Law, the local mediator was expected to assist the two parties to come to some form of a compromise. Mediation was not, however, meant to deter divorce altogether. In the words of Shi Liang:

> The meaning of mediation is that the People's Government and the judicial organs from the standpoint of the new democratic Marriage Law assist the divorcing parties in considering their problems and solving them. The meaning is not that without regard for the actual circumstances, from the standpoint of pity or the old morality, the mediators exercise pressure on the parties to come to a compromise. This would be deviation. Mediation can take into consideration all ordinary circumstances and adopt different devices. It can point out where the practical problems of divorce lie. The authority concerned must investigate the case, penetrate into the inside, probe into the matter in detail and study the case. Only then can it make its decision. For example, it may use either persuasion, education, or explanation, or it may correct mistakes. Mediation devices may bring the parties together and reconcile them; in other cases, when it is clear that no love exists between the man and the woman and that if they continue to live together the result will be to hinder production and work, then mediation is of no avail and the case must be referred to the District or Municipal People's Court for

decision. The mediating authorities *cannot forbid the parties to file a petition for divorce.* (Meijer 1971, 106–7, emphasis mine)

The fact that the local mediators could not forbid divorce proved to be one of the major victories of the Chongqing Coalition, and of Deng Yingchao in particular. As implemented beginning in 1953, however, mediation transpired through moral ideological "criticism" and "education" (Huang 2005, 171) and as such materialized as an "instrument of control" (Lubman 1965). Indeed, Huang (2005, 174) describes mediation as "coercive marriage counseling undertaken by the party-state through its court system." The fact that most marriage disputes did not make it to the courts at all is attributable to mediation's embeddedness in community (Diamant 2000, 158–59), in which local mediators were often well known to both parties (Wolf 1985, 164). After 1953, village women's heads played a central role in keeping women in their marriages.

Village women's heads were pivotal social brokers, or what Ong (2022, 105–7) defines as individuals who fulfill their objectives by mobilizing guanxi and ganqing. As Ferree (2004) argues, the threat of stigma and ridicule can serve as powerful tools for inducement and control, a form of "soft repression" that Deng and O'Brien (2013, 534) call "relational repression." Building on Ferree (2004), Deng and O'Brien identify relational repression as a "cultural strategy to prevent collective action by actively discouraging identification with a group that could make claims against an institution." Operationalized through friends, family, and native-place connections, relational repression rests on "emotional blackmail and feelings of affinity" (Deng and O'Brien 2013, 534), an approach that many village women's heads mastered. Mediation served as a highly effective means of dispute "suppression" (Fu 2014); in the hands of women's heads, it would prove a powerful deterrent to marriage dissolution.[23]

As the instructions on Marriage Law implementation shifted, local women's heads began to draw on their growing familiarity with the inner workings of families to deter women from divorces. Hou Qiuyi discussed the transformation as follows:

> When it was the new society, after marriage registration, the man and woman discussed together, shared everything and they didn't argue about money, they shared everything. But some women didn't understand this and they thought women's status had been raised and so women were allowed to quarrel with their in-laws but this is not permitted. So, after the district Women's Federation was established some women were abusing their mothers-in-law and so leaders gathered everybody together, and the leaders interfered. As soon as the district Women's Federation saw this, they gave instructions, and then

the district Women's Federation gave instructions too and then whoever had a good experience would get the other couples to follow their
example. I had meetings every day to learn how to speak. Whatever the
leaders said, I got it right away, then came back to the village and would
tell other people. Back then [I] learned the leaders' words. If a woman
was abusing her in-laws I went to her to say, "We are good sisters, we
listen to Chairman Mao. We can't abuse/quarrel with our in-laws, this
is not right. Women's status has been raised so that you can work and
contribute to the revolution [but] you can't abuse the elders. A husband
can't quarrel or beat [his] wife either, so everyone in the family must live
together in harmony; if you quarrel every day, other people would laugh
at you." So the husband cannot quarrel or beat [his] wife, you must
point out her or his weaknesses and strengths from solidarity.

The most important role that local women's heads played in the enactment of
the Marriage Law was not that they liberated women from feudal or violent
marriages but rather that they tried to convince couples to "get along" and stay
together. Here, Hou's narrative of emancipation in which husband and wife
"share everything" and "discuss everything" is embedded within a hierarchy of
revolutionary agency, in which women's improved status was not a right in and
of itself, but rather a means to a larger end. Indeed, Hou's embodiment of the
Loyal Soldier was predicated on her capacity to implement instructions given by
Mao Zedong and her local Women's Federation superiors, and operated in part,
through the threat of community ostracism. Persuasion thus served as a form of
political consciousness raising that, in this context, was rendered into an attached
enactment of maternalist tutelage.

Rong Litang, 116, drew on an older form of relational repression when she
sent one young woman back to her father to educate her not to quarrel with her
mother-in-law. In other cases, women's heads applied relational repression by
reminding women of the chaos and loss they would create *for others* by pressing for divorce. Diamant (2000, 149), for example, quotes one former Women's
Federation official as saying to a potential divorce litigant: "Everyone spent a lot
of money to marry you . . . if you divorce, the man will really suffer." These kinds
of speech acts drove home the necessity of prioritizing relational obligations over
individual rights also enshrined in the text of the Marriage Law.

The imperative to remain married, despite the cost, was applied equally to
situations of severe domestic violence. Former Huoyue women's head Hao Lianfen, 131, recounted the following case in which she deterred a survivor of violent
abuse from divorcing her husband:

If the woman ran to the water, her husband would push her under the
water and said: "Drink! Drink!" Her mother-in-law was also really bad.

Later, [the wife] requested to divorce. Our mediation didn't work, and [so we] gave them an introductory letter and [they] went to the commune, and also underwent mediation. [But] that woman still wanted to divorce. They had a boy and a girl. They urged her: "Don't divorce, if you divorce, the husband's family won't let you take the children. They only have you as their daughter-in-law, and only the one son, and one daughter, they absolutely won't let you take them." [The woman] said: "If I don't divorce there is no way I can go on." Later she divorced. I ran into her when I was walking to my elder sister's place and she was walking to her natal family. I said: "Don't divorce, we are the same clan village. If it really can't work, let's sit down and talk about it a while; let's see if we can come up with some suggestions. You go back, everyone in this situation has been hurt, you can't take your son or daughter, aren't you sad?" This woman was good, and said okay. I said: "I am going to stay with my elder sister for no more than two days, you hurry up and return home. If you get there and they don't let you back in, then come get me and I will take care of it for you. If they don't say anything, then don't divorce." Later, she went back, went back home, and she didn't come looking for me. [This] proves that her family was okay again, [they] weren't arguing, and didn't talk about divorce anymore. Now, she's a grandmother. Her husband died last year.

In this situation, Hao Lianfen's enactment of relational repression proved to be a powerful tool to obtain compliance. Hao Lianfen repeatedly "worked on" the woman by reminding her that she would lose access to her children if she did not change her mind. Indeed, the threat of real loss was embedded in the affective circuit of relations to which both of the women belonged—that is, a shared clan village—and within which Hao herself felt she had an obligation to intervene— that is, should the in-laws not accept the daughter-in-law from returning. Hao's sincere belief that she helped the woman because "she didn't come looking for me," however, obscures what was very likely a high cost for the woman herself. It also contradicted the orders of the Women's Federation: local women's heads were instructed to assist abused women seeking to exit their marriages (ACWF 1953 [1999]).[24]

Although the goal was to deter divorce, this is not to say that women's heads were oblivious to the harm of domestic violence. When Tian Min, 85, the former Gaoshan Youth league director first introduced in chapter 4, directly confronted a former veteran who was beating his wife, for example, her approach was to criticize the husband and keep the couple together:

At that time, when neighbors fought, I went to mediate and resolve; when daughter-in-law and mother-in-law fought, I went to mediate and resolve; when man and wife fought, I also went to mediate and resolve. So, I could say that I have done this sort of work for thousands of thousands of families. In the 1950s, there was a family from X Village, the man had been a soldier, serving in the Guomindang army and was later captured by the Liberation Army and later on he became a soldier there. But he was quite hot-tempered. He beat his wife. I learned about this. In my opinion, no matter how high a cadre you are, I will criticize you. If your wife has some shortcomings, you should educate and criticize, but you just can't hold out your hands and hit her.

Tian's pride in her ability to confront this abusive husband is striking, especially given her personal aversion to women-work. As will become increasingly evident, Tian saw herself as a leader who protected women—even when it meant confronting local CCP authority. Tian's agency thus contrasts directly with that of Hou Qiuyi: whereas Hou emphasized her ability to learn the language of the party-state and to follow orders, Tian emphasized her ability to confront it. Ultimately, however, both Hou and Tian evaluated their work on the implementation of the Marriage Law vis-à-vis their capacity to deter divorce. In the case of the violent veteran, for example, Tian stated that she was successful: the couple did not divorce because of her ideological persuasion.

Across Gaoshan, Huoyue, and Wenhe, the message was the same: dissuade divorce whenever possible. Gaoshan women's head Lin Xiaohong, 73, for example, took pride in her ability to keep marriages intact over many decades: "I would always succeed in dissuading them (from divorcing). If one time didn't work, I would do it another time." Similarly, when I asked one former women's head what it meant to be a good women's head, she said: "Persuading couples to stay together" (Yan Zhijuan, 97). Leader Zhang Sumei, 20, echoed this thinking:

> You could only [try] and mediate, and [tell them] not to make each other angry! [You] weren't supposed to encourage them to divorce, or to leave. Even nowadays I am still educating people that [you] shouldn't get angry, shouldn't divorce. Some people [are able to work things out] after [I've] spoken with them, but some people are just too angry, can't work it out, and are determined to leave. Fighting and arguing everyday like that, [someone] has to go to them. The village mediator also takes care of this. There are both men and women mediators, [who] goes to their home and educates them. How can you ignore them when they come to you?

Of course, relational repression was not always applied everywhere, or with success when it was. In Jiangsu, women filed complaints about their domestic

situation with the Letters and Visits Bureau—the numbers of which nearly doubled between 1956 (75) and 1957 (136) (Lu and Miao 2000, 206).[25] Several participants in my study were able to obtain divorces over the course of the 1950s.[26]
According to Niu Shumiao, 52, and some of her former neighbors, getting a
divorce in the 1950s was not difficult. Niu's in-laws, for example, not only criticized her for serving as women's head in her village; they also encouraged her
husband to beat her and tried to prevent her from leaving the house. Eventually
she became fed up and petitioned for divorce. Shortly afterward, she married her
second husband, a cadre in a neighboring village.[27] It was "easy to get a divorce"
(Fang Huayun, 51); all you had to do was "go to the commune" (Wen Xiujin, 39).
Women's head Liu Yuezhen, 10, also insisted that there were many divorces in
cases where people could not be persuaded to make up. When asked if she had
ever helped a woman to obtain a divorce, Niu replied, "Yes. This also happened.
[In this situation] you went and tried to explain things to them. If the situation
really could not be resolved, then the person would divorce."

But these handful of reported divorces pale in comparison with the "thousands
and thousands" of families Tian and her counterparts convinced to remain together.
The numbers in Gaoshan, back this up. Between 1953 and 1954, civil marriage
cases in Gaoshan dropped from 630 to 454, reaching a low of 50 in 1973 (GX 1994,
694). While the actual number of divorces granted is not included in the record, the
overall reporting is suggestive of a marked pattern of decline in people taking their
marital disputes to the courts. Given that Gaoshan's population size was 728,559 in
1953—the actual number of divorces would have been vanishingly low.

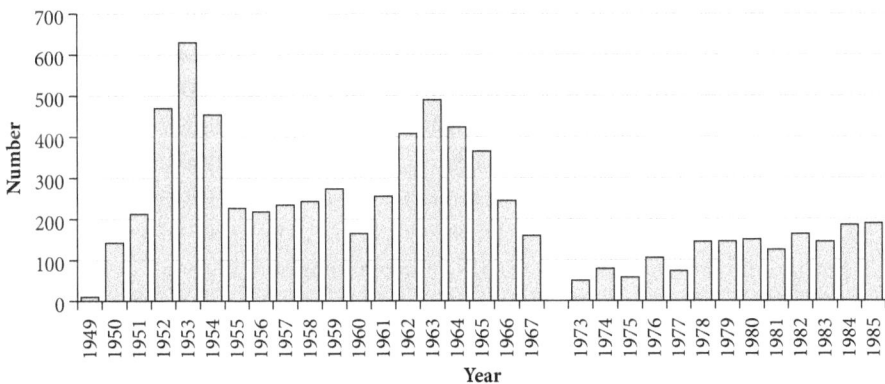

FIGURE 3. Number of marital cases in Gaoshan County, 1949–85. *Source: GX* 1994, 694.

With the exception of the years of the famine and its aftermath, a development I discuss in chapter 9, the number of divorces registered nationally also suggest a marked decline. In 1965, for example, only 395,665 divorces were recorded—less than half the peak of 940,369 in 1954 (Bachman 2006, 939).[28] Whereas both Diamant (2000) and Bachman (2006) view the ongoing practice of divorce as evidence of robust social practices, however, I interpret the numbers somewhat differently. Rather, I see these numbers as evidence of the effectiveness of the local state to curb what would have otherwise been a far more robust culture of legal contention. It is thus no surprise that rural women embroiled in marriage disputes decades later "exhibited little faith in the law as a champion of their rights" (Gilmartin 1990, 207)."

Love, Filiality, and Revolutionary Virtue

The 1950 Marriage Law, and its post-1953 implementation, did not just impact women seeking exit from their marriages. Gail Hershatter argues that in order to understand the impact of the Marriage Law it is necessary to take a wider and longer view of the legislation as it was implemented—one that not only produced shifts in how marriages were arranged and formalized, but also in how marriage itself was practiced (Hershatter 2011, 127). In Shaanxi, for example, arranged marriages gradually began to give way to "half-free, half-arranged" matches, whereby couples were introduced to a matchmaker with parental approval (127). Statistics collected by the Jiangsu Women's Federation similarly suggest that after the mobilization of the Marriage Law 60–70 percent of rural matches made via introduction in the Suzhou District had the consent of the betrothed (Lu and Miao 2000, 134).

Family structures were also changing at this time, with increasing numbers of in-laws and married children choosing to live separately rather within the same household (Cohen 2005). One Gaoshan woman, Ma Mingyu, 128, whose husband was working outside the village, for example, ran away after being mistreated by her in-laws. Pregnant, she took shelter with an aunt who was living in a city nearby. Her parents eventually brought her back to her in-laws who continued to mistreat her. In this case, the ultimate solution was not a divorce but rather family separation. The young couple loved each other and wanted to stay together; indeed, it was the oppression of the elder generation from which they needed to escape, not each other.

As is evident from many of the examples of family conflict already discussed in this chapter, the relationship between couples and in-laws was also undergoing rapid change throughout the course of the 1950s. For the most part, women continued to relocate to the homes of their husbands after marriage. But natal family ties maintained a powerful pull and source of support as well.[29] In some cases women prioritized filial obligations to their parents over their obligations to their marital family. Sun Qinqin, 162, a former women's head and schoolteacher, for example, petitioned for divorce in 1961 when her husband refused to move to her natal village, although she had married him with the understanding that they would live with her natal family. As the eldest daughter in a family of girls, she felt responsible for taking care of her parents. Indeed, her stepfather had wholeheartedly supported her education and treated her as a boy. Thus, even though she had two babies to care for, she pursued the separation. When she encountered resistance from her husband's family, she produced the marriage document on which it was explicitly written that the groom would move to his wife's residence. Sun was ultimately granted her divorce and later remarried. Although the past was difficult, "The most important thing is that my mother and father were happy in their later years—that meant, in the end, I was filial to my parents."

Youth League leader Tian Min's filial commitments led her to make the opposite decision. Tian Min chose not to petition for divorce because to do so would have brought shame on her parents, even though they were the ones pushing her to take advantage of the new law. In a visit to her parents in Kunming, Yunnan, in 1955, Tian's mother, a women's representative herself, tried to persuade her to divorce her husband:

> My mother asked me why I did not end the marriage after the Marriage Law was promulgated: you see how awful they are to you. I answered my mother with one sentence: "Because when I was about to go to Jiangsu [you] said this to me: you can't let people say, 'How can your parents raise a daughter like you!'" After I finished speaking, my parents said: "This is pre-liberation talk. [You should] act in accordance with the Marriage Law." At last, I thought, my mother was the director of the local community since 1952 and when I returned home in 1955 she had been in that position for three years. [But] I always thought about what my parents said before I went to Jiangsu, my parents told me not to let people say, "How can your parents raise a bad daughter?" So I never brought [divorce] up. In fact, I had started working and was able to get divorced if I wanted. That was true.

Tian's comments of filiality and obedience stand in stark contrast to her insistence, also shared during her interviews, that she did not "listen to the commands" of her in-laws. Her refusal to address her in-laws through traditional terms, was an example, in her eyes, of what it meant to be proud of (*zihao*) of being a woman after Liberation.

On the other hand, Tian's insistence that she always obeyed her mother-in-law reinforces the importance of harmonious domestic relations. Tian was particularly worried about not coming between her mother-in-law and her husband's grandmother, who constantly tried to defend her:

> My grandmother[-in-law] cursed: "That old hag didn't give you enough to eat at home, now she's dead, and you are not eating."[30] By that time my stomach was already in bad shape. My mother-in-law was often fighting with my grandmother[-in-law]. My grandmother[in-law] wouldn't put up with my mother-in-law and so they fought a lot. I didn't get involved. I wouldn't tell my mother-in-law what my grandmother[in-law] said and wouldn't tell my grandmother[in-law] what my mother-in-law said. If I got involved, they would have fought constantly.

Tian's journey into activism involved her own fanshen, or liberation, from abused child bride to Youth League director.[31] Through this process, and the work she was assigned to do as a women's representative, Tian developed a strong critique of feudal forms of hierarchical domination. The post-1949 emergence of "woman," or funü, as liberated state subject (Barlow 2004) was anticipated by Tian's own resistance to familial forms of oppression at the same time that funü was reincorporated back into new operations of power within the socialist household. Divorce would have produced a major disruption at a time when household harmony was rapidly becoming the chief goal of women-work, one of the jobs for which Tian was also responsible.[32] It is in this light that Tian's own preference for Youth League work and her description of herself as having a "boy's personality" becomes a little clearer. Whereas women-work kept Tian tied to the family, both in her own life and as a focus of her efforts with other women, the Youth League, the party, and the army offered a form of liberation unencumbered by these concerns.[33]

Tian's decision to stay in her marriage echoes the desire of women, and women activists and cadres in particular, to be perceived as "virtuous" or "good" as they traveled between natal and marital home and between household and the public stage. At the time of her visit back to Kunming, Tian had already been working as a women's representative for three years and was intimately familiar with the Marriage Law, especially as it pertained to women in her situation—a mistreated former child bride. Even though her parents tried to persuade her that it was her obligation to leave the marriage, and even though Tian felt like she could have financially afforded a separation, she never "brought it up" because of her earlier promise not to bring shame on her parents by being a "bad daughter."[34] This logic of virtue would mirror that of former Wenhe Commune leader, Yuan Jinyu, 158, who refused to divorce her husband despite the support of local party authorities and her own father who advised her not to "straddle two boats." When Yuan's mother-in-law locked her out of the house on her late return from meetings, Yuan simply went home to her natal family, who lived "seven doors away," or to the home of another woman model worker. If anyone gossiped about her, she had a witness: "My best condition was that my natal family was in the same village, because I had a place to eat anyway [if my husband's family did not want me]."

In Tian's world, and in the world of Yuan hundreds of kilometers away, the Marriage Law emerged as a fulcrum through which notions of virtue, domestic harmony, and filiality were rearticulated and expressed as central to the emergence of the new socialist family. If Tian and Yuan had chosen to divorce, they would have rendered themselves more vulnerable to accusations of impropriety than if they stayed in unhappy marriages. In this way, and many others, the Marriage Law materialized as an attached enactment of a state capable of producing new expressions of liberation and compliance. Indeed, as local women activists and leaders struggled to understand and implement the Marriage Law through the relationships that most defined them, the law's effect as an expression of state power was also realized—with complex outcomes for themselves and the women they led.

Deng Yingchao's determination to direct the highly controversial and protracted writing of the 1950 Marriage Law built on numerous official appointments and informal ties within the CCP and government to achieve the marriage reform she sought: a law that included one-party petition divorce. But Deng's work on the Marriage Law would meet with extraordinary resistance from within the party and the ACDWF, and violence from those at the grassroots who were opposed to divorce. In the end, the millions of divorces granted to women during the first years of the PRC were only a fraction of those likely sought. Deng Yingchao's early triumph was thus overshadowed by these developments and by the consequent decision to deter divorce.

If one considers the Marriage Law as a tool by which violence against women could be eliminated, through which wives and husbands could become "equals," and through which the "harmonious" socialist family might begin to take shape, we see how these at times contradictory goals thus led to deeply uneven outcomes. There is no question that the specter of divorce haunted local implementation: when the Marriage Law was first introduced, for example, it both emboldened women to attempt to leave unwanted marriages and terrified and infuriated in-laws at risk of losing what they considered a familial investment. Given the lack of clear directives and a revolutionary field marked by male leaders whose own practices defied the spirit of the law, it is thus remarkable that some former soldiers and male cadres were in fact confronted for beating their wives.[35] But it is also true that the capacity of rural women to leave unhappy and violent marriages was seriously hampered by the revolutionary agency of the women leaders tasked with resolving familial conflict. Indeed, as the directives shifted over 1953 and 1954, the Marriage Law may have continued to enable greater freedoms in marriage choice, but when it came to marital dissolution at the local level, the law simultaneously became an instrument of repression. By gatekeeping familial decorum and respectability, local women's heads extended the state's capacity to surveil and manage family relationships.

The efficacy of new institutions with a gender reform mandate can become mitigated by the reinscription of gender norms and relations, "as the authoritative ways in which politics . . . is understood and done" (Mackay 2014, 556). Although elite reformers were able to achieve rapid breakthroughs in the less controversial project of midwifery reform, their efforts were vulnerable to the operation of male homosocial capital as it was enacted in opposition to marriage reform. They were also vulnerable to the objections of senior women officials frightened of losing their husbands to younger, urban wives, and vulnerable to the work of local women's heads whose mandate shifted from enabling divorce to prohibiting it. As different state and party actors contended with the institutional ambiguities (Mackay 2014, 556) of the ACDWF and its relationship to the CCP over the course of the 1950s, the efficacy of the maternalist reform agenda began to recede. For while the Marriage Law opened up new possibilities to enact and contest family ties, its implementation simultaneously contributed to the normalization of relational repression in women-work. Ultimately, the backlash against the implementation of the 1950 Marriage Law compromised the efforts of the Chongqing Coalition to further pursue an agenda of marriages chosen and maintained on the basis of love. Of particular note is the decreasing visibility of Deng Yingchao as a policy champion of women, a development that would run parallel to Cai Chang's increasing visibility as an advocate of the frugal household. As I will show in the chapters that follow, the attached tactics used in divorce suppression would materialize in the urgent push to capture the harvest, while intensifying pressure on household management. Within a few short years, these and other political developments would profoundly complicate the capacity of the maternalist social policy regime to promote, much less protect, the health and welfare of women and children, even as it simultaneously contributed to the state's increasing capacity to surveil and control the socialist household.

HOUSEHOLD MANAGERS

**China's women are a vast reserve of working power. This reserve
should be tapped and used in the struggle to build a mighty socialist
country.**

—Mao Zedong, "Women Joining in Production Solve the Labor Shortage"

**Managing the country is like [managing] family life: it requires
careful and comprehensive planning.**

—Cai Chang, "Be hardworking and thrifty, overcome obstacles, and support the
building of the country"

In the spring of 1957, Li Fuchun, Cai Chang's husband and chairman of the State
Planning Commission, and Bo Yibo, head of the State Economic Commission,
conducted a major inspection tour of Xi'an, Chengdu, and Chongqing. Over
the course of May, the two visited revolutionary sites in Xi'an (Dong, Cai, and
Tan 1992, 308), with Bo Yibo redeploying the Yan'an era slogan of "self-reliance"
(*ziligengsheng*) while they were in Chengdu (Bachman 1991, 122). By focusing
on building smaller and medium-size enterprises, Bo argued that China could
produce more, faster (Bachman 1991, 122).[1]

The trip, and its connection to the origins of the GLF, has been subject to
contested interpretations. Bachman (1991, 121–25), for example, argues that Li
and Bo's 1957 policy "blitz" (121) was a "brilliant political achievement" which
established the basic framework for the GLF (125–26). In his analysis, Bachman
argues that Li and Bo acted as a bureaucratic coalition, shaped in the context of
their organizational roles as planners. Teiwes and Sun (1999) and Chan (2001),
by way of contrast, draw on different sources to largely dismiss Bachman's institutionalist explanation. Instead, they argue that most CCP leaders, including Li
Fuchun and Bo Yibo, were swept along by the Chairman: "[The GLF] was a case
of the whole Party following Mao" (Teiwes and Sun 1999, 54).

In this chapter, I offer an alternative understanding of the trip and its relationship to the politics of the GLF, the 1958–60 mobilization to communize
the countryside, and the capacity of the PRC to control the harvest. Neither the
product of one man's utopic dreams nor the advocacy of one coalition, the GLF
took shape through contending revolutionary attachments that placed Mao at

the center of struggle. And chief among those contending was Cai Chang, Mao's "younger sister," the chair of the ACDWF, and the most senior woman in the CCP.

Prior to 1956, Cai Chang spoke at major events and weighed in on important matters but otherwise left the day-to-day management of the Women's Federation to Zhang Yun, vice chair of the ACDWF (Su 1990, 226). Cai's relative inactivity may have been due, in part, to illness: Cai Chang was treated for health issues in the Soviet Union between August 1952 and June 1953 (Su 1990, 226; Dong, Cai, and Tan 1992, 300).[2] Cai's inactivity may have also been due to her wariness of the more overt feminism of the Chongqing Coalition ascendant during the first years of the PRC. Nonetheless, 1956 proved a turning point. In September, Cai Chang (1956 [1988]) gave a speech at the CCP's Eighth National Congress in which she drew attention to the need to train and promote more women cadres. Among factors challenging the capacity of women to advance included the discrimination women faced from male leaders (a remnant of patriarchal ideology, she said) and the ongoing conflict between the household and work responsibilities of women cadres. While this speech could be interpreted as an endorsement of women's leadership for women's sake, Cai Chang was, in fact, doing what former Women's Federation official, Li Baoguang (1992, 75) suggests Cai Chang always did, which was to properly locate women-work within the overall situation of Central Committee policy. The CCP needed to cultivate women cadres who were both virtuous (committed to CCP ideology) and talented (a recipient of formal education) (de cai jianbei) to strengthen the capacity of socialist construction as it was being redefined by Mao Zedong and the CCP at that historical moment.[3]

In 1956, alongside her husband, Li Fuchun, who was simultaneously seeking to speed up and localize economic development, Cai Chang began to repurpose an urban housework campaign into a national wartime vision of household austerity: "Diligently, frugally build the country, and diligently, frugally manage the family" (the "double diligences") (qinjian jianguo, qinjian chijia). Between late 1956 and 1959, Cai Chang and Li Fuchun worked across their organizations to mobilize households, fields, and factories to fulfill Mao's dream of rapid and frugal development. As part of this larger effort, Cai Chang not only participated in the May 1957 trip to Xi'an, Chengdu, and Chongqing (Dong, Cai, and Tan 1992, 308), but she followed it up with a call for austerity among youth that harkened back to the Yan'an era (Cai 1957).

By reading the work of Cai Chang and Li Fuchun side by side, the couple's cross-cutting policy innovations, and the revolutionary attachments that undergird them, become legible for the first time. Cai-Li's companionate policy making can be understood as coalitional: the couple was deeply invested in the organizational protection and promotion of the Women's Federation, particularly during 1958 when both household and federation would come under attack. And yet, Cai and Li's motives for doing so flowed directly out of their long-standing and close relationship with the Chairman. As Mao's most loyal soldiers, the couple sought to achieve rapid and intensive economic construction by building on Mao Zedong and Cai Chang's earlier collaborations in Yan'an. While Cai Chang was always committed to the welfare of funü, her first commitment was to the task of socialist construction as it was defined and led by Mao Zedong.

Ever since Mao and Cai led the work on the 1943 Resolution, the household had served as an important unit of economic production in the emerging socialist economy. After the foundation of the PRC, the CCP's attempts to harness the resources of rural households for state coffers was activated, in part, through local women's heads. Armed with intimate knowledge produced through other forms of women-work, including midwifery reform and the Marriage Law, local women's heads were in a prime position to increase the state's capacity to control the harvest. Indeed, local women leaders extracted grain from households in much the same way that they worked to keep women in unhappy and violent marriages: through intensive ideological work forged through family and community ties.

Efforts to control the harvest would intensify further under collectivization. Beginning in the mid-1950s, women's labor became an increasingly important feature of the rural economy (Gao Xiaoxian 2006; Hershatter 2011; Thorborg 1978). With the commencement of collectivization, household land ownership was rapidly phased out, a change that compelled the majority of working adults, including women, to "work to eat," or be allocated points for field work that could be redeemed in the form of grain. While collectivization granted the state direct access to the harvest, and thus all but eliminated household procurement, it placed new pressures on women householders already responsible for childcare and housework. It is at this fraught moment that Cai Chang and Li Fuchun's companionate work on the double diligences began in earnest.

The adoption of the double diligences agenda has been variously interpreted as a response to conservative economic policy (Johnson 1983, 160) and as a strategic maneuver to maintain the legitimacy of the ACDWF in the face of critique (Wang 2017, 54–77). In this chapter, I argue that Cai Chang's advocacy of the double diligences was part of a larger effort to centralize austerity generally, and household frugality specifically, in economic policy. By championing the double diligences, Cai Chang put her own stamp on the Marxist maternalist equality that had defined the maternalist social policy regime since the foundation of the PRC, placing renewed focus on the economic role of the household in socialist construction.

The wartime ethos undergirding the double diligences would be further underscored by the launch of a new rectification campaign designed to weed out anticommunist elements among the intelligentsia, the CCP, and society at large. Unfolding throughout the summer and fall of 1957, the Anti-Rightist Movement impacted the lives of more than 550,000 people (Teiwes 1993, 82), unleashing a powerful critique of the Women's Federation from within the CCP and from within the federation itself. As Wang (2017) argues, Cai Chang worked alongside Deng Yingchao and Deng Xiaoping to maintain the organizational integrity of the Women's Federation by upholding the double diligences. In light of Cai Chang's conception and promotion of the double diligences, however, I argue that this defensive move was also already central to Cai Chang's vision of the ACWF's emerging role in the state economy, with the socialist household at its heart. A "Total War" vision of rapid advance that was grounded in the experience of Yan'an, the double diligences served as a major plank of economic policy, rather than a reaction to it.

The fact that Cai Chang played a leading role in the implementation of the 1957 Anti-Rightist Movement within the Women's Federation further complicates her relationship to the double diligences, and the politics of the GLF that followed. As Wemheuer (2011) argues, the Anti-Rightist Movement—called the Socialist Education Movement in the countryside—made hunger an "ideological problem" by forcing cadres and farmers to undertake self-criticisms for "pretending to be hungry."[4] As I will show, the double diligences compounded the politicization of hunger at the rural grassroots. Indeed, the double diligences rendered household managers increasingly vulnerable to the deadly intensification of state surveillance and deprivation in the months leading up to the GLF.

The Attached Politics of Procurement

On July 31, 1955, Mao Zedong made his first major policy statement since 1949.[5] In a landmark speech, Mao called for an acceleration of collectivization that would eliminate household land ownership altogether. Central to the establishment of Mao's emerging vision for the countryside were the Higher-Stage Agricultural Producer Cooperatives (HAPCs), a form of universal collectivization in which ownership and management of land, animals, and tools was transferred to a party-run collective. Suddenly, farmers were no longer just accountable to and dependent on their immediate neighbors but to all the families inside their village as well; indeed, many of the newly established collectives were based on the village as the primary organizational unit (Friedman et al. 1991, 186–87).

The rapid acceleration of collectivization marked a sharp departure from the land reform movement, which had defined and organized political life in the countryside during the earliest years of the PRC. Land reform effectively provided hundreds of millions of farmers with the capacity to work their own land and thus become more self-sufficient. The idea, as Dong Biwu argued, was to provide farmers with the means to support themselves, both in the context of their households and in the form of mutual aid with members of their communities, rather than have farmers rely on the aid of foreign missions and government largesse (Bian and Wu 2006, 281–90).

As discussed in chapter 4, women's heads such as Zhang Sumei played an important role in mobilizing women to participate in field work as part of this effort. Indeed, Zhang Sumei, 20, began tending crops as a teenager, shortly after the arrival of the CCP in Huoyue. This was risky work: circulating gender norms forbade women from working alongside men who were not kin. Zhang proved so adept at cotton planting, however, that the brigade leaders made her a role model and instructor. Before long she was leading groups of women in the fields as part of the nascent mutual aid teams (MATs), or emergent teams in which farmers voluntarily agreed to share farm animals, tools, and labor.

As of October 1952, when Zhang was only three years into her tenure as a local activist and leader, it was estimated that 20–40 percent of rural women in Henan were participating in MATs (Shao 1984, 68). Women who engaged in field work served as powerful representatives of the liberated future. Indeed, the capacity of women to fanshen, flowed from their participation in remunerated labor. Young, laboring women also stood as a symbolic rebuke to an older generation of women who continued to labor from the confines of their courtyards, and/or whose physical capacities compromised their ability to participate fully in collective forms of field work.

Local women's heads were not only mobilizing women to participate in field work; they were also reorganizing the work of household management. Indeed, several household activities were now recognized as nodes of production that contributed to familial survival. Since the promulgation of the 1943 Resolution, local party organizations had largely sought to involve women householders in "sideline" production: household gardening, the raising of livestock, supplemental weaving, and other forms of activities associated with the inner courtyard. Depending on the region, the time of year, family size and composition, and a whole other range of factors, women could be found engaged in any number of activities which contributed to the well-being of their household and communities. Although much of this work, such as weaving, for example, took place "inside" domestic spaces such as courtyards and homes, other work took place outside of the family courtyard. Women from particularly impoverished households were often engaged in subsistence activities that included gathering firewood, searching for wild edibles, tending family plots, collecting manure, and caring for livestock.[6]

In calls reminiscent of GMD-occupied China and base area organizing during the war with Japan, local Women's Federations increasingly involved women in planning for the growth and consumption of household crops.[7] In the early 1950s, for example, the Wenhe Women's Federation exhorted women to help ward off the very real possibility of crop failure by actively developing "household production plans."[8] The Gaoshan Women's Federation also encouraged women to economize alongside efforts to increase production, participate in land reform, oppose counter-revolutionaries, and protect the rights of women and children (*GX* 1994, 634).[9]

The concept of dangjia is distinct from the authority invested in the *jiazhang*, or household head. According to a former Gaoshan Commune accountant Chi Meiying, 115, for example, to "dangjia" meant that the wife took care of detailed inside things, while the husband took care of outside things, and that they discussed and took decisions on big matters together. Indeed, whereas to dangjia indicates responsibility for management of household affairs, the jiazhang represents the family to the outside world.[10] But the concept of dangjia would come to mean much more than household management. It would also come to symbolize a new, domesticated path to realizing women's liberation.

In Deng Yingchao's (1950 [1988], 175) reflections on the Marriage Law, she noted how in the past most rural women had no status in the household. According to Deng, the term *dang jia de*, or head of the household, was virtually synonymous with the word husband in some parts of China. In Deng's text she advocated that husbands and wives share home management, including care of the children. However, over the course of the 1950s, to dang jia de increasingly became a feminized status, assumed by the mother-in-law or daughter-in-law. The shifting of power relations within the household, from older generation to younger, and from men to women, coincided with development measures that relied on household financial austerity to address the problem of rural poverty. As household managers were increasingly being folded into the CCP's strategy for local survival, the very definition of "liberation" was being rewritten. Indeed, to *dang jia zuo zhu*, or to be master of one's house, had a strong revolutionary meaning: to be master of one's destiny. In the rural household where the master was replaced by the mistress, to dang jia zuo zhu offered a newly domesticated version of women's liberation.

Efforts by local Women's Federations to encourage the involvement of women in household budgets reinforced the importance of economic liberation outside of the home as well. In order to be truly free, women needed to be able to feed themselves and their families through remunerated labor in collective fields. But these early developments also indicate that local authorities approached women householders as a latent resource to offset, or at least mitigate, the perennial challenge of natural catastrophes. The ACDWF was increasingly adopting this view as well. In 1955, for example, the ACDWF instructed Women's Federations to advocate that "every woman in the family should plan carefully, improve cooking methods and adjust meals, so as to eat well and save food." Moreover, families with food shortages should adjust their planning "according to the ages of family members and the energy expended on labor" (ACWF 1955a [1999]). It is in this way that women began to interface in new ways with the state: in rare cases, as jiazhang with local party authorities, but more often as household managers in relationship with local women's heads.

At the same time the CCP was urging better economic management of households, they were also trying to extract more from households. In late 1953, the CCP imposed the Central Purchase and Central Supply System (*tonggou tongxiao,* CPCSS) in which farmers came under increasing pressure to participate in collectivization and commit larger and larger percentages of their yields to state coffers.[11] In the context of an insufficient grain supply (Perkins 1966, 42–55), the CPCSS made it impossible for farmers to sell their agricultural products to anyone but the state. Given that farmers received far less for their grain from the state than what they earned when they were still able to sell it in open county markets, the imposition of "forced procurements" and "hidden forms of taxation" meant that cultivators "increasingly lost control over the distribution of the harvest" (Oi 1989, 43–44).[12]

Women's heads served on the front lines of grain procurement, both as models of household contributions and agents of the state trying to convince women householders to sell their grain to state coffers. One young eager Gaoshan activist, for example, leveraged the resources of her natal family with nearly disastrous consequences: in the months prior to her entry into the CCP, Qiu Zhaodi, 74, "led the way" and sold all of the family's grain; with nothing left to eat, her mother had to borrow from neighbors. By way of contrast, Huoyue women's head Hou Qiuyi's, 132, natal family was destitute. In 1953, Hou's grain procurement practices focused on persuading fellow villagers to turn over their grain, through an emergent companionate activism with her husband: "My husband was very energetic and competitive. Around here, we were the famous grain collectors [*women zhe shi you ming de liangshi duo*], we both worked so hard, in shifts! We collected the surplus grain [*yu liang*], we collected it from house to house."

Hou's usage of the term *surplus* suggests that the state was merely taking what was not needed by the household; however, many households were, in fact, barely surviving in 1953. Indeed, just as Hou Qiuyi herself was still scrounging to feed her family well after the establishment of the PRC, the actual welfare of sub-sistence farmers only marginally improved over the course of the early 1950s. For instance, nationally, rural food grain consumption only increased from 192 kilograms per-person-per-year in 1952 to a high of 205 kilograms in 1958, before dropping precipitously to 154 kilograms in 1961 (Selden 1988, 18).[13] As Wem-heuer (2014, 86–87) shows, between 1950 and 1957 somewhere in the range of 20 to 69 million farmers "were affected by spring shortages every year." State-defined "surplus" thus fell far below international standards of what was actually needed for basic subsistence (Oi 1989, 44–49).[14] As Gaoshan women's head Fei Achun, 111, recalled, if the harvest was poor, families were left with nothing after they sold their grain to the state coffers. Implementing the CPCSS, she said, was the most challenging form of work she undertook in the early 1950s.

Hou Qiuyi understood the stakes, but insisted that the CCP was not taking everything, as she said at another point: "The party won't let you starve." Wom-en's heads such as Hou were thus struggling for semantic dominance among families already on the precipice of severe malnutrition. These semantic struggles would only intensify as the decade proceeded (Wemheuer 2011).

Hou Qiuyi's effort to procure household grain was not limited to discursive violence; it also included the threat of punishment. She continues:

> Some people didn't want to hand over the grain, and they swore to the cadres that they didn't have anything left but we didn't believe it. We weren't mistaken: if we said he had it, he must have had it. They hid grain in their house. In 1953, many were punished. Cadres without pure thoughts left their position. When it was the time of selling sur-plus grain we made [a cadre] sell 2900 *jin* [catties] [when] he said he didn't have it, but actually he had more than that. Later he was expelled from his cadre position and then afterward he couldn't become a cadre [again] for many years.

Hou's remarks point directly to the contradictory nature of local state power as it was taking shape during the early years of the PRC. On the one hand, when Hou asserted that grain was, in fact, hidden, she was speaking with the authority of the party-state. Establishing the truth was not open to competing visions of the pos-sible; rather it was determined by cadres who saw their authority flowing from correct positioning within party ideology and practice and who approached their tasks with military vigor.[15]

On the other hand, Hou simultaneously asserted that cadres were *not* always right. Indeed, in this recollection, a cadre was expelled from his position for hid-ing his own grain. Given the attention to cadre malfeasance at the grassroots that was underway during the time of the interview, Hou's remarks may have been intended as a critique on contemporary corruption. But Hou was likely also drawing attention to animosities directed toward lower-level cadres and their clients as they played out across the 1950s, 1960s, and 1970s. According to Oi (1989, 6), the struggle over the harvest during the collective period was mediated via the patron-client ties between brigade heads and team heads. A certain "rationality of collusion" (Oi 1989, 125) enabled both team heads and brigade leaders to maximize their interests:

> A team leader cultivated a relationship with the brigade leader to receive special consideration in matters such as allocating quotas, granting loans, procuring scarce goods, generally acquiring extra resources, and, equally important, regulating policy. Successful cultivation of this relationship increased the team leader's power within the team and made his job easier. In return, the team leader enthusiastically carried out his patron's directives, fulfilled demands for grain and labor, showed support in political campaigns, presented gifts, and gave him "face." (Oi 1989, 128)

Oi's description is consistent with farmers who commented that "those who had good relations with leaders didn't have to work as hard" and "the cadres chose [other leaders] who were close to them. They worked less and got more money" (Sun Suzhen, 14). Huang Lanfang, 28, and Deng Huazhen, 29, both team leaders and members of local party families in Zhang's village, were teased mercilessly in a group interview by some of their neighbors for the privileges they had accrued as a result of their positions and family status. The cynicism that permeated rural life may have prompted Hou to share this story as evidence of her own upright leadership, a claim she made a number of times during the interview.

Grain procurement was thus a semantic and physical exercise in violence that was shot through with informal ties. It was also deeply gendered. In a separate interview, Hou's cousin, Zhang Sumei, 20, recounted her own history with harvest extraction during the early 1950s:

> After I took over, [I] often went to town to participate in model meetings, I also went there to participate in cotton meetings. One time I [even] collected sorghum, at that time it was said that the sorghum would be sold abroad. You have no idea how hard it was! A male cadre and I went together to people's homes to measure the intake, to see which families had how much of a surplus. Oh, it was not easy to do this work! Every day, from morning until night, [we] were at people's homes persuading them, performing our task. One family of our own clan sold over 10,000 *jin* of grain. [We] gave him a big plaque to praise him.

When asked for further clarification she continued:

> [I was] urging wheat collection, leading the women to turn over the grain at home. I was only responsible for urging [wheat collection] in the households. After it had been turned in, there were people who specially took the [wheat] into town.

Zhang's comments here speak to the gendered nature of the household and its shifting positionality vis-à-vis the state. The awarding of a plaque to the head of a family in Zhang's clan reinforced the family as a corporate body in the socialist economic system, with a male head as its representative, or the position of jiazhang. At the same time, the local enactment of family reform was reorienting decision making within families—a shift local women leaders sought to model and leverage in their work. Given the intimate implementation of the Marriage Law and reproductive health reform, local women's heads were ideally positioned to participate in grain appropriation and to draw on and shape local discourses about the responsibility of the good householder to economize family resources. How these processes of reform impacted households depended greatly on many factors, including the social system of the local community; regardless, the impact was profound.[16]

Beginning in 1954, the CCP pressured farmers to join a new form of collective body known as Lower-Stage Agricultural Producer Cooperatives (LAPC). The LAPCs included twenty to fifty households and required all members to pool their animals, tools, and labor. Members were distributed basic grain rations according to individual need and effort. With each stage of collectivization, farmers found it increasingly difficult to avoid or to exit collectives if they later changed their mind. In 1955, for example, some 6,100 Wenhe households residing in four townships (or 98 percent of total households) joined collectives, following Mao Zedong's critique of the slow rate of collectivization, or the problem of "women with small feet."[17] When Mao called for rapidly deepening and expanding collectivization in summer 1956, farmers found themselves facing an offer they could not refuse (Liu Yu 2006).[18]

Households were also being reconfigured within the boundaries of the nation and state in other ways. On the one hand, new regulations guiding movement were pinning people to the regions, and often the villages, in which they were born. The *hukou*, or a population registration system, was instituted just prior to Mao's call to speed up collectivization, effectively limiting the capacity of households to move to urban areas and thus access jobs and benefits otherwise available to urbanites. As argued by Cheng and Selden (1994, 660–61), "By 1956, a many-faceted hukou system, complemented by grain rationing, compulsory grain sales and restrictions on migrant labour, produced a deep but not impermeable divide between urban and rural areas, between workers and collective farmers, between the state sector and the collective sector."

On the other hand, households in Henan were simultaneously being encouraged to move West as part of a program of organized settlement of the "frontier." In Huoyue, for example, 2,069 households (a total of 8,028 people) emigrated to Qinghai and Gansu in 1956 (*HX* 1993, 31). Women's Head Liu Yuezhen, 10, wanted to move her household to Xinjiang, another region targeted as part of the resettlement, but her husband refused on the basis of the poor health of his mother. According to Bao Qinglian, 160, who spent a year in Qinghai with her mother toward the end of the GLF, both youth and women were organized to undertake these militant exercises in national expansion. Bao and her mother were determined to live up to the motto of the moment: "Born in Henan, die in Qinghai."[19]

It is in the context of this rapid economic and spatial reconfiguration that the vast majority of rural, married women found themselves commissioned to simultaneously serve in two capacities: as household managers and as fieldworkers. Between 1955 and 1956, the percentage of women working in collective field work had increased from 40–55 percent to 60–70 percent (Thorborg 1978, 592). In Jiangsu, the percentage of women working in the spring and summer increased 30–40 percent over previous years (Lu and Miao 2000, 215). It is not just that women participated alongside men; in some regions the production of certain crops was feminized. In Shaanxi, for example, women began to assume almost exclusive responsibility for the cotton harvest during this period (Gao Xiaoxian 2006).

As individuals joined collective structures, women's heads became responsible for organizing and leading women's work teams. Liu Yuezhen, 10, a former Huoyue women's head, remembers that her work with women became increasingly challenging after the establishment of the LAPC's: "Women had to work every day, [there was] no time off, not even during Spring Festival; [they] hauled manure, pulled the grinding stone, dragged soil, and put earth in the cow sheds. All this was done with pull carts. It was like this every day with no spare time. Not like today when there's nothing to do during the slow seasons of farming."

As discussed in chapter 5, women's heads were also expected to take care of the health needs of women, including assigning menstruating, pregnant, and lactating women to work that was light, dry, and close by, and to continue the work of mediation within conflict-ridden households. This was a challenge: according to one investigation of twenty-four villages undertaken in Huoyue in early 1957, more than a year before the GLF began, twenty women were injured, nine women suffered from menstrual disease, fifteen women suffered miscarriages, and sixty-two women had experienced uterine prolapse.[20]

But one of the biggest challenges was the need to establish collective child-care services where almost none existed. Indeed, although Liu Shaoqi had identified childcare, alongside marriage and midwifery reform, as a priority for the Women's Federation at the outset of the establishment of the PRC (Luo 1998b [2000], 26; see chapter 2), by 1956 very little rural childcare infrastructure had been developed. Insufficient provision of childcare meant that women with young children were often caught in the dilemma of "having to work to eat" or risk political censure and malnutrition by staying home with their children.

In Huoyue, Wenhe, and Gaoshan, collective childcare was largely undertaken by untrained local women with little support from village authorities. Because the services were so uneven and difficult to access, many parents relied on the assistance of elderly relatives or older daughters to care for younger children.[21] When older children, in-laws, or parents were unavailable, some parents left their children alone to fend for themselves. During the summer of 1956, some 12,281 Gaoshan children were placed in childcare or kindergarten, whereas 17,200 were looked after by relatives and neighbors; a remaining 7,313 children, however, lacked any kind of "collective" care altogether.[22] Accidental injury and death among children was not uncommon: more than 130 unsupervised children drowned in 1956.[23] Accidents in Huoyue and Wenhe County similarly led to the death of children.[24] In the words of former Huoyue farmer Yuan Lei, 136, "At that time children suffered too much, [they were] not like human children at all. When we went to the fields, we just had to set them aside . . . there was no one to look after them. [We] didn't know where they all got to."

As collectivization intensified, and the safety and health of women and children became increasingly compromised, the Women's Federation leadership made repeated calls for restraint in women's mobilizations and for attention to the provision of women's healthcare and childcare, especially during peak planting and harvest seasons. In June 1956, for example, Deng Yingchao, urged that the collective mobilizations better protect women and children by keeping in mind the "specific" characteristics of women's physiology and the ongoing realities of housework (Deng 1956 [1988], 279). Although Cai Chang and other senior ACWF officials encouraged men to help women with housework, they expected women to shoulder most of the work that remained in the home.[25] Childcare continued to remain an unfunded mandate and was, therefore, more often than not ignored or only implemented with half-hearted measures.

By late 1956, the strains of the socialist upsurge were beginning to show. But at the very moment that women were struggling to find ways to care for their children, provide meals, sew and mend clothing while simultaneously working

long days in the collective fields, Cai Chang sought to add an additional responsibility onto their plates: the burden of further economizing already constrained
household budgets.

Revolutionary Household Management: The Double Diligences

In a 1951 speech published in the *People's Daily*, Cai Chang (1951 [1988], 105–7)
warned grassroots activists against "leftist" tendencies to liberate women that
involved mobilizing women to cut their hair or leave their family, and in which
daughters-in-law struggled with their mothers-in-law and wives with their husbands. The consequence, she argued, was to create chaos among the peasants.
Instead, Cai Chang argued, the goal of mobilizing women should be consistent
with the policies and methods established in the 1943 Resolution. Five years later,
Cai Chang would seek to recenter the domestic roles of women in socialist construction, much as she had in 1943.

Cai Chang first began to mobilize around the double diligences in the wake
of a speech Mao gave to the Second Plenum of the Eighth Central Committee
in the fall of 1956 (Su 1990, 182).[26] Mao had identified the need for thrifty collectives and households as early as October 1955—an idea that was given greater
credence in "The Debate Over Agricultural Cooperativization and the Present
Class Struggle" (Mao 1955 [1986], 645). Although the Central Committee issued
a "Joint Directive Concerning Running Cooperatives Diligently and Frugally" in
April 1956, analyses of "waste" as originating in the collective *and* the household
only began to be heeded in earnest in the wake of Mao's talk at the Second Plenum in late 1956. One of Mao's (1956 [1992], 162) criticisms in his November
talk was that newspaper propaganda was placing too much emphasis on improving the people's livelihood in a "one-sided and unrealistic manner" and not giving enough attention to diligence and frugality.

Mao's remarks came at a moment when his push for rapid collectivization and
industrialization had come under fire within the party, and as the economy itself
ran into problems. At its heart, collectivization was an extensive growth strategy that Mao conceived "as a resource mobilizing vehicle for expanding physical
output as required by the industrialization imperative" (Kueh 2006, 709). In the
midst of an economic contraction, when several high-level leaders urged a slow-
down of the pace of development over the winter of 1956–57, Li Fuchun proved
himself to be one of the Chairman's most steadfast supporters (Teiwes and Sun
1999, 27). Unlike Zhou Enlai, for example, who opposed "rash advance" (*fan
maojin*), Li Fuchun "would not express a dissenting opinion" to Mao (Teiwes

and Sun 1999, 50). Instead, Li Fuchun embraced Yan'an values, which by the fall of 1956, were considered "old-fashioned and inappropriate" (Bachman 1991, 138), and alongside Cai Chang, championed them as a solution to the country's economic woes.

As noted in the introduction, the Cai-Li marriage did not project the same aura of uprightness as did that of the Deng-Zhou marriage. But rumors of infidelity, such as they were, did not nullify the real policy and political cooperation that transpired in Yan'an and that would activate again during the latter half of the 1950s. At a time when high-level leaders worked months at a time apart from their spouses, Cai Chang's ten months of medical treatment in the USSR coincided with period in which Li Fuchun was also in the USSR, completing work on the First Five Year Plan (Bachman 1991, 104). Li Fuchun also remained active in women-work. Cai Chang teasingly referred to Li Fuchun as the "son-in-law" of the Women's Federation, with Li Fuchun frequently weighing in on the work of the Women's Federation and sometimes revising drafts of documents on Cai's behalf (Cai Asong 1992b, 189–90). But Li Fuchun needed his wife's support as much as she needed his. Given Cai Chang's long-standing familial relationship with Mao Zedong, she was in a prime position to discern and support the Chairman's vision for the development of the country.[27]

Li Fuchun and Cai Chang were both early promoters of the principle of economy (thriftiness) in socialist construction. According to Bo Yibo (1979 [2002], 115; 1980 [2002], 279), Zhou Enlai proposed in 1956 that industry develop on the basis of the slogan: "duo, kuai, hao" (more, faster, better), which Mao Zedong enthusiastically adopted. After further discussion, Li Fuchun added the word *sheng* (economical), an emphasis that Mao had been making since 1955 when he began to call for diligence and frugality in development. Ultimately, the slogan "more, faster, better, economical" became the general line of the GLF: "Develop all of your energy, strive for the upper reaches, and establish socialism as quickly, efficiently, and economically as possible" (*gu zu ganjing, lizheng shangyou, duo kuai hao sheng di she shehui zhuyi*) (Bo 1979 [2002], 115).

From the outset, Cai Chang linked Mao's emerging attention to thrift to two important themes: scientific household management and wartime sacrifice. The ACDWF had been extolling scientific household management since at least 1952, when the leadership began to train the wives of workers to establish "Five Goods Families," or supportive homes for their husbands by ensuring they ate and rested enough, maintained good relations with their comrades, and improved their hygiene and studies (Ren 1989, 313–14).[28] In late November and December 1956 in one of her first public speeches on thrift, Cai instructed Five Goods activists to prioritize the double diligences as part of this work (Dong, Cai, and Tan 1992, 306–7). Not long after, Luo Qiong argued that the most urgent issues facing socialist construction not only included raising ideological consciousness and strengthening unity, but also to "diligently and thriftily manage the country, diligently and thriftily manage the family, and make a great effort to increase savings" (Luo 1957 [1988], 277; Yang 1991, 92)—a clear signal that the double diligences was emerging as an important area of focus for the federation. Not insignificantly, the ACDWF, the All-China Federation of Trade Unions (ACFTU), and other mass organizations made the double diligences the 1957 theme for March Eighth celebrations (Yang 1991, 94). The Jiangsu Women's Federation records include the 1957 notification in the province's annual history as well (Lu and Miao 2000, 249), further suggesting the increasing importance of the double diligences at this time. Lower levels of the Women's Federation correspondingly took notice: in April 1957, for example, the Gaoshan Women's Federation meted out the following criticism: "If everyone relies on the collective and on the state, no one will think to save, what do you think will happen? Will it be possible to establish socialism under these circumstances?"[29]

By the time Cai Chang, Li Fuchun, and Bo Yibo traveled together in the spring of 1957, Cai Chang and other senior officials in the Women's Federation had spent more than six months propagating austerity. Toward the end of the trip, on May 9, the *Sichuan Daily* published remarks that Cai Chang (1957) gave to the Sichuan Youth Federation. In her speech, "Arduous Struggle, Hard Work, and Thriftiness," Cai Chang could not have been clearer regarding the direction of the economic development of the country: "The policy of how we build the country is through hard work and thrift, it is also our path of construction."

Cai Chang was able to mobilize her effort much in the same way that the Chongqing Coalition had been able to mobilize its earlier efforts—that is, by leveraging multiple leadership appointments simultaneously. Indeed, among other positions, Cai Chang served concurrently as the chair of the ACDWF and as the director of the Women Workers Department of the ACFTU. In the days that followed, Cai Chang participated in a joint ACDWF-ACFTU Spousal Representative Conference, in which she called on participants to uphold the double diligences and to implement the Five Goods in order to aid the country to overcome difficulty and assist in national construction (Su 1990, 183–84). Over the nine-day meeting, delegates discussed the relationship between women's liberation and the much less popular occupation of housework. On June 12, Cai Chang responded to demands for employment and complaints about housework by arguing that housework was a form of work that supported socialist construction. Indeed, she argued, the wives of peasants and craftsmen who engaged in housework were no longer doing so simply for the sake of their individual families; rather, they were contributing to society as a whole. In order to gradually produce more steel and fertilizer, in order to expand water conservation projects, and produce more light industrial raw materials, including cloth, oil, sugar, and paper products, Cai Chang argued, it was necessary to practice thrift and austerity (Cai 1957 [1988], 298–99).

Cai Chang's arguments were in lock step with those of Li Fuchun and Bo Yibo. In a report sent to Mao after the conclusion of their spring trip, Li Fuchun and Bo Yibo urged an economic approach that proceeded from the current situation of the country, avoided comparison with foreign technology, that embraced small enterprises, and that above all, was grounded in thrift and diligence. Bo Yibo and Li Fuchun also expressed concern over the limited capacity to house the family members of workers (Li and Bo 1957 [1992], 194). Cai Chang would note the same challenge for housing in her remarks to spouses a month later (Cai 1957 [1988], 298).

It is in this context that the Five Goods family was redefined in accordance with the double diligences slogan and was expanded to include urban and rural working women and housewives. Echoing the WCTU's 1922 priorities discussed in chapter 1, and the work of wartime home economists discussed in chapter 3, to be a Five Goods family now meant to diligently and thriftily manage the family, mutually unite, educate the children, maintain hygiene, and study with dedication (Yang 1991, 98; Su 1990, 184).[30]

Cai Chang built her vision of the household manager directly on the Total War model of economic development that she had first championed in Yan'an in 1943, and that continued to inform local efforts to organize women. As discussed in chapter 3, Total War mobilized women to support the war effort on the home front through judicious planning of household budgets, thrifty spending and consumption, self-reliance, and military recruitment. The fact that the PRC had been engaged in and/or preparing for war since its foundation, only intensified earlier experiments with the model. Indeed, the outbreak of war on the Korean Peninsula in 1950 contributed to a besieged mentality, which, in turn, resulted in the placation of the military, as is evident in modifications to the Marriage Law, and military recruitment drives through the family members of women householders. The double diligences thus reflected the revolutionary imaginary embedded in the CCP's earlier war with Japan, as well as ongoing mobilizations that placed households on a wartime footing.

Mao Zedong himself extolled thrifty families as patriotic, a message that reinforced Mao's voluntarist vision to rapidly develop the Chinese economy through hardship and sacrifice, as so many party members and revolutionary martyrs had done before. In Mao's speech at the Second Plenum of the Eighth Central Committee in 1956, for example, Mao called on the CCP's revolutionary heritage to encourage practices of economic sacrifice:

> The comrades have suggested that directors of factories and principles of schools can sleep in huts. I think that would be a good idea, especially

in times of difficulty. On our Long March, when we crossed the marsh-lands, there were no houses at all, and we just slept [without them]. Commander-in-Chief Zhu walked forty days to cross the marshlands, and even he slept in that way; and we all made it. When our troops had nothing to eat, they ate the bark and leaves off trees, and they shared weal and woe with the people. This is what we did in the past; why can't we do it now? So long as we do things in this way, we will not be divorced from the masses. (Mao 1956 [1992], 162)

Xu Guangping, the former lover and comrade-in-arms of one of China's great-est modern writers, Lu Xun, similarly reinforced the wartime imaginary dur-ing her International Women's Day Address in March 1957. In a speech largely devoted to extolling the double diligences, Xu reminded her audience of the past wartime sacrifices of women, including sending husbands to the military, tilling the land, making clothing for the army, and economizing household consump-tion. During this peaceful period, she argued, women once again needed to con-tinue the tradition of family frugality to ensure the happiness and well-being of all (Xu 1957 [1999]).[31] In separate talks in May and June, both Shuai Mengqi and Cai Chang also linked the emerging focus on austerity with the CCP's war-time and revolutionary past. Shuai Mengqi, for example, spoke at length about the sacrifices women party members had made fighting the Japanese and the Guomindang, struggling through the Long March and suffering hardship in Yan'an (Shuai 1957 [1988], 288–91). When Cai Chang addressed housewives in June, she made a similar equation: "Relatives of revolutionary martyrs have suf-fered so much for the cause of the liberation of the people; they forsook their parents, wives, and children, and sacrificed their lives, this little bit of difficulty is nothing [in comparison]" (Cai 1957 [1988], 299).

The intensive work on the double diligences was amplified, in turn, by Mao. A month after Mao Zedong, Liu Shaoqi, Zhu De, Zhou Enlai and other senior leaders received the delegates at the June housewives meeting (Yang 1991, 98), Mao Zedong issued his clearest statement yet on the importance of thrifty house-holds: "We must advocate diligence and thrift, [as we] organize the collectives and build the country. Our country must be (1) diligent, and (2) thrifty. Don't be lazy and don't be too prosperous. Lazy is bad, it's not good. To resolve the issue of diligently and frugally managing the family [we should] chiefly rely on women's groups to do such work" (Mao 1957 [1992], 656–57).

In the meantime, Li Fuchun spent much of the summer working with other leaders of the State Planning Commission and the heads of various ministries to conduct research in preparation for the second Five Year Plan. In a report Li Fuc-hun gave early that fall, he discussed the challenges of a large population, limited arable land, and a weak economic infrastructure. Among his recommendations, which included the simultaneous development of industry and agriculture, he also stressed the importance of the double diligences: "The policies of building the country through diligence and thrift, and managing the family through diligence and thrift, must be implemented in an all-round way, so that increasing production and saving will become a social ethos and a regular system" (Fang and Jin 2001, 497). What had begun as a directive issued by Mao Zedong to pay attention to thrift had thus deepened under the attentive work of Cai Chang and the parallel, overlapping efforts of Li Fuchun and Bo Yibo. But Li Fuchun's recommendations that autumn likely reflected an additional development, and that is: the onset of the Anti-Rightist Movement.

The Anti-Rightist Movement

Some six weeks prior to the convening of the ACDWF-ACFTU Spousal Representative Conference, Mao launched the Anti-Rightist Movement. Deeply angered by an outpouring of criticism voiced by intellectuals in the spring of 1957, Mao conceived of the anti-rightist campaign as a means of clamping down on dissent. Once again, Cai Chang rose to the defense of the Chairman, this time leading the initial rectification of the senior leadership of the Women's Federation in three consecutive meetings of the CCWMC and the ACDWF Party Group during the week of May 31–June 6, 1957 (Yang 1991, 97). Kang Keqing (1993, 440–45) served as vice chair of the Rectification Movement Subcommittee and was made responsible for the ACDWF Rectification Movement Office.[32] Deng Yingchao was also present during the meetings. At the conclusion of the internal rectification process, Deng Yingchao is reported to have said, "Everyone's criticisms are mostly good, and have really helped the rectification" (Wang 1990, 75).[33] Nonetheless, it would appear that Cai Chang was in charge of rectifying the women's movement at this critical juncture.

Ultimately, a total of seven senior Women's Federation cadres, including Ding Ling and Liu-Wang Liming, were vilified and labeled "rightists" (Zhang 1996, 252). The singling out of Ding Ling was not surprising. As discussed in chapter 3, Cai Chang had previously made Ding Ling into a poster child of rightist feminism during the first rectification movement in Yan'an.[34] The 1957 attack would have far worse consequences: indeed, Ding Ling lost her party membership and spent most of the next twenty years either engaged in labor reform or isolated in prison. Although her rightist label was repealed in 1978, she was not fully rehabilitated within the party until 1984 (Feuerwerker 2003).

In some ways, however, the attack on Liu-Wang Liming was more surprising. Although Liu-Wang had long been regarded with suspicion by the

ACDWF Party Group (Lead Party Group of the ACDWF 1953), Cai Chang (1947b [1988], 105) had publicly defended her in the past.[35] Liu-Wang had also recently attended the Tenth Conference of the International Women's Christian Temperance Union.[36] But as was the case with Ding Ling, Liu-Wang's past was ultimately held against her. Specifically, Liu-Wang's pre-1949 work with women was brought under scrutiny, as was her attempt to establish a branch office of the WCTU in Chengdu in 1956 (Zhang 1996, 254). In the aftermath of the Anti-Rightist Movement, Liu-Wang became persona non grata, and within a year the WCTU was disbanded. By 1958, only one of the three independent founding women's organizations of the Women's Federation, the YWCA, was still operating.

It was not just the WCTU that was compromised, however; the ACWF itself was in danger of being shuttered as well. In fall of 1956, Cai Chang had pushed back against efforts by male-dominated city committees to weaken urban women's committees (Wang 2017, 30–53).[37] But the attacks were not only emanating from a male-dominated party power structure; they were also materializing within the grassroots of the Women's Federation itself. Collectivization had rapidly increased the demands placed on local women's heads, leading to exhaustion, resentment, and burnout. Moreover, the distaste for women-work that materialized in Yan'an seemingly intensified alongside collectivization, with some rural women leaders refusing to do women-work altogether. The fact that in 1954 local authorities in Wenhe expected the county's Women's Committee to carry out their work as the party committee's "assistant," likely further diminished the efficacy and attractiveness of local women's organizing.[38] Given the challenges inherent in undertaking women-work at this time, it is not surprising that some women were not interested in serving as women's heads or, if they were already active, wanted to quit. A county-level report describes these challenges as they materialized in Wenhe in the spring of 1957:

> [Some] think that women-work is degrading, not glorious, and that it has no future. There is no way, they think, that they will ever be able to achieve anything and that it is not as good as Youth League work. When some comrades come to the county to attend meetings, they don't even bother to go to the Women's Federation. There are also some other cadres who have a self-satisfied and arrogant approach to production. They think that all that matters is their own ability and don't bother to try and learn from others. . . . There are some who think that the Women's Federation should simply be disbanded or that it should be amalgamated with other departments. Everyone criticized these ideological errors

and agreed that right now women have not yet been thoroughly eman-
cipated, that women-work will require many years of bitter struggle;
and they [also] criticized women who are not willing to do women-
work for forgetting their own past suffering.[39]

These were significant challenges, but with the onset of the Anti-Rightist Movement the stakes were raised even higher: indeed, the Women's Federation faced
the threat of outright dissolution.

When Mao launched the Anti-Rightist Movement, the ACDWF plunged into
a flurry of self-examination. It would prove to be a period of extreme disorien-
tation. Internal debate abounded as to how best to prepare the ACDWF Work
Report to the Secretariat of the CCP in preparation for its Third National Wom-
en's Assembly, scheduled to take place in September 1957. Only after a series
of meetings did it finally become clear that the ACDWF could not discuss its
efforts to achieve "women's equality" lest it be perceived as an implicit criticism
of socialist construction (Wang 2017, 57–70).

Now any deviation from the purest form of class struggle, including attention
to questions of sexual inequality, was suspect. Indeed, the CCP Secretariat leadership unanimously agreed that "the socialist system has genuine equality. Raising
[the slogan of] equality between men and women again at present will cause ideological confusion" (Wang 2017, 61–62). Yang Shangkun, a Long March veteran
and senior CCP leader, for example, downplayed the need to discuss women's
liberation: "Women have been liberated, men and women are basically equal.
To talk about equality between men and women again is likely to cause a lot of
conflict. It should not be broadly publicized, it could cause confusion" (Zhang
1996, 246).

The problem quickly became clear: how did the Women's Federation justify its
existence without making it vulnerable to accusations of "rightism"? According to
the historical record, Deng Xiaoping proposed making the double diligences the
major focus of the Women's Federation (Wang 2017, 64–65; Yang 1991, 99–100;
Zhang 1996, 244–48). By directly intervening, Deng Xiaoping strengthened the
hand of Deng Yingchao and Cai Chang, both of whom rejected making reference
to "equality between men and women" (Wang 2017, 58–59, 64). But it was not
until Deng Xiaoping stepped in to instruct the drafters to focus on the double
diligences, that the deadlock was broken.

Whether Deng Yingchao or Cai Chang asked Deng Xiaoping to intervene is
unknown. Also unknown: whether Deng Xiaoping settled on the double diligences as a solution by himself, or whether Cai Chang privately proposed this
direction on the basis of ongoing advocacy. According to Su (1990, 182), Mao's
July comments on the two diligences prompted Cai Chang to initiate "serious

discussions" (*renzhen de taolun*) on the subject among the ACDWF Party Group. Cai Chang also organized four investigation teams to travel to different parts of the country to discuss and publicize the two diligences and personally traveled to Sichuan, Henan, and Shanghai to conduct investigations related to the policy: "Everywhere [Cai Chang] went she directly met with and discussed with women, encouraging everyone to implement the policy of the two diligences" (182).

The Anti-Rightist Movement would have two major consequences for the work of the Women's Federation. First, it strengthened the ACWF's top-down capacity to control lower-levels of the mass organization while weakening the federation vis-à-vis the CCP as a whole. At the Third Women's Congress held in September of 1957, the Women's Federation dropped all reference to United Front work (most specifically the reference to "Democratic" in its name) and adopted a constitution which gave the ACWF secretariat much broader powers over everything from women-related domestic and international activities to the topics covered in the ACWF's major journal *Women of China (Zhongguo funü)* (Zhang 1996, 256–57).[40] It also stipulated that all levels of the organization correspond with state administrative divisions, a change that Zhang Naihua (1996, 255) argues "formally incorporated *Fulian* into the state administrative hierarchy." She continues: "The entire organization, from structure to operation and documents, was formalized and bureaucratized, functioning more like a top-down hierarchy. As a result, the ACWF lost the little autonomy and spontaneity it had under its looser more horizontal structure, functioning more like a state agency" (257). The ACWF's decreasing power vis-à-vis other organs of government and party were not lost on leaders at lower levels of the organization, several of whom recounted versions of the following refrain in interviews:

The party has power
The government has power
Who lacks power? Who lacks power?
The Youth League
And most pitiful of all is the Women's Federation

As Wang (2017, 51–53) notes, this kind of critique, of which there were several different versions circulating, took full stock of the position of institutional peril in which the federation found itself, and in which the ACWF assumed much of the responsibility of government, but none of the authority. These trends were exacerbated by the adoption of the double diligences as the primary theme of the Third Women's General Assembly in September 1957. Indeed, with the advent of the double diligences the household became positioned as a unit of accounting with untapped capacity to conserve consumption. In the context of the Socialist Education Movement, and the GLF that followed, this shift would have deadly consequences.

The Socialist Education Movement

A series of natural disasters struck China in 1956. The situation was particularly dire in Huoyue, where catastrophic flooding destroyed more than 37,500 buildings and 680,000 mu of arable land (*HX* 1993, 31). Flooding was followed in 1957 by a drought so extreme that no wheat was planted.[41] In the fall of 1956, the Huoyue Women's Federation emphasized the urgent need to economize, exhorting that "to conserve grain is each woman's glorious duty."[42] As 1956 came to a close, the Huoyue Women's Federation instructed its grassroots leaders to avoid encouraging dependence on government relief, through a rearticulation of the ideology of harmonious families:

> This past year's natural disaster created dependencies on the collective and government disaster relief and the Women's Federation ignored political ideological education. As a consequence, [you] must organize all of the women in the county to diligently study the "respect the elderly and love the young in harmonious unity" slogan. Hold talks and study sessions to advocate respecting the elderly and loving the young (and advocate) the glories of labor, advocate that family life should be arranged well, oppose wasteful overeating and drinking, oppose not enthusiastically participating in labor and completely relying on the collective and government relief, and that mothers and daughters-in-law, husbands and wives, sisters-in-law, and neighbors should all help one another.[43]

The specific articulations of the need for thrift in Huoyue were magnified as the ACWF made the double diligences an increasing priority of women-work over the course of 1957, and as both problems with flooding and drought continued. The Socialist Education Movement politicized the emerging emphasis on self-reliance and thrift (Wemheuer 2011), cracking down on farmers who, in the wake of the local disasters, requested additional food aid and, more seriously, were trying to exit collectives. The 1957 annual report of the Huoyue Women's Federation noted that although the double diligences had helped to accelerate a Great Leap Forward in agriculture, problems remained: some women were not resolute in loving the collective like their family, while others complained that the CPCSS was not "free"; that there was not enough grain to eat, and that [the state] took too much from the peasants. The report also noted that "some young women think they should enjoy themselves after socialism and not apply themselves to hard work and struggle. This is particularly the case after the natural disaster . . . some women have very confused thinking . . . they are pessimistic . . . and expect the country or the collective to feed them or give them money" (HCAWF 1958).[44]

At the very least, the double diligences contributed to the expectation that women should bear the responsibility for diminishing family finances; at the most, it deflected state-imposed deprivation onto women and their individual capacities to manage their household budgets.

Leader Hou Qiuyi articulated these exact ideological stakes. The first time I raised the double diligences with Hou, she responded: "Back then, in meetings, you couldn't just say: "My family is having a hard time, take care of me. Everyone recognized that."

When I asked her who in the family oversaw the double diligences, she responded:

> If you had 360 jin of grain then you have to calculate; you can't eat it all. Some people had higher work points and some had lower work points, then if you had 360 jin of grain you had to calculate. For some people who only had 280 jin they still had to cover the whole year with that much grain. So what did they do? They had to be frugal, and they had to find something else to mix with the grain to cover the whole year. If you didn't calculate well then you are a bit stupid [*you yi dian ben*].
>
> [Were men or women in charge at home?]
>
> Mostly it is/was men taking care of the outside, and women taking care of the inside. I usually decided how much grain we could eat per month. If we didn't have enough, that just meant that I was not capable of running the household and people would laugh at me. If other people had enough to eat and you didn't, that was shameful. We had many children and we always had 280 jin of grain. Other people had 360 jin. Some people had more than 360. It was shameful if you didn't run your household.

Here, Hou speaks of herself as household manager—the expectation that she should manage the family's grain supply so that it would stretch to feed the household over the course of a year. As both subject to and participant in this state discourse, Hou identified the wife/mother as responsible for the family's survival. If Hou failed to uphold her familial responsibility, she would become a subject of community shame—laughable, incompetent, and ignorant. In this instance, as in many others, the fulfillment of the state's collective project was understood and operationalized through familial and community attachments.

The moral responsibility to be "thrifty" would, in turn, have life and death implications for the members of Hou's community. When I asked Hou about Five Goods and Harmonious Households, for example, she returned to speaking of the double diligences in the following terms:

> Some people say that: "We save and are thrifty." Some people were waste-ful, making steamed buns, and "after they ate everything" they would cry poverty. On the West End of our Brigade there was one idiot, when she ran out of food she went begging and froze to death, and then came the investigation and disciplinary action [for the cadres]. Brigades were not allowed to let people starve to death, there would be disciplinary action if people starved. "The double diligences," [that is] people plan-ning well, [and that way] people were not short of fuel or food, this is the "double diligences." If you were not diligent and thrifty, others don't want to lend you anything. You were not able to repay it because you were too poor to have enough food for yourself, how could you repay them? There were several people like that in each brigade.

Hou Qiuyi makes a direct linkage between wastefulness and starvation, suggest-ing that the woman brought her death on herself by not managing sufficient resources properly. While it is unclear when this incident took place, whether prior to, during, or well after the 1950s, the message was nonetheless clear: star-vation resulted from careless household management.

Hou's cousin, Zhang Sumei, 20, similarly criticized fellow villagers. When I asked about work point equality, she mistook the question as a reference to reward for work expended:

> You earn what you work, is that what you mean? Otherwise, who would expend so much energy working? But there were still some riffraff [*pizi*] [who] didn't care about [getting more], [they] didn't want to work. Some only received food aid [*zhaogu liang*]. In one word, there were people who worked hard and got what they deserved. Those who couldn't work or didn't work, they've never been up to it even until today.

According to Oi (1989, 22), "Political competence was measured by economic performance. Asking for relief, especially grain loans, had negative political con-notations. Few cadres were willing to be labeled backward and risk their political reputation and position." The risks associated with requesting aid became ampli-fied with the Socialist Education Movement, a factor that may well have played into Hou and Zhang's reasoning. But other, ideological processes were at play as well. Both women suggested that one must work hard to get what one deserved, and that those who requested food aid were, in fact, shirking their obligation to socialist construction. Moreover, these ideals were gendered, with women house-holders held morally responsible for managing what little they had. When it was necessary to give "idlers" grain, therefore, Zhang told me that she always com-bined it with a lesson, asking them: "Why aren't you saving and thrifty?"[45]

The lessons of the double diligences made their mark in Wenhe and Gaoshan as well. Qiu Zhaodi, 74, a former Commune women's head in Gaoshan, echoed the need to budget; for her, the double diligences meant to "eat grain according to a daily plan [jihua chifan] so that it was possible to save." Another Gaoshan leader, a former village women's head, offered a similar rationale: "Because men worked outside, women took charge of the home [zhangwo jiating].[46] [If] a woman did a good job taking charge the family could live well. It was bad when some women did not know how to do this" (Yan Zhijuan, 97).

Most striking, perhaps, was the reaction of Pu Congxi, 156, a former women's head from Wenhe. When I asked Pu to tell me about the double diligences, she simply laughed. "That," she said, just means "eating a little less."

In 1956, Cai Chang drew on her multiple official positions and informal ties across government, party, and mass organizations to develop and mobilize sup-port for frugality among women, workers, and youth: a Total War vision of socialist construction. By the time Deng Xiaoping instructed the CCWMC to make the double diligences the leading mandate of its work in summer 1957 (Dong, Cai, and Tan 1992, 308–9), Cai Chang and Li Fuchun had already been making the case for its importance in the development of the socialist economy for more than eight months.

Cai Chang's work on the double diligences asserted a new role for the house-hold, and for women householders more specifically, at the same moment that men's control of the family household was diminishing. Indeed, although house-hold economic decision making was still a family matter in the early 1950s, with male family heads formally representing the household vis-à-vis the state, women were increasingly assuming household budgeting. Under the watchful eyes of local women's heads, women were expected to hand over "surplus" grain and encouraged to tighten already meager household budgets. Simultaneously active in managing marital ties and intrafamilial relations, women's heads enhanced the capacity of the state to surveil and determine economic decisions from within the household itself.

Family reforms were not only transforming "the family," but were also actively redistributing economic power within the household and between the house-hold and the state. Specifically, they were further rendering the socialist family as an embodied and affective site of state-managed kinship ties, with short- and long-term consequences. The CCP's decision to relax birth control regulations and thus slow population growth was one attached attempt to reduce consumption. The CCP's decision to compel frugal household management was another. Indeed, with intensification of collectivization in the mid-1950s, and the state's increasing capacity to control the harvest at its source, Mao Zedong, Li Fuchun, and Cai Chang turned to austerity measures as yet another way to address the growing challenge of an impoverished rural population. Thrifty household management thus served as an increasingly important feature of the socialist economy as it began to reshape local household practices and economic exchange during the first years of the PRC.

And yet, within a few months of the launch of the GLF, the double diligences slogan seemingly dropped off the policy agenda, and the ACWF was once again in the throes of crisis. As Cai Chang and Li Fuchun struggled to shape how the country should make its Great Leap into the socialist future, they would prove central to the politics that followed. Ultimately, these struggles, and the revolutionary righteousness, family ties, and political terror that informed them, would lay the groundwork for the further scarcity and violence to come.

SHOCK TROOPS

It is man that counts; the subjective initiative of the masses is a mighty driving force.

—Liu Shaoqi, "The Present Situation, the Party's General Line for Socialist Construction and Its Future Tasks"

During the GLF, there was a great liberation for women. No women stayed at home. They got used to being outside, they could see people willing to speak, and that everyone had come out [of their homes]. Starting in 1958 everyone came out [of their homes].

—Fang Huayun, 51

Of course, I worked toward the establishment of the communes! If my husband joined the Eighth Route Army and wasn't afraid to die, why would I be afraid to die?

—Tang Xiuying, 37

Just one year after the Third Women's Congress convened and declared the double diligences as its central principle, the ACWF was again embroiled in crisis. Over the winter of 1957–58, Mao began to advocate for new programming to bypass Great Britain and the United States in steel production within fifteen years. With the vocal support of radical provincial party secretaries, Mao led a campaign for the decentralization of economic planning and the building of infrastructure projects in the countryside, including new dams and irrigation works. In March 1958, in the wake of the Central Committee's further endorsement of rapid modernization, rural governments began to experiment with industrialization projects and to establish massive communes. By summer 1958, as "People's Communes" rapidly became the new administrative unit of the countryside, and as women were mobilized on masse into the fields and onto construction sites, the validity of the socialist household, women-work, and the ACWF itself came under attack.

The GLF could not have taken place, much less been conceived, without the labor of rural women. The sudden and spectacular emancipation of hundreds of millions of rural women from some of their household chores through the universal establishment of dining halls, child care, and elder care, and their mass mobilization into field work and onto construction sites, placed women at the center of this utopic experiment.[1] As Hershatter (2011, 237) argues, "A gendered analysis of the Great Leap Forward and its aftermath suggests that this feminization of agriculture undergirded the rural economic development of the Mao years, supporting the central accumulation strategy of the Party-state." To date, however, the politics behind the mobilization of women, and the accompanying provision of social services, has largely been overlooked. Indeed, the most extensive mobilization of women in history has been treated as incidental to a state project that was organized and led by elite men leaders debating steel production targets, and by the grassroots men leaders who procured the grain deemed necessary for rapid industrialization.

In this chapter, I focus on the attachments that undergird the GLF, arguing that the family also materialized as a major site of conflict, if not *the* site of conflict, during this unprecedented state-led mobilization of its citizens. At the heart of the struggle lay contrasting visions of the methods and goals of the state: Total War and War Communism. While participants of the time did not use these terms themselves, I argue that they encapsulate the two overlapping policy frameworks that defined the GLF in 1958 and the first half of 1959.

From a Total War perspective, the goal of the GLF was to strengthen state capacity through mobilizing citizens inside and outside of the household. Insofar as women leaders were made responsible for establishing and running many of the collective structures that would enable women to mobilize en masse, a Total War approach operationalized the ACWF as a key link between the CCP and the new communes, and the communes and households. As the architects of this Total War approach, and Mao's most staunch supporters, Cai Chang and Li Fuchun were deeply invested in the possibilities of the GLF as Total War. Supported by many leaders within the upper echelons of the ACWF and within the provincial Women's Federations, as well as several prominent members of the Central Committee, the double diligences, in particular, was viewed as a key mobilizing principle to meet the goals of the GLF. For Li Dequan, the establishment of the communes offered a related opportunity: the possibility to strengthen the local state's capacity to deliver rural reproductive health services. To this end, the minister of health and vice chair of the ACWF swung into action to realize a second major mobilization of midwifery services across rural China during the summer of 1958.

Whereas Total War approached the GLF by making the ACWF a strengthened arm of the state, War Communism sought to make a Great Leap by strengthening local governance while diminishing or eliminating vertical state control altogether. According to Marx's definition of communism, state and household were expected to wither away as a materialization of "the end of history," or the end of class struggle. With this utopic logic in mind, advocates of War Communism sought to mobilize women directly through commune administrative structures and eliminate the ACWF and household altogether.

First used to describe emergency measures implemented during the earliest years of the Soviet Union (1917–20), War Communism entailed excessive coercion in the purchase and confiscation of grain from the countryside and created a centralized subsistence economy notable for its abolition of money and commodity relations, heavy reliance on compulsory labor mobilization, and egalitarian distribution (Selden 1988, 36–37). In the context of the GLF, War Communism also disregarded gender difference and the family, seeking to build a communist utopia through establishing an industrial army of "shock troops": nondifferentiated state subjects conscripted to undertake projects of rapid development.[2] Championed by radical provincial party secretaries and grassroots women leaders frustrated with women-work, War Communism manifested as a form of radical egalitarianism, incorporating women as "combatants" rather than as "civilians" while pushing for the rapid dissolution of the family and the ACWF.[3]

Ultimately, neither vision would prove totally victorious in the struggles that played out across 1958 and the first half of 1959. Rather, the GLF emerged as a blended implementation of the two visions. As senior Women's Federation and CCP officials sought to defend "the family," women's health, and the ACWF at the peak of the frenzied mobilizations in the summer and fall of 1958, they engaged in a careful dance of negotiation and compromise. Both defensive and proactive, the dance would redraw personal ties and institutional capacities to not only position China to make a great leap in economic production but also a leap in welfare and health care provisions for women and children. As I will show in this chapter and the next, different states of activism and shifting personal ties gave rise to temporary alliances, shaping a kaleidoscope of conflict at the center and on the ground, during the euphoric, chaotic, and fateful mobilizations that constituted the GLF.

Making a Great Leap

The local experimentation that gave rise to the GLF first took root in Xinyang, a prefecture in Henan some two hundred miles south of Huoyue. Mao's strategic jockeying to assert control over economic policy making and to assure big results fast was enthusiastically supported by the secretary of the province, Wu Zhipu, who endorsed the establishment of the first model commune (Chan 2001).[4]

Throughout 1958, Henan featured frequently in the national media with stories highlighting the amazing achievements of Henan's highly mobilized work-
force, communal dining halls, and collectivized childcare services. Henan would
also serve as the destination point of many local officials, including several from
Gaoshan, who traveled across China to learn from the first People's Communes
(Kang Yuesheng, 101).

It is difficult to appreciate the all-encompassing speed with which communization played out across the country during spring and summer of 1958. In
Huoyue, for example, the fourteen districts that were established in April (from
an original thirty established in 1956) became People's Communes in August
(*HX* 1993, 48). With women's participation mandated, some 80–95 percent of
women were mobilized across the country (Thorborg 1978, 592).[5] But it was
not just that more women were working more hours, it was that more women
were assuming responsibility for agricultural production as a whole. In Jiangsu,
by April 1959, for example, nearly 60 percent of agricultural production, 80 percent of sideline production, and 10–30 percent of water conservancy and steel
production, was being undertaken by women (*WW* no. 8 [1959], 4). Seasonal

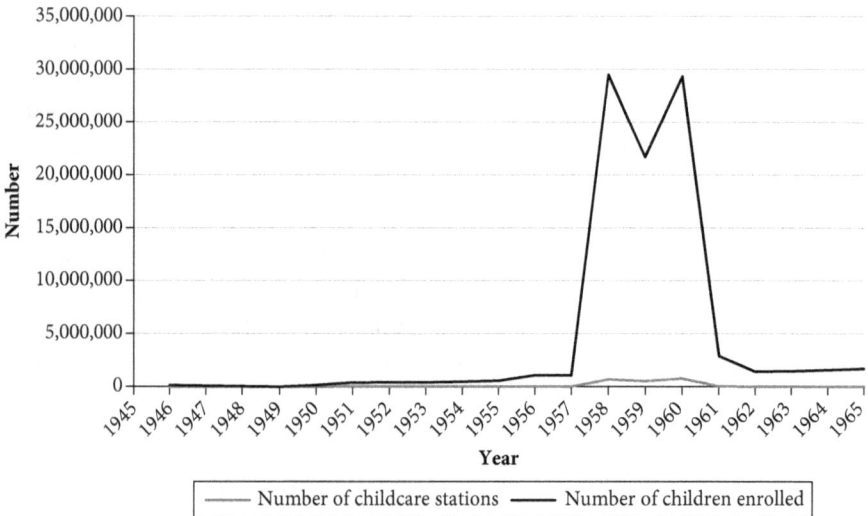

FIGURE 4. Annual national figures for childcare stations and children enrolled.
Source: Zhongguo funü tongji ziliao, 1949–1989 [Statistics on Chinese women,
1949–89], edited by Zhonghua quanguo funü lianhehui funü yanjiusuo [Research
Institute of All China's Women's Federation] and Shaanxi sheng funü lianhehui
yanjiushi [Research Office of Shaanxi Provincial Women's Federation] (Beijing:
China Statistical Publishing House, 1991), 120.

experiments with collective eating and childcare during peak seasons suddenly became year-round mandates. In Jiangsu, by September 1958, 4.22 million pre-school children, or more than 70 percent of preschool children, were attending childcare (Lu and Miao 2000, 219).

The dining halls were set up and running in a matter of hours. According to Hou Qiuyi,

> Party Secretary Li said in a meeting: tomorrow we are going to collect all of the woks, and then gather people to eat in the dining hall. So we built the dining hall overnight then the next day made everyone eat in the dining hall. We had someone in the village, a reliable person, make flour and then we had somebody who was hygienic become the cook. Three women, four men, and an accountant managed the dining hall.[6]

On the new communes, the term *brigade* replaced the word for village, and work teams served as the most basic level of organization in agricultural tasks.[7] Depending on local needs, "platoons," "companies," "battalions" and "brigades" were mobilized to take up additional programs of infrastructure development, including building new systems of irrigation management, steel smelting, and digging for iron ore.

The establishment of brigades and teams signaled that wartime conditions had commenced and that everyone was expected to plunge into the challenge of socialist construction. In fact, Mao Zedong had risked an international crisis by bombing the islands of Jinmen in late August and early September, knowing well that wartime conditions would drum up further support for the GLF (Lüthi 2008, 98–100). And, indeed, many responded with enthusiasm. Hou Qiuyi, described this early period of the GLF as her "glory days" (*guangrong*): a time of plentiful food, hard work, and leadership. Hou understood this moment in the context of war: "If men can defend the nation, why not women?" In a quote that begins this chapter, Wenhe women's head, Tang, offered a similar wartime rationale. As Kang Keqing (1993, 446) recalls, the motto of the time was: "People with great courage, can [produce] land with great yields" (*ren you duo da dan, di you duo da chan*).

During the earliest months of the GLF, patriotism and the promise of a new age energized a whole generation of young people to give their best to the country. The fact that food seemed plentiful and the harvest abundant contributed to the emergence of a kind of utopic fever. In Dafo, Henan, for example, local party leaders saw the GLF as an opportunity to relieve themselves and future genera-tions of the famine and hardship they had known in years gone by (Thaxton 2008, 113). Young women filled the fields wearing their most colorful clothing, with cheeks rouged and lips drawn bright with lipstick, celebrating the mobiliza-tion in a moment of operatic wonder. Former women's head Liang Jinfeng, 57, was delighted with the festival-like nature of the mobilizations: "I loved it! Now it is all over. Back then our village had an opera [wing] room where we would perform the old operas." During this period opera troupes toured the countryside, adding to the aura of festivity and reinforcing the idea that men and women were now equal.

The militarized mobilizations offered young rural women new freedoms beyond the confines of the village and a chance to participate in a revolutionary moment of transformative possibility. Zhou Changfen, 157, an eighteen-year-old women's battalion leader in Wenhe, embraced the shock work with relish and enthusiasm. In the early fall of 1958, she worked round the clock alongside other women—often only breaking to sleep for a few hours at a time—to bring in the harvest of grain and cotton. The women ate and slept together, bringing their quilts with them as they traveled to different villages: "At the time, [I thought] it was great, the women were really happy all working together."

One of the biggest transformations was the opportunity for women to assume new positions of leadership, including within the CCP. In Huoyue, for example, the number of women party members nearly doubled, from 662 in 1958 to 1,237 in 1960 (*HX* 1993, 278).[8] As part of this celebration and promotion of women's leadership, the Woman Warrior was revived. Hou Qiuyi was inspired by a Hua Mulan opera troupe, for example, that traveled through her region. And in Wenhe, Hua Mulan, Mu Guiying, and Liu Hulan, emblematic Women Warriors, were all upheld as role models.[9] Although the work was often backbreaking, the hours long, and the food poor, young childless women especially saw an opportunity to escape the bonds of village and family by running away to "join the army" of young people working on construction sites across the countryside. By the end of 1958, nearly four thousand women in Huoyue were participating in armed, militarized groups practicing military drills on their breaks in order to be ready to defend the country at a moment's notice.[10]

The young women who were swept up in the GLF found pleasure and meaning in the mobilizations. Optimism is a social relation that involves attachments that "organize the present" (Berlant 2011, 14), including through the material and discursive practices of militarism (Chisholm and Ketola 2020). As in the context of armed struggle in Colombia (Nieto-Valdivieso 2017), a certain "joy of militancy" permeated the recollections of women narrating a moment when past, present, and future fetters seemingly fell away. To this end, the utopic promise of a few years of hard work to realize a lifetime of reward was not just about the future that would be, but also an expression of the good life now, including solidarity through hard work and leadership and freedom from the regulations of community and family ties.

Many in the upper echelons of the CCP similarly became caught up in the feverish excitement of the period, with Li Fuchun and Cai Chang being no exceptions. Li Fuchun was the first economic planner to embrace Mao's plans, attacking those who had underestimated China's capacities to develop rapidly (Chan 2001, 33). While Li Fuchun continued to note concerns about the practicality of implementation, he nonetheless enthusiastically threw himself behind the Chairman and was fully supportive of the GLF (Fang and Jin 2001, 506, 511). Cai Chang similarly came out early in support of Mao's vision, exhorting China's women to be more advanced (*xian jin*), to produce more (*duo*), to be faster (*kuai*), to be better (*hao*), and to be more frugal (*sheng*) (Cai 1958a, 1). A colleague, Li Baoguang, who accompanied Cai Chang to the Hebei countryside in the fall of 1958, recalls that as soon as Cai entered a village she greeted the villagers like they were family: calling elderly women "Aunty," picking up children and holding them close to her breast. That year, "when Aunt Cai and the masses were together, the feeling was like that of a fish in water" (Li 1992, 77).

The couple's publications from spring 1958 suggest that although they understood that the GLF was shifting the economic and social terrain, they nonetheless expected to meet Mao's call for a Great Leap on the basis of real continuity. For example, Cai Chang's April article published in *Women of China*, included multiple references to the double diligences and Five Goods families, offering Hubei Province's redefinition as an example: (1) Love the country and collective and produce well, (2) study culture and skills well, (3) budget and plan well, (4) eliminate the four pests and love street committees well, and (5) love and respect the elderly and young, educate children well. In June, Li Fuchun similarly adhered to the goal of building the country (*qinjian jianguo*) through applying the approach of "more, rapid, good, frugal" (Fang and Jin 2001, 510). Li Fuchun and Cai Chang did not view the Leap as a total break with the past, but rather as an unprecedented opportunity to deepen the Total War model of development that the couple had been advocating for well over a year.

The GLF also offered an unprecedented opportunity to deepen the maternalist vision of public health that Li Dequan had been championing since the early 1950s. Although a number of birth planning advocates, including Yang Chongrui, had fallen victim to the 1957 Anti-Rightist Campaign, Li Dequan's standing with the CCP remained strong, and birth control continued to be discussed at the highest levels of the party, Ministry of Health, and Women's Federation.[11] Indeed, Deng Xiaoping gave the Women's Federation Party group explicit instructions to continue to make birth control advocacy a priority of the Federation *after* the Anti-Rightist Movement had commenced (Dong, Cai, and Tan 1992, 308–9). Chen Yun also advocated on behalf of birth control in August 1957 (Chen 1957

[1988], 293). The advocacy of birth control continued within the Women's Federation and the Ministry of Health in early 1958 as well.[12]

By 1958, 40.2 percent of students studying medicine and pharmacy were women (Davin 1976, 188), a continuation of a feminization of medicine that had begun during the Republican era. The availability of knowledge about the health of women and children was expanding rapidly as well. While only thirteen books were published on women's liberation in 1958, for example, eighty-five appeared on the topics of women's hygiene, medicine, women's obstetrics, and caring for children—some 55 percent of the total number of books published on women that year (Zhang, Ru, and Dong 1992, 597). During the heady early months of the GLF, Lin Qiaozhi planned and oversaw a survey of eighty thousand women, with a particular focus on their reproductive health (Zhang 2005, 288–90); an effort that was certainly unprecedented in China, and likely globally as well.

Despite these advances, however, major problems remained. In August, at a National Symposium on Maternal and Child Health, Li Dequan spoke with emotion about the ongoing costs of inadequate health care infrastructure: an annual toll of 3,335,000 infant deaths and 249,375 maternal deaths, largely caused, she argued, by neonatal tetanus (infants) and puerperal fever (mothers) (Li and Zhang 2007, 327). While also blaming "the disasters left by old China," Li Dequan nonetheless critiqued local cultural practices and health cadres, themselves: "The vast majority of working women, due to the long-term oppression of reactionary rule, live a difficult life, have a backward culture, and lack or pay little attention to scientific health or knowledge. Maternal and child health work is a relatively weak link in health construction. It depends on the care and support of all health cadres" (Li and Zhang 2007, 327).

The establishment of the communes and the work point allocation system provided new opportunities. In July 1958, *Women-Work* (hereafter *WW*), the internal periodical (*neibu kanwu*) that the ACWF used to inform and train Women's Federation cadres, reported the opening of 262 *new* birthing clinics in Henan, Jiangxi, and Gansu (*WW*, no. 13 [1958]: 20). Nationwide, 35,290 midwives and 774,983 assistant midwives were providing services to women, mostly in rural areas (Lim Kha-ti [Lin Qiaozhi] 1959). Between 1957 and 1960, women and children's collective health stations increased by 37.8 percent (see figure 2 in chapter 5).

This high-level prioritization of maternal health and birth planning is evident in reporting from Huoyue. In May 1957, for example, Huoyue County urged cadres to lead the way to promote late marriage and birth planning, noting that it was very difficult for leaders to do their work if they had too many children. By April 1958, the Huoyue Women's Federation estimated that 75 percent of men and women had been exposed to birth planning propaganda, and some 8,637 women had started to use birth control.[13] And in August 1958, just as the GLF was heating up, the Huoyue County Women's Federation urged women with many children to undergo tubal ligations and use contraceptives.[14] This mobilization took place, in no small part, through the rapid expansion of birthing stations and trained midwives in Huoyue, as discussed in chapter 5.[15]

Notably, plans to make a "great leap" in women and children's health was mobilized through the double diligences and harmonious family projects already underway.[16] One Huoyue midwife combined midwifery reform and birth control, delivering some 63 babies and distributing 1,230 condoms over a six-month period in 1958.[17] Throughout the summer and fall of 1958, the Huoyue Women's Federation continued to make birth control, midwifery reform, and women's health a clear priority of mobilization, even as the implementation of these priorities was not shared by all within the CCP.

The problem was that Cai Chang and Li Dequan's Total War vision of the GLF—a vision in which gender-appropriate work, women's health care, harmonious families, and ACWF leadership were prioritized—came up against two major challenges. First, was the challenge of Total War itself. Indeed, Total War placed impossible expectations on rural women, effectively boxing them into marriages from which they could not exit, household obligations they could not refuse, and family relations they could not forsake. Unexpectedly, the GLF briefly opened new space within the otherwise constraining dictates of the socialist household. When asked if women were freer in 1958, Li Liping, 17, a young activist in Huoyue at the time of the GLF, responded:

> Yes. In the past women had constraints [yueshu] on the work they could do. In that year women all came out [of their homes]. They became freer at home. The men were gone and so they didn't suffer from men's regulation. In the brigade they could work a lot or work less. Women were really free. In 1958, during the GLF, no matter [whether or not] the food was good we could still get enough to eat.

Li Liping's remark, and the comments made by a number of other former young women activists, production team leaders, and village-level women's heads, reflect and transform critical aspects of the harmonious family. According to the revolutionary logic of the moment, women should have gained their liberation during the GLF because of the unprecedented opportunity for compensated work and the socialization of housework. In contrast, Li Liping suggested that their true "liberation" was from patriarchal villagers and husbands—a temporary stopgap in unhappy, or even violent, domestic relationships.

Second, and related, Cai Chang and Li Fuchun's Total War vision of the GLF was being rapidly overtaken by War Communism. The communes, some believed, would facilitate the early emergence of communism in China through the absorption of all private property, the socialization of housework, and the realization of the all-round Communist man who was simultaneously a soldier, peasant, worker, and intellectual (Manning and Wemheuer 2011b, 6). Indeed, policy confusion reigned, in part, because neither hastily contrived rural development projects nor the imminent arrival of communism had featured in the original "Total War" policy platform; rather, they were the product of local leaders implementing their own vision of Mao's call to rapidly develop the country.

War Communism

In March 1958, Mao Zedong, speculated about the imminent demise of the family:

> In socialism, private property still exists, factions still exist, families still exist. Families are the product of the last stage of primitive communism, and every last trace of them will be eliminated in the future. Kang Youwei perceived this in his Great Harmony.[18] Historically, the family has been a production unit, a consumption unit, and a unit for giving birth to the next generation of the labor force and educating children. Now worker families are no longer production units. . . . This is even more the case for families involved in the bureaucracy and the army . . . it is possible that in the future, the family will no longer be beneficial to the development of productivity. . . . Many of our comrades don't dare to consider problems of this nature because their thinking is too narrow. (Yang 2012, 174)

These remarks, given before thirty-nine of the highest party officials in Chengdu, are believed to have ignited the decision of local officials to implement dining halls (Yang 2012, 174–75). They also contributed to a growing political radicalism among provincial officials who owed their positions to Mao and/ or who were already sympathetic to the idea of radically restructuring society, including the family itself (Chen 2011; Yang, Xu, and Tao 2014). Zhou Enlai, a strong supporter of the ACWF and a recent advocate of the double diligences, suddenly, and somewhat surprisingly, agreed.[19]

When Zhou Enlai visited Henan in July and August, he praised the collective dining halls and nurseries as "the sprouts of communism" and argued that the thorough liberation of women required liberating them from their household duties (Yang 2012, 175). Zhou's invocation of the possibility of a "thorough" liberation, placed him alongside leaders who at this early juncture used the term to argue that the new commune system obviated the need for attention to women's issues and, indeed, for the Women's Federation itself. It was thus an odd moment, and one that may have been produced through Zhou Enlai's own precarious position vis-à-vis the launch of the GLF. Specifically, in March 1958, and under increasing pressure from Mao Zedong, Zhou made a public apology for having "thrown cold water on the enthusiasm of the people" (Barnouin and Yu 2006, 171), a reference to his opposition to rash advance, discussed in the chapter previous.

Given Zhou's difficulties in preparing the self-criticism that accompanied the apology, Deng Yingchao and Zhou's secretary convinced Zhou Enlai to let his secretary write the text himself (Barnouin and Yu 2006, 172). This humiliating exercise in self-criticism only served to embolden the more radical leaders within the CCP while silencing Zhou Enlai and Deng Yingchao from playing any public role in criticizing War Communism as it was rapidly emerging at the grassroots. Indeed, Zhou Enlai's adopted Thai daughter, Sirin Phatanothai, recalls Zhou's incredulity when she reported the steel-making success of her classmates to the premier in the fall of 1958. She also recalls his privately shared distress when famine later beset the country (Phatanothai 1994, 157–58). As Phatanothai also recalled, however, private utterances within Zhongnanhai did not always match public discourse.

In 1980 Deng Xiaoping criticized Liu Shaoqi, Zhou Enlai, and himself for becoming "hot heads" during the high tide of the GLF (Wemheuer 2010, 180). Of the three, Liu Shaoqi proved to be biggest "hot head." Indeed, Liu Shaoqi enthusiastically called for the demise of the family when he appeared before the ACWF Lead Party Group on June 14, 1958, endorsing the importance of socializing household labor as a means of increasing productivity and insisting that "embarking on Communist society should liberate women from all household labor" (Yang 2012, 174–77); he also sent his own children to work on a commune near Beijing that summer (MacFarquhar 1983, 131). Liu Shaoqi understood that Mao was envisioning nothing short of the "end of history" in which state and family would dissolve into the fullness of communism.

With the enthusiastic support of a number of provincial officials and some of the CCP's highest officials at the center, War Communism quickly became reality on the ground. Almost overnight, women were deployed to work wherever and whenever the team or brigade leader determined was best, regardless of whatever additional responsibilities a householder might have been already carrying, of which there were many. Although childcare provision expanded exponentially during the earliest months of the GLF, it differed little from the makeshift forms of care that had been piloted during 1956 and 1957. For the most part, childcare work was allocated to older women who were not physically strong enough to undertake demanding physical labor or to women who had connections to the brigade leadership. Even with the provision of childcare, communal dining, and, in some places, "happiness homes" for the elderly, women householders were still making and mending clothes and were preoccupied with elder care, care for young children, and countless other tasks.

Former Wenhe women's head, Zhou Changfen, 157, who was overjoyed to work alongside women outside the brigade, describes the challenges mobilizing women householders:

> Women's thinking was too backward. Whatever work you tried to implement was really difficult. You wanted her to work in the fields, she wanted to stay at home and make clothes, [she] also had children in the way. Adults and children needed clothes. At that time trying to liberate women from the house to work was really difficult. The young people without any burdens were all very happy to work in the fields. Back then there was no family planning. In our village a woman had ten children; six boys, four girls. Do you think she could come out to work? But at that time the brigade needed this labor, it was really difficult.

Zhou told me that she herself locked her own child at home with some pancakes when she had to attend meetings as there was no one to look after him when he was small.

Zhou's analysis of the burden faced by women householders is astute. There simply was too much household work to do for women to be "liberated" to engage in field work. And yet, she simultaneously critiques the ideological limitations of women themselves. In Zhou's view, the Maoist vision of being able to overcome obstacles through subjective initiative, to liberate oneself, was impeded by the backwardness of the country woman herself.

The dismantling of family cook stoves and the massive disruption to people's living quarters was extremely difficult as well. According to former Huoyue women's head Liu Yuezhen, 10, some people were forced to move from their homes during this period: "For instance, if your house was going to be turned into a cowshed, then you would have to move out and move to wherever there were spare houses or to whichever place they wanted you. [Then] the cattle were kept in your house."

Even more troubling, some "model" communes waged an unparalleled campaign of destruction. In Macheng County in the province of Hubei, for example, homes were destroyed and families forced to live in barracks (Dikötter 2010, 38; Wang 2011, 151).

For many women who already had children, being conscripted as "shock troops" to work outside of the brigade was a disaster. When militarized units were deployed, whether to forge steel, bring in the harvest, or to build new dams, they would often spend weeks or even months away from their home villages. Some people said that the term "to stress the situation of women" (zhongshi) transformed into "emphasizing their usefulness" (zhongshi) (Jin 1993, 2:552–53). The conditions in Huoyue were often terrible, including mass sleeping arrangements and no toilets, leaving workers no choice but to relieve themselves in the ravines, absent of privacy.

When Miao Murong, 129, led several hundred women to work on steel smelting she found herself constantly trying to placate unhappy conscripts: "Many of the women hadn't left home before and were crying and screaming, they missed home, [and] wanted to go back. [But] when I took two of the troublemakers home, the party secretary told me that I had to bring them back." As many women hated being deployed, desertion was not uncommon. When Song Lijuan, 60, for example, left the steel works because her child was sick, the leadership deprived her of food: "They held big meetings to struggle against me. I had no choice, I kowtowed to the cadres—I made a big fuss. They said that I wasn't working, me and X's mother, they said I wasn't working and wouldn't give me [food] tickets, [they] wouldn't let me eat. At that time people with kids were really to be pitied."

But one of the worst parts of the GLF for many women was the labor conditions. Despite the fact that regulations guiding the establishment of the model Weixing commune in Henan, for example, included staffing a health officer and midwife at lower levels (*The People's Daily*, August 7, 1958), and despite continued calls to implement the "three transfers" by provincial and county women's federations, reproductive health deteriorated rapidly.

According to Tian Min, 85, the attempts to create new irrigation systems in Gaoshan took an especially harsh toll on her body and the bodies of other women:

> The water conservation projects were extremely difficult. At liberation there was no fish bank. All of the fields had been flooded away, so people had to go down to . . . to dig mud. Everybody lined up, row after row to put the mud on a steamer. After we got the earth, we built up the fish bank. It rained really hard while we were working. Drenched us so thoroughly that we couldn't see the face in front of us. I got my period in the pouring rain and had a constant belly ache, and it lasted a long time. Back then people didn't care about any kind of hardship. They still had to participate in work and put up with an incredible amount of hardship. . . . I led my own youth team to work on the river. Women comrades were supposed to be the same as men and they suffered a lot.

When asked if there were health protections for women, Wenhe Brigade party secretary Dai Jingzong, 61, retorted:

> That was during the GLF! You have no idea how extreme things were then; how in the hell could you take care of women's health? It wasn't just the women but also us cadre party secretaries [who had it rough]. If we said one wrong thing at the commune, we'd immediately get struggled against. At that time the struggle sessions were the most terrifying thing.

It anguished him, he said, to watch the women with children work:

> At that time the struggle meetings were really extreme. There was just no way. After eating dinner, women would line up to pick the cotton. Oh

my! The women would bring their babies to the fields and they would also stay at the side of the fields. That really broke our hearts. Some of the women were really strong. After picking they could go home. They needed to pick three rows of cotton—at least 0.8 mu. Some women were really worried that they couldn't finish.

When asked if women ever slept while they were working, Niu Shumiao, 52, a Wenhe women's head, replied,

> Yes, because they worked during the day and then made clothes for their children at night and so some women had a nap when they were working. Back then women were really pitiful, and their children were wearing broken shoes with toes peeking out and so at night they had to make shoes for children and the children need shoes to wear the next day. Some people joked "you were stealing cows last night" which means they didn't sleep.[20]

Niu worked on the same brigade as the party secretary who spoke of his fear of the struggle sessions. Here, Niu's comments suggest that she tried to find ways to accomplish her work targets so she could make her report to "the higher-ups," while accommodating the total exhaustion of the working mothers—a very common problem at the time, and one that contributed to mounting health costs. Both Niu and the party secretary were responding, in no small part, to the political atmosphere of fear that was rife during the GLF. For while the utopic exuberance of the early months of the GLF was very real, equally real was the political fallout from the Socialist Education Movement that had been carried out in the fall of 1957. Local leaders knew that if they did not comply with orders to meet production targets, they could risk the public humiliation of a struggle session, the loss of their position, or much, much worse. In contrast with Dai and Niu who struggled to comply with their orders, however, Tian Min, 85, prided herself on protecting women during the height of the labor mobilizations.

Tian Min is the Gaoshan Youth League secretary who chose to remain with her in-laws, despite her dream of joining the army. By the time of the GLF, Tian had become a mother herself. Although she had been advised to sacrifice her children for the good of her work by a superior who had abandoned, or perhaps even killed her own child during the throes of a military engagement, and although Tian herself did not especially like women-work, she strove to protect the women in her care:

> The [brigade] work team wanted me to mobilize women to go to [another brigade] for the night shift, to thresh the rice. [The night shift] was from seven at night until seven in the morning: the whole

night. I myself am very stubborn. For example, if you are mobilized to participate [in the night shift], just when your child is nursing, I wouldn't mobilize you to go, I would go [instead]. For example, when X had given birth to her first child. How can [you] let her work all night when the baby was left at home? What would [the baby] eat? So I went [instead]. The work [leader] came to get me with the flashlight, [and] ordered me to quit and return home to sleep. I myself am very stubborn [*wo zhege ren shi ge xing hen ying de*]. I don't pay attention to what the leaders say, I have my own will power [*ziji de yizhi*], I do what I want. [If] you, the leader, won't let me work, [you can] forget it. [When the] working group [leaders] wanted me to get off of the threshing machine, I didn't get off. Why did they want me to quit? Because after working all night, [I will] sleep tomorrow. If I sleep during the day, there is no one to manage the work during the day. I didn't care if they had someone to manage the day shift or not. It is not my business. I absolutely refused to get down. The leaders had no way to make me go [home] to sleep. [So] I didn't go back. I just couldn't go and get nursing mothers to work the night shift. I myself was extremely considerate of all of the women.

In this example, Tian embodied the activist who was able to overturn (*fanshen*) her status through sheer force of will or, as she described it herself, through the force of her "stubborn personality." Tian's determination to protect the women in her care is especially notable given the highly militarized climate of the period, and the expectation that good leaders followed orders. Instead, Tian refused: "I didn't obey orders, [I] didn't listen to the commands, you can punish me as you like. I did the right thing. That child was still nursing, who was going to take care of [the baby] left home at night? No one!"

Tian's actions were unusual, but not necessarily without parallel elsewhere. In July 1958, for example, *Women-Work* (no. 14 [1958]: 11) shared a report from Hunan about a woman cadre who refused to mobilize menstruating and breastfeeding women on an irrigation site, facing down a male cadre to do so. Miao Murong, 129, and Tang Li, 159, also strove to assist breastfeeding mothers during this period. Similar to Tian, Miao educated the team leaders to let women nurse their children: "Some children ate so frantically they threw up." Rather than assuming the figure of heroic male, however, Tang's response was decidedly maternal: suckling the babies of other women and providing them with the cast-off clothing of her own children.

Tian's comments are extraordinary for several additional reasons, most notably her self-narration of Woman Warrior heroism. Indeed, even as she sought to protect other women from its demands, Tian practiced a Maoist ethic of self-sacrifice and of overcoming all odds. Tian's comments are also extraordinary given the way they contrast with the Wenhe party secretary's fear of the "terrifying struggle sessions," struggle sessions Tian later insisted did not take place in her locale at this time. This is not to say that struggle sessions did not occur, for, indeed, they did all over China at that time.[21] But it is to note the decided contrasts in gendered agency as narrated by former leaders, Dai, Niu, Tian, Miao, and Tang. These are contrasts that would be mirrored at the party apex as well. Over the course of the summer and fall of 1958, an emerging Total War coalition actively challenged the excesses of War Communism, attempting to recenter the family and the ACWF at the heart of the GLF.

The Struggle to Protect Women-Work

The belief that Mao Zedong supported the immediate dissolution of the family was not shared by everyone in the CCP. Throughout Mao's tenure as chairman of the CCP, he was prone to make statements or set forward ideas that were, at best, public musings. As Teiwes (1984, 40) argues, "Leaders who wanted to please Mao for their own reasons were frequently at a loss as to how to go about it." Politics at the apex of the CCP was thus in no small part shaped by how one interpreted Mao's remarks, and how one shaped a policy agenda through those interpretations.[22] One could therefore be wildly supportive of Mao's call for a Great Leap while simultaneously advocating for the importance of the socialist family and the ACWF in the process. This was the case for Cai Chang and Li Fuchun, two of Mao's most loyal comrades, who simultaneously embraced the Leap's rapid approach to development while nonetheless seeking to moderate the approach to women and the family that was being taken on the ground. It was also the case for a number of other officials, both inside and outside of the ACWF, who actively sought to ground the GLF in Total War.

The first to step forward was Song Qingling. Since the foundation of the PRC, Song Qingling's greatest contributions were to advance the reputation of the new regime on the international stage (Lee 2003e, 471–72). Although she seldom traveled internationally after 1949, she frequently wrote about the early successes of the PRC in *China Reconstructs*, an English periodical designed for foreign readership that she helped to found and edit. She also remained active in organizations that supported the welfare of women and children. When the "mother of the nation," spoke up in defense of mothers, therefore, she was able to leverage significant symbolic and emotional capital behind her.

In June, Song Qingling (1958 [1988], 365–66) commemorated International Children's Day by publishing an essay in *Women of China*, that highlighted the important role that mothers played *in the family*, raising moral, upright, and socialist citizens. Although Song's text was short and would not have received a wide audience beyond its housewife readership, her effort to reaffirm the family at a moment when many grassroots and some senior CCP leaders were speaking of its imminent demise was either a sign that she was out of touch with the political winds that were blowing, or an early maternalist intervention.

Song Qongling's mentee, Kang Keqing, also stepped into the fray. In her autobiography, published shortly after her death, Kang Keqing describes her outrage when a "responsible comrade," spoke to the ACWF Party Group during the GLF (Kang 1993, 451–52); the unnamed "responsible comrade" was likely Liu Shaoqi, on his June visit to the ACWF, discussed earlier in the chapter. Although Kang later regretted not speaking out on other occasions during the GLF, she did not hold back when the official suggested that all children and students should live at their day cares and schools full-time rather than returning to their families at night, and that postnatal mothers should hand their infants directly over to the commune childcare system after they completed their period of confinement. Kang Keqing vocally denounced the proposal at the meeting and would later attempt to moderate public understanding of the relationship between family care and collective care in the provisions of childhood education, as I will discuss shortly.

In the meantime, Dong Bian, editor-in-chief of *Women of China* and member of the ACWF's secretariat, sought to protect the ACWF against what was clearly a growing chorus of criticism coming from within and outside of the Women's Federation (Dong 1958 [1988], 363–65; Luo 1998a [2000], 59).[23] At a major conference on women-work that began on June 30, 1958, Dong Bian faced a number of questions from within the ranks of the ACWF: Why hadn't the ACWF raised the socialization of housework at the Third Women's Congress? Why had it not declared that women's "thorough" liberation had been achieved? Some officials suggested that, since housework had already been socialized and the family itself was already being eliminated, there was no need for the double diligences. In parts of the country, local women's federations were being disbanded, and even where they remained, local cadres feared being labeled rightists if they addressed women's issues (Liu 1992, 115).

The threat to the Women's Federation was not without precedent. As discussed in the previous chapter, Cai Chang, Deng Yingchao, and Deng Xiaoping had mobilized to protect the Women's Federation from dissolution in 1957; in doing so, they were not only trying to protect it from the critiques of senior male party officials but also from the dissatisfaction of grassroots women leaders. The GLF gave new life to criticisms focused on women-work, with a small number of women officials arguing, for example, that the Women's Federation should be eliminated because its historical mission had been completed (Luo 1998a [2000], 59). In Wenhe, some lower-level women leaders seemingly agreed. In February 1958, for example, the county Women's Federation reported receiving complaints that women-work had "no future" and was "troublesome." The county federation worried that they were losing the trust of the masses and that these feelings could challenge their efforts to implement the double diligences.[24] Several reports published in *Women-Work* over the course of the summer of 1958, suggest a distaste for women-work was continuing to plague the strength of local Women's Federations across the country (for example, *WW*, no. 14 [1958], 21). The fact that the establishment of the communes generated open speculation about the rapid demise of the state, and the centrality of governance within the commune structure itself, likely contributed to a political environment in which the Women's Federation was increasingly viewed by some as irrelevant.

But this time the threat to the ACWF was delivered in a one-two punch: an attack on the ACWF, and an attack on the family itself. In her address to the conference delegates in June 1958, Dong Bian sought to show that a year previous conditions in the economy had been fundamentally different and thus had merited the adoption of the double diligences. While conditions had changed and the socialization of housework was now an important slogan of the ACWF, however, not all problems had been resolved. According to Dong Bian, two basic challenges continued to make the "thorough liberation" of women an ongoing issue: the low skill level of women compared with that of men and the feudal patriarchal ideology that permeated the thinking of both men and women. The thorough liberation of women, Dong continued, would not be realized until communism was realized in China—something that was still far off in the future. In the interim, she argued, the work of the Women's Federation was necessary to achieve equality. She also cited Mao Zedong and Liu Shaoqi, both of whom had previously supported the role of women leaders and women-work in the PRC.

Several senior CCP male officials actively contributed to the Women's Federation's July work conference that followed. Members of the senior CCP leadership, including Mao Zedong, Deng Xiaoping, and Peng Dehuai, met with the conference delegates. More important, however, was the active participation of several members of the Central Committee and the Party Secretariat in the conference. The vice director of the Central Committee's Propaganda bureau, Zhou Yang, for example, gave a report on how to conduct ideological education with women. But it was the CCP Secretariat that would prove most central to the discussions. Li Fuchun and Tan Zhenlin, the main official responsible for guiding the GLF and a recent addition to the Politburo (Yang 1996, 37), represented the CCP Secretariat at the meetings, delivering reports on the economy and providing important guidance on how to proceed (Cao 1958, 2; Yang 1991, 112–13).

The close involvement of the CCP Secretariat in women-work marked a significant departure from previous ACWF conferences and itself reflected the important changes underway during the GLF. Li Fuchun and Li Xiannian, another economic czar, had just been appointed to Party Secretariat a few months prior—the first time that an economic official had become a member of this powerful body. Bachman (1991, 209) argues that the appointment of Li Fuchun symbolized "the great role the Party saw itself playing in economic affairs." I would add that the growing presence of the CCP in the workings of the ACWF and Li Fuchun's assignment to represent the CCP Secretariat at the women-work conference symbolized the important role that some within the CCP leadership placed on women and women's organizations in the GLF even as the leadership of the ACWF and CCP remained conflicted about their role. Specifically, the appointment undergirded a Total War approach to the mobilization of women, including the interventions by Deng Xiaoping that followed.

After the ACWF Party Group submitted a report on its deliberations to the CCP Secretariat, Deng Xiaoping requested that the ACWF Party Group meet with the Party Secretariat on the morning of July 24 (Luo 1998a [2000], 60).[25] In a "very serious" manner, Deng Xiaoping told the Party Group that the Women's Federation *must* uphold the double diligences. Furthermore, Deng Xiaoping also clearly stipulated that the call to socialize housework "should not be advocated for at least another decade or two." Deng Xiaoping's views were echoed by two senior CCP officials also present at the meeting, namely Peng Zhen and Liu Lantao. Peng Zhen stated: "The family will remain for a long time, even during the time of our children and grandchildren it still won't have withered away. Even though the socialization of housework is underway, the family is still the basic economic unit of society!" Liu Lantao similarly remarked, "In the past you never really had a good discussion about the double diligences, but this is really the long-term direction of women-work and the Women's Federation should strengthen this aspect of its work. Right now there isn't a question about whether or not to dismantle the Women's Federation, but rather [about] how to strengthen and improve [your] work, work that will not end during your lifetime" (Luo 1998a [2000], 60).

Peng Zhen's remarks in support of the Women's Federation are noteworthy given that just one year prior he had argued that women's problems were no longer special social and political issues: namely, that the problems of women workers concerned reproduction and children, and that "there is nothing special about female students, except menstruation" (Zhang 1996, 246–47). Peng Zhen would also prove himself to be one of Mao's most loyal supporters during the GLF itself (Chung 2015). Peng Zhen's about-face may also have reflected international pressure. Yang (2012, 176) suggests, for example, that senior CCP officials scaled back their comments about the coming elimination of the family in the wake of foreign criticism in the summer of 1958. The involvement of the Party Secretariat, however, did not end the conflict. In many ways it was only beginning.

In the wake of the meeting, the published conference summaries, penned by Cao Guanqun and Liu Jialin, the ACWF propaganda director, strengthened many of the same themes that Dong Bian had outlined earlier. Cao and Liu were particularly concerned that women leaders understood how to correctly propagate the meaning of the socialization of housework. Neither the family nor all labor within the home, they stressed, had been eliminated. Leaders must not say, therefore, that, "women are liberated from the home" nor that "women have been freed from the burdens of housework." The family remained "the planned economy's basic unit of consumption." They also stressed that although the different conditions had slightly shifted the meaning of the double diligences, it was still necessary to continue to advocate the slogan. Despite the recent increase in production, they expected that the family would continue to practice reasonable consumption and oppose wastefulness. Both leaders were also emphatic: the commencement of collective living did not mean the advent of communism (Cao 1958, 2–12; Liu 1958, 13–18).

Liu's article went further than Cao's. Specifically, she strategically reminded the reader that Liu Shaoqi had always valued women-work by citing his founding instructions that propaganda should be the most important aspect of women-work. After referencing Mao Zedong's call to correctly handle the contradictions among the people, Liu Jialin said it made "us" feel that "the ACWF, as an organization of the women masses, is a link between the Party and the women masses, [which must] strengthen women's political and ideological work" (Liu 1958, 15). In closing she expressed that the mood was comfortable (*shufu*) and that women-work was promising (*dayoukewei*), perhaps an expression of relief that the ACWF was seen as having a continuing role during this historical moment of rapid transition. Interestingly, however, she did so while separating Liu Shaoqi's instructions to the Federation: organize production and organize living conditions, from the instructions of the CCP Secretariat (which went unnamed, but as Cao discussed at length in the same issue, included explicit instructions to continue the double diligences). In so doing, Liu Jialin may have been acknowledging in print what former Jiangsu Women's Federation chair, Shi Jian, 110, referred to as the "two different opinions" (*liang zhong bu tong de yijian*) at play within the Central Committee at that time.[26]

Shortly after, the CCP Secretariat committed to the path of War Communism. Indeed, at a meeting at Beidaihe, the summer seaside resort for senior leaders, the CCP leadership surged behind the Chairman, whose enthusiasm for the utopic promise of a militarized countryside was now at a peak. Over the course of the meeting, Mao spoke of the transition to communism while enthusiastically endorsing military-style mobilizations replete with dormitories, dining halls, and twenty-four-hour work cycles. He also intensified the implementation of "harsh administrative measures" by endorsing the discipline of those who failed to meet production targets (Teiwes and Sun 1999, 110–11). The "communization and militarization of society as innate organizational methods" (Lüthi 2008, 89) were seemingly adopted wholesale. In addition to Liu Shaoqi and Zhou Enlai, other members of the Party Secretariat who supported the Chairman's plans for increasing steel and agricultural production through mass mobilization included Deng Xiaoping, Li Fuchun, Bo Yibo, and Peng Dehuai (Teiwes and Sun 1999, 110–12).

At the same time, the CCP leadership seemingly caved in to calls to reduce the power of the ACWF. In August, the CCP Secretariat eliminated the CCWMC from the Central CCP, a move that reduced some of the overlap in connections that the ACWF Leading Party Members Group maintained with the Central CCP, and thus the ACWF's access to the central corridors of power (Zhang 1996, 301–5).

The ACWF leadership also seemingly acquiesced to War Communism. In September and October, *Women-Work* ceased to publish articles that referenced the double diligences. Instead, the journal primarily focused on the successes of the new communes and accompanying mobilizations, limiting mention of problems that were concurrently arising. The lead editorial published in *Women-Work* (no. 18 [1958], 2–3) shortly after the Beidaihe meetings set the tempo: "The commune has become a large collective living unit, realizing the socialization of housework, breaking the restrictions imposed on women by individual family life, and enabling them to participate in social labour without fatigue." But the battle over the importance of the family and of the ACWF was not over. In the same editorial, both family and ACWF were reasserted: "We should educate women not only to be mistress [*zhufu*] of their own family, but also to be a good mistress to the larger socialist collective family." The gendered and familial language of "mistress" was key. Key members of the ACWF's leadership were not ready to give up the Federation's historical role in the development of socialist construction generally, and in the GLF, specifically.

Over the course of the fall of 1958, Cai Chang mobilized to recenter the ACWF in the GLF. Her work began almost immediately, in September, with a joint investigative trip undertaken with Li Fuchun and Lü Zhengcao, vice minister of railroads (Dong, Cai, and Tan 1992, 312). Distressed by the discovery that some Women's Federations at the county level and below were being dismantled (Liu 1992, 115), Cai Chang subsequently organized nine working groups to investigate the organizational problems besetting local women-work in eleven provinces and one autonomous region (Dong, Cai, Tan 1992, 312; ACWF 1958b [1999]), dispatching her more competent secretaries to relevant meetings to make the case (of the Federation) (Liu 1992, 115). The work was extensive, involving thirty-two leaders, including Cai Chang, Kang Keqing, Zhang Yun, Cao Mengjun, Dong Bian, and others (*WW* no. 22 [1958], 13). Cai Chang herself traveled to several provinces including Henan and Hubei to hold meetings with Women's Federation cadres. She was not pleased with all that she saw: indeed, Cai Chang was deeply alarmed to learn that, on the new communes, husbands and wives were being organized into sex-segregated barracks and that children and the elderly were being neglected (Gao Jian, 6).

In Henan, Cai Chang directly intervened with her provincial counterparts, arguing that because the decision to establish the ACWF in 1948 had been made by the Central Committee and Mao Zedong; the provinces did not have the authority to dismantle the Women's Federation (Liu 1992, 115). In the meantime, however, debate rocked the highest levels of the ACWF, with members of the ACWF Party Group continuing to argue among themselves about the need for women's organizations at a meeting on October 21 (Zhang 1996, 299). Also divided were provincial leaders, who expressed conflicting views at a national organization work forum October 26 (299). By the end of the forum, Cai Chang had nonetheless garnered enough internal consensus from within the ACWF Party Group to argue that "our opinion is" that the ACWF should be maintained at the county level and below (ACWF 1958b [1999]; Dong, Cai, and Tan 1992, 312).

Liu Lantao agreed with Cai Chang and assigned Luo Qiong and one other to attend the Sixth Plenum of the Eighth Central Committee held in Wuhan from November 28 to December 10 (Dong, Cai, and Tan 1992, 312). At the meetings, Luo Qiong discussed the findings of the investigative working groups, arguing that, "although the cause of women's liberation has significantly advanced with the GLF and the communization movement, a number of problems specific to women and children continue" (Yang 1991, 114). Luo emphasized that local women leaders played an important role in the organization and provision of social welfare services, especially the development of childcare and kindergartens, and that local women's organizations were necessary to strengthen and improve the People's Communes to ensure that a great leap in agricultural production was not interrupted and to drum up the enthusiasm of the rural women masses. Cai Chang was also in attendance and presented her report to Deng Xiaoping (Liu 1992, 115). The attendees of the meeting unanimously agreed with the findings of the investigations, and the Disciplinary Committee "clearly stated" that organizations *at all levels* of the ACWF *must* continue to exist and were not permitted to be abolished (Dong, Cai, and Tan 1992, 312, italics mine).

In the meantime, *Women-Work* accompanied this intensive spate of advocacy by publishing articles addressing problems on the ground, including dissatisfaction with the working conditions on construction sites, the need for health protections for women, and the problems with (the lack) of women's organizations on some communes (*WW* no. 19 [1958], 8–9). In early November 1958, *Women-Work* republished Kang Keqing's (1958) essay on Liu Shaoqi's September call to place all children into twenty-four-hour collective care (it was originally published in the periodical *Chinese Youth*). In what at first reads as a profound repudiation of over a decade of work focused on maternal and infant care, Kang Keqing vigorously critiqued the "greatness" of motherhood, and those who would exaggerate the usefulness of a mother's love for children. Whereas mothers, specifically, and parents, generally, ran the danger of privatizing the practice of family life and thus disrupting the transmission of socialist morality, she argued, fully collective day care and schools were much better able to raise future generations of communist citizens.

But, as was often the case during highly politicized moments, the devil lay in the details. In the article, Kang simultaneously argued that "mothers should love their own children *and* love the children in the "big family of socialism"; a specific recognition of the subjectivity of motherhood, and its relationship to the larger project of socialist construction. Even more significant were Kang Keqing's expectations regarding such a roll-out: "In the *future*, day cares *could gradually* establish twenty-four-hour care, *according to the conditions and needs of locali-ties*. Primary schools *could* also *gradually* change from day schools to residential schools" (Kang 1958, 9, italics mine). This was not a call to immediately eradicate motherhood or the family, rather, just the opposite: a careful moderation of Liu Shaoqi's public statements on the future of the family.

To that end, Kang Keqing strategically quoted Liu's September remarks on the family, in the less radical form they had become: "We advocate and emphasize socialist education, but that does not mean we don't want family education. Liu Shaoqi also instructed in his remarks: family education is still necessary. Chil-dren will still spend a certain time living in the family, the family [thus] still has responsibility for educating and caring for children" (Kang 1958, 9).

In the following issue, *Women-Work* published pieces that directly challenged War Communism's disregard for the health and welfare of women and children, and the ACWF. In the lead article in the November 22 issue, for example, *Women-Work* published a wide-ranging discussion of conditions in Jiangsu, as prepared by the Jiangsu Women's Federation (*WW* no. 22 [1958], 2–4). Unlike many of the reports published in *Women-Work* in the wake of the Beidaihe meetings, which largely extolled the early successes of the GLF, the Jiangsu Women's Federation discussed at length problems in the communal dining halls, and openly critiqued the quality of food, canteen-related corruption, and caregivers who lacked train-ing: with over 90 percent of the staff illiterate, "the only way to deal with the children was to coax and scare them." The article also included a plea for the development of more overnight childcare, primarily as a measure to address the needs of mothers working nightshifts.

In the same issue, *Women-Work* (no. 22 [1958], 7, 17) published a report from the Xuchang Women's Federation Office, under the auspices of the Henan Women's Federation, that criticized conditions on the steel-making site in the mountains, including the lack of unisex bathrooms and menstruation products, and the imperative to carry out heavy work while menstruating. Finally, and in the same issue, the periodical also published a brief report of the investigative findings of the working groups that had been conducted earlier that fall (*WW* no. 22 [1958], 13–14).

The timing of the publications was important. During October and November, Mao Zedong had grown increasingly concerned about the excesses of the GLF, suspicious that he was not being given a true picture of what was transpiring on the ground. Many in the most senior echelons of the CCP, including Zhou Enlai and Chen Yun, did not feel themselves in a position to speak truth to power—even as they harbored doubts about the GLF's ability to meet production targets (Teiwes and Sun 1999, 121–22). Mao Zedong thus undertook an inspection tour in the latter half of October, meeting with local cadres to try and assess the situation. He also relied on members of his own household for information about conditions on the ground (122–24). In late November, fear to be seen to the "right" of the Chairman was so high "it was now the Chairman who seemingly dragged other radicals to more 'reasonable' positions" (135). By way of contrast, Cai Chang and her allies were already airing their concerns about the toll of the mobilizations on women and children, including their concerns about the fate of the ACWF.

How could this have been? How could the least powerful CCP leaders have had the courage to speak out when so few others would?[27] It might have been that Mao's comments in Anhui in September emboldened the advocacy that followed. Specifically, Mao argued:

> Women cannot be thoroughly liberated when there are still women who do not have one or two thousand jin per year, when [some women] have no [access to] public dining halls, nursing homes, childcare, when [some women] have no [access to] literacy training, primary school, middle school, and university.

And further:

> It is only possible to thoroughly emancipate women *when the People's Communes are run well*. The People's Communes adopt the free supply and free wage [system], in which the wage is issued to the individual and not the patriarch, (something that makes] young people and women very happy. It is in this way that patriarchy and the right of bourgeois ideology is destroyed. (ACWF 1958b [1999], emphasis mine)

It could also be that Mao heard directly from Li Fuchun and Cai Chang on the issues of women and children, the family, and the ACWF. Li Fuchun, for example, may well have found a receptive audience in Mao Zedong when they met in early November—the only central leader consulted by Mao at this time (Teiwes and Sun 1999, 130). As an adopted member of Mao's household, it is also possible that Cai Chang herself may have also had a frank personal exchange with Mao Zedong during this time as well. What we do know is that in the wake of weeks of intense advocacy, the Chairman specifically addressed Cai Chang's criticisms about the separation of husbands and wives into barracks. In the third week of November, Mao instructed party leaders to

> Abolish the patriarchal [family] system [that derives] from history. Ensure that homes are built which are conducive to men and women, old and young living together; when [work] is intense, they may be separated. Building homes without proper arrangements is a coercive method. Abolish only the patriarchal [family] system [deriving] from history. At present a family still needs a head, namely the most capable, not necessarily the most senior (Mao 1958 [1989], 456).

Less than a week later, Cai Chang sent a report from the ACWF Party Group to the Central Committee Secretariat, with a personal note attached (ACWF 1958b [1999]). Similar to Luo Qiong's arguments, the ACWF Party Group report was explicit regarding the costs of dismantling organizational support specific to women and children. Insufficient, subpar, and understaffed social services undermined both women's liberation and the GLF itself. The ACWF Party Group was also able to politically strengthen this argument by referring directly to comments that Mao Zedong had made while touring Anhui in September.

Ultimately, the advocacy was successful. Before the year came to a close, both the family and the ACWF were affirmed as central to the project of socialist construction. Indeed, Peng Dehuai, acting as a representative of the Central Committee, gave a public address to a conference of women activists in December highlighting the important responsibility that women played in educating the next generation both at home and on the collective care structures (Peng 1958, 2–3). The "thorough liberation of women" was "*becoming* realized" (*chengwei xianshi*), he argued, in the context of socialism that enabled a "happy, democratic, and united family life." Cai Chang also directly disputed the idea that the advent of collectivization meant the end of the family. In Cai Chang's publications in December and in the months that followed she was unequivocal on the importance of the family and its relationship to the project of women's liberation and the GLF (for example, Cai 1958b; 1959a).

Just as important, the ACWF's status as an independent mass organization received the backing of the CCP leadership. In early December the Central Committee instructed grassroots governments to maintain local women's federations. Specifically, the final version of the December 7 memo issued to provincial, municipal, and autonomous party committees, and signed by Deng Xiaoping, stipulated that women's federations were not to be disbanded at the county level and above (ACWF 1958b [1999]; Dong, Cai, and Tan 1992, 313).

Three days later, the Central Committee issued its "Resolution on Some Questions Concerning the People's Communes" (CC 1958 [1960]). The resolution not only sought to moderate some of the goals and methods of the GLF (Yang 1996, 44), recognizing that the transition from socialism to communism, was a "gigantic and extremely complex task" that could take "fifteen or twenty years" (CC 1958 [1960], 216), but simultaneously reaffirmed the role of the state in guiding the people's communes in carrying out the necessary "division of labour in production and exchange of commodities with other people's communes and state-owned enterprises" (CC 1958 [1960], 223), and in accordance with the principle of "running the communes industriously and thriftily" (CC 1958 [1960], 224). While not repudiating the military methods of mobilization, the resolution nonetheless emphasized democratic management: "It is absolutely impermissible to use 'getting organized along military lines' as a pretext or to make use of the militia system—which is directed against the enemy—to impair, in the least, democratic life in the commune and the militia organizations" (CC 1958 [1960], 231). And while not naming the ACWF specifically, the resolution nonetheless devoted an entire section (section 5) to addressing the multitude of problems raised by Women's Federation leaders during the fall. The CCP must "care for the people and correct the tendency to see only things and not human beings"; "it is wrong to set production and people's livelihoods against each other and to imagine that attention to the livelihood of the masses will hamper production" (CC 1958 [1960], 226). Collective services should be run well, couples and families should be permitted to reside together, and the health of women should be protected. With respect to the "people's livelihood" the resolution thus adopted wholesale the Total War position being advocated by Cai Chang, Li Fuchun, and their allies.

There was one final signal that Total War was in the ascendance: namely, Li Dequan was finally accepted to join the CCP on December 1, 1958 (Li and Zhang 2007, 338). Given the fate of other senior Women's Federation leaders during the Anti-Rightist Movement, and Li Dequan's own social gospel roots, this was no small matter. But it was a crucial one. If nothing else Li's admittance to the CCP was a signal that at least some of the most senior party brass viewed the welfare of women and children as key to the welfare of the PRC during this historic moment of rapid transition.

The GLF has largely been studied through the seemingly gender-neutral lens of political-economy, a mass mobilization that catastrophically failed to meet the utopic production targets set by Mao and the central and provincial leaders who supported him. In this chapter I have sought to tell a different story about the earliest months of the GLF, and that is one centered on the attachments that fueled it. While many elite and grassroots leaders became caught up in the emancipatory possibilities of the communes and the collectivization of social services, opinions diverged as to the consequences of the communes for the status of the family itself. From the perspective of Li Fuchun, Cai Chang, and others invested in Total War, the social support on the communes was a welcome solution to the problems faced by women that had become apparent during the Socialist High Tide. The universal introduction of dining halls and childcare was meant to support householders; it was not intended to supplant their role in the family nor supplant the family altogether. From the perspective of a number of other officials, including Liu Shaoqi and radicalized provincial leaders, the social support enabled military-style mobilizations regardless of physiological gender or family circumstances. The rapid imposition of War Communism at the grassroots thus ran roughshod over the some of the most sacred values of the federation, including protecting the health of women and children and cultivating harmonious socialist families.

As two of Mao's most loyal friends and supporters, Cai Chang and Li Fuchun, worked closely to rearticulate the mobilization in a way that maintained the importance of the socialist household in support of the project of rapid development. Cai Chang's determination to maintain household and ACWF was part of a decades' long effort to interpret and fulfill Mao's direction for the CCP, through the crafting of a "correct" position on women, and women's leadership. At first glance, Li Fuchun's role is a little more curious. He was, after all, the same economic czar who worked feverishly throughout the fall of 1958 producing fantastic projections in steel production, projections that, in turn, spurred forward the twenty-four-hour work schedules at the grassroots. And yet, his policy views did not flow in lockstep with some of his provincial comrades. The couples' deep involvement in convening meetings, leading investigations, and subsequent reporting to Mao may well have influenced Mao's statement: "Abolish *only* the patriarchal system from history" (italics mine). In the context of this companionate advocacy, the enactment of the Loyal Soldier meant defending the family and the ACWF, even as the couple's own exuberance for aspects of War Communism, including utopic production targets, undermined their capacity to fully do so.

But it was not only Li Fuchun and Cai Chang articulating and advocating for a Total War approach to making the Leap. Others took considerable risk to speak up as well. Tian Min and Kang Keqing proudly recall defying their leadership: in Tian's case her local party leaders; in Kang's, the second most powerful official in the country. In both cases, a Woman Warrior state of activism mediated the defense of vulnerable women and children, even as these same two women themselves remained far more committed to the work of the Youth League and military than women-work. Provincial Women's Federation leaders also took risks, publishing concerns about the collective facilities and the conditions women were facing on irrigation and steel-making projects. Overall, the ACWF's fall campaign to moderate the impact of War Communism was nothing short of extraordinary, with Women's Federation leaders at the provincial level and at the center collaborating to reassert the health and well-being of women, children, and the family in the unprecedented mobilization that was the GLF.

And Li Dequan, against all odds, launched a new national mobilization of maternal and infant health care delivery in August 1958. Indeed, at the same moment party leaders across the country were denying any physiological or historical differences between men and women, Li Dequan organized to address reproductive health and the mother-child bond. Her reward? Party membership, a status which she had longed to assume for years. It is in this way also that the ACWF served as a central arena for articulating an alternative approach to making a GLF, even as it withstood attack from officials who saw its role as a remnant of history. Indeed, the fact that the Huoyue Women's Federation continued to implement midwifery reform and birth control through the double diligences and harmonious family slogans in the fall of 1958 suggests that the Total War effort continued even as War Communism engulfed the countryside, and even as total investment in reproductive and children's health care seemingly declined (see graph earlier in chapter).

The mass militarized mobilizations that took place in 1958 nonetheless dealt a catastrophic blow to family-centered reform in Wenhe, Huoyue, and Gaoshan. This is not only because of the extractive demands inherent in War Communism as it transpired on the construction projects, but also because of the attached imperatives inherent to the Total War model as it was simultaneously implemented on the brigades. War Communism imperiled an ACWF-centered approach to the GLF at the grassroots and at the party center, yes, but did so in the context of a Total War project that advocated familial austerity and imposed domestic harmony, and in the wake of the terror unleashed through the Socialist Education Movement. The ongoing tension between the two visions, and the personal ties through which they were enacted, contributed to the disastrous outcomes in the months and years to follow.

9

LEADERS

> Don't write about me, write about Chairman Mao! [You] must propagandize Chairman Mao. The accomplishments of women-work have been achieved under the correct leadership of Mao Zedong and the Central Committee.
>
> —Cai Chang, quote from Su, *The Biography of Cai Chang*

> I have been a cadre for all my life, and I haven't had many difficulties. . . . A good man is meant to be a soldier, and good iron is meant to make nails [*hao nanzi yao dang bing, hao tie yao da ding*].
>
> —Hou Qiuyi, 132

> When I first started, I was rather impatient. I didn't believe that women were inferior to men. You only needed to show men that you could do some work, in the end no one was stronger than the other. I relied on subjective initiative to move forward, and similarly carried out my work in this way.
>
> —Yang Junxia, 83

In July and August of 1959, the CCP leadership gathered at Lushan, the same Jiangxi mountaintop where the Chongqing Coalition had first coalesced in 1938. The leadership was meeting to discuss the progress of the GLF, which had been officially underway for a year. The prognosis, many agreed, was not good. The drive for rapid industrialization was proving more costly than anticipated. The extraction of rural laborers from fields to work on steel making and irrigation projects in home counties and in urban factories, reduced the capacity to harvest while simultaneously increasing the demand for grain. Despite attempts to moderate the communization movement, however, local cadres continued to make procurement promises on which they could not deliver. When the state came to collect on those promises, many villages were left with nothing.[1]

The CCP leadership knew that its legitimacy rested in large part on its ability to feed the population. Both the Qing and Guomindang governments had been largely discredited because of their inability to cope with crises of both national and international origin. Natural disasters were especially perilous, given the long-standing belief that rulers who did not protect the people could lose their mandate to govern (Perry 2002a, ix). And yet, the CCP did not pivot from War Communism in 1959. In contrast with 1938 and 1949, when elite women leaders effectively mobilized personal and family ties to address domestic crises, Lushan ushered in a second wave of mobilization and procurement that decimated the health and welfare of rural women, men, and children. The subsequent losses were staggering; as the GLF was finally brought to a halt in 1961, more than 20 percent of the female rural labor force were suffering from uterine prolapse. In areas with wet rice cultivation, 50–80 percent of the female rural labor force were suffering from amenorrhea (Luo 1980 [1988], 558).[2] The famine that unfolded between 1959 and 1961 thus lay waste to a rural population already suffering from overwork and exhaustion. It was a deadly combination.

The GLF, and the starvation, disease, and injury that it precipitated, can be understood as a massive failure of state capacity.[3] Even as the capacity of the PRC to achieve other goals remained strong, the state's inability, and in some cases outright refusal, to recognize and respond to the crisis would have devastating consequences for the women and children at the heart of its revolutionary project. It need not have turned out this way. In the months leading up to Lushan, Women's Federation officials at the center and provincial levels of the polity challenged the brutality of mass mobilizations and rural conditions of increasing scarcity. Working through both informal and formal channels of communication, these leaders became an important part of an emergent internal warning system. Were it not for Lushan, the ACWF, and the broader maternalist social policy regime in which it was embedded, might have played a major role in the prevention of further famine and injury. It was only when the Chairman felt his power challenged that he threw down the gauntlet: either side with his belief that he was under attack or be subject to political ostracization. In the disastrous months following, the central leadership chose Mao.

Cai Chang and Li Fuchun were among those who most fervently backed the Chairman, placing both the central planning apparatus and the Women's Federation at the center of the revival of the GLF. In the ACWF, Cai Chang's leadership of a new Anti-Rightist Movement contributed to a climate in which few dared to critique the policies that were leading the country on the road to disaster. Instead, longtime friends and allies, including outspoken provincial Women's Federation chairs, fell victim to another purge, and the federation itself became one of the primary vehicles through which the GLF's mass mobilization could continue unchecked. After Lushan, a deadly combination of fear and loyalty prevented the elite women leaders, who had for so long served on the frontlines of relief and social welfare work, from speaking about and directly addressing the crisis. Just as deadly, the ACWF reinforced famine conditions by labeling criticisms of hunger as "rightism" and by continuing to push household austerity when there was nothing left to consume, much less save.

The catastrophe that engulfed rural China did not, however, impact everyone equally on the ground. The mortality rates in 1960, the worst year of the famine, for example, were more than triple in Anhui (68.6 per 1000) and double in Henan (39.6 per 1000) than they were in Jiangsu (18.4 per 1000) and Jiangxi (16.1 per 1000) (Yang 1996, 38). While ecological advantages and favorable tax regimes improved survival rates across provinces (Chen 2011), what Chen (2011) calls the "leadership factor" was of greatest importance (see also, Yang 1996; Yang 2008; Yang 2012; Yang, Xu, and Tao 2014; Cao and Yang 2015). Leadership at the local level also saved lives, including in the hard-hit province of Sichuan (Bramall 2011), where mortality rates were 47.0 per 1000 (Yang 1996, 38).

During the 1957 Anti-Rightist Movement and the GLF that followed, radical provincial and local leadership has been variously explained as an expression of clientelism and of provincial-central struggles (Bramall 2011; Cao and Yang 2015; Domenach 1995; Forster 1997; Teiwes 1979; Yang 2012). Yang (2012, 397) also argues that radicalism was more likely in contexts in which "the leading cadre's political attitude most closely matched Mao's." The radicalism of the first secretaries in charge of Henan (Wu Zhipu), Sichuan (Li Jingquan), and Anhui (Zeng Xisheng), for example, was produced by Mao's cultivation of these leaders, and each was rewarded by his loyalty. Xicun's history of violent conflict and dedication to the teachings of Mao similarly produced a local leadership marked by militancy. This was true for the Huoyue cousins, Zhang and Hou, first introduced in chapter 4, one of whom beat the women in her charge and the other who, in one instance, justified starvation as an expression of revolutionary sacrifice.

As I have already argued, however, loyalty to Mao should not be conflated with radicalism nor with self-serving clientelism per se. By 1958, the PRC was a Mao-centered polity in which personal commitments to Maoist ideology and to Mao himself, produced both War Communism and Total War as underlying policy frameworks for the GLF. In the face of hunger and injury in 1959, officials at multiple levels of the party-state similarly sought to reprioritize the health and welfare of the masses as an expression of Maoist leadership. In the province of Jiangxi, for example, the provincial Women's Federation chair and sister-in-law of Mao, Zhu Danhua, was protected by the province's second party secretary and governor, Shao Shiping. The Jiangxi provincial leadership consequently staved off calamitous death rates by refusing some of the excesses encouraged in more radical provinces (Chen 2011). The party secretary of Gaoshan's Mu Guiying brigade, whose own leadership was marked by the Maoist conception of subjective initiative, courageously advocated for a grain loan on behalf of her community. Local enactments of a Woman Warrior state of activism did make a difference in the lives of women and children in rural China, even if the highly charged fields in which they materialized limited the impact of those isolated interventions of Maoist resistance.

Critique and Contention, December 1958 to September 1959

Few global leaders have acknowledged much less publicly addressed menstruation as a matter of national importance. And yet, in December 1958 Mao Zedong, chairman of the CCP, insisted that menstrual health be protected in the new regulations guiding the governance of the communes: "We must protect both pregnant women and women who have just given birth by ensuring that they get plenty of rest. Moreover, we should make sure that menstruating women also get plenty of rest; they must not do taxing work, work in cold water, or work throughout the night" (Shi 1988, 137).

Mao's recognition of reproductive health followed on the heels of the intensive advocacy that Cai Chang led during the autumn of 1958. Over the winter and spring of 1959, Cai Chang continued to stress the importance of protecting women's health in her major writings, suggesting that some leaders' thinking about women's health protection was "conflicted," a condition that needed to be rectified (Cai 1958b; 1959a). Vice chair of the ACWF and minister of health, Li Dequan, similarly acted across her portfolios, exhorting medical authorities to avoid exaggerated claims and to adhere to a scientific spirit (Li and Li 2015, 62). In an essay devoted to women's health published in *Women of China* in early 1959, Li Dequan (1959) wrote at length about the vulnerabilities that women faced, arguing that women's physical capacities were less than men, and that they were endowed with specific physiological characteristics that required special protections. As the CCP moved into the new calendar year, however, it quickly became clear that neither women's health nor women's organizations were being universally protected. One of the first to come under attack was the Jiangsu Women's Federation.

In early 1959, and in flagrant violation of the orders of the Central Committee to maintain the Women's Federations at the county level and above, the Jiangsu Provincial Party Committee amalgamated the Jiangsu Women's Federation with the Labor Department and Workers' Union into one Worker's Ministry (Lu and Miao 2000, 8). The rationale? Women's equality had all but been achieved. The decision came on the heels of months of push and pull within the provincial leadership, and between the Jiangsu Women's Federation and the leaders of the new communes below. An initial blow had landed nearly a year earlier when the provincial CCP had reduced the staff of the provincial Women's Federation from forty-three to twenty-six, while simultaneously eliminating the connected propaganda and social welfare departments. In April 1958, and in anticipation of a similar change instituted at the center in September, the Jiangsu Provincial Central Committee abolished its Women's Committee, establishing the Party Group of the Provincial Women's Federation in its place (Lu and Miao 2000, 249). And then, during the fall of 1958, Jiangsu commune leaders began to disband women's organizations on the commune structures. This cascade of organizational diminishment could have neutralized the Jiangsu Women's Federation. Instead, its leadership came out swinging.

Throughout the late fall of 1958 and for the first half of 1959, the Jiangsu Women's Federation leadership countered the onslaught underway by leveraging close personal ties to the senior leadership of the ACWF, and to Cai Chang, in particular. Cai Chang herself had deep roots in the province, having served as chair of the Jiangsu Women's Committee in the late 1920s (Lu and Miao 2000, 70). Shi Jian, vice chair of the Jiangsu Women's Federation, was in turn deeply devoted to Cai Chang and Deng Yingchao. Indeed, and as recounted in chapter 3, Shi Jian joined the CCP in 1939 at the age of eighteen, inspired by revolutionary stories about the two women leaders. In Shi Jian's words, she was "really loved" (*feichang de ai*) by both Cai Chang and Deng Yingchao, and the relationship between the ACWF and the Jiangsu Women's Federation was relatively close (*bijiao qinmi*).

Shi Jian attended the first meetings of the ACWF in 1949, held the role of chair of the Subei Women's Federation during the early 1950s, and in 1956 assumed the position of chair of the newly established Jiangsu Women's Federation. Shi Jian also became a member of the Standing Committee of the ACWF (Lu and Miao 2000, 82). According to Ge Ying, 109, and Shi Jian, one of Shi Jian's staff had worked as Cai Chang's secretary during the 1950s. In addition, Zhang Yun, who became a vice chair of the ACWF in 1953, had a long history of working in the province (Zhao 2003c, 700). Correspondence between the ACWF and the Jiangsu Women's Federation, which was frequent, took place through internal reporting and telex, and through official visits, including an official visit made by Cai Chang on at least one occasion. The Jiangsu Women's Federation generally, and Shi Jian specifically, were strong advocates of the double diligences, with 80–90 percent of the population reportedly having received education about the policy by spring 1958 (Lu and Miao 2000, 156–57); Shi Jian herself gave a major speech on the double diligences during the GLF. In early June 1958, Shi Jian also traveled to Vienna as part of a fifteen-member delegation to the Fourth Congress of the International Democratic Women's Federation (Lu and Miao 2000, 82), a meeting at which Cai Chang was reelected vice chair; Li Dequan and

Xu Guangping were elected directors; and Cao Mengjun and Yang Yunyu were elected alternate directors (Yang 1991, 111–12).

In short, Shi Jian embraced the central precepts of Marxist maternalist equality and strongly identified with the women who were the ACWF's most important leaders: "If it had been up to me rather than the [Party], I would have spent my whole life doing [women-work], especially because the ACWF's Deng Yingchao and Cai Chang really loved me." These expressions of love and sisterhood are critical for understanding Shi Jian's early political engagement and subsequent losses during the GLF. For Shi Jian, the ACWF was an affective site of belonging; the revolution's maternalist vehicle for social transformation *and* cohesion.

The close ties between Cai Chang and the Jiangsu Women's Federation became vividly apparent in November 1958 when Cai Chang's advocacy to maintain the integrity of the Women's Federation and to protect women's health was at its peak. Indeed, the ACWF published a short introductory editorial urging readers to reflect on the Jiangsu Women's Federation's November 1959 essay, the first in a series of increasingly critical reports in *Women-Work* identifying challenges in the provision of social services and in the protection of women's health at the grassroots. At a moment when few in the CCP hierarchy were willing to challenge any aspect of the GLF, the Jiangsu Women's Federation's efforts to articulate and publicize a critical counternarrative was no small matter.

The successful advocacy that Cai Chang undertook to maintain the lower levels of the Women's Federation, and that Deng Xiaoping partially affirmed, in turn, provided Shi Jian with the backing she needed to persuade county leaders to restore women's organizations and thus "continue the independence of the Women's Federation." And while the Jiangsu Provincial Party Committee's sudden decision to combine the Jiangsu Women's Federation with the Labor Department and Worker's Union in January 1959 would prove another significant setback, the Jiangsu Women's Federation was nonetheless able to maintain its independence and name (Lu and Miao 2000, 250). Shi Jian argues that the amalgamation took place in the absence of approval by the ACWF and the National Party Committee (*guojia dangwei*). Shi Jian personally felt supported by Deng Xiaoping's key interventions at that time, quoting him as saying, "Capitalist societies permit mass organizations, permit the masses to organize; how can we not have mass organizations and a Women's Federation?" Under the leadership of Shi Jian, who now held the position of executive minister in the new Worker's Ministry, the Jiangsu Women's Federation continued to advocate for the protection of women's health. In April 1959, for example, *Women-Work* published an article prepared by the Jiangsu Women's Federation that urged women cadres to "boldly use and carefully protect women's labor" (*WW* no. 8 [1959], 4). Consistent with a Woman Warrior ethic of heroism and care, the article called on women cadres to rectify cadre indifference to women's health and to persuade cadres, and the women in their charge, of the need to protect "natural and physiological phenomena" such as pregnancy and menstruation. The article also sought to correct the "misunderstanding" that production tasks could not be completed if women's labor was protected, and emphasized that women's health was a leading cause of the health crisis at the grassroots.

Over the first eight months of 1959, the intense exchange and sharing of information that marked the Jiangsu Women's Federation relationship with the ACWF was not unique. During this key period, multiple provincial federation leaders shared investigative findings through back channels, publications in *Women-Work*, and at organizational conferences. The research and reporting undertaken by Women's Federation leaders at all levels of the organization would prove critical at a moment when reliable information was in short supply. As recently argued by Ghosh (2020, 258–59, 265), data gathering during the GLF underwent a process of decentralization and indigenization in which each level of the administration was expected to participate in statistical work through the adoption of the "typical survey" (*dianxing diaocha*). Insofar as this method relied on the "quality of the investigator and the duration of the survey" (Ghosh 2020, 276), however, it fell prey to the politics of the moment. The only way that central and provincial leaders could rely on data, itself often subject to wild exaggeration (Yang 1996, 65), was to undertake investigations themselves and to demand accuracy from their direct reports. The ACWF played a key role in this process.

In January 1959, senior ACWF leaders formed six working groups to survey conditions on the ground, mobilize women to participate in the technological revolution, and to protect women's health in Guangdong, Guangxi, Zhejiang, Shanxi, Hunan, Jiangxi, Fujian, Yunnan, Inner Mongolia, Ningxia, and the Beijing suburbs. Kang Keqing and Zhu De, both deeply concerned about the state of the dining halls and the need to consolidate the family system, traveled to Guangdong and Hunan in early 1959. The working groups, some of which continued their investigations until March, reported their findings back to the Women's Federation secretariat (Kang 1993, 446–47; Yang 1991, 117).

The accuracy of investigative reporting was of particular concern to former Jiangxi Women's Federation chair, Zhu Danhua, who sought to avoid false production claims by requiring Women's Federation cadres to personally confirm the results of experimental fields or face sanctions (Ma 2013, 166). "In this way," she said, "the figures reported by the Women's Federation were generally more accurate." In this way also, Zhu Danhua was documenting and reporting the unsustainability of the food supply at the grassroots at a time when few other leaders dared to do so.

Zhu Danhua was the widow of Mao's younger brother, Mao Zemin, who was killed in 1943. Unlike Cai Chang, whose siblinglike relationship with the Chairman sent her running to Mao's defense during moments of intense party rectification, Zhu had the opposite response. Indeed, Zhu adamantly refused to purge a comrade who had shared critiques with the provincial federation during the 1957 Anti-Rightist Movement: "At that time I felt her opinions were aiding our work, what she said was the truth. Chairman Mao said, 'punish the former and save the latter, to cure the disease and save the life [*chengqianbihou, zhibingjiuren*],' we [thus] should be thanking her." When pushed further to meet the quota for rightists in the unit, Zhu said she would take full responsibility for failing to meet the quota, which, she noted, shut everyone up (Ma 2013, 159). Zhu's willingness to validate and protect "truth-telling" in 1958 was likely also reinforced by Jiangxi's unified provincial leadership. As argued by Chen (2011, 214–15), Jiangxi's governor and second party secretary, Shao Shiping, and first party secretary, Yang Shangkui, both maintained strong ties with the local Jiangxi populace and took early steps to moderate the impact of the GLF. After attending an important set of party meetings in Zhengzhou in late February and early March, Shao Shiping set about rectifying exaggerated production claims and coercive mobilization practices, a moderation of the GLF that Shao understood as being ordered by Mao Zedong himself (Ma 2013, 164–65). Yang Shangkui consequently dissolved more than eighty thousand dining halls in 1959 (Chen 2011, 214), an act that reinforced the more moderate political environment that marked Jiangxi governance throughout the period of the GLF.

Women-Work also played a role. During this period, provincial, county, and commune investigative reports were being forwarded to the ACWF, some of which were published in the internal journal. The reports offered snapshots of the brewing crisis on the new communes, including reproductive injury, poorly managed dining halls, neglect of childcare, exhausted caregivers, and malnourished nursing mothers. Analysis of the cause of the problems as they were shared in *Women-Work* over the winter and spring of 1959, however, ranged widely. The high incidence of uterine prolapse (19 percent) in one Sichuan village, for example, was attributed to both "past exploitation of the reactionary ruling class" and women not resting after giving birth (*WW*, no. 3 [1959], 12), while the spread of infectious diseases among children in the Beijing suburbs, including whooping cough and measles, was attributed to "unusual weather" (*WW*, no. 4 [1959], 12). But many of the problems reported, including insufficient health protections for women and shoddy social services, were not explained away with euphemistic references to the past or to the weather. Instead, they were attributed to the continued implementation of mobilization practices that reinforced War Communism at the rural grassroots.

The conflict between meeting production goals and implementing health protections that the Jiangsu Women's Federation highlighted in its April report was echoed in many other reports across the winter and spring. One of the biggest issues was the practice of male brigade and team leaders prioritizing production before all else, while at the same time minimizing or even mocking steps being taken to protect reproductive health. Fear also continued to be a factor, with some cadres dreading punishment if they did not complete their tasks. In an incisive report, Zhu Danhua drew on Cai Chang's words to argue that protecting women's health was a way to improve production: "Urgent production needs cannot be made into an excuse for ignoring labor protection" (*WW*, no. 6 [1959], 7). But insofar as the capacity to attend to the needs of women was predicated on whether male cadres were also "paying attention," as one county report from the province of Fujian described in the same issue (*WW*, no. 6 [1959], 11), protecting women's health proved a tall order indeed. Instead, "commandism" (*qiangpo mingling*) continued to prevail.

The direct consultations by the ACWF with regional Women's Federation leaders (province, autonomous regions, and cities) also revealed serious problems on the ground. Those consulted expressed concerns about steel works mobilizations that involved everyone (men, women, old, and young), leaving only the women, elderly, and weak to manage the agricultural harvest. As a consequence of overwork, women's reproductive health was also compromised, with women suffering from uterine prolapse. Critical commentaries included: "What kind of main force [*zhu li jun*] is this? A main force of suffering [*shou zui*], [that should be] pitied [*kelian*]." Some Women's Federation officials were also openly questioning the makeshift steel production and the dining hall system (Kang 1993, 450).

With some 25.17 million people lacking food in fifteen provinces (Yang 2012, 447), by April 1959 it was clear to many at the provincial level and in the central leadership that the economic system was failing. It was at this time that Mao Zedong, with Chen Yun's full involvement, initiated a series of reforms that included reducing steel targets and the numbers of rural workers in urban factories by some ten million people and reprioritizing agricultural production (Yang 1996, 46–47; Teiwes and Sun 1999, 154–55). Regional experiments in Anhui and Henan also took place, whereby authority over land, animals, farm tools, and grain was returned to the household, or an accounting system called "household contracting" (*baochan daohu*). Dining hall participation was also broadly relaxed (Yang 1996, 48–50).

In June, the Total War conception of the household was revived to support these reforms. According to Kang Keqing's (1993, 447) recollections of Zhu De's critique, "It is impossible to live without a family. There are so many wives and children. If the family is not responsible [for them], who will be?" Similar to many other officials, Zhu De's critique was twofold: the obliteration of the capacity of the household to accumulate resources and manage its consumption was harming the enthusiasm of the masses and leading to wastefulness. It was the responsibility of the family, and not the state, to manage household resources: "It is better to return to the family" (*haishi hui jia hao*) (Kang 1993, 447–49). Zhu De's concerns were shared by others, including Dong Biwu and Lin Feng, who sent a joint letter in June to the Central Committee advocating that grain be redistributed to households as but one measure to address the severity of the problems in the countryside (447). This effort to recentralize the household as an economic unit was matched by the ACWF. The lead editorial in *Women-Work* in June 1959 urged women's federations to recommence the double diligences policy, arguing that it could help overcome the unfolding "temporary difficulties," including natural disasters, through avoiding wastefulness and developing side household production (*WW*, no. 12 [1959]).

Scholars suggest that Mao arrived at Lushan prepared to work with his comrades to slow down the pace of change; indeed, his intention was to consolidate, not expand, the GLF (Lieberthal 1993, 104; MacFarquhar 1983, 160–72; Teiwes 1993, 306–11). However, a closer examination reveals not only contradictions in Mao's own thinking (Teiwes 1993, 308) but also a certain melancholy for the revolutionary past when the cause was clearer. On his way to Lushan, Mao visited his hometown, where he met with a number of old comrades, including the widows of close friends who had died for the revolution many years earlier (Li 1994, 301–12; MacFarquhar 1983, 181–90). Shortly after his arrival at Lushan, Mao also asked Zhu Danhua and Zeng Zhi to arrange for He Zizhen, Mao's ex-wife, who was at that time living in nearby Nanchang, to meet with him (Ma 2013, 168–70). The meeting was not a success; He Zizhen sobbed most of the hour they spent together. In the aftermath of the meeting, she suffered an emotional breakdown that mirrored one she had years earlier while incarcerated in a Soviet psychiatric hospital (Wang 1997, 209; Wei 2004, 34–38; Zeng 2011).[4] All in all, it was not an auspicious start to the Lushan gathering. But what happened next defied the expectations of even the most seasoned CCP veterans.

Some two weeks into the Lushan meeting, Peng Dehuai sent Mao a personal letter articulating his concerns about the GLF. During Peng's inspection visits to Gansu, Jiangxi, and Anhui in spring of 1959, he had seen many disturbing problems that he described and attributed to the excesses of the GLF. Peng, a revolutionary general with almost no involvement in economic planning, said little in the letter that was different from the discussions already underway. Results of the provincial and county-level Women's Federation investigations were shared in a meeting that took place at the same time as Lushan. Zhu Danhua herself expressed her deep reservations about the GLF with Deng Yingchao just prior to Lushan

(Ma 2013, 167), and with Kang Keqing and Zhu De during the meetings themselves (Kang 1993, 448). Deng Yingchao, in turn, asked Zhu Danhua to prepare materials to give to her at Lushan.

Despite the strong support within the central leadership for a more measured and careful approach to the GLF, Mao Zedong came to understand the content and meaning of Peng Dehuai's letter as a personal attack. In private meetings with Mao, several provincial leaders insisted that Peng's letter amounted to nothing short of a full-frontal assault on the GLF (Luo 2021, 15–16). Shortly after reading the letter, the Chairman shifted from being receptive to Peng's concerns—all of which Mao had expressed himself—to interpreting Peng's letter as part of a factional attempt to hijack the leadership of the CCP (18). Mao consequently went after the general "with a vengeance" (Lieberthal 1993, 105), setting aside goals of achieving policy consensus in favor of buttressing the party against the onslaught of the class enemy (Luo 2021, 18). The Chairman's furious response spun the meetings into an uproar, propelling senior party leaders to either run for cover or to the Chairman's defense.

Upon hearing of the political crisis that had broken out, Mao's wife, Jiang Qing, rushed to Lushan and made separate and lengthy house calls to Deng Yingchao and Zhou Enlai, and to Cai Chang and Li Fuchun (Li 1994, 318).[5] Deng Yingchao, who had arrived at Lushan in poor health, quickly departed (Wang 1990, 76).[6] Under the stress of the Lushan conflict, Deng Yingchao's heart condition flared up. She did not participate in the ACWF rectification (Jin 1993, 2:555).

Cai Chang, by way of contrast, shifted into high gear. While it is unknown what was said at her meeting with Jiang Qing, we do know that in later years Mao would defend Cai Chang as one of the most "loyal and kind" people (Huang 2004, 64). Indeed, when Red Guards criticized Cai Chang during the Cultural Revolution, Mao Zedong was reportedly very upset and consequently declared, "Cai Chang is an honest and kind person, if she is struggled against then there are no good people left" (Su 1990, 220).[7] For her part, Cai Chang's support for Mao remained "unwavering" throughout the Anti-Rightist Movement, the GLF, and the Cultural Revolution (Su 1990, 219).

Cai Chang's first response to the Lushan crisis was to phone the ACWF and instruct the staff to prepare for a new round of rectification. This time the primary victim was Cao Guanqun, a long-serving senior Women's Federation official. Cao's crime? Her willingness to criticize commandism, the dining hall system, and the steel works (Kang 1993, 450–51) were criticisms that many of her colleagues had also expressed at the ACWF meeting of Women's Federation chairs while party officials gathered at Lushan (Ji 1992, 177). Kang Keqing (1993, 450–52) and Zhu De were also in deep trouble. When the Lushan meetings imploded, both Zhu De and Kang Keqing were criticized for having "rightist thinking."[8]

Years later, and even though she had agreed with Cao's criticisms of the GLF, Kang Keqing (1993, 451) recalled being too frightened to fully speak her mind.

The recommencement of the Anti-Rightist Movement directly impacted provincial Women's Federation chairs as well. The ACWF meetings in September targeted three leaders: the chairs of the Jiangxi, Fujian, and Sichuan women's federations. Zhu Danhua was accused of rightism for having compiled documentary materials on the dining halls for Deng Yingchao at Lushan. Whereas in 1957, Zhu Danhua had defended her comrade against charges of rightism, this time it was Zhu Danhua who was vigorously defended by both her comrades within the Jiangxi Women's Federation and by the province's second party secretary and governor, Shao Shiping. In the wake of Shao Shiping's judgment that Zhu's research findings were "truthful" (*shi shi*), she was spared. The chairs of the Sichuan and Fujian women's federations, however, were condemned as rightists by the ACWF and purged (Ma 2013, 182).

The 1959 Anti-Rightist Movement also destroyed Shi Jian's career. By her own account, Shi Jian had managed to maintain the quality of provincial women-work despite the diminishment of the Jiangsu Women's Federation earlier that year and despite the complicated lines of authority marking the new Worker's Bureau. Shi Jian's new boss, minister of the Worker's Bureau Xu Min, had little experience and relied heavily on Shi Jian. Xu Min was also the wife of the first party secretary of the province, Jiang Weiqing. Shortly after returning from the Lushan meetings, Jiang Weiqing accused Shi Jian of being a rightist for organizing a meeting that had been "requested by the masses." Although Jiang Weiqing had asked that Shi Jian take charge of the organization of this meeting, the revival of the Anti-Rightist Movement seemingly provided the provincial leader with an opportunity to purge Shi Jian. According to Shi Jian, he had always resisted the reinstatement of the lower levels of the Women's Federation, and after Lushan, "said that I opposed him." He said that "I wanted to be the minister," and that "I wanted to be a leader." Shi Jian and forty or fifty other senior leaders were consequently purged from their posts.

The shift in political tides at Lushan not only decimated the ranks of officials who had been attempting to document and to respond to the crisis, but it also broke down and tarnished the formal and informal lines of communication between localities and center. In *Women-Work*, the rapidly deteriorating political environment was such that resistance to the dining halls and/or declining food rations was framed as "right-leaning sentiment." In October, for example, *Women-Work* (1959 no. 20, 13) published a county report from Taihe, Anhui, that criticized rightist thinking behind a push to disband the dining halls. One of the "excuses" criticized in the report was that people did not have enough to eat. Given that by this time, the famine in Anhui was "teetering on the brink of reaching epic proportions" (Cao and Yang 2015, 1697), the report merely reinforced rather than sought to address the crisis underway.

The information exchange among party family networks also broke down. At the party center, Deng Yingchao and Kang Keqing ceased the investigative and reporting work they had begun before Lushan. At lower levels, blockades on movement prevented the passage of information, especially in areas that were afflicted with mass starvation. When the Women's Federation chair of Xinyang Prefecture sought to inform a comrade, an official in the CCP's North China bureau, of the starvation underway in Xiping County, for example, she sent a note to the official's wife, "to avoid discovery" (Yang 2012, 51). Although the note was written innocuously, ("I have something important to tell you"), it was returned the next day, indicating, as Yang (2012, 51) argues, "the extent of controls on information at that time."

Instead of responding to the crisis, the CCP launched a second phase of the GLF, with Li Fuchun and Cai Chang leading the charge. In September, Li Fuchun, still one of the most powerful economic czars in the country, argued that "speed is the fundamental issue of socialist construction" and urged his comrades in the agriculture ministry to "give full play to subjective initiative" and set "advanced indicators" in agricultural production (Fang and Jin 2001, 531–32), a position that reignited War Communism at the grassroots, reinforced inequities between city and countryside, and further depleted diminishing food stores. While Cai Chang's approach to the GLF continued to be marked by a Total War vision of social transformation, with women as frugal householders, enthusiastic fieldworkers, and social welfare keepers at its center, it was as though the forced mobilizations that she had previously criticized had somehow magically disappeared. Thus, while Cai Chang and Li Fuchun joined Deng Xiaoping, Bo Yibo, Liu Lantao, and other leaders on an investigative tour in Dongbei in fall of 1959 (Dong, Cai, and Tan 1992, 315–16), anything they might have found did not moderate the path that Mao had set, and that Cai Chang and Li Fuchun were now determined to implement. Indeed, Cai Chang (1959b) called on the ACWF to support the CCP to complete the second five-year plan, three years ahead of schedule.

In 1959, the CCP leadership chose to prioritize the state's capacity to produce and procure over the state's capacity to protect. In the absence of any structural changes to the economy or state provision of famine relief, and in the ongoing implementation of the renewed Anti-Rightist Movement, Li Dequan's continued calls for health protections, including the elimination of pests and diseases, amounted to little more than spitting in the wind (see, for example, Li 1960).[9] The ACWF's call to women householders to combat "natural disasters" through frugality and saving, as they did throughout the latter half of 1959 and 1960, was equally egregious. Indeed, the exhortation not to waste a "single grain of rice" (*WW*, no. 22 [1959]: 10), and to adopt frugal recipes (*WW*, no. 3 [1960]: 15), effectively minimized the responsibility of the leadership of the CCP, while throwing the burden of familial survival onto women householders themselves.[10] The consequences were particularly stark in Xicun and its surrounding hamlets.

Party Family Ties, Loyal Soldiers, and Famine

In Xicun, the famine was well under way when the villagers rose up in anger against Zhang Sumei, the women's head, and her husband, the village accountant. Shouting insults and wielding sticks, the group sought to avenge the accountant's murder of a man in a neighboring village. They were also angry with Zhang herself. Since becoming women's head in the village several years before, she had tyrannized women and men villagers—forcing women to carry out heavy field work while pregnant and humiliating people who arrived late to the dining hall. But while Zhang was always looking for opportunities to criticize others for their lack of adherence to collective principles, she herself was said to have dipped into the grain in the village's storage container kept next to her house. The villagers wanted to strike back against the hypocrisy and the abuse that they had experienced under the couple's leadership.[11] In the aftermath, Zhang, her husband, and Zhang's brother-in-law, a commune official, were all removed from their posts for their roles in the GLF.

Zhang frequently repeated that she never forced villagers to do anything against their will, nor did she ever take advantage of her leadership position to enrich herself: "At that time, the more you worked, the more you would get. If you don't work, you have nothing to eat. I never forced anyone to work, if they didn't come out to work, I did not do much about them. Do as they like. Whoever wanted to work, work; if you work, you get points. I didn't embarrass others. Just like that, I am always like that. I didn't criticize anyone because she was late, never!"

And yet, conversations with many other villagers and with Zhang's cousin suggest that her leadership was infused with violence.

In my first two visits to the village in the spring of 2001, two women, whom I interviewed separately, condemned Zhang as having treated villagers harshly in the fields and in the dining halls. For example, Li Xiaoyue, 24, who was newly married and in her early twenties at the start of the GLF, was furious with Zhang and Zhang's husband for their poor treatment of her family during the mobilization. Zhang, she told me, punished Li and her sister-in-law for being late to the dining hall by ordering them to pick sweet potatoes in the field until dark. Zhang was also very cruel to her own aunt. According to Li, after Zhang's aunt was seen taking two beans from the field to use as a salve for a sore on her lips, Zhang berated her in front of all the other villagers. When Zhang's aunt tried to explain, Zhang cried, "If everyone behaves like you what will become of the collective?"

Zhang forced Li Ailing, 30, to work through her first pregnancy and did not allow her to take any time off after giving birth. Like Li Xiaoyue, she accused Zhang of being a poor leader. Li Ailing held Zhang responsible for the starvation in the village because she "took others' rice and noodles away." Zhang also had access to resources other villagers did not. When Zhang gave birth to her first child in 1959, for example, the staff at the obstetrical clinic offered her a little extra. According to Zhang: "At that time even the chickens were collectivized, there were no eggs. I was at a higher level than other people. Although the eggs were collectivized, the brigade people gave me some eggs and gave my husband a little liquor. If I was a regular person then I wouldn't have received [that care]. I was higher than the others [so] they respected me and gave me some eggs. [laughs]"

The perception that Zhang ate better than other villagers and went out of her way to pick on individuals only seems to have exacerbated villager resentment and anger in the midst of famine. But it may well have been Zhang's violence that ultimately turned the villagers against her. As Zhang herself noted, when she worked on constructing a reservoir, "some people said I was a mad person, shouting and yelling all day long at the worksite." Hou Qiuyi, Zhang's cousin, however, suggested that Zhang's violence was physical as well: "Sometimes she beat people who were working hard, and [she] still beat them. If people were not working hard she should have been more persuasive and called them out. Beating [people] didn't work."

The conditions in Zhang's village may have been extreme—Li Xiaoyue, 24, for example, says the leaders were far worse in Zhang's village than they were in her natal village—but they were not uncommon. At a time when militias guarded the grain reserves (Li Liping, 17) and cadres humiliated and beat people for "hiding" or "stealing" grain, cadre violence was epidemic (Liang Jinfeng, 57; Wang Xiaosu, 16; Ji Hui, 124). Women cadres elsewhere were also perpetrators. A 1961 report by the ACWF suggests that during the GLF a small number of women cadres scolded and beat farmers in their charge, as well as publicly paraded people and deprived them of food, among other forms of punishment. Some did not care whether the masses lived or died (ACWF 1961c [1999]).

In Wenhe, as in Huoyue, daily rations were reduced to almost nothing by 1959:

> What was really hard was calling people. The dining halls were all empty so when you called people they didn't come out [to work]. Some people

couldn't get enough to eat or drink. They wanted to come here but there was only soup. It was only soup that the dining hall served at each meal. You'd call them and those stubborn folks would curse you. This is when women work was hardest. (Fang Huayun, 51)

Between 1958 and 1960, the population growth rate of Huoyue County decreased from 15 to -6.6 per thousand. In spring of 1959, the province sent Huoyue 3.5 million kilograms of grain to help with the "production shortage" (*HX* 1993, 32). As hunger engulfed Huoyue, Wenhe, and Gaoshan, edema took hold and many farmers resorted to scavenging for roots and secretly taking what they could from the collective fields.[12]

To a large degree, survival was determined by one's connections (guanxi) and familial background. In Gaoshan, for example, families with relations working in a nearby city could access rations not available to those whose family members only farmed (Lin Xiaohong, 73). To be assigned to work in the dining hall or in the childcare facility was a particular privilege—a privilege that in Zhang's village went to several women who were married to village leaders.[13] When I asked whether there were any difficulties with the day care facilities, Zhang Sumei retorted,

> The wife of the party secretary was taking care of the children there; the wife of the head of the local bank was there taking care of the kids. That was to say they did not have to work in the fields. It was later on when it was no longer in practice that [the day care] was disbanded. I donated

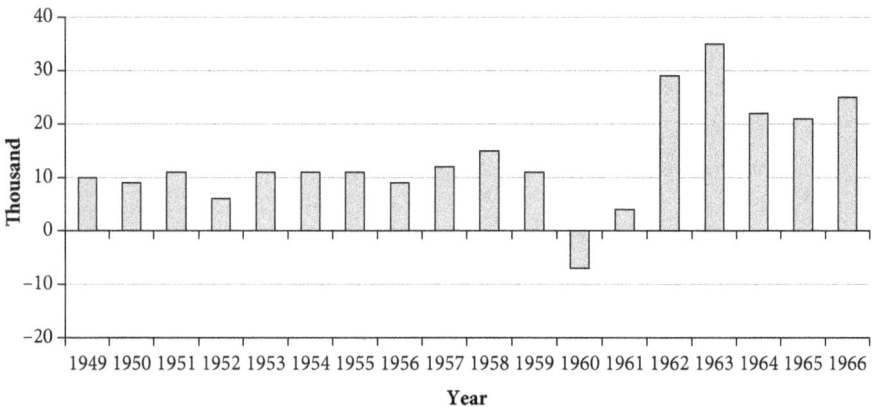

FIGURE 5. Natural growth rate of the population in Huoyue County, 1949–66, expressed per thousand. *Source: HX,* 1993, 404.

some tables, bamboo chairs to them and decorated very cozily for them. The wife of the secretary and the bank head were working there. Who would give them fewer points? Taking care of kids there and having enough to eat, how comfortable!

In an interview with Yan Shuqun, 43, and Pu Congxi, 156, in Wenhe, Yan recalled eating after meetings finished late at night, at the day care where they were held. Pu, who had earlier teased Yan for wanting her to establish a day care so that cadres like her could eat, laughed and said: "Wasn't I right? Back then the cadres were very special." Fang Huayun, 51, who resided in Yan's village, explained further in a separate interview:

> The cadres clearly ate more and took more. After eating supper they would still have night meetings so the cook would also cook for them. Then at night they would eat another meal; otherwise they wouldn't eat well. Sometimes when we women cadres would hold meetings and the masses had departed, two women cadres would come and one would make dough and the other would make the noodles and would brew it and then eat it. So this is the advantage for the cadres. When trying to improve the life of the commune members we would also fry dough for the members; there would be some leftover and the cadres would eat them. Well, the cook, [he] would eat the most but he wouldn't dare to eat them up since if he ate all of them the cadres would know.

Many of the retired leaders I interviewed complained at great length about contemporary corruption, holding up their own service records to contrast with reform-era officials living high on the backs of ordinary villagers. And yet one could argue that in places such as Huoyue, Wenhe, and Gaoshan, GLF-era leaders and their families were able to reap the benefits of the greatest privilege of all: survival.[14]

Party family ties not only worked to protect some over others; they also worked to exclude the politically undesirable. The relatives of individuals ascribed a landlord status or other politically suspect categories were at an extreme disadvantage when the food supply ran out. According to Zhou Changfen, 157, the only people who died in her area were "landlords, wealthy farmers, or historical bad elements." Unlike villagers with politically acceptable backgrounds who pilfered from collective fields to survive, the politically marginalized did not dare to try and steal food.[15] Former Gaoshan Commune women's head Qiu Zhaodi, 74, for example, described how she saved a nursing mother and her newborn from what otherwise would have been sure starvation because of the political sins of the baby's father:

> The husband had some kind of political black mark. When I went to visit the mother after giving birth she was very upset as she wasn't producing milk and the child was crying like a cat; she was afraid it would starve to death. She hadn't been given her 14 jin of grain because of her husband's political history. So I went to the leaders, they said that she was the relative of a counterrevolutionary, the masses did not want to give them grain. I said that no matter what the circumstances, you can't let them starve, otherwise you will be held responsible. They gave the grain, and the child was saved. [That child] is now more than forty years old.[16]

It is clear that family configurations and their embeddedness within local enactments of revolutionary privilege and exclusion often meant the difference between life and death. But while party family power grew during this period, the hardships party families inflicted cannot be explained on the basis of self-interest alone. Also at play were ideological and affective rubrics of meaning making. This is as true of Qiu Zhaodi, who defended a famished young woman and her newborn, as it was of Zhang, who abused women in her charge, and of Hou, who continued to serve with pride as vice party secretary and women's head for many more years. Hou's comments about the famine, speak directly to this point:

> Some people came from Xi Ping. They came and picked up sweet potato scraps and ate them. Some would stick them in the compost, and then come back and go to the river and wash them to eat. There were a number of brides who came back from Xi Ping and settled here. In some places people starved to death. Not just regular folk, but also some in the army couldn't handle it and came back. One guy who came from a middle-upper peasant class, couldn't handle being in army, couldn't handle the living conditions. If he hadn't come back, he would have been an officer. The poor and middle peasants had experienced hardship, could endure it, and stayed in the military and became officers. If you yourself can't *jianjue* [endure], you can't become an official. If you come back, you can't achieve anything.[17]

Xiping residents endured some of the worst effects of the famine.[18] A tight control on the movement of people meant only the lucky were able to slip past militias and escape to other regions to beg (Yang 2012, 49–52). Hou's judgment of the soldier for having escaped the famine is telling. If the soldier had stayed, he might well have died. As discussed in chapter 7, Hou blamed one woman's death from starvation as an outcome of her own lack of thrift; here, Hou's comments suggest that the soldier's problem was a lack of capacity to *endure* starvation. Hou's discussion of the sacrifices necessary to be a good cadre, repeated several times during the interview, underline this perspective further: "Listen to what Chairman Mao says, keep your feet planted on solid ground [work hard] so there will be no difficulties. If you say you have difficulties that means you didn't work hard. I have been a cadre for all my life, I didn't have many difficulties. To become a soldier—a good man is meant to be a soldier, and good iron is meant to make nails."[19]

In Hou's retelling of severe deprivation, both Marxist maternalism (house-holder wastefulness) and Maoist militancy (weakness) rationalize an unthink-able event, and a determination to follow both CCP and Mao Zedong. As Hou repeated several times over the course of the interview, "[Treat] the tasks assigned to you by the party, [with] firm and unswerving [resolve]" (*Dang jiao gei ni de renwu, jianding er bu yi*). But just what were those tasks when the party itself, as Hou insisted, "would not let anyone starve to death"? Hou shared that in her role as vice party secretary she resisted exaggerating the harvest yield in her reports: "A challenge [*tiaozhan*] is just a challenge, it cannot be overstated. What if the masses starve to death?" And yet, Hou also acknowledged that people had died of starvation in other parts of the province, and that in her own village, people were so desperate that they ate tree bark and leaves, and women were so malnourished that they lost their capacity to menstruate. She also shared that no one dared to suggest that the dining halls should be dismantled. "[We] had one person who made some comments and he was struggled against something fierce." In Hou's retelling, terror provides a partial explanation, alongside and intertwined with the complex ideological and affective contradictions that were simultaneously at work in the conditions through which the famine unfolded.

The militancy of Hou and other local-level leaders in the context of extreme deprivation would only further undermine the harmonious family as the basic unit of socialist society. This was not due to the establishment of the dining halls, day care, or other forms of collective social services—all services that would mark the life of work units in urban China for the remainder of the Maoist period; rather, War Communism undermined the "harmonious family" through mobi-lizations that did not recognize the maternal-child tie as revolutionary attach-ments worthy of cultivation and protection. War Communism did not recognize Marxist maternalist equality nor the maternalist social policy regime constructed to realize it. In Wenhe, in 1961, for example, when a local cadre's child died of starvation, she was promptly reprimanded for requesting a resignation.[20] She was also relayed a story of a "revolutionary martyr" who protected the position of troops by suffocating her infant under a quilt. In this didactic narrative, one remarkably similar to that heard by former Gao Shan youth league leader and women's head, Tian Min, losing one's child to famine had been reshaped into a form of revolutionary sacrifice.

Maternal loss nonetheless emerged as an important theme within the narratives of some former leaders. Ding Xueqin, 64, the young Wenhe woman recruited by the CCP in 1949 who would go on to become a commune leader, for example, believes that work conditions in the GLF caused her infant son to contract polio. With no childcare available, Ding brought her baby to the steelworks, and he somehow ended up falling in the rushing waters of a river. Although the infant survived, he would develop polio two months later, an illness, Ding believes, he would not have contracted if she had not taken him to the work site. Although the two events were likely not connected, in Ding's mind they are, and the memory serves as a permanent source of loss for Ding who continued to care for her adult disabled son at the time of our interviews.

Maternal regret was also expressed by former commune Women's Federation head Yuan Jinyu, 158, who lost her daughter to suicide. Yuan said that her daughter blamed Yuan for making her take care of her younger siblings, a burden which prevented her from performing well at her studies. Yuan also relied on her mother and sister for childcare, "All of my children grew up in my sister's home. They are not my children." And: "I feel that my revolutionary work made my children [suffer from] heavy losses."[21]

The famine itself also cast a long shadow on the capacity of women to protect themselves and their children. A retired teacher and former women's head from Meihua County, Henan, Sun Qinqin, 162, recalled the famine as a period of stark gender inequality: "During the famine they said things were equal but actually men had more food than women, [they] said things were equal but they weren't." When compensation was distributed through grain rations, enduring, and in some cases, worsening sexual inequality placed women at a deadly disadvantage.[22]

Family breakdown skyrocketed both during and in the aftermath of the famine in no small part because women were being denied the little food that had been begged, borrowed, or stolen.[23] Indeed, divorce cases filed in Henan increased 43.3 percent between 1960 and 1961 (Shao 1984, 101). A similar spike in civil marriage cases occurred in Gaoshan County, as noted in chapter 6, figure 3. Whereas it had been almost impossible to obtain a divorce for most of the 1950s, desperate young and middle-aged wives were now bypassing local women's heads and fleeing their marital homes—a phenomenon Hou directly references in her famine description in chapter 7 as well. The Henan Women's Federation notes that marital problems increased dramatically during the years 1959–61, with the former practice of bride selling experiencing a particularly strong resurgence.[24] As a consequence, the provincial Women's Federation initiated a large-scale Marriage Law education mobilization in 1963 (Shao 1984, 95).

Pu Congxi, 156, a former Wenhe women's head who was very critical of the Maoist past, scoffed at the idea that any form of women's liberation was achieved during this era: "Women had the right to liberate themselves [*fanshen le*]. What kind of right? The right to work. If you didn't liberate yourself you didn't work. [Laughs] Women were liberated, little feet became big feet, and the big feet could work. If you had bound feet then you could carry manure. [Laughs]"

Pu's response summed up how many former women farmers looked back on this period: an extended mobilization of forced drudgery, hardship, and deprivation. Her sarcastic response, however, contrasts sharply with the memories of a former Gaoshan women's head who recalls the emergence of women's power on the communes: "I was really happy. In the past it was all according to family [structures], this time was collective. The communes all had women's power. I felt like this: [whereas in the past] women were always at home, now they had the right to speak, and societal status. They could speak, could be in charge. So my work was always very good" (Yan Zhijuan, 97). Yan's comments celebrate the replacement of the family with a feminized form of collective power, an emphasis that reflects the narratives of the leaders of a nearby woman-led brigade: the Mu Guiying Brigade.

The Woman Warrior

> Proud and alert, they carry five-foot guns,
> The first rays of the morning sun illuminate the drill-field
> The Daughters of China are filled with high resolve,
> To red garments they prefer the uniform.

—Mao Zedong, untitled poem (1961 [1974], 339)

Mao Zedong's 1961 poem is a powerful tribute to the Woman Warrior, a tribute made just as the GLF itself was being repudiated by the leadership of the CCP. The poem speaks directly to the revolutionary imaginary on decidedly familial terms: young women as China's daughters who long for a military life over a life of marital domesticity (red garments being the color of bridal clothes). To this end, the poem speaks directly to the desire of young women's head and Youth League leader, Tian Min, who herself considered escaping her marital home by joining the army, and to the ongoing circulation of the Woman Warrior state of activism as it became central to the articulation of women's liberation and women's leadership in the context of the GLF. I finish this chapter with a focus

on this powerful liberatory state of activism as an important ongoing historical development in its own right, and to illuminate its role in simultaneously
contributing to and offsetting the impact of the GLF on women and children as
enacted on the Mu Guiying Brigade.

Gaoshan County's Mu Guiying Brigade received its new name in 1957 when
the primary leadership posts, party secretary, women's head, and brigade accountant, were held by women. Yang Junxia, 83, became party secretary in 1957, just
a year prior to the commencement of the GLF. This was an extraordinary development: as of 1956, only 67, or 1.21 percent, of the 5,556 party secretaries in
the province were women (Strauss 2020, 35). Since Yang had been recruited and
trained as a Youth League member in 1953, she had served as a committee member of a LAPC, committee head of a HAPC, women's head, and Youth League
secretary. Prior to becoming party secretary, she said, she had found it challenging to implement equal pay for equal work because she lacked the authority of a
primary cadre. After she became a party secretary, however, she found the work
much easier for two reasons: the new authority that came with her position, and
the fact that other women were running the brigade as well. "You can say what
you want but equality wasn't realized back in the mid-1950s. [Equality] was only
realized when the most important leaders were women. Women were in charge
[dang jia] of everything. The collective was in women's hands [jiti dangjia shi nü
de], we liberated ourselves [fanshen le]."

In this narrative, it was women's leadership that enabled the realization of
equality within the brigade. Moreover, Yang's terminology of dang jia suggests a
powerful image of managing the brigade as a household, an expression that she
used in reference to the liberation of ordinary women as well. But the presence
of fanshen, a word she also used frequently during our first interview, disrupts
the maternalist flow of care. The female leadership of the brigade enabled women
to chu lai or "emerge," and thus fanshen, as she commented again a moment
later. Indeed, Yang repeatedly emphasized the intense hardship involved in being
a leader at this time; she would also speak of the real suffering that ordinary
women endured.

Accountant Fan had had six years of primary education when she was
recruited to record work points during collectivization in 1956. In the GLF, she
was first assigned to be an assistant accountant before being promoted to primary accountant. Fan recalled the challenge the women faced in amalgamating
two natural villages into a brigade in 1958. Their youth was a significant draw-
back: Yang was only twenty and Fan just nineteen. Leader Lin, the women's head,
on the other hand, was twenty-seven. A young widow with a small child, Lin had
been the first in the district to join a Mutual Aid Team (MAT) and was eventually
recognized as a "pace-setting" MAT head. She became a women's head in 1956.

All three women expressed a deeply felt need to prove themselves as capable despite their youth and gender. According to Yang, some on the brigade had questioned whether a "little girl" could become a brigade head, others thought her leadership strange, and still others initially dismissed her altogether.

> The work back then was simply complicated. Especially since when I emerged I was a woman. I had to get that many people to believe and trust in me, I really had to be careful with everything, had to be an example everywhere. Emerging as a woman, no one wanted to trust me. Among the masses, there weren't only one or two, but several thousand people. Getting the people to trust in me really wasn't easy. It required that I myself had to do it.

In one of the quotes that begins this chapter, Yang drew on the Maoist conception of subjective initiative to outperform male workers and other male leaders. She continues:

> At that time there was so much to do. For example, I was this brigade's party secretary, our commune had nineteen brigades and I was the only woman. When the party committee ordered that a task be completed in three days, I completed it in two. I wanted to have a target to struggle toward, you must have subjective initiative to move forward, be determined.

For Yang, overcoming the limits of her female physiology was not an issue. Despite the propagation of slogans that clearly warned of the health risks to menstruating women who worked in cold water, Yang plunged into canal construction during the early months of the GLF:

> We all continued with our work, regardless of menstruation. I carried the weight. To this day I've never been ill. At that time the brigade party secretary went to the fields and picked up the seedling samples. The weather was extremely cold. But even with my period I still picked the seedlings and sent them to the commune. I was barefoot then and the water was deep. I thought I would develop arthritis. In the end I didn't.

Leader Lin Xiaohong, 73, also sought to defy local and official limitations on her body, although her perspectives on the liberating joys of household/collective management differed somewhat from Yang's. Like Yang, Lin was extremely proud of the achievements made by the Mu Guiying Brigade: "In our brigade women had the power" (*women dui li shi nü de dang quan de*). She spoke of the brigade's determination to implement equal pay for equal work, and of the extreme happiness of ordinary women in 1958 when they were able to emerge and take charge (*dangjia zuo zhu le*):

> At that time we women responded whole-heartedly to the call of over-turning the "three big mountains": one was imperialism, one was the inequality between men and women, and one was men's bullying and oppression of women.[25] Overturning the three big mountains means realizing the goal of the equality between men and women and realizing equal payment for equal work. However, it was impossible for men and women to get equal payment for equal work because women are physically weaker. But in our small brigade, it was realized because the power was in the hands of us women and we had strong labor power. We worked shoulder to shoulder with men no matter what work it was. For example, when men carried a bit more seedlings, women would thin more of them faster. Because carrying seedlings was physical labor, men did more of it whereas women were faster in thinning the seedlings, so women did more of this work. Men and women would help each other.

But Lin was never able to fully embody the leadership she sought, despite the early encouragement and rewards. In her own words, she could not become a formal cadre (*zhengshi ganbu*) because of the early death of her husband and the fact that she had a child to raise on her own: "I had no one at home. I had to do all of the housework." When I mentioned that other women's heads had said to me "women's heads had it tough" she commented:

> You could say that men did not have it as hard as women. . . . At that time the work women had to do was really hard, but they were very enthusi-astic about their work. On the one hand there was a lot of pressure from above to implement [directives]. We implemented pretty well over here. Women really had it harder than men. Because there was no childcare back then, women had to do housework, take care of the children, cook dinner, and go and work in the fields.

Ultimately, Lin's lack of decision-making power prevented her from partici-pating in what she deemed the more exciting and manageable work as a leader during the GLF: canal construction. Despite trying to convince the brigade leadership otherwise, she was assigned to "manage the elderly, women, and children" at home, a job she considered far more onerous than leading work teams on irrigation sites:

> Because constructing canals was done by young people and also they are physically strong and also they have that kind of collective ideology. Everyone lived together, ate together and we stayed at home. There were

953 mu of rice fields left for the three types of people who stayed at home: women with children, old men, and old women, and you had to mobilize them to come out to work. Some still had housework, cooking, it was very difficult. I argued with the brigade about this, I asked to go out to construct canals, as a leader, but they disagreed and made me stay at home, because people liked me. It was not easy to stay at home. Every time they went to give aid, I stayed at home to take care of this awful mess.

Lin's comments regarding the deficiencies of the brigade-as-household reveal some of the fundamental contradictions of the dangjia path of liberation, and the Total War mobilization in which it was embedded. When she juxtaposes physically and ideologically strong young (men) against the "awful mess" at home, the brigade emerges as a feminized site of lack. In so doing, Lin's comments speak volumes about the status of women-work and the household in the 1950s: policy relied on both, but neither was valued as a true form of revolutionary work in practice. No matter how much Yang and Lin may have tried to implement an expanded domesticity of liberation, the ongoing denigration of household work within socialist construction barred its realization.[26]

The lack of access to education was a further barrier to liberation. To follow the path of dangjia, rural women would have had to acquire new literacy skills and thus improve their level of ideological consciousness.[27] But while the GLF included much-publicized campaigns to increase the literacy levels of rural women, most women were far too overwhelmed with work to have time to attend study sessions, a finding consistent with Tong's (2003) research on women's literacy attainments during this period. This was the case of one former production team leader, Yu Xialian, 121, who wanted to become women's head but felt inadequate because of her illiteracy and because she did not know how to ride a bike (and thus presumably get to meetings). "You can't do it if you aren't capable," she said. Wu Qiugui, 120, interviewed at the same time as Yu, was also somewhat sceptical about the realization of sex equality after 1949. When I asked her if she had heard of feminism (*nüquan zhuyi*) she remarked,[28]

> Feminism is [when] women manage the household [dangjia]; today all women are in charge of the household. Things were better after Liberation [when] sex equality was advocated. Before Liberation when women had no power to speak, there was no point in women speaking.

But when I subsequently asked if she thought sex equality had been realized she said, "Things were hopeless before Liberation. Things were definitely unequal before Liberation. But after Liberation, it was mostly a lot of talk."

At the same time, the path of fanshen was blocked to most country women as well. Given that the bodies of rural women were supposed to be protected, they were, by definition, foreclosed from liberation through fanshen unless they were able to transform themselves into sites of male heroism, as did Yang and Lin. In fact, many young women's bodies did transform when they ceased menstruating under the stress of overwork and severe malnutrition.[29] But even then, they received little reward for their sacrifice. Despite Yang and Lin's insistence to the contrary, ordinary women on the brigade rarely received the same number of work points as men.[30]

How one practiced liberation, and thus embodied funü, depended on a range of factors, not all of them stable. As Chen has suggested, CCP discourse was "rife with slippage from one body to another, one subject position to another" (Chen 2003, 291). Although Yang was functionally illiterate, a point Lin stressed at several points during our conversations, she fully inhabited the subjectivity of Maoist activist. Yang's full-body expression of this activism, however, may have foreclosed the possibility of a shared appreciation of liberation among the ordinary women in the brigade. When I asked two local women to evaluate Yang's leadership, they did not comment on her status as a *woman* leader but rather noted that she was a "hard worker" who did her job much better than did the current generation of leaders (Wu Qiugui, 120; and Yu Xialian, 121). Their lack of interest in Yang's gender or in the history of the Mu Guiying Brigade suggests that, unlike Yang, Lin, and Fan, they did not celebrate their past through the lens of a shared socialist sisterhood.

Thornton (2007) argues that the projection of the state as a moral actor has played a central role in the Chinese state-making process. As the processes that constituted this state morality began to break down during the GLF, however, so did the legitimacy of the state project itself (Thaxton 2008). Party Secretary Yang Junxia's final act of heroism in the GLF speaks of both the excesses and the limits of her personal embodiment of the local state. Gaoshan County had experienced a similar population decline to Huoyue: dropping from a high of 23 in 1958 to a low of -4.3 per thousand in 1961 (GX 1994, 177). Faced with the threat that the members of her brigade might starve, Yang sobbed and pleaded with the commune authorities for a loan of grain in 1961, a brave act given the taboo against naming hunger at that time. She also dismantled the dining halls:

> In 1961 the average grain [ration] was very low, we'd been eating in the dining halls for two years then. At that time [I] broke up the cafeteria because the average grain [ration] was so low. One person could only eat eight or nine jin of grain a month. The situation was becoming extremely intense. People in our brigade say that we got grain because

I wept. At that time the commune had some grain from Subei. The party committee secretary said I still had grain. At that time, I was extremely worried—the peasants didn't have any grain, everyone was sick, I was so worried that tears began to pour out. There was no grain, we couldn't run the dining halls any longer. The porridge was just like water. The pressure was tremendous. I was responsible for over a thousand people on the brigade who had nothing to eat. The peasants really sympathized with [and were really appreciative of] me. They said that my getting the grain was a really difficult task.

Although the commune finally relented and provided her with grain to redistribute, Yang found herself attacked five years later by some of the same villagers she had fought so hard to save.[31] Yang, a "good leader," thus became subject of a violent politicized struggle, much as had Zhang Sumei just a few years earlier. And it is exactly here that the state's project as moral agent runs aground, for even the "good leader," villagers knew, had contributed to the construction of a local state socialism marked by deep deprivation, injury, and loss. Indeed, Yang may have been a "woman in charge" during the GLF—but who was she in charge of? None other than exhausted, sick, and ignorant "country women," rendered powerless by the overwhelming burdens of household management in a utopic age of fanshen.

Neither the death of tens of million people from famine nor the reproductive injury of tens of thousands from overwork was inevitable. Over the first seven months of 1959, central, provincial, and regional leaders undertook grassroots investigations and reported back their findings through personal and official channels; some, consequently, reversed important policy planks of the GLF. The ACWF played an important role in this process. While Women's Federations were subject to the authority of the CCP at every level of the administrative structure, and thus "lacked power," they nonetheless enjoyed two key advantages during the highly politicized struggles that played out in the months prior to Lushan. First, they had a semantic capacity to address health. Over the course of 1958 and the first half of 1959, the ACWF frequently published reports on health that, in turn, called into question excessive mobilization tactics and even began to give voice to malnutrition. The ACWF's recognized responsibility for the welfare of women and women's bodies, as well as social welfare more broadly, enabled a semantic slippage in which an analysis of the causes of the problems, including excessive mobilization tactics and the specific harm they produced, could be named.

Second, the webs of personal and family ties in which Women's Federation leaders were embedded at all levels of the polity served as important conduits for sharing and mobilizing information about what was transpiring on the ground. Cross-gender sibling, sororal, and companionate ties were all well in evidence. Both Cai Chang and Zhu Danhua enjoyed a siblinglike relationship with Mao Zedong that enabled them to advance critiques, and offer alternative policy solutions, that others could not. At the same time, and despite facing an unsupportive first party secretary, Shi Jian's relationship of mutual support with the ACWF empowered the Jiangsu Women's Federation chair to continue to advocate strongly on behalf of women. The companionate tie shared by Kang Keqing and Zhu Du was also activated during the spring and summer of 1959. These attachments were an important part of a moderating impulse underway that could have shifted the outcome, had Mao Zedong, at Lushan, not suddenly narrowed what was semantically and politically possible.

The responsibility for the famine rests largely with Mao Zedong (Bernstein 2006; Chan 2001; Teiwes and Sun 1999). It was Mao who reignited the Anti-Rightist Movement in which so many of the leaders who had dared to speak out that spring were criticized and purged. It was thus Mao who heightened the risk to speak about, much less attempt to address, the starvation, disease, and injury already marking much of the countryside. But Mao Zedong did not act alone. The central, provincial, and regional leaders who reproduced the semantic and political conditions that foreclosed acknowledgement of the growing disaster also directly contributed to the death and harm that it produced. Clientelism and ideological fervor explains this outcome among the most radical provincial leaders and their local clients. Cai Chang and Li Fuchun's post-Lushan behavior, however, was not enacted through the pull of self-serving righteousness, but rather as an expression of the loyalty and love that had long defined their revolutionary state building. In the wake of Lushan, Cai Chang's devotion to Mao Zedong effectively disabled the ACWF's capacity to advocate on behalf of the women and children in its charge.

More than three million people were purged during the second Anti-Rightist Movement (Yang 1996, 52), including Shi Jian. Shi Jian received the protection and support of the ACWF, and by proxy Deng Xiaoping, until Jiangsu's first provincial party secretary turned on her after Lushan. In Shi Jian's view, her purge was an outcome that the ACWF was powerless to prevent. By way of contrast, Anhui's second provincial party secretary, Shao Shiping, protected Zhu Danhua from the ACWF. If Shao had not stepped in, the ACWF anti-rightist committee would have purged Zhu Danhua alongside the chairs of the Fujian and Sichuan women's federations. In the wake of Lushan, a reassertion of the localization of power within the hands of provincial, regional, and local leaders, and Cai Chang's rectification of the ACWF, meant that the fate of outspoken women leaders rested with lower-level male authorities rather with the ACWF itself.

Cai Chang's rectification of the ACWF produced another outcome that would worsen conditions on the ground: a reassertion of the language of thrift while famine was gripping the countryside. The two diligences and its discourse of austerity was never a benign slogan, but part of Cai Chang's comprehensive effort to control consumption at its source, whether in the home or in the dining hall. The two diligences was Cai Chang's major contribution to economic policy making; it was also her major contribution to the conditions that shaped the famine, and as I will discuss briefly in the conclusion, the conditions of continued deprivation that followed.

Finally, and related, it is critical to recognize the role of Mao and Maoism in the complicated attachments that marked the struggles over family and state during the GLF. Shao Shiping, one of the most notable provincial leaders to speak out in 1959, deployed Mao's leadership as he sought to address the crisis besetting his province. By "raising the flag to oppose the flag" he called attention to what he saw as the true meaning and legacy of the Chinese revolution: the state's capacity to protect the livelihood of the people. Zhu Danhua deployed a similar rational when she delivered 50 million jin of grain to neighboring Shandong in 1960. Despite having personally witnessed famine victims in Shandong and on the streets of Nanchang, Zhu Danhua was at pains to blame the cause of the famine on the workstyle of leaders who capitulated to leftist excesses after Lushan, and not on Mao himself (Ma 2013, 184–85). Time and again, Zhu's resistance to Maoist excess was enacted through Mao's own words; she, like so many others, could not have conceived of a lifetime of revolutionary sacrifice without Mao at its center.

But, and this is a very large "but," Mao could not have conceived of, much less enacted, the GLF, and the recovery from the GLF, without women at its center. This is as true of the young militants and householders who took charge of the agricultural sector during the GLF as it is of Mao's female kin and comrades, who struggled to shape the conditions in which those women mobilized. Mao Zedong, however, never acknowledged his ideological and material debts when he popularized the term, "women hold up half the sky" (*funü neng ding ban bian tian*).[32] Indeed, when Mao began to use the term during the Cultural Revolution, he was drawing on a version first published by the Xiushui County Women's Federation in the province of Jiangxi, and that Zhu Danhua rearticulated at a women-work conference in December 1958 (Ma 2013, 160–63). It was an apt omission. Yes, women held up half the sky, but when that sky crashed to the ground, they were expected to clean up the catastrophic mess left behind. This unacknowledged history of attached labor not only proved central to the state's capacity to "make a great leap," but also to recover and, much later, to reform.

CONCLUSION

The Attached Politics of State Capacity and Contention

> I myself am a woman. If I don't do women-work, won't it be hard to get men comrades to do it? There are a lot of women comrades who are unwilling to do women-work. I've spent a lifetime doing women-work without resentment. I'm not willing to leave the battle front of women.
>
> —Liu Yinting, Handan County Women's Federation official, from Jin, *Biography of Deng Yingchao*

In late spring of 1961, Deng Yingchao and Zhou Enlai undertook a joint investigation of rural living conditions in the Handan region of Hebei Province. At first, all seemed well (Jin 1993, 2:556–70). Indeed, as leaders and farmers gathered around "Grandpa" and "Elder Sister Deng," community members spoke only of the achievements of the GLF. After several days of patient and determined questioning, however, a few brave souls began to open up about the wretchedness of their living conditions. The dining halls were a sham, local farmers reported; only the leaders were able to eat their fill while everyone else had to survive on watery gruel. People were so hungry that they were reduced to eating tree leaves and had little energy to work. One man had lost his wife to a starvation-induced illness and did not know how he was going to care for his four children. As the crowds began to gather to meet the officials from Beijing, an elderly man collapsed on the ground before the premier, pleading to this "angel" from God to save them.

Aghast at what they found, Deng Yingchao and Zhou Enlai gave immediate instructions to provide food provisions to those who had spoken honestly. Deng Yingchao also offered to adopt one of the widower's children. After their departure, Zhou Enlai ordered the local Handan authorities to immediately disband the dining halls. Hebei Province, and the remaining provinces still operating dining halls, quickly followed suit. In the following months, Deng Yingchao personally oversaw the effort of the ACWF to address the health crisis that plagued so many rural women and children, including treating the malnourishment, disease, and injuries women had developed from overwork in difficult conditions. In her parting words to local Women's Federation leaders, Deng apologized: "We leaders really let down the masses" (Jin 1993, 2:570).

266

To date political scientists and historians lay the majority of blame at the feet of Mao Zedong and the elite male officials that surrounded him, including Premier Zhou Enlai, who had firm knowledge of the disaster that was playing out across the country well before his trip to Handan.[1] Among the hundreds of scholarly works published on the high politics of the Maoist period, only a handful consider the role of women officials. Indeed, the dominant scholarly perspective assumes that the ACWF was a passive pawn in a larger field of struggle—that it was "mobilized" to participate in the GLF and, when the GLF collapsed, it supported a recovery organized and led by men. This book has offered a different portrait, both of women leaders and of the families in which they were embedded. As I have argued, women leaders were full participants in the politics of the GLF, including concerted efforts to moderate the impact of the mobilization, and concerted efforts that led to its direct extension. Central to these maneuverings, I argue, was "the family" itself, both as a means of and a subject of struggle.

In the 1950s, state capacity in the PRC took shape not despite family ties, but through them. By decentering the focus on individual agency that has for so long dominated analyses of feminist and factional struggle, and foregrounding instead the affective relations that produce and mediate political purpose and practice in the context of fields, this book shows how previously overlooked ties underpinned the early state building of the PRC. Insofar as the circulation of affect is "bursting with potential" (Gould 2009, 20), and insofar as family ties are nothing if not an "intimate and creative practice" (Brandtstädter and Santos 2009, 10), the affective enactment of family ties are a key part of political transformation. Indeed, and as Stoler (2004, 6) argues of Dutch colonial rule, "structures of feeling" are not incidental distractions from the operation of statecraft, they are rather its "true plot."

Long before the rise of Second Wave feminism in the West, the CCP made women's leadership a central part of its governance structure. At the state apex, senior women officials ushered in one-party petition divorce, led extraordinary improvements in maternal and infant health outcomes, and championed new economic roles for women in the household and in the fields. At the grassroots, hundreds of thousands of women activists and leaders, in turn, undergirded the implementation of the policies that flowed from this strategic work. The stunning and rapid achievements are a testament to the connectedness of a highly determined elite, and its capacity to mobilize a new generation of committed, and equally connected, activists at the rural grassroots.

How is it that these globally unprecedented developments have received so little attention by political scientists to date? Given that these reforms affected the lives of hundreds of millions of women, both for good and ill, it is striking that so few have considered their origins and consequences. A part of this oversight stems from the canonization of people, policies, and events intrinsic to the self-historicization process, or the "historically specific means by which some domains and not others are understood as political" (Murphy 2012, 178). Insofar as the primary preoccupations of party men became the primary preoccupations of the historians and political scientists who studied them, the fields of social policy itself have been largely overlooked. But political attachments are at play as well. As Ko (1994, 11) observes of an earlier era, "The appearance of kinship hierarchy and formal structures of power mask the realities of the exercise of power."

When I first began to study elite revolutionary politics, I assumed, as so many had before, that both Song Qingling and Li Dequan served as little more than symbolic figureheads. And in many ways this was true: their status as elite nationalist widows *was* highly symbolic. But to dismiss this symbolism as having no real political import is to miss Song Qingling's contributions to the forging of the Second United Front, and to miss the role Li Dequan played keeping the Second United Front together. It is also to miss how they drew on their symbolic status to great effect in international diplomacy both before and after the establishment of the PRC. Li Dequan may well have wielded little power within the MOH, as power is commonly understood. As neither a physician nor a member of the CCP, she held very little sway over the majority of deliberations that transpired in the MOH during the early 1950s. But, if one considers the issues she cared about most, and that is the health and welfare of women and children, the picture suddenly changes dramatically. It is highly unlikely that infant and maternal mortality would have become an early preoccupation of the new PRC, were it not for the widely accepted truth that a state's civilizational status was grounded in its capacity to improve the health and welfare of women and children. Song Qingling and Li Dequan symbolized and enacted this preoccupation.

International fields of maternal and infant health, social work, education, and law constituted maternalist state building in the first half of China's twentieth century. Early experiments in social policy reform and relief work were thus not only linked to those taking place in the Soviet Union, but also to those in Japan, Europe, and North America. Although many future officials would spend significant periods of time studying Soviet solutions to the challenges faced by mothers and their children, maternalist norms and ideas central to suffragism, continental feminism, and social gospel feminism would have a significant impact in the unfolding of the New Woman and Social Reformer states of activism. As I have argued, social gospel feminism would play an especially important role in shaping emerging ideas about the moral authority of women's leadership in social service reform generally, and relief work specifically.

Song Qingling's connection to the faith of her natal family receded over time. Nonetheless, her preoccupation with social welfare, and particularly the welfare of women and children, suggests that her Methodist upbringing and Wesleyan College days continued to resonate in her left-leaning politics. Li Dequan maintained a much more active connection to Christianity and social gospel activism than did Song, at least for the first years after the founding of the PRC.[2] The central preoccupations of the Chongqing Coalition, an early issue network, were in this way as much a product of religious reform as of the writings of Chinese liberal feminists and Marx, Lenin, and Stalin. The religious influences on state building generally (Gorski 2003) and social policy development specifically (Charrad 2001; Morgan 2006) have been established in the context of Europe, North America, and the Middle East; the addition of post-1949 China, only adds weight to the argument that religious struggles and ideas have played a central role in the emergence of the modern state.[3]

If the preoccupations of the Chongqing Coalition were grounded, in part, in a social gospel vision of the world, it was personal ties that enabled advocates to realize this vision. In post-1949 China, senior women officials were appointed to key, mutually reinforcing portfolios on the basis of their expertise, stature, and preexisting ties with each other, and with the senior leadership of the CCP. These appointments, in turn, enabled the coalition to create and expand a bureaucratic infrastructure that reached directly into rural households. The Chongqing Coalition not only accessed the autonomy necessary to achieve politically mandated policy ends, a basis for strong bureaucratic performance as argued by Fukuyama (2013), but were, from the outset, institutionally and relationally positioned to shape and realize the social policy priorities of the new regime. This early form of "embedded autonomy" (Evans 1995) realized a high degree of state penetration, the second condition necessary, after autonomy, to reduce infant and maternal mortality, as recently argued by Brieba (2018).

The attached politics that shaped the advocacy of the Chongqing Coalition were also complemented, fragmented, and at times, overturned in the context of a revolutionary field saturated with a multiplicity of emotional pedagogies and ideological critique. Indeed, Maoist states of activism informed the work of elite officials and grassroots activists alike. The deployment of new vocabularies and techniques of anti-oppression enabled several generations of Chinese women to see themselves as part of a larger project of constructing a more just society for themselves, their families, their communities, and other women. The rise of the Iron Girls, women who were celebrated for engaging in physically demanding and sometimes dangerous work in urban and rural areas beginning in 1964, is but one example (Jin 2006; Wang 2017). Chinese socialist anti-oppressive techniques would reverberate around the world for decades to come, including in the consciousness-raising sessions of American Second Wave feminists.[4] Today critical socialist feminisms in China are drawing on memories of local socialism as "an empirical legacy and a potential resource for theory building" (Spakowski 2018). Song Shaopeng's searing critique of "virtue" as it has been redeployed as an aspirational value for women/mothers in contemporary China, for example, builds on a rich heritage of Chinese socialist feminist theorizing. As Song (2015b, 107) argues, "'Virtue' cannot become a cover for oppression and exploitation."

Attending to the deeply textured interplay between founding stories, personal relationships, ideology, and the moral imperatives of the state-building mission, an analysis of attachments not only contributes to new understandings of state capacity and Maoist contention, but also contributes to new understandings of the origins of state-produced catastrophe. The degradation of bureaucratic norms and relations offer a partial explanation, as anticipated by Evans (1995, 71). Over the course of the 1950s, the Chongqing Coalition lost its autonomy to set priorities, while Cai Chang, relying on a distinct, albeit intersecting, set of informal and organizational ties, increasingly imposed her own vision of socialist construction on the ACWF. But insofar as the maternalist social policy regime extended and deepened the civilizing mission that had begun under the GMD, the loss of bureaucratic autonomy was not the only dynamic at play. With its longstanding focus on family reform, maternalist state building gave rise to the discursive, organizational, and relational conditions that simultaneously made possible the privileges and privations that came to define the socialist household.

In the 1940s and 1950s, the PRC was built through the struggles of women activists and leaders operating as symbols and participants in the violent creation of a new socialist order. Women-work, a much maligned and often resisted form of "non"-revolutionary work, nonetheless enabled the state to materialize militarily, financially, and morally, both within and beyond its borders. Whether one considers recruitment drives to fight in Korea or to settle the "frontier," whether one considers divorce dissuasion or the imposition of household austerity, or whether one considers Cai Chang's repeat implementation of rectification campaigns, it becomes clear that the tissue and sinew of the state's capacity to mobilize and extract was enacted, in no small part, through the gendered hierarchies of family ties. Since its founding, the ACWF has served as the organizational embodiment of a complex trifecta: women's movement, CCP handmaiden, and moral bureaucracy all wrapped up in one. Neither maternalism nor Maoism were innocent in the attached politics that enabled the famine to unfold.

The quote that begins this chapter exemplifies these profound contradictions. When Deng Yingchao visited Handan in 1961, she and County Women's Federation leader, Liu Yinting, discussed the challenges of women leaders refusing to do women-work—a phenomenon that continued throughout the GLF.[5] Liu's response, when Deng asked if she liked women-work, was telling. On the one hand, Liu's proclamation of allegiance to women-work was made in the terms that Deng Yingchao and other senior male officials had made count-less times before: women-work was women's work. On the other hand, the actual expression of devotion was uttered through the language of militarism, not maternalism: "I'm not willing to leave the battle front of women" (Jin 1993, 2:568). The resentments that were reinforced through the mass mobilizations of the GLF did not subside with the cessation of the movement. Rather, they con-tinued to fester as women's heads were mobilized to tend to a traumatized and exhausted population through the reimposition of the thrifty household. Before sharing some final thoughts on the party family, I briefly discuss the attached politics of famine recovery and its relationship to socialist household manage-ment under revolution and reform.

The Socialist Household, Redux

By the time Deng Yingchao and Zhou Enlai visited Handan in 1961 and ordered the disbanding of the dining halls, some rural leaders and farmers had already taken matters into their own hands. As discussed in chapter 9, Yang borrowed grain to distribute to the villagers in her charge when she disbanded the din-ing halls; in a neighboring commune, former commune official Lei Junming, 102, told me he disbanded the dining halls as early as 1959. One Wenhe county official, Meng Yongyu, 67, traveled to neighboring Shaanxi to buy cooking uten-sils, after secretly disbanding the dining halls on a remote commune, leading farmers, many of whom were suffering from edema, to cry out "We're liberated!" Although neither the district nor province agreed to the experiment, Meng was able to gradually dismantle the dining hall system throughout the county with the backing of at least one other county leader. Meng said that he simply could not have otherwise continued in his role as a leader.

The disbanding of the dining halls has long been heralded as an important, if insufficient, step in the cessation of the famine. In the wake of the GLF, local and national leaders deplored the inefficiencies of the dining hall system, arguing that the policy of "eating without pay" generated an overconsumption of grain (Xie Changfa, 78). As Zhu De had argued in 1959 (Kang 1993, 449), and would con-tinue to argue again in 1961 (Yang 1996, 78–79), the dining halls were wasteful and farmers were better off eating at home. Lei Junming's argument for disbanding the dining halls on his commune also reflected this rationale: preparing food at home rendered greater control over decision making, in contrast with the dining halls, "which were really wasteful."[6] Although, dining hall consumption may have contributed to the famine, other factors, including the decline in grain availability, and the prioritization of rapid urban industrialization, have been identified as being more important (see, for example, Yang 2008; Wemheuer 2014). The persistence of the narrative of over overconsumption would nonetheless justify the reimposition of the socialist household as the basis of the rural economy, with the woman householder as its frugal center. In so doing, the narrative simultaneously elided what had been one of the central rationales for the establishment of the dining halls in the first place: lessening the double-burden of women, so that they might increase the number of hours that they worked outside the home.

There is no question that the disbanding of the dining halls, whether by stealth or by fiat, was welcomed by the vast majority of farmers. The dining hall had become a dreaded and reviled institution, in no small part because it was not able to feed the people. But the return to household eating in 1960 and 1961, just like the return to family farming in 1979 (see Shue 1988), did not diminish the state's oversight of family and household; rather, it strengthened it. The revival of the two diligences and birth planning would play an important role in this process.

The two diligences was propagated in the context of the Anti–Five Winds Campaign, a 1961 rectification targeting grassroots cadres who had veered into extreme leftism (referred to as "the communist winds," *gongchanfeng*), commandism (*mingling zhuyi*), exaggeration (*fukua*), blind direction of production (*xiazhihui shengchan*), and privilege seeking (*ganbu teshu*). It was also revived in the context of experiments with household contracting.[7] In a report dated October 10, 1961, the ACWF argued that the Communist winds had produced a total lack of accountability, in which "what is yours is mine, what is mine is yours, and no one is responsible" (*ni de ye shi wo de, wo de ye shi ni de, ziji shenme dou bu dangjia le*). The ACWF also criticized women cadres who disregarded the fact that women-work flowed directly from party policy, and who continued to believe that women-work had no policy nature (*zhengce xing*) (ACWF 1961c [1999]). Two months later, the Women's Federation invited Deng Xiaoping to speak to a large meeting of Women's Federation chairs from the provinces, cities, and special districts regarding the future direction of women-work. Luo Qiong, one of the only Women's Federation leaders to speak up for Kang Keqing when she was attacked after Lushan (Kang 1993, 451), presided; Cai Chang was present as well (Luo 1998a [2000], 59–64). In his address, Deng apologized for the mistakes committed during the GLF: "This wasn't the fault of everyone here, but [the fault] of the Central Committee." He then went on to reassert the double diligences as the primary policy around which to orient the long-term work of the federation, reaching both backward and forward in revolutionary time: "The two diligences is the regular and long-term work [of the ACWF]. During the Anti-Japanese War, during the period of war within the country, this was the focus of the work, in the past few years [we] have neglected this, [and instead been] keen on lively spectacles" (Yang 1991, 141). According to Deng Xiaoping, women now, and well into the future, needed to support socialist construction through good household management, including conducting housework, childcare, and care of family finances.

Responsibility for household survival thus was largely placed back on the shoulders of rural women, who were themselves depleted, and in some cases recovering from injuries endured during the large-scale mobilizations. Given that per capita caloric consumption barely inched up over the two decades that followed (see, for example, Wemheuer 2014, 229, 235) the temporary renewal of the two diligences, and the accompanying discourses of thrift, would continue to place extraordinary pressure on the women who had been "liberated" to manage household budgets, or *dangjia zuozhu*.[8] Former women's head Zhou Changfen, 157, remembers the two diligences being advocated in 1960 when life was difficult. Women needed to sew and repair clothes at home, she said, and to be more frugal and careful with meal preparation because things were expensive. Li Shuangshuang, the heroine of a novella first published during the GLF, was Zhou's role model. While the 1958 and 1959 versions featured Li Shuangshuang breaking down gender barriers inside and outside the village, in the 1960 version of the publication, Li Shuangshuang makes collective "great leap noodles" that are fashioned from sweet potatoes, instead of wheat, because of extreme food shortages (see King 2011, 61–65). Li's evolution thus reflected the return of the "mistress" of the collective, just prior to the reassertion of the household manager, in a seemingly seamless evolution of redomestication.

While Deng Xiaoping set the two diligences as the line for women-work, and Luo Qiong enthusiastically propagated it, Cai Chang also played a major role in its development and impact. Indeed, it was Cai Chang who been the two diligence's original champion, and it was Cai Chang who continued to propagate thrift in the context of absolute deprivation. The narrative of liberation from above thus not only needs to be reexamined vis-à-vis farmers who survived through the sheer force and strategy of their own efforts (Thaxton 2011), but also read against the attached politics of household consumption, at play before, during, and in the wake of famine. To do otherwise, is to idealize the rural household as situated outside of and external to the politics of revolution and reform, when the household, and the women assigned to uphold it, have been so central to these state projects of transformation.

The household would, in fact, become subject to additional forms of regulation and oversight in the decades following the famine. Most important, birth planning was renewed with an urgency not seen previously, as policymakers, including Zhou Enlai, interpreted the famine through the lens of overpopulation.[9] New resources were devoted to publicizing birth planning, and new contraceptive technologies were developed and distributed as well. To name but one example, Lin Qiaozhi (1964) seemingly moved past her religious opposition to abortion and became involved in the study of its application.[10] While many women welcomed the increasing availability of contraception (Hershatter 2011, 206–7), by the early 1980s, birth planning, like the two diligences, had assumed a more ominous role. Under the auspices of the One Child Policy, women of childbearing age became subject to regulations managing who could birth, when, and to how many. Techniques of persuasion that had once been used by local women's heads to convince women to remain in their marriages and maintain thrifty households were now redeployed to convince women to use an IUD or to undergo a late-term abortion (Manning, forthcoming). Under the politics of opening and reform (*gaige kaifang*), relational repression would assume an unprecedented role in strengthening the state's capacity to manage its population.

The Attached Politics of the Party Family

When asked in 2004 if there were any women leaders who did not do women-work during the GLF, former Gaoshan Commune women's head Chi Meiying, 115, turned the tables on my question: "At that time there were clear rules that the government had to have women participate in politics, not [just] in women-work. Clinton's wife Hillary participates in politics [but doesn't do women-work], it's the same here in China."

Women's leadership was a hallmark of the GLF, a time when women were expected to lead great feats in socialist production. Chi's remark bears examining not only for what it says about China during the GLF, however, but also what it says about America's present. Despite a long track record of high-level positions in politics, including serving as senator from New York, head of the US State Department, and a presidential candidate, Hillary Clinton has also always been a "Clinton," forever implicated in her husband's former presidency. Whether one considers Hillary Clinton's attempt to reform US health care in the early 1990s, Bill Clinton's much-publicized infidelity-sexual harassment, or Hillary Clinton's 2016 run for the presidency in which her husband campaigned extensively, Hillary Clinton's marriage has remained an important part of her political past and present. For Hillary Clinton and thousands of other North American women serving as elected officials, public life produces daily reminders of their familial ties, including to their children and spouses, as they try to navigate the still male-dominated world of parliamentary and republican democracy.

The party family is perhaps one of the most ubiquitous but understudied phenomena in modern political life. If, as I argue, politics are enacted through family ties pretty much everywhere, how party families emerge and take shape is nonetheless specific to the fields in which they are enacted. Indeed, what makes these affective enactments different one from the other, are the stories, commitments, and regulatory processes that shape how these politics play out. When thinking about how culture affects politics in China or elsewhere, we thus need not only to attend to existing practices and norms, but also to the ways those practices and norms are being reinvoked or proscribed in the context of a particular field of struggle. In other words, studying the role of culture in politics cannot just be about what officials and activists say culture is about, or what Weber says it is about, but rather an analysis of how culture itself is a site of continuity, struggle, and rupture.

Whether inspired by the stories of Hua Mulan and/or encouraged and supported by relatives, many of the young grassroots women who became activists in the 1950s would not have materialized as liberated subjects without the CCP mobilizing familiar stories and relational ties to meet their revolutionary ends. Neither a patrimonial nor a neopatrimonial analysis can explain this particular outcome or their effects on the revolutionary politics of rural villages. The complex political struggles that animated the rise and fall of Women's Head Zhang and Party Secretary Yang are powerful testaments to the centrality of practical kinship, even as they are also powerful testaments to the local enactment of ideological transformation.

The emphasis on transformation is key: ascribing an individuated and constant consciousness to participation in movements and policy processes can blur the affective engagement necessary to become and remain an activist or leading party official. In revolutionary China states of activism were produced through the process of participation itself. This does not mean, of course, that women activists and officials were the willing dupes of male-dominated party organizations and movements, but rather that their projects of self-determination and class struggle can be more fully understood through a careful study of the vocabularies, emotional pedagogies, and relational ties through which those projects were produced.

When an investment in one project ends, or interweaves with another, as in the case of some Christians who became party members, and party members who became Christians, the "self" is quite literally subject to change as well. This was the case for Zhou Changfen, 157, a retired Wenhe women's head and vice party secretary, who converted to Christianity in the 1990s, and found great solace in her new religion's capacity to protect her health and uplift her family's financial well-being. This was also the case for Zhou Jianglan, 144, who shared that sexual equality was only achieved after her conversion to Christianity, well after the 1950s. Viciously beaten by her husband in the earliest years of her marriage, the beatings only stopped, she said, once she turned to God.

Read across the decades, the protocols regulating the Chinese Communist Party family have, in fact, been subject to significant transformation. Indeed, while male homosocial capital has been a constant feature of PRC politics, its expression has nonetheless shifted, suggesting that the rules, norms, and practices of informal institutions may not always endure as has previously been suggested.[11]

As revolutionary participants aged, as CCP organizations strengthened and weakened, and as new expectations of relational obligation were established, both the party family and the state itself were transformed. The rise of companionate couples in the 1930s and 1940s, for example, took shape, in part, as a way to uphold sexual equality while offsetting a perception of factionalism and corruption. The rise of companionate couples also enabled the CCP to build its governance structure, with women officials assuming responsibility for women-work. The post-GLF recovery initially continued this practice. As has been previously noted by Yang (1996, 78–79), senior male leaders fanned out to undertake investigations in 1960 and 1961. Zhu De and Zhou Enlai did so in the company of their spouses: Kang Keqing and Deng Yingchao (see, for example, Kang 1993: 455–58). At the same moment, Cai Chang organized ACWF cadres to participate in investigative groups of the central government, including one led by Li Fuchun, at the Beijing Capital Iron and Steel Plant. Cai Chang would also directly intervene when the ACWF working group sympathized with women who did not want to be sent back to the countryside, as part of the economic policy of retrenchment. Cai Chang lectured her comrades that while it might appear that the CCP was asking women to sacrifice their immediate interests, in fact this effort was protecting the interests of all of the people, including the fundamental (*genben*) interests of women (Liu 1992, 115–17). At another moment, Cai Chang asked Li Fuchun to speak to senior Women's Federation officials to help them to understand the new economic emphasis. According to Li (1992, 75), elder sister Cai helped them to understand how to situate women-work in the context of the overall situation.

As is evident in the description of Deng and Zhou's visit to Handan that begins this chapter, and the collaborations of Cai Chang and Li Fuchun, the investigative tours enabled the couples to unite their offices, share recommendations, and shore up the state's capacity to roll out recovery. This recovery included an intense focus on attending to uterine prolapse and restoring menstrual health, activity that had begun well before the GLF was quietly ended in December 1960.[12]

The separate but equal functioning of the companionate tie, however, began to come under increasing strain in the context of repeat Anti-Rightist Movements, the GLF, and the famine. Beginning in the late 1950s, clientelist behavior began to assume greater importance in defining the Chinese Communist Party family. This shift is evident, for example, when Shi Jian was replaced by the wife of the provincial party secretary who had her purged. It is also evident in the politics of the Cultural Revolution (1966–1976), when the ACWF was shuttered for seven years, and clientelism informed the attached struggles that ensued (see Jin 1999).[13]

When the Reform era commenced, yet another shift in the practice of the party family took shape: that is, the elimination of women spouses from elite politics altogether. Indeed, only the most senior and revered women party leaders were granted a seat at the table in the earliest years of the post-Mao era. It was in 1978, for example, that Deng Yingchao was finally able to ascend to the Politburo, as Zhou Enlai's widow (Rosen 1995, 317). Since the death of the most senior women members of the CCP, including Deng Yingchao, Cai Chang, and Kang Keqing, the party family has largely been transformed into a vehicle of dynastic advancement. This is true at both the grassroots and at the apex of the CCP.[14] Many interviewees discussed offspring or grandchildren who are now party members.[15] The most powerful man in the CCP today is Xi Jinping, son of Xi Zhongxun, the revolutionary who assisted Deng Xiaoping to widen access to contraception in 1954. Now, after three decades of intensive and, at times, violent, birth planning, it is Xi Jinping who is leading efforts to curb access to birth control and abortion in a bid to encourage Han women to birth more babies (see Dou 2021). At the same time, scholars are raising serious questions about genocide among Uyghurs, based on the rapid increase in IUD insertions, sterilizations, and abortions in Xinjiang (Smith 2021). What began as an attached effort to increase women's access to reproductive options in the early 1950s has thus come full circle, with the regulation of women's bodies and households once again adapted to the economic and political priorities of the CCP.

Beyond the politics of the PRC, countless other enactments of party families that have shaped the politics of the twentieth and twenty-first centuries, perhaps none more celebrated than the joint leadership of Juan and Eva Perón of Argentina. Juan Perón first held the Argentinian presidency between 1946 and 1955. Both prior to assuming the presidency and during the first six years he was in office, Juan worked closely with his second wife, Eva, to build the Peronist movement, and in particular, to involve women in the grassroots development of "social action." While they oversaw passage of the first suffrage law for women in 1947, and Eva personally spearheaded the selection of six women candidates for senator on the Peronist ticket in 1951 (all of whom won office), the couple was highly critical of feminism (Deutsch 1991). Instead, the Péron valorized the ideal that women could best support the state and national development through their commitment to motherhood—their role of wives and mothers "qualified them to take part in political life" (Grammatico 2010, 128). To this end, Eva herself ran the ministries of Labor and Health, founded and oversaw the Eva Perón Foundation and the Female Peronist Party, and made an unsuccessful bid for the vice presidency in 1951. At the same time, the Peróns undertook a number of reforms, including deploying health measures to protect mothers and new-borns, providing women subsidies for giving birth, reducing taxes for big families, enforcing strict repression of abortion, and providing training for women in modern childcare practices (Grammatico 2010, 128).[16] Eva Perón's wild popularity with lower-class women fueled the Peronist movement both before and after her early death in 1952, and her legacy has continued to influence Argentinian politics up until the recent past.[17]

As enactors of social policy, and as symbolic representations of the nation and state, the political struggles in which the Peróns were engaged was highly personalized. Similar to other aspiring and new leaders, the Peróns sought to strengthen their legitimacy and gain compliance, in part, through establishing themselves as parental figures of the nation and state.[18] The fact that party families have deployed themselves in this way, of course, does not mean that they have not also operated to advance the welfare of family members as well. The "First Lady Syndrome," whereby the wives of African heads of state have strategically deployed "women's issues" as a means of advancing familial power, is but one contemporary example (Abdullah 1995; Ibrahim 2004). The "Princelings" (*taizi dang*), or the adult and now ageing children of the original Chinese revolutionary leadership, including Xi Jinping, is another. Rich and powerful the Princelings have held considerable influence in behind-the-scenes elite negotiations in the Reform Era (Chung 1991; Tanner and Feder 1993; and Shih, Adolph, and Liu 2012). But while clientelism may be the most visible enactment of family ties in politics in the PRC and elsewhere, it is only one dimension of a much more extensive relational fabric that continues to course through contemporary politics today.

On May 23, 1989, and just weeks after celebrating the seventieth anniversary of May 4, Deng Yingchao (1989) published an open letter in the *People's Daily* to the hundreds of thousands of university students protesting in the streets of Beijing, urging them to return to their classrooms. As a retired member of the Politburo and Zhou Enlai's widow, Deng Yingchao was intimately involved with the elite decision-making that took place that spring, including the decisions to declare Martial Law, to fire Zhao Ziyang, and to appoint Jiang Zemin as the new general secretary of the CCP (see, for example, Zhang 2001, 74, 83, 479 and Nathan 2001, xxx–xxxi). In her letter, Deng Yingchao made an emotional appeal to the students to restore order and unity, "which everyone wants." She also sought to discredit rumors flowing, including about herself (though she does not indicate what those rumors were). Most important, Deng spoke to the students much in the way a mother would to her wayward offspring, "I am an old member of the Chinese Communist Party, and have always held deep feelings (*shenhou ganqing*) toward children, I hope that when [you] children grow up [you] will make [your] talents useful to the nation and make great contributions to the people, become patriots, love the people, and construct the nation" (Deng 1989).

When it became clear that the students were not responding to martial law or the appeals of the elders, Deng Yingchao herself urged the senior CCP leaders to show restraint:

> Let's take a moderate approach. We can persuade the students to go back to their campuses, use the PLA in the city to maintain order, and show the common people and the majority of the young students that the party and government are determined to address their concerns and are confident of success. This will make us popular. I hope we can restore order quickly. (Zhang 2001, 313–14)

The elders and the new Standing Committee of the Politburo, of course, did not embrace moderation, deciding, as they did, to violently clear Tiananmen Square beginning on the evening of June 3. While it is unclear whether Deng Yingchao participated in the final decision to mobilize the troops, in Deng's speech at an expanded meeting of the Political Bureau of the Central Committee on June 19, she fully endorsed Deng Xiaoping's and Li Peng's speeches which justified the military onslaught, while condemning the counterrevolutionary rioters (*fangeming baoluan fenzi*) (Deng 1989 [2019]). Deng's biographer praises her for helping to keep China strong and united even as communism collapsed in Eastern Europe that same year (Jin 1993, 2:965).[19]

Deng's role in the crisis of spring 1989 points to some of the enduring elements of China's revolutionary attachments as they have materialized over the past century. When Deng called the students "children" and attempted to persuade them to return to their campuses, she was enacting the same form of relational repression that she and thousands of women activists and officials have engaged since well before the founding of the PRC. What neither Deng Yingchao, nor her adopted son, Li Peng, who also personally failed to persuade the students to be "reasonable," seemed to understand is that the students resented being treated like children, just as so many women activists had resented being treated as women before them. The attached underpinnings to Deng's responses to the events of 1989 and 1961, both recounted by Deng's biographer, speak to the maternalist linkages between these moments of violence and loss, and their ultimate contestation. In the wake of the June 4 massacre, the Tiananmen Mothers, the bereaved mothers and fathers of young people killed on June 3 and 4h,

1989, would give renewed meaning to the language of maternalism, demanding information about and accountability for their murdered and missing offspring (see Lim 2014).

Attached politics are as common as they are consequential. Regardless of regime type, the ongoing enactment of party families, the adoption of familial terms and histories, and the regulation of family life has been central to the realization and imagination of the modern state. This is as true of Canada, where Canadians have elected two Trudeaus during my lifetime, as it is of the United States, where party families from both political parties have defined the Oval Office for decades. When querying the origins of state power the question is thus not simply whether the state can operate distinct from family ties, but rather which family ties matter, when, and how, in ongoing processes of state formation. During a moment of rising populism and leadership cults, struggles over transgender children and reproductive rights, and here in Canada, the recovery of mass graves of residential school children, understanding the familial foundations of state power has become a more urgent task than ever.

GLOSSARY

Anhui 安徽

bai mao nü 白毛女

baochan daohu 包产到户

baozhang 保长

baoyu houdai 保育后代

Beidaihe 北戴河

Beijing 北京

biaoxian 表现

bijiao qinmi 比较亲密

Bo Yibo 薄一波

bu heli de shehui zhidu 不合理的社会制度

bu ruyi de pei'ou 不如意的配偶

bu tai anxin de qingxu 不太安心的情绪

bu zhengpai 不正派

buxu e si yi ge ren 不许饿死一个人

Cai Chang 蔡畅

Cai Hesen 蔡和森

Cao Guanqun 曹冠群

Cao Mengjun 曹孟君

Cao Zhuxiang 曹竹香

Changsha 长沙

Chen Boda 陈伯达

Chen Shaoyu (Wang Ming) 陈绍禹 （王明）

Chen Yi 陈毅
Chen Yun 陈云
cheng 撑
Cheng Wanzhen 程婉珍
Chengdu 成都
chengqianbihou, zhibingjiuren 惩前毖后，治病救人
chengwei xianshi 成为现实
chi qing 吃青（to eat unripe crops）
chi shitang de shihou 吃食堂的时候
Chiang Kai-shek (Jiang Jieshi) 蒋介石
Chongqing 重庆
chongxin xunzhao xin'ai de duixiang 重新寻找心爱的对象
chufen 处分
chu jia 出家
chu lai 出来
cihou 伺候
culü 粗滤
Da Fo 大佛
da jiating 大家庭
da yue jin 大跃进
da zhangfu 大丈夫
da zhuang 大壮
dajie 大姐
dang jia 当家
dang jia de 当家的
dang jiao gei ni de renwu, jianding er bu yi 党交给你的任务，坚定而不移
dangjia zuozhu 当家作主
dangjia zuozhu le 当家作主了
danwei 单位
dayoukewei 大有可为
de cai jianbei 德才兼备
Deng Xiaoping 邓小平
Deng Yingchao 邓颖超
Deng Yuzhi 邓裕志
dianxing diaocha 典型调查
Ding Ling 丁玲
diu ren 丢人
Dong Bian 董边
Dong Biwu 董必武
Dongbei 东北

duli renge 独立人格

dundian 蹲点

duo 多

ertong wansui 儿童万岁

fan maojin 反冒进

fandui si zhong yapo 反对四种压迫

fangeming baoluan fenzi 反革命暴乱分子

fanshen 翻身

feichang de ai 非常的爱

Feng Yuxiang 冯玉祥

fengjian de shufu 封建的束缚

Fudan 复旦

Fujian 福建

fukua 浮夸

funü 妇女

funü gongzuo 妇女工作

funü neng ding ban bian tian 妇女能顶半边天

Funü shenghuo《妇女生活》

Funü zazhi《妇女杂志》

Fuping阜平

furen 夫人

fuying weisheng xue妇婴卫生学

gaige kaifang 改革开放

ganbu teshu 干部特殊

ganqing 感情

ganqing shen 感情深

Gansu 甘肃

Gaoshan xian 高山县

Ge Jianhao 葛健毫

geming lao zumu 革命老祖母

genben根本

Gongaihui 共爱会

gongchanfeng 共产风

gu lü 顾虑

gu zu ganjin, lizheng shangyou, duo kuai hao sheng de jianshe shehui zhuyi
     鼓足干劲力争上游，多快好省地建设社会主义

Guangdong 广东

guangrong 光荣

Guangxi 广西

guanxi 关系

Guo Tengyun 郭腾云
Guojia dangwei 国家党委
Guomin canzhenghui 国民参政会
Guomindang 国民党
gupo 姑婆
haishi hui jia hao 还是回家好
Han Youtong 韩幽桐
Handan 邯郸
Hangzhou 杭州
hao 好
hao nanzi yao dang bing, hao tie yao da ding 好男子要当兵，好铁要打钉
hao nan bu da bing, hao tie bu da ding 好男不当兵，好铁不打钉
He Long 贺龙
He Xiangning 何香凝
He Zizhen 贺子贞
Hebei 河北
Henan 河南
Hu Binxia 胡彬夏
Hu Jingfu 胡经甫
Hua Mulan 花木兰
Huaiyin 淮阴
Huang Qizao 黄启璪
Huanqiu wenhui 《环球文汇》
Hubei 湖北
hukou 户口
Hunan 湖南
hunyin ziyou 婚姻自由
Huoyue xian 活跃县
Jiang Qing 江青
Jiang Weiqing 江渭清
Jiang Zemin 江泽民
Jiangnan 江南
Jiangsu 江苏
Jiangxi 江西
jianjue 坚决
jianjue fandui 坚决反对
jianku fendou 艰苦奋斗
jiashu 家属
jiating guanli 家庭管理
jiating hemu 家庭和睦

jiazhang 家长

jiazu 家族

jiefang 解放

Jiefang ribao《解放日报》

jiemei hui 姐妹会

jihua chifan 计划吃饭

jiji 积极

jin 斤

Jinmen 金门

jiti dangjia shi nü de 集体当家是女的

jiu bu jiao wairen 就不叫外人

Kaifeng 开封

kaiwanxiao de 开玩笑的

kang 炕

Kang Keqing 康克清

Kang Sheng 康生

Kang Youwei 康有为

Ke Qingshi 柯庆施

kelian 可怜

kuai 快

Kunming 昆明

laodong funü 劳动妇女

Li Baoguang 李宝光

Li Dequan 李德全

Li Fuchun 李富春

Li Jingquan 李井泉

Li Peizhi 李培之

Li Peng 李鹏

Li Shuangshuang 李双双

Li Tete 李特特

Li Xiannian 李先念

liang zhong bu tong de yijian 两种不同的意见

Liao Chengzhi 廖承志

Liao Mengxing 廖梦醒

Liao Zhongkai 廖仲恺

Lin Biao 林彪

Lin Feng 林枫

Lin Jiamei 林佳楣

Lin Qiaozhi 林巧稚

lingdao ren 领导人

Liu Hulan 刘胡兰
Liu Jialin 刘加林
Liu Jingfan 刘景范
Liu Lantao 刘澜涛
Liu Qingyang 刘清扬
Liu Shaoqi 刘少奇
Liu Yinting 刘银廷
Liu-Wang Liming 刘王立明
Lu Xun 鲁迅
Lü Zhengcao 吕正操
Luo Qiong 罗琼
Lushan 庐山
Ma Yinchu 马寅初
Macheng 麻城
Mao meizi 毛妹子
mao qian 毛钱
Mao Zedong 毛泽东
Meihua 玫花
meiyou diaocha jiu meiyou fayan quan 没有调查就没有发言权
Meng Qingshu 孟庆树
mingling zhuyi 命令主义
Minzhu funü lianyihui 民主妇女联谊会
minzu 民族
mishu 秘书
mofan de kanhu, Zhongguo de Nan ding ge'er 模范的看护，中国的南丁格尔
mofan de muqin 模范的母亲
mu 亩
Mu Guiying 穆桂英
mujiao yundong 母教运动
muqin yingxiong 母亲英雄
muxing 母性
muzhi 母职
Nanchang 南昌
Nanjing 南京
nannü cuowu 男女错误
nannü pingdeng 男女平等
Nanyang 南阳
neibu kanwu 内部刊物
ni de ye shi wo de, wo de ye shi ni de, ziji shenme dou bu dangjia le 你的也是
    我的，我的也是你的，自己什么都不当家了

niangjia 娘家

Ningxia 宁夏

nongcun funü 农村妇女

nongmin 农民

Nongmin hui 农民会

nü tongzhi fan de shen zui da 女同志翻的身最大

nüquan zhuyi 女权主义

nüzi 女子

Ou Mengjue 凶梦觉

pa si bu dang Gongchandang 怕死不当共产党

paibie douzheng 派别斗争

Peng Dehuai 彭德怀

Peng Pai 彭湃

Peng Zemin 彭泽民

Peng Zhen 彭真

pigu niu li 屁股扭哩

pin ku baixing 贫苦百姓

pizhun 批准

pizi 痞子

poche 破车

poxie 破鞋

qiangpo mingling 强迫命令

Qing 清

Qinghai青海

qinjian jianguo, qinjian chijia 勤俭建国，勤俭持家

Qiu Jin 秋瑾

Quanguo minzhu funü lianhehui 全国民主妇女联合会

Ren Bishi 任弼时

ren you duo da dan, di you duo da chan 人有多大胆，地有多大产

renjia 人家

renqing 人情

renzhen de taolun 认真的讨论

Shaanxi 陕西

shan ye 山野

Shandong 山东

Shanghai 上海

Shanghai pingmin nü xuexiao 上海平民女学校

Shanxi 山西

Shao Lizi 邵力子

Shao Shiping 邵式平

Shen Junru 沈钧儒
Shen Zijiu 沈滋九
sheng 省
shengli shang de texing 生理上的特性
shenhou ganqing 深厚感情
shensheng de muxing 神圣的母性
Shi Liang 史良
shishi 事实
shixing zhenzheng nannü pingdeng 实行真正男女平等
shiyi xing 适宜性
shou zui 受罪
Shuai Mengqi 帅孟奇
shufu 舒服
Sichuan 四川
sixiang 思想
sixiang gongzuo 思想工作
sixiang kumen 思想苦闷
Song 宋
Song Ailing 宋蔼龄
Song Jiaoren 宋教仁
Song Meiling 宋美龄
Song Qingling 宋庆龄
Song Ziwen 宋子文
su le 酥了
Subei 苏北
Sun Yat-sen (Sun Zhongshan) 孙中山
Suzhou 苏州
taitai 太太
Taihe 太和
taipo 太婆
taizi dang 太子党
Tan Zhenlin 谭震林
Tao Zhu 陶铸
taoyan 讨厌
tiandixia pao de shi zhenjie nü, xiulou shang xiu de shi yang han jing 天底下跑
    的是贞节女，绣楼上绣的是养汉精
Tiananmen 天安门
Tianjin 天津
tianzhi 天职
tiaozhan 挑战

tonggou tongxiao 统购统销

Tongmenghui 同盟会

Wang Guangmei 王光美

Wang Huiwu 王会悟

Wang Ming (Chen Shaoyu) 王明 (陈绍禹)

Wang Ruqi 王汝琪

Wang Shijin 王诗锦

Wang Shiwei 王实味

Weixing 卫星

Wenhe xian 温和县

wo bushi he tamen yiyang shi ren, a? 我不是和他们一样是人，啊？

wo genben bu hui zuo nüren, wo bu neng zuo funü gongzuo 我根本不会做女人，我不能做妇女工作

wo zhege ren shi gexing hen ying de 我这个人是个性很硬的

women dui li shi nü de dangquan a 我们队里是女的当权啊

women zhe shi youming de liangshi duo 我们这是有名的粮食垛

Wu Yaozong 吴耀宗

Wu Yunfu 伍云甫

Wu Zhipu 吴芝圃

Wuhan 武汉

wuhui 污秽

wuxian ganqing 无限感情

Xi Jinping 习近平

Xi Zhongxun 习仲勋

Xi'an 西安

Xiang Jingyu 向警予

xianjin 先进

xiao 孝

xiao jiating 小家庭

Xiao Hua 萧华

xiazhihui shengchan 瞎指挥生产

Xibaipo 西柏坡

Xicun 西村

Xiehe 协和

xieqi 泄气

Xin Zhongguo funü 《新中国妇女》

Xinhua ribao 新华日报

Xinjiang 新疆

Xinyang 信仰

Xiping 西平

xitong 系统
xiu 羞
Xiushui 修水
Xixing Manji 西行漫记
Xu Guangping 许广平
Xu Min 徐敏
Xu Yunbei 徐运北
Xuchang 许昌
xue huai 学坏
Xue Ming 薛明
Yan Renying 严仁英
Yan'an 延安
yang 阳
Yang Chongrui 杨崇瑞
Yang Kaihui 杨开慧
Yang Shangkui 杨尚奎
Yang Shangkun 杨尚昆
Yang Yunyu 杨蕴玉
Yang Zhihua 杨之华
yangge 秧歌
Yanjing 燕京
yao 腰
Ye Jianying 叶剑英
Ye Qun 叶群
yi song, er cui, san piping 一送，二催，三批评
yi ziyou wei yuanze 以自由为原则
yin 阴
yinggai 应该
you ganqing 有感情
you yi dian ben 有一点笨
youshengxue 优生学
yu liang 余粮
Yuan Yuying 袁玉英
yueshu 约束
Yunnan 云南
Yuying tang 育婴堂
Zeng Guofan 曾国藩
Zeng Xisheng 曾希圣
Zeng Zhi 曾志
Zhang Jieqing 张洁清

Zhang Qian 张茜
Zhang Qinqiu 张琴秋
Zhang Xichen 章锡琛
Zhang Yun 章蕴
zhangfu 丈夫
Zhangjiakou 张家口
zhangwo jiating 掌握家庭
Zhanshi ertong baoyu hui 战时儿童保育会
Zhao Xian 赵先
Zhao Ziyang 赵紫阳
zhaogu liang 照顾粮
Zhejiang 浙江
zhengce xing 政策性
zhengfeng yundong 整风运动
zhengpai 正派
zhengshi ganbu 正式干部
Zhengzhou 郑州
Zhonggong zhongyang funü yundong weiyuanhui 中共中央妇女运动委员会
Zhongnanhai 中南海
zhongshi 重视
zhongshi 重使
Zhou Enlai 周恩来
Zhou Yang 周扬
Zhounan nüxiao 周南女校
Zhu Danhua 朱旦华
Zhu De 朱德
zhu guan nengdongxing 主观能动性
zhu li jun 主力军
zhufu 主妇
Zhumadian 驻马店
Zhuo Lin 卓琳
zihao 自豪
ziji de yizhi 自己的意志
zili gengsheng 自力更生
ziyou 自由
zizhu 自主
zuo yuezi 坐月子
zuofeng 作风
zuofeng bu hao 作风不好

INDIVIDUALS INTERVIEWED

	POSITION	LOCATION	DATE OF INTERVIEW
1	Party/federation apex (Zhu Hong, 朱红)	n/a	1/17/01
2	Party/federation apex (You Qing, 尤青）	n/a	3/10/01
3	Party/federation apex (Xue Yiwei, 薛忆伟）	n/a	3/10/01, 3/19/01
4	Party/federation apex (Xie Junhong, 谢军红）	n/a	3/10/01
5	Party/federation apex (Cai Ming, 蔡明）	n/a	3/19/01, 6/23/01
6	Party/federation apex (Gao Jian, 高剑）	n/a	3/19/01
7	Party/federation apex (Li Lan, 李澜）	n/a	3/19/01
8	Village party secretary (Zhao Kaitai, 赵开泰)	Huoyue Village 1	2/14/01, 2/16/01
9	Woman (Mu Fengxi, 母凤熙)	Huoyue Village 1	2/14/01, 2/16/01
10	Women's head (Liu Yuezhen, 刘月珍)	Huoyue Village 1	2/14/01, 2/18/01, 7/10/04
11	Militia leader/cafeteria accountant （Ma Guilin, 马贵林）	Huoyue Village 1	2/16/01
12	Bachelor （Zhang Furen, 张富仁）	Huoyue Village 1	2/16/01
13	Man Accountant (Chen Zongze, 陈宗泽）	Huoyue Village 1	2/17/01
14	Work point model (Sun Suzhen, 孙素珍）	Huoyue Village 1	2/17/01
15	Work point model's husband (Li Guifu, 李贵富）	Huoyue Village 1	2/17/01
16	Woman (Wang Xiaosu, 王小素)	Huoyue Village 1	2/17/01
17	Young activist (Li Liping, 李 丽萍)	Huoyue Village 1	2/18/01
18	Women's head's husband （Xiao Erhei, 肖二黑）	Huoyue Village 1	2/18/01

(continued)

(continued)

	POSITION	LOCATION	DATE OF INTERVIEW
19	Militia leader (Xue Gui, 薛贵)	Huoyue Village 2	2/20/01
20	Women's head (Zhang Sumei, 张素梅)	Huoyue Village 2	2/20/01, 7/7/04
21	Childcare worker (Ai Yue, 艾月)	Huoyue Village 2	2/20/01
22	Childcare worker's husband (County statistical clerk) (Cheng Haiting程海亭)	Huoyue Village 2	2/20/01
23	Accountant (Zeng Xiaofan, 曾小凡)	Huoyue Village 2	2/20/01
24	Cafeteria worker and woman team leader (Li Xiaoyue, 李小月)	Huoyue Village 2	2/20/01
25	Party secretary (Gao Yunxi, 高芸熙)	Huoyue Village 2	2/21/01
26	Woman (Jiang Wenli, 蒋文丽)	Huoyue Village 2	2/21/01
27	Party secretary's wife (Cai Qingfang, 蔡清芳)	Huoyue Village 2	2/21/01
28	Woman (Huang Lanfang, 黄兰芳)	Huoyue Village 2	2/22/01, 7/7,04, 7/12/04
29	Woman team leader (Deng Huazhen, 邓花贞)	Huoyue Village 2	2/22/01, 7/8/04, 7/12/04
30	Woman (Li Ailing, 李爱玲)	Huoyue Village 2	7/4/01
31	Women's head (He Jinxiu, 贺金秀)	Huoyue (near Village 1)	2/15/01
32	Women's head (Peng Xiufen, 彭秀芬)	Huoyue (nearby commune)	2/19/01
33	District women's head (Feng Shuyun, 冯淑云)	Huoyue Village 2	7/4/01
34	District leader (Gu Mingjun, 古明军)	Huoyue Village 2	7/4/01
35	Man Commune administrator (Tao Xizong, 陶析综)	Huoyue (from Village 2)	2/20/01
36	County women's head (Yang Chunlan, 杨春兰)	Huoyue	7/1/01
37	Women's head (Tang Xiuying, 唐秀英)	Wenhe (neighboring commune)	3/29/01
38	Party secretary (Wang Chengli, 汪成礼)	Wenhe Village 1	3/31/01, 6/27/01
39	Woman team leader (Wen xiujin, 文秀金)	Wenhe Village 1 (a)	3/31/01, 6/27/01
40	Accountant (Gao Qinguo, 高勤国)	Wenhe Village 1 (a)	3/31/01
41	Woman (Ma Meiying, 马梅英)	Wenhe Village 1 (a)	3/31/01, 6/27/01
42	Woman team leader (Gu Xiulan, 谷秀兰)	Wenhe Village 1 (a)	4/2/01
43	Women's head (Yan Shuqun, 严淑群)	Wenhe Village 1	3/31/01, 6/27/01, 7/20/04
44	Woman (Liu Chunxia, 刘春霞)	Wenhe Village 1 (a)	4/2/01
45	Woman (Li Hongmei, 李红梅)	Wenhe Village 1 (a)	4/2/01
46	Woman (Zhao Xuemei, 赵雪梅)	Wenhe Village 1 (a)	4/2/01
47	Woman (Guo Yunyue, 郭云月)	Wenhe Village 1 (a)	4/2/01
48	Woman (Wang Fangfang, 王芳芳)	Wenhe Village 1 (a)	4/2/01

	POSITION	LOCATION	DATE OF INTERVIEW
49	Woman (Fu Yongzhen, 付永珍)	Wenhe Village 1 (a)	4/2/01
50	Man (Xiang Zhengjun, 向征军)	Wenhe Village 1 (b)	4/2/01
51	Woman team leader (Fang Huayun, 方华云)	Wenhe Village 1 (b)	4/2/01, 4/6/01, 7/17/04, 7/18/04
52	Women's head (Niu Shumiao, 牛淑苗)	Wenhe Village 1	4/2/01, 7/17/04
53	Party secretary/women's head (Xiu Yuefeng, 修月凤)	Wenhe Village 2	4/4/01
54	Party secretary (Wu Fazhong, 吴发忠)	Wenhe Village 2	4/4/01
55	Man (Xiao Wanxing, 萧万兴)	Wenhe Village 2	4/4/01
56	Woman team leader (Lu Guizhen, 卢桂珍)	Wenhe Village 2	4/4/01
57	Women's head (Liang Jinfeng, 梁金凤)	Wenhe Village 2	4/5/01, 6/28/01
58	Women's head (Du Shuzhen, 杜淑贞)	Wenhe Village 2	4/6/01
59	Man (Luo Fugui, 罗富贵)	Wenhe Village 2	4/6/01
60	Childcare worker (Song Lijuan, 宋丽娟)	Wenhe Village 2	4/6/01
61	Party secretary (Dai Jingzong, 戴敬宗)	Wenhe Village 2	4/6/01, 6/28/01
62	County women's federation (Ye Xiaoxin, 叶小欣)	Wenhe	3/30/01
63	County women's federation (Qiu Mingli, 邱明丽)	Wenhe	3/30/01
64	Commune women's federation (Ding Xueqin, 丁雪琴)	Wenhe	3/30/01, 6/25/01, 7/22/04
65	County women's federation (Cao Fengzhu, 曹凤珠)	Wenhe	3/30/01
66	Man commune leader (Jia Pinggui, 贾平贵)	Wenhe (neighboring commune)	6/25/01
67	Man Vice county leader (Meng Yongyu, 孟永玉)	Wenhe	6/25/01
68	Women's head (Liang Ling, 梁玲)	Gao Shan	5/25/01
69	Man team leader (Hu Lingzhu, 胡林柱)	Gao Shan Village 1	5/30/01
70	Man (Zhu Jitang, 朱基堂)	Gao Shan Village 1	5/30/01
71	Man (Gu Xiangju, 顾祥驹)	Gao Shan Village 1	5/30/01
72	Brigade head (Shen Qingfang, 沈清芳)	Gao Shan Village 2	5/30/01
73	Women's head (Lin Xiaohong, 林小红)	Gao Shan Village 2	5/28/01, 6/1/01, 6/21/04, 6/23/04, 6/24/04, 6/28/04
74	Commune women's federation leader (Qiu Zhaodi, 邱招弟)	Gao Shan (neighboring commune)	5/28/01, 6/25/04, 6/27/04
75	Cafeteria accountant (Tan Xiangmin, 谭向民)	Gao Shan Village 2	5/30/01
76	Woman team leader (Deng Langui, 邓兰桂)	Gao Shan Village 2	6/1/01
77	Woman (Mao Xiaoling, 毛小玲)	Gao Shan Village 2	6/1/01

(continued)

(continued)

	POSITION	LOCATION	DATE OF INTERVIEW
78	Man team leader (Xie Changfa, 谢长发）	Gao Shan Village 2	6/1/01
79	Woman (Su Huijuan, 苏惠娟）	Gao Shan Village 2	6/1/01
80	Woman team leader (Qian Yindi, 钱银娣）	Gao Shan Village 2	6/2/01
81	Woman cafeteria worker (Yao Yuling, 姚玉玲）	Gao Shan Village 2	6/2/01
82	Woman accountant (Fan Xinyue, 范歆月）	Gao Shan Village 2	6/4/01
83	Women's head/party secretary (Yang Junxia, 杨君霞）	Gao Shan Village 2	6/4/01, 6/25/04
84	Woman accountant (Xu Hongmei, 徐红妹）	Gao Shan Village 3	6/6/01, 6/29/04
85	Youth league rep/women's head (Tian Min, 田敏）	Gao Shan Village 3	6/6/01, 6/29/04, 6/30/04
86	Woman (Dong Biyu, 董碧玉）	Gao Shan Village 3	6/7/01
87	Woman (Wei Zhaoyun, 魏朝云）	Gao Shan Village 3	6/7/01
88	Childcare worker (Ren Dongmei, 任冬梅)	Gao Shan Village 3	6/7/01
89	Woman team leader (Guo Liangyu, 郭良玉）	Gao Shan Village 3	6/7/01
90	Woman team leader (Lu Xiaoyun, 陆小云）	Gao Shan Village 3	6/7/01
91	Woman team leader (Tang Jieyu, 汤捷玉）	Gao Shan Village 3	6/7/01
92	Man youth league party secretary (Ning Jicai, 宁吉财）	Gao Shan Village 3	6/7/01
93	Man team leader (Zuo Gongming, 左功名）	Gao Shan Village 3	6/7/01
94	Woman (Mei Xingning, 梅香凝）	Gao Shan Village 3	6/8/01
95	Woman (Yi Xiaoai, 易小艾）	Gao Shan Village 3	6/8/01
96	Man brigade head (Qi Tianhong, 齐天宏）	Wenhe Village 1	3/30/01
97	Women's head (Yan Zhijuan, 严志娟）	Gao Shan Village 3	6/8/01, 6/28/04
98	County women's federation head (Lan Jieru, 兰洁茹）	Gao Shan	6/8/01
99	Man county leader (Wen Xiangyang, 温向阳）	Gao Shan	6/8/01
100	Man commune party secretary (Wu Fengyi, 吴凤仪)	Gao Shan	6/8/01
101	Man commune accountant (Kang Yuesheng, 康月生）	Gao Shan	6/8/01
102	Man commune leader (Lei Junming, 雷俊明）	Gaoshan (neighboring commune)	6/11/01
103	Commune leader (Gong Dongsheng, 龚东生）	Gaoshan (neighboring commune)	6/11/01
104	City women's federation (Bi Lirong, 毕俐蓉)	Gao Shan	6/11/01
105	City women's federation (Nie Chunyan, 聂春燕）	Gao Shan	6/12/01
106	City women's federation (Zhu Xiaoming, 祝晓明）	Gao Shan	6/12/01

	POSITION	LOCATION	DATE OF INTERVIEW
107	County women's federation head (Ke Yanrong, 柯燕蓉）	County near Gaoshan	5/18/01
108	Husband to 107/county leader (Shang Xianggui, 尚祥贵）	County near Gaoshan	6/18/01
109	Jiangsu women's federation (Ge Ying, 葛英）	Nanjing	6/10/01
110	Jiangsu women's federation head (Shi Jian, 石坚）	Nanjing	6/19/01
111	Women's head (Fei Achun, 费阿春）	Gao Shan Village 2	5/30/01
112	Man brigade vice head (Sha Xiangrong, 沙向荣）	Huoyue Village 2	2/22/01
113	Brigade vice head's wife (Sang Baoling, 桑宝玲）	Huoyue Village 2	2/22/01
114	Man village leader (Tu Guizhu, 涂贵柱）	Huoyue Village 2	2/22/01
115	Women's head and commune accountant (Chi Meiying, 迟美英）	Gaoshan	6/21/04, 6/22/04
116	Women's head (Rong Litang, 荣丽棠)	Gaoshan Village	6/21/04, 6/23/04, 6/24/04
117	Women's head (Chu Xiaohan, 楚小寒）	Gaoshan Village	6/21/04
118	Man (Han Jinbiao, 韩金标)	Gaoshan Village 2	6/23/04
119	Man (Lu Changwei, 路长伟)	Gaoshan Village 2	6/23/04
120	Woman team leader (Wu Qiugui, 吴秋桂）	Gaoshan Village 2	6/24/04, 6/26/04
121	Woman team leader (Yu Xialian, 于夏莲）	Gaoshan Village 2	6/24/04, 6/27/04
122	Women's head (Yang Yulian, 杨玉莲）	Gaoshan	6/26/04
123	Women's head (Zong Haixia, 宗海霞)	Gaoshan	6/26/04
124	Woman teacher (Ji Hui, 季惠)	Gaoshan	6/26/04
125	Male production leader '63 (Qin Xueming, 秦学明）	Gaoshan Village 3	6/29/04
126	Woman (Xiao Feng'e, 肖凤娥)	Gaoshan Village 3	6/30/04
127	Woman (Dou Guiying, 竇桂英）	Gaoshan Village 3	6/30/04
128	Woman (Ma Mingyu, 马明玉）	Gaoshan Village 3	7/02/04
129	Women's head (Miao Murong, 苗慕蓉）	Huoyue	7/06/04, 7/07/04
130	Cafeteria accountant (Xi Junchang, 席俊昌）	Huoyue	7/06/04
131	Women's head (Hao Lianfen, 郝莲芬）	Huoyue	7/06/04
132	Women's head/party secretary (Hou Qiuyi, 侯秋艺）	Huoyue	7/08/04, 7/12/04
133	Woman (Ma Xiaogui, 马小桂)	Huoyue Village 1	7/09/04
134	Man (Tong Hongcai, 童宏才）	Huoyue Village 1	7/09/04
135	Woman (Zha Xiaopei, 查小珮）	Huoyue Village 1	7/09/04
136	Woman (Yuan Lei, 袁蕾）	Huoyue Village 1	7/09/04
137	Man (Li Changhong, 李长宏）	Huoyue Village 1	7/09/04
138	Woman (Jiang Lili, 江丽丽）	Huoyue Village 1	7/09/04
139	Woman (Chang An, 常安）	Huoyue Village 1	7/09/04

(continued)

(continued)

	POSITION	LOCATION	DATE OF INTERVIEW
140	Man (Shao Yonggang, 邵勇刚）	Huoyue Village 1	7/09/04
141	Man (Teng Renfu, 滕仁富）	Huoyue Village 1	7/09/04
142	Man accountant (Cheng Jiashan, 程家山）	Huoyue Village 1	7/10/04
143	Woman (He Xiaolu, 贺小露）	Huoyue Village 1	7/10/04
144	Woman (Zhou Jianglan, 周江兰）	Huoyue Village 2	7/12/04
145	Woman (Sun Heling, 孙荷玲）	Huoyue Village 2	7/12/04
146	Woman (Chu Anqin, 储安琴）	Huoyue Village 2	7/12/04
147	Man (Tan Yaoxian, 谭耀祖）	Wenhe Village 1 (a)	7/17/04
148	Production leader woman (Fu Youmei, 伏幼梅）	Wenhe Village 1 (a)	7/18/04
149	Man (Zhao Guangzong, 赵光宗）	Wenhe Village 1 (a)	7/18/04
150	Woman (Han Lingmei, 韩岭梅）	Wenhe Village 1 (a)	7/19/04
151	Woman (Zou Dandan, 邹丹丹）	Wenhe Village 1 (a)	7/19/04
152	Woman (Kong Yanyun, 孔燕芸)	Wenhe Village 1 (a)	7/19/04
153	Man (Sheng Yunchang, 盛云长)	Wenhe Village 1 (a)	7/19/04
154	Man (Dong Xuesheng, 董学圣）	Wenhe Village 1	7/20/04
155	Woman (Wang Dangui, 汪丹桂）	Wenhe	7/20/04
156	Women's head (Pu Congxi, 蒲从熙)	Wenhe	7/21/04
157	Women's head (Zhou Changfen, 周长芬）	Wenhe	7/21/04, 7/22/04
158	Commune women's federation leader (Yuan Jinyu, 袁锦玉)	Wenhe	7/24/04
159	Women's head (Tang Li, 唐莉)	Wenhe	7/24/04
160	Commune women's federation leader (Bao Qinglian, 包清莲）	Meihua	12/15/06
161	Woman youth league party sec (Ni Changqing, 倪小青）	Meihua	12/15/06
162	Woman teacher/women-work responsibilities (Sun Qinqin, 孙琴琴）	Meihua	12/15/06
163	Commune women's federation leader (Zheng Xiuwen, 郑秀文）	Meihua	12/15/06

Appendix 3

RESEARCH METHODS AND SOURCES

The work on this book originally focused on women's mobilizations in the GLF, which I initially explored through a focus on Henan, a leading model province during the GLF, and Jiangsu, which did not stand out as a leading province at that time. In the earliest iteration of this research, I sought to understand how the CCP and the ACWF related to one another at each level of government, at center, province, prefecture, county, commune, and village, as well as the organizational and family dynamics among leaders and peasants within six villages, through a methodological "anthropology of the state" (Migdal 2001). During the more than twenty years I have spent working on this project, I have expanded beyond the original scope of the book both in source and methodology, to focus on the larger question of the gendered origins of state power itself.

Interview participants included a wide range of individuals who had been involved in and/or impacted by women-work in the 1950s.[1] In 2001, 2004, and 2006 I interviewed retired party officials within the Women's Federation, two retired chairs of the Jiangsu Women's Federation, as well as retired county, township (commune), and village-level women leaders. Where possible, I also interviewed retired party and government officials at the county and township level. Interviewee participants included twenty-five former village-level women's heads who served before or during the GLF years, plus two additional village women's heads (one whom started after the GLF ended and one whom went on to serve as an accountant on her commune).[2] A total of forty-three women interviewed served at the village, commune, or county level before or during the GLF.[3] I also sought to develop a sense of local understandings of women-work by interviewing a wide swath of villagers, activists, and leaders from the six communities.

The interviews I conducted were semistructured and lasted anywhere from minutes to three hours at a time. Although I did not start out to conduct life histories or revolutionary testimonials per se, the further I continued in the work, the more my explorations moved in this direction. As della Porta (1995, 19) suggests, revolutionary testimonials "allow us to observe the way in which history forms . . . individual consciousness, how public events intervene in private life, and how perceptions [of such events] shape behavior."[4] I sought to better understand how the revolution and the state were understood and enacted at the local level. In each interview I thus tried to cover a specific set of questions about an individual's work and life, questions that continually expanded as I understood more about women-work and the local contexts in which it took place, and as I matured as a scholar. Indeed, and many thanks to the advice and assistance of senior colleagues, the interviews I conducted in 2004 and 2006 proved much richer and deeper than my first awkward and anxiety-ridden attempts in 2001. Instead of starting the interview with the rather formulaic, and in some cases off-putting: "In what year were you born?" for example, I shifted my first questions to focus on early childhood and married life.

Over the course of my research I worked with five different assistants who helped me set up interviews and translate from the local dialect into Mandarin. Following the protocol of the Institutional Review Boards at the universities under which I conducted my research, I gained oral consent prior to each interview. All interviews were given and recorded by myself and transcribed by assistants and are held in my possession.[5] Some interviews, especially when I first began to spend time in a village, also included the presence of curious neighbors, friends and relatives. Once the fascination of our presence wore off, however, my assistant and I were often able to meet and talk with interviewees alone (except in instances when I purposefully organized several group interviews, one of which I discuss in Manning (2005; 2007). I not only selected village sites based upon clan history (discussed in chapter 4) but also upon whether or not the former women's head from the GLF period was available to speak to, and the village's proximity to the county seat. In each case I tried to obtain access to villages that were approximately the same distance in travel time from the county seat.

When interviewing in village settings I always received my initial introductions through official channels, often the county or township Women's Federation. Village officials, usually the local women's head, assumed responsibility for providing me with introductions to local leaders from the 1950s.[6] These leaders would then provide initial introductions to ordinary villagers, although I also met and subsequently interviewed a number of villagers without the aid of local officials. I also met a number of former local women's heads through the introduction of women's heads I had already interviewed. When interviewing retired Women's Federation officials at the township (commune) level and higher, I primarily worked through the introduction of local Women's Federation officials. However, my interview with Shi Jian, retired chair of the Jiangsu Women's Federation, was made possible through a series of personal introductions. I conducted the majority of interviews in people's homes.

As a number of scholars have argued in recent years, the politics of remembering the past is a highly complex and contingent exercise.[7] This is particularly the case in contexts where grave violence or trauma has occurred (Weigelin-Schwiedrzik 2003). The famine that started in 1959, and deepened in 1960, marked where and how I conducted interviews. Although members of my personal network gave me the option of doing research in Zhumadian, a region that was devastated by famine, for example, I chose to confine my work to regions that, although deeply impacted by the famine, did not suffer the same loss of life. Neither my training, nor my methodology, were suitable to conduct interviews with individuals whose communities were decimated during the latter part of the GLF. I nonetheless have felt an acute sense of responsibility to those whom I interviewed who suffered greatly during this period, as well as to those who shared experiences of liberation made possible before, during, and after the GLF.

The issue of drawing on historically mediated memory does not so much produce a problem to be resolved as it points to new puzzles to be explained and interpreted, a process thoughtfully rendered in the emergent social histories focused on the PRC.[8] To this end, I have endeavored to explore and explain recollections as constituting part of the field of struggle. In the context of interviewing, the task became to develop robust understandings of a person's narrative(s), and thus, when possible, following up with some individuals either in the days following an initial interview or, in some cases, three years later. Regardless of the length of elapsed time, repeat meetings almost always brought new insights through deeper levels of discussion, since the majority of interviewees told additional stories that were detailed and layered in ways that our initial discussions were not.

Interviews were coded with the support of a research assistant. The primary purpose of the coding was to establish a basic set of descriptors about the individuals interviewed (birth date, sex, leadership position, etc.), a task, I might add, that has proven extremely challenging. Indeed, given the local variations in dialect, the sweeping changes in village administration that took place across the first decade of the PRC, and given that some women held multiple leadership positions within their village (and at higher levels as well) it has been difficult to classify leadership positions with precision; my accounting has been imperfect at best. Also—while I attempted to cover a preset series of questions, the interviewees often set off in tangents I had not originally anticipated. While these tangents added richness, depth, and further understanding, they sometimes came at the cost off covering "all the bases" of my preset interview protocol. Ultimately, over the many years of transcript analysis I have sought to engage in a reflective, interpretative process and have refined my conclusions accordingly.[9]

I triangulated the use of oral interviews with a study of a wide range of documents from the 1940s and 1950s. Materials drawn on include Women's Federation reports and speeches from the three counties and county and provincial gazetteers. In addition, I have collected and drawn on previously published CCP and CCP women's movement documents from both before and after the establishment of the PRC. I also read and analyzed the journal *Women-Work* for the second half of 1958, 1959, and parts of 1960 and 1961. While the ACWF journal *Women of China* has been analyzed extensively by feminist historians and political scientists studying the 1950s, the journal *Women-Work* has not appeared in many bibliographies. I was nonetheless able to acquire copies of *Women-Work* (1958, 1959, and parts of 1960) from the Beijing National Library, even though it had originally been marked as an "internal document." Insofar as the latter journal was published as a resource for ACWF officials and local leaders, it offers an excellent source of insight into policy debates and new directions in women-work as they unfolded prior to the Cultural Revolution. Former Wenhe Women's Federation commune head Ding Xueqin, 64, for example, read *Women-Work* during the 1950s and early 1960s.

Although I was unable to gain direct access to the ACWF archives, one collection I have accessed, a CD-ROM published by the ACWF, also includes reports from the ACWF archives, with a useful reference to file numbers. In addition, I was able to obtain several ACWF documents from Chongqing Municipal Archives. Finally, and not insignificantly, I have also drawn extensively on published memoirs and biographies of retired Women's Federation and CCP officials, and official histories of the ACWF.

The construction of official CCP history began well before the foundation of the PRC. When Deng Yingchao (1964 [1988], 304–7) reflected in 1964 on the task of writing the history of the women's movement, she herself pointed to Mao Zedong's Yan'an instructions, written during rectification, as the primary model from which to undertake this work. The many official histories and memories published during the Reform Era, therefore, but must be read with political objectives in mind. They must be "layered," or explained in the context of their production and circulation (Schmalzer 2021, 777), which in the case of this book, I argue, means read as part of the story of attachment politics itself. Can one imagine, for example, an edited volume about Mao Zedong, Zhu De,

Zhou Enlai, and their comrades entitled, "Blood and Tenderness: The Stories of the Life and Death of Ten Elder Brothers of the Chinese Communist Party"? (*TR* 2004) No—because their official histories do not employ these particular relational modes of kin-based belonging, nor do they invoke the same vulnerability and emotional register of the revolutionary conflict as is presented in this collection's title and contents. It is in this light, therefore, that He Zizhen's resurrection in the volume cited above and in other Reform-era produced histories, can be understood as part of the work of rewriting Chairman Mao's story.[10] And it is in this light that the ACWF has undertaken its own ongoing quest to legitimize its existence, through the documents senior ACWF historians release in its collections and through public battles over who gets to claim authorship of the original Marriage Law, for example.[11] Given these complexities, I have simultaneously sought to map the fields of struggle through exploring incidents of "what actually happened" (Brown 2021b, 697) and through exploring "why certain things matter and to whom" (Schmalzer 2021, 778). This is a fine line to walk, but a necessary one, even as that line so often is as forcefully intangible as the state is, itself.

Notes

INTRODUCTION

1. Although estimates of the actual number of famine deaths continues to be a subject of scholarly dispute, most would agree that at least thirty million people perished as a consequence of the famine. See Ghosh 2020, 251, for a recent summary of studies of famine estimates.

2. See also Bourdieu and Wacquant 1992, 97.

3. See Patil's (2013) transnational feminist emphasis on colonial modernity in the emergence of the modern nation-state.

4. For other examples of studies that grapple with the multiplicity that is the modern state, see Brooke and Strauss 2018; Frödin 2012; Migdal 2001; Strauss 2020; Thornton 2007; and Vu 2010. Hershatter's (2011) path-breaking monograph on the "state effect" in rural Sha'anxi is also an important touchstone for this book.

5. See, for example, Remick's (2014, 188) discussion of Kunming's sex work policy, which "was rooted in a particular set of gendered social relations, shaped local state development, expanding the coercive power of an already dominant militaristic local government and creating a set of state institutions that were unique at the time in China."

6. Albeit the difference between affect and emotion can be one of degree (Yang 2014, 11; Yang 2015, 94). Following Ahmed 2004 and Yang 2014 I am more interested in exploring what emotions do than I am in demarcating a sharp boundary between affect and emotion.

7. On revolutionary emotions in Maoist mobilization, see Liu 2010 and Perry 2002b. See also Lee's (2007, 275) discussion of the revolutionary structure of feeling promoted by those affiliated with the CCP and GMD: "The revolutionary subject needs first of all to establish itself as an affective subject, one that feels, loves, and, as it is increasingly necessary, hates; one that is capable of loyalty, devotion and self-sacrifice; and one that can transcend its (class) limitations and empathize with the suffering masses."

8. This is not to say that later years could not also be classified as "revolutionary" but for the purpose of this book, my usage of the term "revolutionary China" encompasses this particular time period.

9. Zylan (2000, 612) defines state maternalism as "the discourse of state responsibility to protect and aid mothers and children." See O'Connor, Orloff, and Shaver 1999, 12, for a fuller discussion of the concept of social policy regime and Skocpol 1992 for discussion of women's leadership in state maternalism.

10. The All China Women's Federation (ACWF) was called the All China *Democratic* Women's Federation (ACDWF) from 1949 until 1957. I discuss the elimination of the word *democratic* from the organization's title in chapter 7.

11. Leftist regimes with a strong state have historically had greater success in addressing infant and child mortality (see, for example, Caldwell 1986; Moon and Dixon 1985). I return to this literature, with a specific discussion of infrastructural capacity, in the book's conclusion.

12. The numbers of interviewees reported here differs slightly from those reported in an earlier publication (Manning 2011). Counting interview participants, and coding for formal roles, has proven to be a highly challenging process throughout the project. This

is, in part, a reflection of having undertaken several group interviews (see, for example, Manning 2007; 2005), regional variations among different sites, and lengthy leadership histories that often reflected overlapping and shifting roles across years, if not decades.

13. My usage of the term *event* here is to be distinguished from Barlow's (2021, 3) introduction of "in the event of women," which she defines as "prolonged efforts to demonstrate a truth." Similar to Barlow (2021, 6), I assume that "people act under given conditions beyond which, in most circumstances, nothing else is thinkable." A "state of activism" builds on this recognition, and the relational ties through which thinking and acting also flow. As I mobilize the term here, an "event" is thus neither simply a meta historical event, nor a "context," but rather a relationally situated process through which agency is enacted at a historically specific moment.

14. See Charrad's (2010, 517–18) discussion of the structure-agency dilemma with respect to feminist analysis. See Myra Marx Ferree 1992 for one of the first important critiques of rationality in the context of social movements.

15. The black and racialized feminists who introduced and have continued to advance intersectionality as a tool of analysis and social transformation, is long. Crenshaw 1991, among others, is often cited as a foundational text. See also Wemheuer 2019 for a recent application of intersectionality to Maoist China.

16. As Jasper (1998, 413) argues, affective ties give networks "much of the causal impact they have."

17. See Wu's discussion (2014) of Red Guard struggle over revolutionary bloodlines during the early years of the Cultural Revolution.

18. See Adam and Galinsky 2012, for example, for a discussion of what they call "enclothed cognition," which they define as "the systematic influence of clothes on the wearer's psychological processes and behavioral tendencies."

19. As Mahmood (2005, 15) argues, "What may appear to be a case of deplorable passivity and docility from a progressivist point of view, may actually be a form of agency—but one that can be understood only from within the discourse and structures of subordination that create the conditions of its enactment. In this sense, agentival capacity is entailed not only in those acts that resist norms but also in the multiple ways in which one *inhabits* norms."

20. Solomon (1969) considers the psychological foundations of Chinese attitudes toward dependence as a way of explaining authority relations in the PRC. Both Solomon (1969) and Weakland (1958) focus in particular on Mao's rebellion against his father. Although my analysis does not engage directly with these arguments, Hunt's psychoanalytic reading of the "family romance" of the French Revolution is an important reminder of the "centrality of narratives about the family to the constitution of all forms of authority" (1992, 8).

21. See Lan and Fong's (1999) edited collection that includes Mao's three essays on "Miss Zhao's Suicide."

22. Scholars do not agree on the exact start and end of the May Fourth Movement. I am following Rana Mitter's more long-term view of this cultural moment (2004).

23. Spakowski (2022) directly questions the concept of "state feminism" as applied to the PRC. While I share many of Spakowski's concerns regarding how to best conceptualize state, society, and indeed, agency, I do not agree that these concerns, when addressed through a state-in-society approach to the state (see Wang 2021), and when written with attention to shared historical linkages (Kaplan, Alarcón, and Maoallem 1999), negates the conceptual power that a partial focus on state feminism can bring to questions of state capacity and conflict.

24. In her study of American maternalism, Ladd-Taylor (1993, 110) argues for a more limited definition, in which maternalists advocated for men to be the primary

breadwinners, with wives and children at home. My own view of maternalism as a source of national and international mobilization, however, conforms with a more complex and expansive understanding of maternalism such as discussed by Koven and Michel 1993; Van der Klein and Plant 2012; and Zylan 2000.

25. Yang (2015, xiv) argues that "the ambiguity of the heart and its moral and psychological agency allows it to be framed to serve various purposes, including as a medium of sustaining social and political order and as a site for regulation and value extraction. It constitutes a resource that government projects can mobilize."

26. See Diamant 2000 for an extended critique of the application of the concept of "patriarchy" to midcentury politics in China.

27. According to Calhoun (1995, 146), "The revolution does not mark a break with the habitus, but is based on it, even though it breaks the pattern of stable reproduction."

28. Adams's (2005) study of the patrimonial foundations of early Western state building has been an important source of inspiration in the writing of this book. Although I decenter patrimonial/neopatrimonial frameworks in my own analysis, Adams work is a significant feminist intervention for rethinking common assumptions regarding the relationship between family ties and the origins of state power.

29. Eisenstadt's early work (1973) is one of the foundational texts in this literature. See also Wai's (2012) searing critique of the neopatrimonialism literature as applied in studies of African politics.

30. Jin's study (1999) of the Lin Biao Affair, arguably one of the most comprehensive examination of elite political families in Maoist China, questions the official CCP factional account of the event while nonetheless seeing factions (and other factors, such as senile paranoia) as also playing a role in the Affair.

31. As Luo (2021) argues, Chinese Communist themselves have a highly articulated understanding of factions, which Western scholars have built on to explain informal struggles within the CCP apparatus.

32. See, for example, Rosen 1995, 317. The first individual I interviewed in 2001 shared this exact account when I asked about her observations of senior CCP women officials in the 1950s. Zhu Hong, 1, the adult child of one of the most influential CCP elders of the Maoist and Reform Eras, told me that the top wives of male senior officials did not participate in politics but merely supported their husbands on special trips or investigations as *jiashu* (family members). They surmised that frequent ill-health and the "time of life" (menopause) also likely impacted their capacity to participate in politics. As will become clear in the chapters that follow, my critique of this narrative is deeply indebted to the path-breaking research of Kay Ann Johnson (1983), Naihua Zhang (1996), and Wang Zheng (2017). See also Gilmartin's foundational study (1995) of women leaders and family ties in the CCP during its first decade.

33. This definition is a marked departure from my earliest conception of the party family, which I first introduced as a family with two or more members active in party organizations (Manning 2005; 2007).

34. This book builds upon contributions by feminist institutionalist scholars, including Bjarnegård's introduction (2013) of male homosocial capital. For additional discussions of gender and informal institutions, see also Banaszak and Weldon 2011; and Waylen 2017.

35. On dynastic succession, see, for example, Dal Bó et al. 2009; and Purdey et al. 2016.

36. In the comparative study of political parties, the term *party family* is used to classify parties who share certain characteristics, often ideological in nature (see Mair and Mudde 1998). By introducing a new conceptual framing for the term, I recognize that I risk muddying the waters of the field of comparative politics. However, I hope that the two conceptualizations can exist independently of one another, informing understanding of what are otherwise distinct arenas of study.

37. The feminist literature on this point is vast. See, for example, Bacchi 1999; Lombardo and Forest 2015; Kantola 2006; and Lombardo, Meier, and Verloo 2009.

38. For an exploration of attached advocacy in contemporary Canadian politics, see Manning 2017.

39. Joseph (2011, 151–52) makes this case as well. Joseph's discussion of "political familism" in Lebanon, offers an important alternative to patrimonialism in considering the complex and dynamic ways that families engage in state-society relations.

40. For an early analysis of familial symbols in the PRC polity, see Weakland 1958. See also Steinmüller's discussion (2015, 88) of family and kinship metaphors in Maoist governance.

41. See also Kipnis 1997; Yan 1996; and Yang 1994.

42. Plotkin (2003) and Kampwirth (2010, 15) discuss women in populist movements as missionary "outsiders" to politics, able to link family and movement, in ways that men cannot.

43. Sageman (2004, 107–13, 139) uses the term *small-world* network structure in his study of individuals recruited to Jihad terrorist activities.

44. See Thomas and Bond 2015 for a discussion of supply-side factors that draw women into violent political organizations.

45. In revolutionary China, women spies also had a role to play, albeit as "honey traps" who used their "feminine charms to seduce their targets" that contravened otherwise strict moral codes regulating sexuality (Edwards 2020, 217).

46. The two-volume study of Wugong Village in Hebei offers one of the most impressive accounts of the intricate workings of local party family networks to date (Friedman et al. 1991; Friedman et. al. 2005). Indeed, as I commenced my doctoral research in 2001, the detailed depiction of politically "strategic marriages" (Friedman et al. 1991, 180) alerted me to the central role these ties played in the building of the local party and state.

47. See Ying's discussion (2009, 236) of an earlier generation of women who would redefine filiality in relationship to their natal family.

48. See Evans 2008, 17–22, for a review of scholarship on this subject.

49. It is unclear who sold her into bride service, but Bao shared that her paternal grandmother always said that "girls belong to other people."

50. Fraternal ties played an important role in Chinese state building under the Mongols (Barfield 1989) and in the early Qing (Wang and Adams 2011).

51. Cai Chang was four years older than Deng Yingchao and assumed a higher status within the CCP structure (Su 1990, 222, 225).

52. Personal communication with Wang Zheng, March 7, 2015.

53. Personal email communication with Song Shaopeng, March 15, 2015. According to Averill (2006, 55–56) sworn brotherhoods in the Jinggangshan region of the late 1920s were "modeled on kinship relations and aimed by linking their members (who generally included unrelated people) through notional kinship bonds to provide them with much the same solidarity and mutual assistance benefits that in other circumstances were typically obtained through family ties." The Triads and the Elder Brother Society, for example, were common in South China and the Yangzi Valley (Chesneaux 1972, 11–13; Polachek 1983, 813–14). See Perry's study (1980, 69) of bandit gang members in the Huaibei region who "often underwent sworn brotherhood ceremonies and addressed one another with fictive kinship titles."

54. Stephan (2010) introduces the concept of "couple's activism" in her study of Lebanese women's rights activist Laure Moghaizel. Insofar as Stephan emphasizes this form of activism as emerging in family feminism (Fernea 2003), it parallels the companionate activism I introduce shortly.

55. In the absence of laws criminalizing sodomy, local authorities responded in divergent ways to their perceived "errors," including "reform through education and/or labour" (Li 2006, 82–83).

56. See also Kang's (2022) study of male same-sex relations in China during the Mao era.

57. See Goodwin 1997; Klatch 2004; and Bjarnegård 2013 for discussion of some ways that perceptions of affective loyalties can disrupt social movement and party cohesion. I return to this issue in later chapters.

58. Mao was first married at the age of fourteen to a woman four years his senior. They apparently never consummated the arranged marriage, and she died a little over a year after their marriage. Gilmartin (1995, 105) suggests that Yang Kaihui was likely made one of the first four women members of the CCP due to her preexisting relationship with Mao.

59. The recipient of a missionary education, He Zizhen joined the Communist Youth League in 1925 and participated in one of the armed uprisings of 1927. Once she married Mao in 1928, however, she became Mao's secretary and gave birth to several of their children. Of ill health and sidelined by Mao's passionate interest in other women, including Jiang Qing, He Zizhen left Mao for Moscow in 1937, only to be divorced by him shortly thereafter (Jin 1999; Wiles 2003c).

60. Goodwin and Pfaff (2001, 288) argue that intimate support networks can have the contradictory effect of simultaneously generating a strong sense of collective purpose, while, at times, giving rise to factional and organization divisions and thus undermining that unity. See their discussion of the conflicts among East German activists (often romantic in origin) in the revolution of 1989.

61. Deng Xiaoping's second wife, to name another example, joined a political attack on Deng while he was fighting in the Jiangxi mountains, and left Deng for one of the CCP officials that was responsible for Deng's temporary ouster from his official posts (Vogel 2011, 29). See also Gilmartin 1995 for further discussion of the instability of these early love matches and Zheng's (1997, 138–56) discussion of the impact of some of these love affairs on inner party struggles.

62. Among those who served in this capacity included Ye Qun (for Lin Biao); Wang Guangmei (for Liu Shaoqi); Li Shuyang (for Chen Boda); and Zhang Jieqing (for Peng Zhen) (Jin 1999). He Zizhen also served as Mao's secretary, albeit unwillingly (Wei 2004, 11, 19).

63. The CCP Central Committee made Jiang Qing pledge she would not participate in politics for thirty years (Jin 1999, 143–44). According to Witke (1977, 172–73), Jiang Qing did not participate in official functions in Yan'an. Prior to the Cultural Revolution (1966–76) Jiang Qing leveraged her official appointment to the Ministry of Culture and her role as *mishu* to keep herself connected to politics and to Mao (Lee 2003c, 261).

64. On the phenomenon of dynasties and the roles of Aung San Suu Kyi, see for example, Fleschenberg 2009.

65. See also Diamant 2001b, 177, for a discussion of political widowhood in the Maoist context.

66. During the Ming and Qing dynasties, official kinship dictated that widows not remarry (see, for example, Mann 2005, 607–13). It is interesting to note that not one of these three widows remarried, including Song Qingling who was in her late twenties when her husband died.

67. See Li's (2007) analysis of the role that Chinese wives of diplomats have played in the PRC.

68. See also Wiles 2003a, 22, for a discussion of Li Fuchun's affair with a worker while they were still in France.

69. This dynamic is also evident in the postwar treatment of women spies by the CCP, in which "in order to assert the level of fidelity required of a national hero, the party must be the ultimate object of woman's devotion" (Edwards 2020, 230).

70. Zhou Enlai, for example, did not inform his wife about China's developing atomic capabilities before the test of China's first atom bomb was held in 1964 (Zhao, Lan, and Zhang 1985, 137), an anecdote retold in a number of publications.

71. Also see Jin 1993, 1:327–32, for a discussion of this and related talks.

72. Deng Yingchao's (1942) essay on young people and love and marriage, for example, serves as the preface to a 1985 collection of hagiographic portraits of revolutionary marriages (Deng 1942 [1985], 1–7).

73. See Guo's analysis (2019) of the political, professional, and friendship networks of women elites in wartime China. As Guo (2019), Li (2010), and many others have argued, the CCP's narrative about the corrupt, bankrupt, and selfish behavior of the GMD government has long overshadowed a remarkable history of mobilization and state building during the late 1930s and early 1940s.

74. Other senior male party officials who married much youngers wives included Lin Biao (Ye Qun), Liu Shaoqi (Wang Guangmei), Chen Yi (Zhang Qian), Deng Xiaoping (Zhuo Lin), Li Xiannian (Lin Jiamei), and He Long (Xue Ming) (Jin 1999, 141).

75. Specifically, out of twenty-four former women's heads, thirteen reported the support of their husbands, five reported "neutral" support, and three were in direct opposition. Among thirty-seven former women's federation leaders on whom I have data, twenty-seven reported having a politically active husband whereas nine did not.

76. The work of Bjarnegård 2013 and Wedeen 1999, are important exceptions, as is the work on political dynasties. The handful of other scholars who study contemporary political families largely work outside of the discipline of political science: for example, McCoy's edited volume (2009) on political families in the Philippines (history), Charrad's work (2001; 2011) on political families in the Maghreb and Iraq (sociology); Joseph's study (2011) of political familism in Lebanon (anthropology); Stephan's study (2010) of couple activism in Lebanon (sociology).

1. THE MAY FOURTH MOVEMENT

1. For a discussion of the scholarly literature on maternalism, including its more recent global turn, see Van der Klein and Plant 2012.

2. Johnson, Litell-Lamb, and Manning 2018 examine some of this activity.

3. Judge (2008, 115) notes that Shimoda emphasized the development of physical strength over intellectual development in the quest to create a strong Chinese nation-state. Throughout the first decades of the twentieth century, physical education studies became extremely popular among young Chinese women. See Gao Yunxiang 2006 for a discussion focused on the 1930s.

4. St. Hilda's School for Girls, originally called the Jane Bohlen School for Girls, for example, was founded in 1875 by Episcopalian missionaries with some of these goals in mind (Liu and Kelly 1996).

5. The number of foreign missionaries in China grew rapidly at the turn of the century, doubling between 1890 and 1905 (Ross 1996, 215). But it was the number of single women missionaries that grew the most rapidly. By 1910 there were 1,500 single women missionaries in China; an increase of 671 women from two years previous (Latourette 1967).

6. According to Hunter 1984, 10, by 1911 some 50 percent of American missionaries in China were no longer engaged in direct evangelism but were rather serving their mission through teaching.

7. See Cong's (2007) detailed discussion of the development of women's education during the first decades of the twentieth century.

8. See also Saich's (2021, 47–49) discussion of the first party congress, which he argues took place at a member's house.

9. See Zarrow 1988 and Liu, Karl, and Ko 2013 for discussions of anarcho-feminism in China.

10. Jasper (1997, 106) defines a moral shock as a moment "when an unexpected event or piece of information raises such a sense of outrage in a person that she becomes inclined toward political action."

11. Although many women, including Deng Yingchao, contributed to the intellectual discussions focused on women's issues, it was men scholar-activists who often led the debates in the important journals of the day (Gilmartin 1995; Wang 1999).

12. Gilmartin (1995, 154–55) argues that Luxemburg, killed in Berlin in 1919, came to represent the ideal of women's emancipation in Chinese women's mobilizations by 1927.

13. In the post-Mao era, Deng Yingchao continued to emphasize the "inextricable relation" between proletarian national revolution and communist women's liberation (Barlow 1994a, 344).

14. Zhou signed his March 8 card using his pen name from the May Fourth Era.

15. The discussion of Liu-Wang that follows builds on Edwards 2002, 2008; Kwok 1992; Schneider 2011; and Wang 1999. Liu-Wang is also known by the name "Wang-Liu" and "Wang Liming."

16. See Barlow's (2004) discussion of Chinese theorists engaged in discussions of female sexuality, evolution, and eugenics, and the relationship of these subjects to the well-being of the nation as a whole.

17. See Barlow 2004; Chiang 2006; Pan 2015; Sakamoto 2004; Schneider 2011; and Wang 1999 for discussions of how the work of Key and other European and Japanese eugenic theorists was rearticulated by Chinese theorists in the 1920s and 1930s.

18. For an example of an English translation of one of Key's central works, see *Love and Marriage* (1911). According to Tyrrell 1991, 67, Key did not ally with the WCTU, because of the "conventional conception of sexual morality that underlay the theme of purity in the Temperance movement."

19. Cited in Wang 1999, 337.

20. According to Sakamoto 2004, Cai Hesen was particularly interested in biometrics—a form of eugenics.

21. Hu was a member of the Common Love Society (*Gongaihui*), a revolutionary organization established to overthrow the Qing government (Kwok 1992, 133).

22. St. Hilda's forbid their students from participating in the demonstrations (Liu and Kelly 1996, 232). The majority of McTyeire students seem to have chosen not to join the demonstrations on their own accord (Ross 1996, 218). And yet, in other Christian schools, especially at the college-level, the protests set off heated debates. Despite their missionary teachers' disapproval, for example, women students from Christian colleges took to the streets (Kwok 1992, 134).

23. See Littell-Lamb 2011 for her discussion of how the YWCA sought to regulate employment conditions of women and children in Treaty Port factories.

24. See, for example, Littell-Lamb's (2010) discussion of the Chinese YWCA's relationship with the World YWCA.

25. Cited in Shang and Tang 1990, 155.

26. A little more than thirty years later, US vice president Nixon and Nikita Khrushchev, the premier of the Soviet Union, publicly disagreed over which system, capitalism or

communism, enhanced women's welfare more. The so-called "kitchen debate" is widely recognized as an important instance of gendered Cold War articulation (see, for example, Koikari 2008, 102; Reid 2005, 290).

2. THE CHONGQING COALITION

1. See Wang's (2021) call for the importance of mapping elite social terrains in understanding the social foundations of state development.

2. This argument builds on the foundational work of Guo 2019; Zhang 1996; and Johnson 1983, all of whom argue that personal ties forged among key women leaders during the war with Japan contributed directly to the early work of the ACDWF.

3. The earliest work on welfare in the PRC was analyzed through the lens of socialism (Dixon 1981; Dixon and Macarov 1992) and, indeed, Chinese policies were seen as based on Soviet policies (Caldwell 1986, 207). Soviet women featured frequently in New Women of China (*Xin Zhongguo funü*), the primary magazine for Chinese women after the foundation of the PRC (Chen 2003; Zhang 1996).

4. See also Guo's (2019) extensive discussion of the Sino-Soviet Cultural Association Women's Committee, in which Deng Yingchao, Li Dequan, and Cao Mengjun all played an important role after its establishment in 1940.

5. Enloe (1989, 97) suggests, for example, that the responsibility of foreign service wives has often included "creating an atmosphere where men from different states can get to know one another 'man to man.'" Baldez (2002, 24) similarly observes, "Parties previously engaged in fierce competition with one another look to women to legitimize the formation of coalitions among them."

6. Song Qingling and her brother Song Ziwen were involved in several efforts prior to the Xi'an Incident to help the GMD make contact with the CCP (Kampen 2000, 85).

7. The question of whether Feng and Li actually met Stalin is subject to debate (Zhang 2017).

8. Unlike many of the women who comprised the Chongqing Coalition, Song initially fled to Hong Kong, not Wuhan, when war broke out in 1937. On Song's periodic trips to Chongqing she publicly toured bombsites, air-raid shelter systems, and hospitals with her two sisters (Lee 2003d, 470).

9. Further biographical treatment of Shen can be found in Zhao 2003b, 448–50; and Guo 2019.

10. According to MacKinnon 2001, 127, the most widely noted and reprinted articles were penned by Song Meiling, Shen Zijiu, and Shi Liang.

11. See also Cao's 1939 [1991] report on the WACW's first year of work.

12. Plum's (2015) research suggests that the actual care that children received was uneven. In some cases caring teachers provided children with education and employment opportunities that they might not otherwise have had. In other cases, children were subject to abuse and neglect.

13. See also the work of Rong 2010 and Li 2010, both of whom focus on efforts of women in Chongqing and beyond during this period.

14. See Schneider's discussion of *tianzhi* as it was being articulated in the field of home economics at that time (2011, 64–66).

15. Zhou's words echo the Soviet writer Sol'ts, who in a 1936 essay wrote: "Soviet woman is not free from the great and honorable duty that nature has given her: she is a mother, she gives birth. And this is undoubtedly not only her personal affair but one of enormous social importance" (cited in Hoffman 2011, 125).

16. During the first seven years of the PRC, the most powerful decision-making body was the Political Bureau (Politburo) of the Central Committee of the CCP. Teiwes (1984, 5)

stresses the importance of Mao's role as the "unchallenged pivot of elite politics," which created a sense of unity on which broader stability could be built (Teiwes 1990, 17). Teiwes (1990, 18) describes the relationship style between Mao and other high-ranking leaders during this early period as "generally consensual."

17. Rosen (1995, 317) suggests that Deng Xiaoping promoted Deng Yingchao to the Politburo as an expression of gratitude to Zhou Enlai, his political mentor.

18. O'Connor, Orloff, and Shaver's definition of a social policy regime includes social provisions and regulations as well as a broader range of state intervention not normally included in welfare state analysis, such as policies regarding reproductive health and family law reform (1999, 12).

19. In the mid-1950s, when the Thai prime minister sent two Thai children to the PRC in a secret bid to establish relations between Thailand and the PRC, for example, Zhou Enlai placed the children under the care of Liao Chengzhi and his family. Both Zhou Enlai and Liao Chengzi "adopted" the children as their own during the tumultuous years they lived in China (Phatanothai with Peck 1994).

20. Xu Guangping was a May Fourth activist and widow of literary icon, Lu Xun. Although Cai Chang was officially named chair, she remained in the Northeast. Deng Yingchao thus led the proceedings (Luo and Zuo 1997, 101).

21. Luo Qiong was in Wuhan for the inception of the WACW but was reassigned to another part of China on the eve of the evacuation to Chongqing (Luo 1989 [2000], 218).

22. *Xitong* refers to "groupings of bureaucracies that together deal with a broad task the top leaders want performed" (Lieberthal 1995, 194). See Barnett 1967 for the original introduction of this term and its usage in the PRC.

23. For discussion of Deng Yuzhi's participation at foreign meetings, as well as discussion of other women's conferences during the 1950s, see Gu 2013, 160–69.

24. This international exchange and collaboration was part of a much wider network of activity during the Cold War. See Ghodsee 2019 for a recent discussion.

25. For more extensive discussions of the origins of organizational work among women in the pre- and post-1949 period see Davin 1976 and Zhang 1996.

26. See also Jin 1993, 2:486–92.

27. Teiwes (1984, 41) defines "waving the flag" as advancing Mao's slogans while pursuing conflicting objectives. Similar to Wang 2017, however, I see this practice being adopted to party statements as a whole.

28. See also Li and Wong (2020) who analyze stasis and change in birth planning policy through the lens of advocacy coalitions during the Reform Era.

29. A birthday celebration for He Xiangning in the 1950s, for example, included Zhou Enlai, Deng Yingchao, Zhu De, Chen Yi, and Song Qingling (Phatanothai with Peck 1994, 151–52).

30. See also Bachman 1991, 104.

31. Deng Yingchao's advocacy on behalf of mothers and children is evident in earlier speeches as well. For example, Deng's commemoration essay marking the third anniversary of the establishment of the PRC highlights the increased protections afforded mothers and children as one of the new regime's major accomplishments (Deng 1951 [1988], 130–33).

3. THE LONG MARCH TO YAN'AN

1. For an extensive discussion of Kang Keqing during this period, see Lee and Wiles 1999.

2. On this front, Kang Keqing was by no means alone. As Spakowski's research (2005, 154,) shows, many women had been attracted to the military in the first place. Kang

Keqing was also likely well attuned to the mythical legends of Women Warriors (Lee and Wiles 1999, 78).

3. Witke (1970, 45) labels this process as the "Mulan complex" or the "unflagging popularity of the type of legendary heroine who rejects domestic femininity without protesting against it and adapts herself to a man's career without attempting to attract a movement of women in her wake." Of course, stories about Women Warriors are not exclusive to China. See Cothran, Judge, and Shubert's analysis of the myth of the Woman Warrior as a "transnational and global phenomenon" (2020, 3).

4. Judge (2008, 14) calls the women revolutionaries of Qiu Jin's era "presentists." By drawing on the stories of Chinese Women Warriors and Western female revolutionaries and anarchists, "presentists overrode what they described as the crippling morality of the past with a new mode of female heroism that would release China's latest latent political power."

5. See also Spakowski's discussion of the difficulties of pregnancy and childbirth for women guerrillas in the Jiangxi Soviets (2005, 150–51). Many children did not survive childbirth; of those that did, most were given away.

6. See Benton 1995; Lee and Wiles 1999; Spakowski 2005; and Young 2001 for detailed accounts of some of the complex gender dynamics during this period of dislocation and warfare.

7. Contrary to Zhu De's assertions, both women and men became physically compromised by the perilous conditions in the Jiangxi Soviets and on the Long March. Mao Zedong himself, for example, suffered from frequent bouts of malaria (Lee and Wiles 1999, 20–21).

8. According to Gao 2007, 48, Deng Yingchao nearly died when she aborted her first foetus. Deng Yingchao and Zhou Enlai did adopt several children, however, including future party leader Li Peng. See also Barnouin and Yu 2006, 125–26.

9. He Zizhen gave birth to her last child in the Soviet Union in 1938, but the child contracted pneumonia and died while still a newborn (Lee and Wiles 1999, 124).

10. Lee and Wiles (1999, 125) suggest that the mental anguish that He Zizhen later suffered was caused in no small part by the onset of postpartum depression.

11. See Zhonghua suwei'ai gongheguo hunyin tiaoli [Chinese Soviet Republic Marriage Act] (1931 [1991], 151). See also Johnson 1983 for a more extensive discussion of Mao's views on women's rights during the Jiangxi Soviet period.

12. Quote by Mao Zedong cited in Schram 1974, 135–36.

13. See Goodman 2000; Stranahan 1983; and Davin 1976 for more extended discussions of women's organizing on the base areas in the late 1930s and early 1940s.

14. See CCWMC 1939 [1991], 138–46.

15. See also Spakowski's documentation of activists resisting women-work duties (2005, 155–60).

16. And those responsibilities were often overwhelming: according to Apter and Saich many women felt that they could not study, work, chop wood for cooking, grow their own vegetables and make their own clothes while raising children in Yan'an (1994, 149).

17. Zeng Zhi would prove one of the few senior women CCP leaders able to establish a career outside of women-work. During the Cultural Revolution Tao Zhu was criticized for demanding that female cadres wear skirts and for his love of dance parties (Diamant 2000, 293), an indication, perhaps, that his "latent chauvinism" persisted.

18. Cai Chang held the post of party secretary of the CCWMC from June 1941 until November 18, 1958, when the Central Committee disbanded the CCWMC altogether (Su 1990, 259).

19. Apter and Saich (1994, 264) define exegetical bonding as "an engagement with words and ideas in a context of immediate social learning, [resulting] in an emotional and symbolic intensity that includes the consciousness of self in terms of others."

20. See Cong's detailed discussion of the origin of the term *ziyou*, Mao Zedong's more general critique of ziyou, and the practical experiments with the alternative concept of *zizhu*, or self-determination, that courts implemented in the base areas of the 1940s (2016, 139–71).

21. As Stranahan (1983, 101) notes, however, Wang Ming himself was not averse to drawing on a revised vision of "good wives, wise mothers" to achieve policy goals. In fact, it may have been under his leadership that the CCWMC first used the term "harmonious households" (*jiating hemu*). See CCWMC, 1939 [1991], 138–46.

22. Ding Ling's essay, "Thoughts on March 8th" has long been seen as a feminist critique of the CCP's position on women. Originally drafted in August 1941, she chose not to publish it until March 1942 (Barlow and Bjorge 1989, 316–17). See also Davin 1976, 36–39.

23. I interpret Gao's usage of the term *leftist* here to mean "radical" rather than to mean rejecting women-work, as discussed below.

24. See Zhongguo gongchandang zhongyang weiyuanhui (CC 1943 [1991], 647–49).

25. Peng also served from 1941 until 1943 as secretary of the CCP North China Bureau. See also Goodman 2000, 919.

26. In one of the most extensive studies of women in Yan'an to date, Stranahan (1983, 99), for example, argues that there was no evidence that Cai Chang played any role in developing policy. Stranahan undertook her study just prior to the publication of archival material, biographies, and memoirs that led to the different conclusions drawn in this chapter.

4. LAND REFORM

1. A colleague of Ding's (Ye Xiaoxin, 62) experienced a very similar start. Because many people tried to return the land that the CCP had distributed, her father was terrified and sought to convince his daughter not to participate in political activities in the wake of the Red Army's retreat. She persisted in her work, however, and quickly rose through the administrative hierarchy. By 1959 or 1960, she was working for the county's Women's Federation.

2. The father of former women's head Tang Li, 159, for example, was beaten to death by the GMD after the Red Army retreated. Thaxton (2008, 78) argues that the CCP used land reform as a political instrument in the civil war with the Guomindang during this period. See also Ruf 1998, 69.

3. The province of Henan was embroiled in violence from the 1920s through to the early 1950s. For extensive discussions of the origins and manifestations of revolution, the Anti-Japanese struggle, and civil war in Henan, see Wou 1994; and Thaxton 1997.

4. The following discussion is based on Luo 1993, 233–38; and Jin 1993, 1:391–411.

5. See also Deng's landmark speech given at a conference devoted to women-work in the CCP-occupied areas (Deng 1948 [1988]).

6. According to one land reform investigation, for example, more than eighty widows in a small village were labeled "whores." In another context, some widows were also called whores for having hired out their labor to men or having hired men to labor for them (Wang, Zhou, Liu 2007).

7. In one letter Zhou Enlai wrote Deng in 1947, he inquired into the outcome of a women's organization and working committee decision, as he had "not yet seen the telegram." Based on this, and other published correspondence, I assume their exchanges were frequent and detailed.

8. For analysis of the implementation of land reform in different parts of China, see Friedman et al. 1991, 80–89; and Unger 2002, 29–37.

9. The CCP also targeted more privileged community members, including those who had some form of education. Indeed, despite its desire to mobilize the poorest individuals in a village, the CCP often relied on those with some education. See Chan, Madsen, and Unger 1992. Also see Thaxton's 2008 discussion of the role that educated cadres originally played in Dafo Village, Henan.

10. In Gaoshan, the percentages of poor peasants involved in women-work were lower: some 62 percent of a total of 178 women's heads in 1961 were from poor peasant backgrounds (GCAWF, "Untitled." 1961. B21–2–1961–7).

11. Deng Yingchao (1948 [1988], 146) also stipulated that women's organizations were not to be established below the county level.

12. Similar to many other student intellectuals (Wou 1994, 384), visiting women cadres were indispensable "seeders" of the revolution.

13. "Funü gongzuo bannian zongjie" [Bi-annual women-work report] (1950?, 9–1–1, 14–24), WCAWF. I do not have a year recorded for the reports listed under folio "9–1–1." However, based on the content of the reports I assume that they were written in late 1950 or early 1951.

14. "Yi jiu wu san nian gongzuo zongjie ji wu si nian gongzuo yijian" [A summary of work in 1953 and recommendations for work in 1954] (1954, 9–1–3, WCAWF).

15. "Shi ge yue yilai gongzuo zongjie ji jinhou gongzuo yijian (Cao'an)" [Work report from the last ten months, along with work suggestions from here on out (Draft)] (1954, 9–1–5, WCAWF).

16. "Funü gongzuo bannian zongjie" [Bi-annual women-work report] (1950?, 9–1–1, WCAWF).

17. A "broken shoe" is an insult implying sex work or another perceived form of sexual misconduct on the part of a woman; it is usually translated as "whore."

18. Liu Yuezhen, 10, and Niu Shumiao, 52. For an early discussion of the story of the White-Haired Girl, a young woman raped by a landlord, and its evolution into a revolutionary opera, see Wilkinson 1974.

19. See also Hershatter 2011, 75, 89.

20. See Cohen 1993; and Schoenhals 1992 for their early and path-breaking discussions of the importance of Maoist vocabulary in shaping politics. For the gendered terrain of language politics in the context of rural Shaanxi, see Hershatter 2011, 99–101.

21. "Funü gongzuo bannian zongjie" [Bi-annual women-work report] (1950?, 9–1–1, WCAWF).

22. See Perry 2002b, 114–15, for a full discussion of this process in the context of early communist mass mobilizations, and see Goodwin and Pfaff's (2001, 293–95) discussion of how mass meetings were also used as a form of "fear management" in the American civil rights movement of the 1950s and 1960s.

23. Manning (2006a, 87; 2011) discusses the challenges faced by one former Wenhe women's head [Interviewee 53] who was essentially forced out of her leadership role by her husband's family.

24. Comparisons were not available for the other two counties.

25. "Quanxian funü tuanjie qi zhengbian sharen xiongfan X wei bei hai X bao-chou" [Women from the entire county unite in condemning the murderous criminal X regarding his killing of X) (1950?, 9–1–1, WCAWF). In this case, a young woman was murdered by her husband after she joined the Peasants Association and petitioned for a divorce.

26. Li Xiaoyue, 24. See also Diamond 1983 and Judd 1989.

27. Of course, political affiliations mattered as well. He Xiaolu, 143, would have joined the Youth League but was unable to because her elder brother had been a local headman under the Guomindang. Her sisters, on the other hand, lived further away where no one

knew about the family's complicated past and so were able to become politically active. In this instance, "marrying out" had greater benefits than staying close to home.

28. Among the fifteen women's heads who discussed their relationship with their mothers-in-law, five had a close relationship, six had a difficult relationship, and the remaining four were ambivalent.

29. Among the twenty-four former women's heads on whom I have data, twelve had family members active in party organizations prior to their own emergence as activists and leaders. Among the forty-one former Women's Federation leaders on whom I have data, a total of nineteen came from families in which members were already politically active.

30. "Funü gongzuo bannian zongjie" [Semi-annual women-work report] (1950?, 9–1–1, WCAWF).

31. Diamant (2000) slightly modified this finding, suggesting that male court and district officials in rural townships and counties tended to grant divorces to women more readily than did their village counterparts.

32. Lü (2000), whose primary interest is official corruption, argues that traditional norms did not begin to undermine state ideology until the Great Leap Forward. I draw on this quote to illustrate the theoretical assumption that traditional norms and practices necessarily undermine state ideology.

33. Zhang's family owned its own land and was designated as belonging to the "middle-upper peasant class." The fact that her father had enough money to buy her a satin outfit, and that some of their belongings were distributed to other families during land reform, suggests that they were comparatively well off.

34. See also Hershatter 2011, 232, for a similar case of a parent drawing on the story of Liu Hulan to dissuade their child from activism.

35. One of the reasons that the couple might have always been seen together was a way to offset suspicion about Zhang's morality.

36. When Yuan Jinyu, 158, a former commune women's head, became the target of gossip after being sexually harassed in the course of her work, her husband discounted the talk: "My husband was a good man."

37. In Wenhe, "young and healthy peasants," were found to be 82.2 percent illiterate at the time the PRC was established (WX 1992, 707).

38. Hou's husband became politically active after he was captured and enlisted into the guerrilla forces of the Eighth Route Army. It is unclear whether or not he was a soldier fighting for the Guomindang when he was captured.

39. According to Hou the two families undertook a "bride swap" in order to avoid the cost of a dowry.

40. Yangko (yangge) is a form of folk dance.

41. In this story, Hou Qiuyi refers to shame as xiu. In others, she used the expression "diu ren."

42. I was not able to corroborate Hou's assertion that local cadres were Long March survivors. Given the extreme violence that characterized the region prior to 1949, however, many were likely battle-hardened soldiers. For the purposes of my analysis, I am less interested in the veracity of the claim than I am in exploring its relationship to Hou's understanding of the revolutionary work in which she was engaged.

43. In its infancy, the Chinese Communist Youth League was comprised of various branches of what was then called the "Socialist Youth Corps"; Zhou Enlai, for example, founded a Socialist Youth Corps while in France in 1921 (Pringsheim 1962, 75–76). A nationwide organization was first established in 1922.

44. On the question of turnover see Funnell 1970, 108–12, and for membership numbers, see Pringsheim 1962, 90–91.

45. "Gaoshan xian minzhu funü lianhehui (gongzuo yebao)" [Gaoshan County Democratic Women's Federation (work report)] (July 31, 1957, B21–1–1957–6, GCAWF).

46. "Funü gongzuo bannian zongjie" [Bi-annual women-work report] (June 5, 1950? 9–1–1. WCAWF).

5. MATERNAL BODIES

1. The Korean War would last until 1953. See Chen 1994; Stueck 2013; and Whiting 1968.

2. "Funü gongzuo bannian zongjie" [Bi-Annual Women-work Report] (1950?, 9–1–, 14–24, WCAWF). The CCP's reliance on women householders to recruit their male relatives into military service dates back to at least the Jiangxi Soviet era. See, for example, Yong Xin Xianwei 1931 [1991].

3. The Gaoshan Women's Federation would continue to make military recruitment a focus of its work after the ceasefire was signed on the Korean Peninsula in 1953, which would continue to draw the ire and resentment of the mothers and wives who were being targeted. "Gaoshan xian??? chong binyuan gongzuo Zhong funü gongzuo zongjie" [Summary of women-work in the work of recruiting soldiers in Gaoshan county] (April 7, 1955, B21–1, GCAWF).

4. In March 1951, some 4.13 million women, or more than 50 percent of adult women in Jiangsu, participated in demonstrations against American aggression (Lu and Miao 2000, 124). More than 100,000 women took part in a demonstration against the Americans in Huoyue in 1950 (*HX* 1993, 322). In Wenhe, women were organized to contribute clothing and other resources to the war effort. ("Funü gongzuo bannian zongjie" [Bi-Annual Women-work Report] 1950?, 9–1–, 14–24, WCAWF).

5. Dong Biwu was born in 1886, a full fourteen years before Cai Chang, for example.

6. On the intersections of women's movements and eugenics in China, see Chung 2002 and David 2018. See also Barlow's 2004 extensive discussion of the evolutionary foundations of progressive Chinese feminism.

7. Wang Shijin was a public health lecturer in the National Central Midwifery School in the mid-1940s and coauthor, with Yang Chongrui, of *Fuying weisheng xue* (The study of maternal and children's health), from which this passage derives (Barnes 2018, 182–84).

8. Wu Yaozong, a strong advocate of the social gospel and a senior leader in the YMCA, would also play a role in coordinating public and private relief resources during this period, while holding a number of government posts (Boorman et al. 1967, 3:459). As in many other areas of state building, the CCP initially relied on individuals who were supportive of the revolution but were not necessarily members of the CCP themselves (Dillon 2007).

9. Dong Biwu's April 1950 official report on relief and health services served as the guiding principle in national relief work (Bian and Wu 2006, 694–95).

10. In middle school, Dong boarded with a revolutionary society that was run by devout Christians (Snow 1972). He subsequently studied in Japan and in the Soviet Union (Snow 1972, 35–43; Klein and Clark 1971, 2:874–75).

11. Dong would also serve as the first Chinese Communist to attend an important international meeting. Indeed, he sat on the Chinese delegation to establish the United Nations in San Francisco in 1945 (Klein and Clark 1971, 2:876–77; Bian and Wu 2006, 159).

12. In addition, in 1950 more than 60,000 cases of kala-azar were treated in Shandong Province and more than 30,000 cases of schistosomiasis along the Jiangsu-Zhejiang border were treated involving "more than a half-million intravenous injections and 444,459 stool examinations" (Li 1952, 16).

13. See also, for example, Kang Keqing's (1993, 407–8) discussion of the nationalization of American and missionary-funded orphanages (*yuying tang*) after the establishment of the PRC.

14. See Smith's discussion (2013) of these reform efforts and the resistance it elicited.

15. See Wang, Liu, and Chang 2002, 320–21, for discussion of China-wide efforts to undertake social reform in the cities. See Hershatter 1997, 304–24; and Wang 2017 for discussions of early PRC organizing among Shanghai sex workers and urban housewives, respectively. A more general discussion of sex work reform can be found in Gu 2013, 31–38.

16. See Dixon 1981; and Wang 2017.

17. The most renowned pre-1949 medical institution, Peking Union Medical College (PUMC), was established by Christians with the support of the Rockefellers in 1915. PUMC trained many physicians in China, some of whom would go on to run other medical colleges and work for the GMD's Ministry of Health, continuing on in the MOH after the foundation of the PRC. According to Bullock 1974, 100–101, PUMC faculty and alumni dominated the Chinese Academy of Sciences throughout the 1950s.

18. One reason Li Dequan may have been overlooked is that Taylor 2005, Lampton 1977, and others have focused on the contentious status of Chinese medicine within the MOH. Li Dequan's primary contributions took place in maternal health medicine, an arena that managed to avoid controversy until birth control became an issue and even then, Li Dequan avoided the criticism that fell on others.

19. According to Lampton (1977, 13), the PRC never allocated more than 2.6 percent of total budgetary expenditures to health in the 1950–56 period.

20. For in-depth discussions of the Patriotic Health Movement, see Rogaski 2004; and Yang 2004.

21. By way of contrast, Johnson (2011, 176) cites an infant mortality rate of 114 per 1000 births in 1948 in areas served by trained midwives. See Li's 2014 discussion of midwifery investigations and training during the early PRC.

22. One key innovation promoted by local governments in northwest Zhejiang, for example, was the usage of bamboo steamers to sterilize delivery kits (Fang 2017, 433–34).

23. Earlier attempts at midwifery reform had been hampered by war and the limited bureaucratic reach of the GMD government. Johnson (2011, 156) suggests that midwifery services were only used by about 25 percent of Beijing's childbearing population during the height of its operation under the GMD.

24. See also, Huang Qizao 1997, 126–27, who praised Li Dequan's coordinated approach to maternal and infant health care.

25. According to oral investigations conducted with forty women in Huoyue 1953, the infant mortality rate prior to 1949 was 52.2 percent (*HX* 1993, 392).

26. *HX* (1993, 394–95). Wenhe County reported having established a ten-worker prevention and vaccination station in 1956 (*WX* 1992, 810).

27. Shi ge yue yilai gongzuo zongjie ji jinhou gongzuo yijian (Cao'an) [Work report from the last ten months, along with work suggestions from here on out (Draft)] (1954, 9–1–5, pp. 1–8, WCAWF).

28. For an in-depth discussion of midwifery reform in rural Shaanxi, see Hershatter (2011, 154–81).

29. The clinic included two rooms, two beds, and birthing equipment. This part of Yan's recollection is paraphrased from notes.

30. The determination to keep birthing within the family was evident in the birthing practices of other nearby families. The births of a former women's head from the same brigade, Niu Shumiao, 52, for example, were attended by her husband.

31. It is not clear whether these numbers refer to rural areas or the national context as a whole. While Li Dequan (1952) notes that sample figures from many counties showed a half to two-thirds decrease of infant deaths from neonatal tetanus. See Li 2014 for a detailed discussion of regional declines in maternal and infant mortality during the 1950s.

32. For in-depth discussions of the history of birth control in China before 1949, see Barnes 2018; Chung 2002; and David 2018. For discussions of policy developments in the 1950s, see White 2006; Greenhalgh and Winckler 2005; and Shi (1988).

33. The timing of this submission followed on the heels of the Second ACDWF Congress held in March 1953.

34. An important exception to this trend took place in 1942 when several articles published in the *Liberation Daily* argued that CCP members should postpone marriage and childbirth because of wartime conditions (Shi 1988, 49–52).

35. By way of contrast, the highly influential Scientific Committee of Medical Sciences, the committee that set largely set medical research priorities, was made up primarily of women doctors (Lampton 1977, 31).

36. On this point, see White 2006, 24–25n20.

37. Dr. Shao Lizi gave a talk on birth control in September 1954 at the People's Congress and in the following months published articles on this issue as well (Shi 1988, 118). For an excerpt of an article published in the *People's Daily* at that time, see Shao 1954 [1997], 529. See also Greenhalgh and Winckler 2005, 69.

38. Ma Yinchu was an economist and President of Peking University. For his views on population growth, see Ma 1957 [1997], 551–57.

39. It is unclear whether Li Dequan participated in these meetings herself; the ministry seems to have been represented by Vice Minister Xu Yunbei. Kang Keqing, the head of the Women and Children's Welfare Department also contributed to the drafting of a report that Liu Shaoqi would publish in December 1957. Lin Feng, deputy secretary general of the CC and head of the Second Office of the State Council, was in charge of drafting the birth planning regulations (CC 1954 [1997], 471).

40. Yan Renying, a protégée of Lin Qiaozhi and Yang Chongrui with a background in eugenics, spent four months with a medical team in a labor camp treating sex workers. Yan would subsequently join Li Dequan on a tour of North Korea during the early part of the war with the United States (Qinghua xiao you zong hui, 2014).

41. See Shi 1988, 18, for a discussion of Shao's 1954 advocacy to remove most restrictions on abortion. The majority of the costs associated with receiving an abortion or tubal ligation were significantly reduced beginning in April 1964 (Shi 1988, 149).

42. See Shi 1988, 127–31, for further discussion of the easing of abortion regulations in 1957.

43. Women's Federation reports either advocated the practices addressed by the slogan, and/or cited the slogan in all three counties: "Huoyue xian 1957 nian hao zuo you fuli weisheng gongzuo yijian" [Suggestions on how to properly accomplish welfare and sanitation work for the children of Huoyue County] (May 7, 1957, 9–5, 40–45). "Wenhe xian fulianhui guanyu guanche zhuanqu fugong huiyi mingque qingkuang zongjie huibao" [Wenhe County Women's Federation summary report on the implementation of the clarification of women-work meetings in the County's special zones] (April 7, 1957, 9–1–8, 38–45, WCAWF). "Guanyu jiaqiang dangqian nongmang tuoer zuzhi he funü laodong baohu gongzuo lingdao de yijian" [Suggestions on strengthening the nursery groups and the protection of women's labour practices] (November 7, 1957, B21–2, 55–57, GCAWF).

44. Li Xiaoyue, 24; Li Ailing, 30; and Hou Qiuyi, 132.

45. Zhang was not alone in this desire: many of Hershatter's Shaanxi interviewees (2011, 206), for example, commented that the burden of multiple pregnancies and caring for numerous children had simply worn them out.

46. Lin Xiaohong, 73, attributes a "lifetime of health problems" to the harmful effects of planting seedlings in water while menstruating during the time of the Higher-level Agricultural Producer Cooperatives.

6. FILIAL BRIDES

1. Glosser (2003, 170) attributes commonalities in GMD and CCP Marriage Reform efforts to "similarities that stemmed from their Leninist party-organization and their common roots in the New Culture Movement."

2. Maternalist reform long included attention to women's legal rights. In 1910, for example, the British Women's Cooperative Guild led a campaign for divorce-law reform (Thane 1993, 356–57).

3. Wang was a graduate of the law department at Fudan University (Wang, Zhou, and Liu 2007).

4. See Diamant 2000, 84–85, for a discussion of the rash of divorces initiated by male Chinese Communist cadres after they assumed office in Shanghai, and the complaints of the Shanghai Women's Federation who sought to stop them.

5. Diamant (2000, 107–8) explains the logic of "distribution" as a kind of linguistic residue of land reform. See his discussion of this phenomenon in the periurban region of Jiangnan as well.

6. Lampton (1992, 34) argues that bargaining is "most in evidence when one is dealing with two or more bureaucracies of approximately equal resources, none of which can carry out an undertaking without the cooperation of the other(s), but which cannot compel the cooperation of the other(s) and cannot persuade a senior authoritative leader or institution to compel the other(s) to cooperate."

7. Wang Ming's role in the drafting of the Marriage Law is still subject to debate. Luo Qiong argued vigorously in 2002, for example, that Wang Ming was not involved in the original drafting of the law, after the journal Global Literary Exchange (*Huanqiu wenhui*) published a story that he had played a significant role in the work on the law (Luo 2002). Wang Ming, who served as director of the Legislative Affairs Commission of the Government Affairs Council, was likely involved but it is unclear whether or how he contributed to the formulation of the first draft. See Meijer (1971) for an extended discussion of Wang Ming's commentaries on the divorce articles.

8. Given the significant role that the military played in policy making during this period (Shambaugh 1997), this particular capitulation is not surprising. According to Shambaugh, "It is not much of an exaggeration to say that the military ruled China from 1949 to 1954" (1997, 131). See also Hu 2017 who discusses the origins of this policy and its impact on women during the war with Japan.

9. The *baozhang*, or the head of the lowest level of administration under the Guomindang government, was a powerful local figure. Whether or not his daughter actually slept with multiple sexual partners is unclear, but more important is the discourse of promiscuity and its conflation with class.

10. As Lampton (1992, 57) notes, "Even once a policy is formulated and adopted, the implementation process is characterized by negotiation among and between levels of the hierarchy, sometimes all the way down to the grassroots."

11. On implementation of the Marriage Law, see also Altehenger 2018.

12. The Beijing Municipal Marriage Law Office, for example, organized some 211 show trials attended by 103,800 people (Diamant 2000, 43).

13. "Quanxian funü tuanjie qi zhengbian sharen xiongfan X wei bei hai X baochou" [Women from the entire county unite in condemning the murderous criminal X regarding his killing of X) (1950?, 9–1–1, WCAWF).

14. See also Diamant's discussion of violent militias in southwest China (2000, 151–52). According to archival reports from Chuxiong County, for example, village cadres incarcerated and sexually assaulted women divorce petitioners. Militia squads also reportedly beat, humiliated, and struggled against individuals accused of promiscuity as well.

15. Similar to the findings of other investigative teams at that time, Shi Liang's final report found that localized factors, and specifically local cadres, often impacted the quality of implementation (Johnson 1983, 133).

16. In his capacity as premier Zhou Enlai oversaw the appointments of senior government positions and portfolios.

17. Liu Qingyang had worked closely with Deng Yingchao and Song Meiling in the early days of the WACW, and later with Liu-Wang Liming in Hong Kong (Wiles 2003d, 359).

18. Shi Liang and Cao Mengjun formed the Association of Democratic Women (*Minzhu funü lianyihui*), and Shi Liang was elected to the Central Committee of the China Democratic League at its inaugural meeting in 1944. Shi Liang also worked underground for the party in Shanghai after the Democratic League was outlawed by the GMD in 1947. See Lee's discussion of Shi Liang's extensive pre-1949 political activities (2003d, 450–55).

19. Another woman ally was the jurist Han Youtong who argued that marriage freedom must include the freedom to divorce; Han also contributed to the drafting of the law (Luo, Huang, and Yang 1986 [1997], 325–37).

20. Specifically, they decided not to organize the campaign "separately." In practice, however, this meant that the second mobilization campaign did not take place.

21. Shen Zijiu had been concerned about the high rates of suicide among women since at least the 1930s. See her study of this issue in Shen 1935 [1991], 223–26.

22. See Lubman's 1967 extensive discussion of the ideological work of mediation. In most cases, mediation was deemed preferable to litigation not only because the latter could "interrupt production" and "create bitterness," but because mediation itself could raise the political consciousness of participants, and even recruit new activists (Lubman 1967, 1317).

23. Judd's 1998 research in northern China found that only childless women could petition for divorce. She furthermore argues that many women and women activists did not see the Marriage Law itself as very significant in their lives, a finding that is not surprising, perhaps, given the primary emphasis on keeping couples together during that time.

24. Diamant (2000, 157) argues that "women seeking divorce often viewed mediators with utter contempt and distrust." Giving the complex enactment of local women-work and the attachments in which it was embedded, however, this was no doubt true for some but not so clear cut for all.

25. It is unclear why there was a sudden jump in numbers.

26. Guo Liangyu, 89, for example, was a child bride who divorced in 1959. Her first husband, a worker in Shanghai, "looked down on rural people." She remarried in 1960.

27. Although Niu was asked to serve as women's head in her husband's village again, she declined. She explained that her caregiving responsibilities were too great and that she just didn't have the heart for it any longer.

28. The major exception is the years of the famine, during which time divorces spiked. I will discuss this phenomenon in chapter 9.

29. In Shaanxi mothers continued to prefer that their daughters marry nearby, for both emotional and material reasons (Hershatter 2011, 127).

30. I understand this as a metaphoric death rather than a real death, for the mother-in-law lived many years after she separated with her daughter-in-law.

31. Tian noted that after "liberation" the poor people (*pinkü baixing*) were liberated (*fanshen*), but that the greatest liberation was experienced by women comrades (*nü tong-zhi fan de shen zui da*).

32. On "domestic filialty" and virtue among women cadres, see also Hershatter (2011, 119–20; 189).

33. Judge's discussion (2008, 177–86) of turn-of-the century intellectuals, including He Xiangning, "who depicted Mulan as fiercely brave and *almost regrettably* filial" (emphasis mine), provides an interesting contrast with Ying's 2009 argument that some of these same women (including Qiu Jin) adopted male forms of filiality in order to advance nationalist and feminist causes.

34. See Duara 1998, 307, on embodying the authentic virtue of self-sacrifice and Hershatter 2011, 28, on prerevolutionary notions of female virtue "reworked and intertwined with more recent categories of self provided by the revolution."

35. In Wenhe, for example, one local leader was fired after being accused of spousal abuse (Ye Xiaoxin, 62).

7. HOUSEHOLD MANAGERS

1. Bo Yibo and Li Fuchun gave a number of speeches and published articles outlining their economic proposals, which highlighted self-reliance, emphasis on building medium-sized and small factories, decentralization, and industry aiding agriculture (Bachman 1991, 26).

2. One Women's Federation historian, interviewee 5, told me that Cai Chang struggled with various ailments in the early 1950s. See also Luo 1983 [1997], 69. Cai Chang's convalescence in the USSR coincided with Li Fuchun's stay in the USSR during this period, as he completed work on the First Five Year Plan (Bachman 1991, 104).

3. See Strauss's (2020, 48–57) discussion of the challenge that the CCP faced in cultivating state administrators with these qualifications.

4. Cadres were also criticized. As Cao (2015, 99–100) shows was the case in the Nanyang region of Henan, people designated as rightists or those with "serious rightist tendencies" more often than not had complained that the rations for farmers were too low.

5. It should be noted, however, that Mao's policy interventions had begun earlier that spring. Indeed, Teiwes (1993, 61) suggests that the decision to rapidly increase collectivization had been made by late May of that year.

6. See Thorborg 1978; Davin 1976; and Hershatter 2011.

7. Although the field of Home Economics was dismantled after 1949, the work of home economic professionals was repurposed into education, child welfare, and nutritional sciences (Schneider 2011, 196–210).

8. "XX funü shengchan jingyan jieshao" [Introduction to the production experience of women in XX] (May 3, 1950?, 9–1–1, 30–31, WCAWF).

9. "Jian sheng er nian lai Gaoshan xian funü gongzuo de jiben zongjie" [A basic summary of women-work in Gaoshan County since the establishment of the province two years ago] (1954, B21–1–1954–3, 1–11, GCAWF).

10. See also Yan 2003, 103.

11. Hou's study (2016) of early collectivization in Shanxi suggests that these policies also derived from experiments conducted at the local level.

12. Compare with Shue 1980, 214–45.

13. See also Oi 1989, 32–42, for her discussion of the share of the harvest and per capita grain availability.

14. Retired Gaoshan commune party secretary, Wu Fengyi, 100, noted that the grain situation began to get increasingly tight after 1954.

15. Hou Qiuyi was not alone in her approach. In 1950, the Huoyue Women's Federation criticized younger women for forcing older women to hand over their grain to the government. The *culü* (rude) work style alienated the older generations of women and men. "Huoyue xian funü ganbu zhengfeng xunlian ban zongjie" [Summary of the rectification training class for women cadres] (October 24, 1950. HCAWF).

16. Mueggler (2001, 88) shows, for example, that collectivization stripped Lolop'o women of the social status and power that they had formerly enjoyed. Prior to collectivization, the female maintenance of household granaries meant that "women sheltered both the sense of a powerful and dangerous feminine reproductive capacity and their own muted transmissive lines of descent." See also Hershatter's (2011, 88) discussion of how women were made targets of grain appropriation in rural Shaanxi.

17. "'X' Xiang 1949–1958 nian da shiji" [Events of X Township, 1949–1958] (March 1959, 106–1–4, 1–111, WCA).

18. See also Friedman et al. 1991, 185–91; and Thaxton 2008, 101–6, for the difficulties this imposed collectivization generated at the grassroots.

19. Hou Qiuyi, 132, shared that during land reform, former landlords were sent to Xinjiang for labor reform. While my capacity to trace out these internal movements went well beyond the scope of this project, I note them here in the hope that others might explore them as an important part of the constitution of the early PRC.

20. "Huoyue xian fulianhui guanyu kaizhan 'wu hao' xuanchuan he heli tiaopei shiyong funü laoli de zongjie baogao" [Huoyue county Women's Federation summary report on the promotion of the "five goods" and the reasonable allocation and deployment of women's labor] (April 10, 1957, 9.4, 32–39, HCAWF).

21. Former Huoyue farmer Jiang Lili's, 138, daughter blames her mother that she was never able to study well because her little brothers always followed her.

22. Or at least that is my supposition in so far as the report identified a total of 36,794 children in the county as in need of care.

23. "Gaoshan xian yi jiu wu qi nian funü gongzuo yijian" [Gaoshan County women-work suggestions for the year 1957] (B21–1–1956–6, GCAWF).

24. For example, on nine brigades in Wenhe some eleven children fell into wells and one had died. "Wenhe xian fulianhui guanyu guanche zhuanqu fugong huiyi mingque qingkuang zongjie huibao" [Wenhe County Women's Federation clarified summary report on the implementation of women-work prefecture meeting], (April 7, 1957, 9–1–8, 38–45, WCAWF). "Huoyue xian 1957 nian hao zuo you fuli weisheng gongzuo yijian" [Suggestions on how to properly accomplish welfare and sanitation work for the children of Huoyue County] (May 7, 1957, 9–5, 40–45, HCAWF).

25. See, for example, Cao Guanqun 1957 (1988).

26. Unlike the two-volume official biography of Deng Yingchao (Jin 1993), the official biography of Cai Chang is much shorter and lighter on specifics. The fact that Cai Chang's biographer, Su Ping (1990, 182–86), allocated several pages to Cai Chang's advocacy of the double diligences is but one indication that Cai broke from a period of relative inactivity to one of concerted policy making and implementation at this time

27. See also Bachman 1991, 104.

28. See also Song's piece (2006) on the state discourse on housewives.

29. "Tuo'er gongzuo jiji fenzi da hui shang de baogao" (cankao ziliao) [Summary of the meeting held for nursery activists (reference material)] (April 9, 1970, B21–2, GCAWF).

30. Yang Zhihua (Member of the Standing Committee of the ACDWF and Minister of the Women's Labor Department of the ACFTU) also delivered a talk, titled: "Diligent and Thrifty Housekeeping to Support Construction." (Yang 1991, 98).

31. By 1957, Five Goods Family activities had spread to 103 cities (Ji 1992, 169). In Shanghai alone, there were reportedly 1,200 Five Goods Family activists (Xu 1957 [1999]).

32. See also Kang 1993, 441, for a full discussion of who actually led the proceedings.

33. By way of contrast, Shuai Mengqi, one of the most highly ranked women CCP members, spoke out against labelling Guo Tengyun, head of the Foreign Affairs Office and Foreigners in China, as a rightist (Luo 2004, 255).

34. See also Edwards's discussion (2012) of the attacks on Ding Ling made by literary critics.

35. See also Guo's (2019, 180–81) discussion of Liu-Wang's political challenges after the establishment of the PRC.

36. Liu-Wang headed the four-member delegation to the meetings and was elected vice-chair of the International WCTU (Wang 1999, 141). In 1954, Liu-Wang represented the PRC at the International Asian Women's Conference in Beijing (Edwards 2003, 376).

37. Between November 20 and December 22, Cai Chang and Luo Qiong traveled to Nanjing, Shanghai, and Hangzhou in order to conduct firsthand investigations of urban grassroots women-work. During the trip Cai Chang also made a major intervention to defend the autonomy of local Shanghai Women's Congresses, which were at that time under threat of dissolution. See Wang's (2017, 30–53) discussion of Shanghai women's congresses in the early 1950s.

38. "Yi jiu wu san nian gongzuo zongjie ji wu si nian gongzuo yijian" [Work report for 1953 and work suggestions for 1954] (March 24, 1954.9–1–3, 1–5, WCAWF). Struggles over defining lines of authority proved a major challenge in urban areas as well.

39. "Wenhe xian fulianhui guanyu guanche zhuanqu fugong huiyi mingque qing-kuang zongjie huibao" [Wenhe County Women's Federation clarified summary report on the implementation of women-work prefecture meeting] (April 7, 1957, 9–1–8, 38–45, WCAWF).

40. This was a change that other mass organizations adopted as well.

41. "Fadong guangda funü jiji touru kanghan zhong mai yundong de yijian" [Opinion on mobilizing women to actively participate in the drought-resistant wheat movement] (September 27, 1957, 9–8, pp. 61–65. HCAWF).

42. "Huoyue xian minzhu funü lianhe hui dui shengchan jiuzai gongzuo de yijian" [Opinions of Huoyue County Democratic Women's Federation on production and disas-ter relief] (October 7, 1956, HCAWF).

43. "Huoyue xian fulian guanyu kaizhan "zun lao zi you, tuanjie huzhu" jioayu gong-zuo de yijian" [Opinion of Huoyue County Women's Federation on carrying out the educational work of "respecting the old, loving the young, solidarity and mutual aid"] (December 11, 1956, HCAWF).

44. "1957 nian funü gongzuo zongjie" [1957 women-work summary report] (Febru-ary 25, 1958, 9–12, 112–23, HCAWF). In early 1958, Xuchang Prefecture also undertook a two-month campaign to save grain. According to provincial records, more than 1,779,000 kilos of grain were saved (Shao 1984, 125).

45. Former Huoyue women's head, Liu Yuezhen, 10, similarly recalled that the double diligences entailed saving two liang every day.

46. Working "outside" here may have been a reference to the employment that a num-ber of men held in nearby cities.

8. SHOCK TROOPS

1. When interviewing, the "Great Leap Forward" (*da yue jin*) and "the time of eating in the dining halls" (*chi shitang de shihou*) were used interchangeably by myself and those participating in interviews. See Hershatter 2011 for her extensive discussion of memory related to campaign time.

2. On the establishment of industrial armies, see also, Wang Yanni 2011, 148.

3. Egalitarianism was not unique to the CCP; Nicaraguan FMLN commanders, for example, believed in a "revolutionary utopia," pretending "that the equality desired for the future existed already in the revolutionary nuclei, where all types of differences were decreed eliminated, for example, those existing between men and women. . . . With such a conviction, the leadership of the guerrilla groups rejected the validity of an analysis [focusing] on the different situations of men and women within the group" (Luciak 2001, 11).

4. See also Chen 2011; Kung and Chen 2011; and Yang, Xu, and Ran 2014 for analyses of the origins of provincial radicalism.

5. These numbers are consistent with the estimates of former Jiangxi Women's Federation chair who suggested that in Jiangxi in 1958 women's labor force participation ranged from 85 to 100 percent (Ma 2013, 162).

6. The "building of the dining hall" meant different things in different places. Sometimes it involved the actual construction of a new building, but most commonly it involved the appropriation of a preexisting structure (often someone's home) to feed up to several hundred people a day. The actual administration of the dining hall depended on the locality as well. In some places, the women's heads assumed responsibility for running the dining halls while, in others, accountants and village leaders figured in this role, a role that became increasingly politicized as the food available began to decline in 1959 and 1960.

7. A brigade sometimes included two or three smaller villages.

8. The number of men party leaders also jumped, albeit not quite as drastically: from 5,439 to 8,198.

9. "Yuejin yilai funü gongzuo zongjie yu jinhou gongzuo yijian" [Report on women-work since the beginning of the GLF along with suggestions for future directions] (August 2, 1958, 9–1–9, 19–30, WCAWF); "Wenhe xian fulianhui 1958 nian funü gongzuo zongjie" [Wenhe county women's federation summary of 1958 women-work] (February 1, 1959, 9–1–9, 1–7, WCAWF).

10. "1958 Nian funü gongzuo zongjie" [Summary of women-work for the year 1958] (December 1958, HCAWF).

11. Ma Yinchu and Yang Chongrui were among the many who fell victim to the Anti-Rightist Movement. Yang Chongrui's political demise was especially shocking to those who had for so long advocated a new approach to birth control and who saw Yang as a national leader in the struggle to improve conditions for women (Zhang 2005, 282). For brief discussions of the politicization of birth control during the Anti-Rightist Movement, see Deng, Ma, and Wu 1986, 234; and Shi 1988, 135–38.

12. See ACWF 1958a [1999] and Qi 1958 [1997].

13. "Huoyue xian funü yundong chuxian xingaochao" [On the new upsurge of the women's movement in Huoyue County] (April 21, 1958, HCAWF).

14. "Huoyue xian funü gongzuo weiyuanhui "fu you weisheng gongzuo yuejin guihua"" [Work Committee of the Huoyue County All-China Women's Federation "working plan for the advancement of women and children's health] (August 26, 1958, HCAWF).

15. See chapter 6 for a discussion of Yan Shuqun, 43, who was trained in midwifery in Wenhe County during the GLF. Zhou Changfen, 157, a former Wenhe women's head, insists that there was no birth planning in Wenhe during the Great Leap Forward although archival records suggests that it had, in fact, begun. "Wenhe xian fulianhui guanyu guanche zhuanqu fugong huiyi mingque qingkuang zongjie huibao" [Wenhe County Women's Federation clarified summary report on the implementation of women-work prefecture meeting], (April 7, 1957, 9–1–8, 38–45, WCAWF).

16. "Di si ji du funü gongzuo anpai" [Women-work planning for the winter season] (October 8, 1958, HCAWF).

17. "1958 Nian shang ban nian funü gongzuo de jiben chengji he jingyan" [Report for the First Half of 1958 detailing women-work experiences and results] (October 8, 1958, HCAWF).

18. Kang Youwei, a political theorist and reformer during the final years of the Qing Dynasty, advocated the elimination of private property and the family. See Wemheuer's 2012 intellectual history of the origins of the GLF.

19. In December 1957, for example, Zhou Enlai advocated the double diligences when attending a women's forum in Shanghai (Ji 1992, 167).

20. Eyferth (2015, 133–34) estimates that sixty labor days were needed "to provide a family of five with the absolute minimum of clothes." In the Guanzhong area of Shaanxi Province, the state's expectation that women would produce textiles and clothing for their families contributed to chronic levels of exhaustion during the Maoist era (147–48, 151).

21. Women's heads rarely mentioned fear of political reprisal as an obstacle to protecting women's health during the GLF. See also Thaxton 2008, 143–47, for his vivid description of public criticism sessions in Da Fo village.

22. In many ways the chaos of the GLF anticipated the breakdown of the Cultural Revolution, a time in which, as Wu (2014, 11) argues, "Mao's ideas, ambiguous and fragmentary as they were, were interpreted in different ways by different agents."

23. Dong Bian was appointed editor-in-chief of *Women of China* in 1956 (Wang 2017, 84).

24. "Jiehe dangqian zhongxin gongzuo qinjian chijia yi zhiyuan shehui zhuyi jianshe da yuejin—xian fulian zhuren X fayan" [Combining the current central work raising up thrifty households with supporting the socialist construction of a great leap forward— speech by the county women's federation head X] (February 4, 1958, 9–1–9, WCAWF).

25. Luo Qiong was too ill to attend this meeting (and the July Women's Federation conference). Her reconstruction of these discussions is thus based on archival documents and discussions with colleagues who were present at that time.

26. Wang (2017, 74–75) offers a somewhat different interpretation of Liu and Cao's articles.

27. Women-Work was not the only publication raising the alarm; articles published in other *neibu cankao* periodicals were airing contrary views as well (see Yang 1996, 44).

9. LEADERS

1. Scholarly discussion of the inner debates among the central CCP leadership during the "cooling off" period between November 1958 and July 1959 can be found in Teiwes and Sun 1999; and MacFarquhar 1983.

2. From 1960 to 1961, 4,354 women from Gaoshan County were diagnosed with uterine prolapse; 3,142 of these women were treated and 1,302 were successfully cured. In addition, 13,626 women were found to have ceased menstruating (*GX* 1994, 915). In Huoyue, a 1961 investigation found 11,170 women suffering from uterine prolapse (*HX* 1993, 392).

3. Frödin (2012, 283) argues of North Korea that it "can be classified as a largely governed order failing to supply its members with a range of vital goods."

4. Li Zhisui (1994, 382–84), Mao's personal physician, remembers He Zizhen visiting Mao at Lushan in the summer of 1961, after she wrote him a letter warning him that the Wang Ming faction might cause him trouble. Given that Zeng Zhi (2011, 254–57) and Zhu (Ma 2013) helped to arrange the meeting between Mao Zedong and He Zizhen in 1959, there may have been two meetings or it may be that Li confused the two summers.

5. Jiang also visited Shanghai Mayor Ke Qingshi and Lin Biao, Peng Dehuai's successor (Li 1994, 318).

6. See also Jin 1993, 2:553. Her illness in the spring of 1959 does seem to have been severe enough that she was prevented from attending March 8 festivities in Beijing.

7. In another version of this event, Mao addressed Cai Chang by her childhood nickname: *Mao meizi* (Huang 2004, 64).

8. Unlike Zhu De, however, Dong Biwu was spared the wrath of Mao. Dong had a very close relationship with the Chairman, which seems to have protected him on this occasion, and during the Cultural Revolution as well (Song 2013, 69).

9. In early August 1959, for example, *Women-Work* (no. 15 [1959], 12) published a notice by the MOH urging local Women's Federations to undertake steps to prevent uterine prolapse that was accompanied by an article from the Henan Women's Federation with instructions on how to treat the injury. While expressions of concern about reproductive health continued to receive mention in *Women-Work* in the fall of 1959, however, the Anti-Rightist Movement temporarily muffled any sustained effort to address the mounting reproductive health crisis at the grassroots.

10. Although the language of thrift disappeared in the immediate wake of the second Anti-Rightist Movement, by late fall urban women's organizations were urging frugality at home. In January 1960 the two diligences was once again being advocated in relation to the home and the dining hall in the countryside. See *Women-Work* for the period November 1959–January 1960.

11. Various versions of this story were told to me by Leader Zhang, 20, a male former district-level party secretary; Gu Mingjun, 34; and two women villagers, Li Xiaoyue, 24, Li Ailing, 30. Given the response of the local authorities, i.e., the block dismissal of Zhang, her husband, and several other village leaders, my best guess is that the incident took place in spring of 1959. In March 1959, the county began to rectify leftist tendencies as the cause of some of the worst excesses, and villagers may have taken advantage of this political opening to rise up. The opening did not last long, however. Indeed, Wu Zhipu, first party secretary of the Provincial Party Committee, and a strong proponent of War Communism, visited the county in May. By August 1959 the county was embroiled in another rectification movement to combat rightism within the CCP (*HX* 1993, 32).

12. In figure 5, the term *natural* is used in the gazetteer. According to the first Huoyue Census undertaken in July 1953, the county population totaled 550,779 people, or 446 people per square kilometer (*HX* 1993, 30).

13. Huang Lanfang, 28, worked in the dining hall, for example, and Ai Yue, 21, worked in the daycare.

14. On this point, see also Friedman et al. 1991, 246; Thaxton 2008, 233–34.

15. In Huoyue, as in other parts of Henan, for example, some villagers resorted to eating unripe crops (*chi qing*) right out of the fields; much of one year's wheat crop was devoured before it even had a chance to ripen (Liu Yuezhen, 10, and Fan Junxia, 83). On the practice of eating unripe crops see Thaxton 2011. Both Thaxton (2008; 2011) and Gao Wangling (2011) offer extensive discussions of the survival strategies of farmers during this period which seriously undermined the state's capacity to procure grain from the countryside.

16. As Yun (2013) argues, the application of "guilt by association" has a long history in China.

17. Tan Yaoxian, 147, a retired soldier who had worked on an air force base in Xinyang during the famine, was deeply troubled that he was provided with an abundance of food while people were starving and looting outside the gates.

18. During the summer of 1958, Xiping county's bumper harvests drew the praise of Zhou Enlai (Yang 2012, 76). See Qiao Peihua's 2009 and Yang's 2012 discussion of the

Xinyang Incident, a region further to the south of Xiping, which also experienced extensive famine.

19. This saying and other related revolutionary versions date back to the Anti-Japanese War, if not earlier. The prerevolutionary version reverses the meaning: *hao nan bu da bing, hao tie bu da ting* (a good man doesn't become a soldier, good iron is not used to make nails.)

20. The report blamed the child's death on "conditions in the countryside"—a euphemism for the famine at that time. "Wenhe xian peixun fulian ganbu huiyi zongjie baogao (cao gao)" [Meeting summary regarding cadre training for the Wenhe County Women's Association (Draft)] (1961, 9–1–12, WCWFA).

21. These explicit expressions of regret sit in stark contrast to the experience of former regional labor model, Cao Zhuxiang as discussed by Hershatter (2011, 202–6).

22. See also, ACWF (1961c [1999]) for details of this behavior as well.

23. On family breakdown, see also Bachman 2006, 939; Diamant 2000, 256–67; Dikötter 2010, 258–62; Friedman et al. 1991, 240–43.

24. Kathryn Edgerton-Tarpley (2004) argues that women in the North China famine of 1876–79 were actually valued for their bride price during the onset of famine and were not systematically discriminated against as has been suggested in a previous literature.

25. "Moving the Three Big Mountains" is an expression that was popularized during the Cultural Revolution.

26. See Tamara Jacka 1997, 34–36. As previously discussed, the work sites also offered adventure and, in some instances, better food.

27. As of 1957, 83 percent of Gaoshan county's illiterate and semiliterate population were women. ("Guanyu jiaqiang dangqian nongmang tuoer zuzhi he funü laodong baohu gongzuo lingdao de yijian" [Suggestions on strengthening the nursery groups and the protection of women's labor practices], (March 1957, B-21–2–1957–3), GCAWF. In 1957, girls accounted for 32.5 percent of the total number of primary school students in the province of Jiangsu as a whole (Lu and Miao 2000, 141).

28. *Nüquan zhuyi* was not a term frequently used in post-1949 China. I specifically raised this question with former women's heads in Henan and Jiangsu as I was interested in exploring whether or not the concept of "feminism" had entered local vocabularies, before, during, or after 1949. For the most part it had not.

29. For discussions of the impact of the famine and overwork on women's health, see for example, Dikötter 2010, 255–62; Liu 2008, 104–5; and Thaxton 2008, 139–43.

30. See Andors 1983.

31. As in many other villages across China during the Cultural Revolution, factional conflict tore apart the Mu Guiying brigade. Yang told me that she was accused of being a capitalist roader but did not provide further details. Leader Lin, 73, by way of contrast, told me that she refused to participate in the conflict and went and stayed in her mother's village during this period.

32. For a discussion of the life of this slogan during the Cultural Revolution and beyond, see Honig 2015.

CONCLUSION

1. Reports of famine were circulating at the apex of the CCP since at least the spring of 1959 (Wemheuer 2014, 119; Dikötter 2010, 89). In mid-1959 Zhou Enlai forbid officials in Tianjin and Hebei to lend food without prior approval (Brown 2011). The CCP put down popular revolts in Henan, Gansu, Qinghai, Sichuan, Yunnan, Tibet, and Xinjiang in 1961 and 1962 (Teiwes 1967, 59). As discussed in chapter 9, Deng Yingchao also had

firsthand knowledge of the increasingly perilous conditions on the ground, since at least Lushan, if not prior.

2. When attending the International Conference of Red Cross Societies in Toronto in July 1952, Li made the following statement to a group of inquisitive reporters regarding her faith: "Yes, I am a Christian and my family have been Christians for three generations" (Endicott and Endicott 1953, 40). She would have renounced her faith, however, prior to being accepted as a member of the CCP in 1958—a condition for CCP membership at that time.

3. See also Roces 2010, who emphasizes the important role that religion has played in the emergence of women's activism in Asia throughout the latter half of the twentieth century.

4. See Hochschild 1975, 298, for a discussion of the 1960s consciousness-raising groups. Self-directed group work, a form of empowerment-based research that can be traced back to the anti-oppressive techniques deployed by the CCP, has also shaped my own writing and advocacy with parents of transgender children. Gender Creative Kids, an organization in which I was deeply involved for five years, came into being in the wake of directed group work with parents in Montreal. See, for example, Pullen Sansfaçon and Manning 2015; and Mullender and Ward 1991, 92.

5. See, for example, *WW*, no. 19 (1959): 5.

6. Yang (1996, 55) describes the GLF as a "tragedy of commons," in which free supply led to excessive food consumption. Wen and Chang (1997) similarly identify the dining hall system as an important cause of the famine.

7. See Yang 1996, 73–97, for an in-depth discussion of the elite politics of recovery.

8. Although the policy of the two diligences would disappear two years prior to the Cultural Revolution, Luo Qiong would endeavor to revive its importance during the Reform era (see Luo 1998a [2000], 64). See also Wang's 2017, 112–39, discussion of the 1964 attack on *Women of China* by Chen Boda, a leading party theorist of the time.

9. See White's extensive discussion of these developments (2006, 42–61).

10. See also Murphy's compelling account of how mobile abortion techniques that originated in China during the 1960s were taken up by radical American feminists and in the overseas population control efforts of USAID (2012).

11. See, for example, Chappell and Mackay 2017, 27.

12. In January 1961, for example, the ACWF disseminated to lower levels of the federation a report from the Sichuan Women's Federation that addressed efforts to attend to rural women's diseases, urging treatment and care in all localities (ACWF 1961a [1999]). The original report, completed in December 1960, drew on investigative work that would have been undertaken in the months prior. The ACWF Party group followed up in February with a report to the Central Committee on the urgent need to attend to the ongoing epidemic (my words) of uterine prolapse. Based on previous experience, the report noted, success was dependent on party committee leadership and political leadership, among other factors (ACWF 1961b [1999]).

13. See also Barlow's analysis of some of these struggles (2021, 191–219).

14. See also Chan, Madsen, and Unger 2009; and Hillman 2014 for discussions of kinship in village governance (and conflict) since the onset of economic reforms.

15. The son and two grandsons of former women's head Rong Litang, 116, for example, are party members.

16. As Guy's 2009 work shows, much of the maternalist social policy framework that the Perón's enacted originated in the local and state-level activism of feminists and philanthropists.

17. See, for example, Grammatico 2010; and Auyero 2011.

18. For example, Nyerere represented himself as "father" of the Tanzanian nation (Schneider 2014). According to Tripp et al. (2009, 25–28), political motherhood has played an especially important role in Africa and is a particularly resonant trope in postconflict Africa contexts. See also Charrad's discussion of symbolic fatherhood in the Maghreb (2011) and Kampwirth's discussion of how political opponents Daniel Ortega and Violeta Chamorro both sought to cast themselves as parental figures in the 1989–90 campaign for the Nicaraguan presidency (2004, 38–46).

19. See Brown's rich historical treatment (2021a) of the Tiananmen protests and Beijing massacre of 1989.

APPENDIX 3. RESEARCH METHODS AND SOURCES

1. Seven important exceptions were the first individuals I interviewed. These individuals were either active at the apex of the party during the 1950s, served as official party historians, or were the relatives of central leaders.

2. By including these two additional women's heads in the coding analysis for this book, my final numbers are slightly different than those I reported in an earlier publication of the same interviews (Manning 2011).

3. I included Nie Chunyan, 105, and Zhu Xiaoming, 106, both former Gaoshan City Women's Federation officials, in this group of forty-three as they lived in rural Jiangsu during their childhoods.

4. As Reed (2004, 663) notes, "Testimonies are a useful way to access and partially to 'read' the very complex emotional dimensions connected to revolutionary action." See also Jasper's 1997 early and influential work on the importance of biography in social movements as well.

5. Several participants, such as Ding Xueqin, 64, and Yan Shuqun, 43, did not want to be recorded the first time we met in 2001 and so I took handwritten notes instead. When I returned in 2004, however, they were comfortable with me recording our conversation.

6. Some women had served as women's head prior to marrying and moving away from the village. Others had died. Adding to the complexity was the fact that turnover among women's heads in some villages was extremely high. This was especially the case in the second Wenhe village which had at least two women's heads, Yan Shuqun, 43, and Niu Shumiao, 52, over the course of the GLF.

7. See Olick 2003; Passerini 1992; and Lee and Yang 2007.

8. See, for example, *Positions: asia critique* 29 (4), November 2021, for a special issue on "The Maoism of PRC History."

9. See Wedeen 2010; and Kuhonta, Slater, and Vu 2008 for in-depth discussions of the interpretivist tradition in political science.

10. See also Wang 1997.

11. See Luo Qiong's public refutation (2002) of the idea that Wang Ming played any role in the drafting of the first Marriage Law. In fact, as I note in chapter 6, Wang Ming did play an important role, although likely not until after the Women's Committee submitted its first draft to begin the review process.

Works Cited

Abdullah, Hussaina. 1995. "Wifeism and Activism: The Nigerian Women's Movement." In *Challenges of Local Feminisms*, edited by Amrita Basu, 209–25. Colorado: Westview Press.

ACWF. 1950 [1999]. "Zhongguo zhengfu baohu funü de zhengce yu shishi" [The Chinese government's policies and methods for protecting women]. In *ZFWN*, E8–27.

ACWF. 1953. "Zhongguo funü jiezhihui quanguo zonghui ji qi fen hui qingquang" [The general situation of the Chinese WCTU and other matters]. 1031–1–6. CMA.

ACWF. 1953 [1999]. "Guanyu guanche hunyin fa yundong hou nongcun zhong yin hunyin wenti jixu fasheng zisha bei sha qingkuang de baogao" [A report on the aftermath of the implementation of the Marriage Law in the countryside in which suicides and murder are continuing due to marital problems]. In *ZFWN*, E11-31.

ACWF. 1955a [1999]. "Guanyu dongyuan quanguo funû nuli zengchan lixing jieyue xiang geji minzhu fulian de zhishi" [Instructions to the ACDWF at all levels on mobilizing women across the country to increase production and practice economy]. In *ZFWN*, E13–44.

ACWF. 1955b [1999]. "Guanyu jiezhi shengyu wenti gei ge sheng shi fuwei de tongzhi" [On the problem of birth control: A report given to provincial and municipal women committees]. In *ZFWN*, E13–78.

ACWF. 1958a [1999]. "Jiu shanxi wenshui xian fulian 'guanyu kaizhan biyun xuanchuan gongzuo de baogao' gei ge sheng, zizhi qu, zhixia shi fulian de tongbao" ["A report regarding the beginning of publicization work for contraceptive methods" that the Wenshui County (Shanxi province) Women's Federation gave to many provinces, autonomous regions, and directly-controlled cities]. In *ZFWN,* E16–86.

ACWF. 1958b [1999]. "Quanguo fulian dangzu dui xian fulian zuzhi cunzai wenti de yijian" [Thoughts of the ACWF party group on the problems existing in the county women's federation organizations]. In *ZFWN*, E16–41.

ACWF. 1961a [1999]. "Jiu Sichuan sheng fulian 'guanyu tuji zhiliao nongcun funûbing de baogao' gei gesheng, shi, zizhiqu fulian de tongbao" [A notice given to provincial, city, and autonomous region women's federations on the Sichuan women's federation "report on the intensive treatment of rural women's diseases"]. In *ZFWN*, E19–51.

ACWF. 1961b [1999]. "Guanyu nongcun zhiliao funü zigong tuo chui, bijingbing chubu jingyan de baogao" [Report on the preliminary experience of treating women with amenorrhea in rural areas]. In *ZFWN*, E19–11.

ACWF. 1961c [1999]. "Zai guanche zhongyang shi'er tiao zhishi guocheng zhong, youguan fulian ganbu he funü qunzhong de qingkuang he wenti" [Situations and issues regarding Women's Federation cadres and the women masses while implementing the twelve directives of the CC]. In *ZFWN*, E19–11.

Adam, Hajo, and Adam D. Galinsky. 2012. "Enclothed Cognition." *Journal of Experimental Social Psychology* 48: 918–25.

Adams, Julia. 2005. *The Familial State: Ruling Families and Merchant Capitalism in Early Modern Europe*. Ithaca, NY: Cornell University Press.

Ahmed, Sara. 2004. "Affective Economies." *Social Text, 79* 22 (2): 117–39.

Alison, Miranda. 2003. "Cogs in the Wheel: Women in the Liberation Tigers of Eelam." *Civil Wars* 6 (4): 37–54.

Altehenger, Jennifer E. 2018. *Legal Lessons: Popularizing Laws in the People's Republic of China*. Cambridge, MA: Harvard University Press.

Andors, Phyllis. 1983. *The Unfinished Liberation of Chinese Women, 1949–1980*. Bloomington: Indiana University Press.

Apter, David E., and Tony Saich. 1994. *Revolutionary Discourse in Mao's Republic*. Cambridge, MA: Harvard University Press.

Auyero, Javier. 2011. *Poor People's Politics: Peronist Survival Networks and the Legacy of Evita*. Durham, NC: Duke University Press.

Averill, Stephen C. 2006. *Revolution in the Highlands: China's Jinggangshan Base Area*. Lanham, MD: Rowman & Littlefield.

Bacchi, Carol. 1999. *Women, Politics, and Policy: The Construction of Policy Problems*. London: Sage.

Bachman, David M. 1991. *Bureaucracy, Economy, and Leadership in China: The Institutional Origins of the Great Leap Forward*. New York: Cambridge University Press.

Bachman, David M. 2006. "Aspects of an Institutionalizing Political System: China, 1958–1965." *China Quarterly* 188 (December): 933–58.

Bai Lang. 1988. *Zhonghua nü yinglie* [Female martyrs of China]. Beijing: Wenwu chubanshe.

Baker, Hugh D. R. 1979. *Chinese Family and Kinship*. London: Macmillan.

Baldez, Lisa. 2002. *Why Women Protest: Women's Movements in Chile*. New York: Cambridge University Press.

Banaszak, Lee Ann and S. Laurel Weldon. 2011. "Informal Institutions, Protest, and Change in Gendered Federal Systems." *Politics and Gender* 7 (2): 262–73.

Banister, Judith. 1987. *China's Changing Population*. Stanford, CA: Stanford University Press.

Banning, Margaret Culkin. 1942. *Women for Defense*. New York: Duell, Sloan and Pearce.

Barfield, Thomas J. 1989. *The Perilous Frontier: Nomadic Empires and China*. Cambridge, MA: Blackwell.

Barlow, Tani. 1994a. "Politics and Protocols of Funü." In *Engendering China: Women, Culture, and the State*, edited by Christina K. Gilmartin, Gail Hershatter, Lisa Rofel and Tyrene White, 339–59. Cambridge, MA: Harvard University Press.

Barlow, Tani. 1994b. "Theorizing Women: Funü, Guojia, Jiating (Chinese Woman, Chinese State, Chinese Family)." In *Body, Subject and Power in China*, edited by Angela Zito and Tani Barlow, 253–89. Chicago: University of Chicago Press.

Barlow, Tani. 2004. *The Question of Women in Chinese Feminism*. Durham, NC: Duke University Press.

Barlow, Tani. 2021. *In the Event of Women*. Durham, NC: Duke University Press.

Barlow, Tani, and Gary J. Bjorge. 1989. *I Myself Am a Woman: Selected writings of Ding Ling*. Boston: Beacon Press.

Barnes, Nicole Elizabeth. 2018. *Intimate Communities: Wartime Healthcare and the Birth of Modern China, 1937–1945*. Berkeley: University of California Press.

Barnett, A. Doak. 1967. *Cadres, Bureaucracy, and Political Power in Communist China.* New York: Columbia University Press.

Barnouin, Barbara, and Changgen Yu. 2006. *Zhou Enlai: A Political Life.* Hong Kong: Chinese University Press.

Beahan, Charlotte. 1976. "The Women's Movement and Nationalism in Late Ch'ing China." PhD diss., Columbia University.

Beckwith, Karen. 2000. "Beyond Compare? Women's Movements in Comparative Perspective." *European Journal of Political Research* 37 (4): 431–68.

Bennett, Gordon. 1976. *Yundong: Mass Campaign in Chinese Communist Leadership.* Berkeley: Center for Chinese Studies: University of California.

Bentley, Amy. 1998. *Eating for Victory: Food Rationing and the Politics of Domesticity.* Champaign: University of Illinois Press.

Benton, Gregor. 1995. "Under Arms and Umbrellas: Perspectives on Chinese Communism in Defeat." *New Perspectives on the Chinese Revolution,* edited by Tony Saich and Hans J. Van De Van, 116–43. New York: Routledge.

Berlant, Lauren. 2011. *Cruel Optimism.* Durham, NC: Duke University Press.

Bernstein, Thomas P. 2006. "Mao Zedong and the Famine of 1959–1960: A Study in Willfulness." *China Quarterly* 186: 421–45.

Bian Yanjun and Wu Shaojing, eds. 2006. *Dong Biwu zhuan* [The biography of Dong Biwu]. Beijing: Zhongyang wenxian chubanshe.

Bjarnegård, Elin. 2013. *Gender, Informal Institutions, and Political Recruitment: Explaining Male Dominance in Parliamentary Representation.* Basingstoke, UK: Palgrave Macmillan.

Bo Yibo. 1979 [2002]. "Shenqie huainian Zhou Enlai zongli" [Heartfelt yearning for Premier Zhou Enlai]. In *Lingxiu yuanshuai yu zhanyou* [Leaders, marshals, and comrades-in-arms], edited by Bo Yibo, 108–19. Beijing: Renmin chubanshe.

Bo Yibo. 1980 [2002]. "Fuchun tongzhi yong zai" [Comrade Fuchun forever]. In *Lingxiu yuanshuai yu zhanyou* [Leaders, marshals, and comrades-in-arms], edited by Bo Yibo, 273–82. Beijing: Renmin chubanshe.

Bock, Gisela, and Pat Thane. 1991. "Introduction." In *Maternity and Gender Policies: Women and the Rise of European Welfare States 1880s—1950s,* edited by Gisela Bock and Pat Thane, 1–20. London: Routledge.

Boorman, Howard L., Richard C. Howard, Joseph Kai Huan Cheng, and Janet Krompart. 1967. *Biographical Dictionary of Republican China.* New York: Columbia University Press.

Bourdieu, Pierre. 1977. *Outline of a Theory of Practice.* Translated by Richard Nice. New York: Cambridge University Press.

Bourdieu, Pierre. 1980. *The Logic of Practice.* Translated by Richard Nice. Stanford, CA: Stanford University Press.

Bourdieu, Pierre. 1986. "The Forms of Capital." In *Handbook of Theory and Research for the Sociology of Education,* edited by John G. Richardson, 241–58. Westport, CT: Greenwood Press.

Bourdieu, Pierre, and Loic J.D. Wacquant. 1992. *An Invitation to Reflexive Sociology.* Chicago: University of Chicago Press.

Bramall, Chris. 2011. "Agency and Famine in China's Sichuan Province, 1958–1962." *China Quarterly* 208: 990–1008.

Brandtstädter, Susanne and Gonçalo D. Santos. 2009. "Introduction: Chinese Kinship Metamorphoses." In *Chinese Kinship: Anthropological Perspectives,* edited by Susanne Brandtstädter and Gonçalo D. Santos, 1-26. New York: Routledge.

Brazelton, Mary Augusta. 2019. *Mass Vaccination: Citizens' Bodies and State Power in Modern China*. Ithaca, NY: Cornell University Press.

Brieba, Daniel. 2018. "State Capacity and Health Outcomes: Comparing Argentina's and Chile's Reduction of Infant and Maternal Mortality, 1960–2013." *World Development* 101: 37–53.

Brooke, John L., and Julia C. Strauss. 2018. "Introduction: Approaches to State Formation." *State Formations: Global Histories, and Cultures of Statehood*, edited by John L. Brooke, Julia C. Strauss and Greg Anderson, 1–22. New York: Cambridge University Press.

Brown, Jeremy. 2011. "Great Leap City: Surviving the Famine in Tianjin." In *Eating Bitterness: New Perspectives on China's Great Leap Forward and Famine*, edited by Kimberley Ens Manning and Felix Wemheuer, 226–50. Vancouver: University of British Columbia Press.

Brown, Jeremy. 2021a. *June Fourth: The Tiananmen Protests and Beijing Massacre of 1989*. New York: Cambridge University Press.

Brown, Jeremy. 2021b. "PRC History in Crisis and Clover." *Positions: Asia Critique* 29 (4): 689–718.

Brubaker, Rogers, and Frederick Cooper. 2000. "Beyond Identity." *Theory and Society* 29 (1): 1–47.

Bullock, Mary Brown. 1974. "A Brief Sketch of the Role of PUMC Graduates in the People's Republic of China." In *Medicine and Society in China*, edited by John Z. Bowers and Elizabeth F. Purcell, 99–101. New York: Josiah Macy Jr. Foundation.

Butler, Judith. 1990. *Gender Trouble: Feminism and the Subversion of Identity*. New York: Routledge.

Butler, Judith. 2002. "Is Kinship Always Already Heterosexual?" *Differences: A Journal of Feminist Cultural Studies* 13 (1): 14–44.

Cai Asong. 1992a. "Cai Dajie yongyuan huo zai wo xin zhong" [Elder sister Cai is always in my heart]. In *WHDCC*, 213-225.

Cai Asong. 1992b. "Gongtong lixiang xian zhongsheng bingjian fendou wushinian" [Dedicated to a shared dream and struggling side-by-side for fifty years]. In *WHDCC*, 186-203.

Cai Chang. 1942 [1988]. "Ruhe shi kangri genjudi de funü tuanti chengwei geng guangfan de qunzhong zuhi" [How to make women's groups become more extensive in the anti-Japanese bases]. In *CCDYKK*, 76–79.

Cai Chang. 1943 [1991]. "Yingjie funü gongzuo de xin fangxiang" [Welcoming the new direction in women-work]. In *ZFYLZ (1937–1945)*, 650–54.

Cai Chang. 1947a [1988]. "Ge le fengjian de ming, hai yao ge shengchan de ming" [We have accomplished the revolution against feudalism, but we still need to accomplish the production revolution]. In *CCDYKK*, 125–32.

Cai Chang. 1947b [1988]. "Wei zhengqu duli, minzhu, heping er fendou de Zhongguo funü" [Chinese women struggle for independence, democracy, and peace]. In *CCDYKK*, 102-16,

Cai Chang. 1951 [1988]. "Zhongguo gongchandang yu Zhongguo funü" [The CCP and Chinese women]. In *ZFYWZH*, 2: 105–7.

Cai Chang. 1956 [1988]. "Jiji peiyang he tiba geng duo geng hao de nü ganbu" [Actively train and promote more and better female cadres]. In *CCDYKK*, 291–96.

Cai Chang. 1957. "Jianku fendou qinjian jianguo" [Build the country with hard work, diligence, and thrift]. *Sichuan ribao* [Sichuan Daily].

Cai Chang. 1957 [1988]. "Keqin kejian, kefu kunnan, zhiyuan guojia jianshe" [Be hardworking and thrifty, overcome obstacles, and support the building of the country]. In *CCDYKK*, 297–300.

Cai Chang. 1958a. "Sixiang yuejin, jishu yuejin" [Making an ideological leap, making a technological leap]. *Women of China* 4: 1–3.

Cai Chang. 1958b. "Tigao juewu xue hao benling wei jianshe shehui zhuyi fenyong qianjin" [Raise consciousness and study skills well in order to forge ahead courageously in the construction of socialism]. *WW* 24: 4–11.

Cai Chang. 1959a. "Quanguo fulian Cai Chang zhuxi zai shoudu gejie funü jinian 'san ba' jie dahui shang de jianghua" [ACWF Chair Cai Chang's speech at the capital Conference of Women from All Walks of Life commemorating the 'March Eighth' holiday]. *WW* 6: 2–5.

Cai Chang. 1959b. "Relie xiangying dang de haozhao, wei tiquian san nian wancheng di er ge wu nian jihua de zhuyao zhibiao fenyong qianjin" [Warmly respond to the party's call to forge ahead and complete the main indicators of the second five year plan three years ahead of schedule]. *WW* 17: 2–4.

Caldwell, John C. 1986. "Routes to Low Mortality in Poor Countries." *Population and Development Review* 12 (2): 171–220.

Calhoun, Craig. 1995. *Critical Social Theory*. Oxford: Blackwell.

Cao Guanqun. 1957 [1988]. "Guanyu heli zuzhi yu shiyong funü laodongli wenti" [The problems regarding reasonably organizing and using women's labor]. In *ZFYWZH* 2: 272–75.

Cao Guanqun. 1958. "Quanguo funü gongzuo huiyi zongjie baogao" [Summary of a meeting on the situation of All-China women-work]. *WW* 16: 2–12.

Cao Mengjun. 1939 [1991]. "Zhanshi Ertong Baoyu yi zhou nian" [The first year of the Wartime Association for Children's Welfare]. In *ZFYLZ (1937–1945)*, edited by Wang Menglan, 238–42. Beijing: Zhongguo funü chubanshe.

Cao Shuji. 2015. "An Overt Conspiracy: Creating Rightists in Rural Henan, 1957-1958." In *Maoism at the Grassroots: Everyday Life in China's Era of High Socialism*, edited by Jeremy Brown and Matthew D. Johnson, 77-101. Cambridge: Harvard University Press.

Cao Shuji and Bin Yang. 2015. "Grain, Local Politics, and the Making of Mao's Famine in Wuwei, 1958–1961." *Modern Asian Studies* 49 (6): 1675–1703.

Cathcart, Adam, and Patricia Nash. 2009. "War Criminals and the Road to Sino-Japanese Normalization: Zhou Enlai and the Shenyang Trials, 1954–1956." *Twentieth-Century China* 34 (2): 89–111.

CC. 1943 [1991]. "Zhongguo gongchandang zhongyang weiyuanhui guanyu ge kangri genju di muqian funü gongzuo fangzhen de jueding" [The CC's decision regarding the current direction of women-work in the anti-Japanese Base Areas]. In *ZFYLZ (1937–1945)*, 647–49.

CC. 1948 [1991]. "Zhongguo gongchandang zhongyang weiyuanhui guanyu muqian jiefangqu nongcun funü gongzuo de jueding" [Decision of the CC on rural women-work in the Liberated Areas]. In *ZFYLZ (1945–1949)* 299–306.

CC. 1953 [1999]. "Zhonggong zhongyang guanyu pifa 'Zhongyang fuwei guanyu guanche hunyinfa yundong hou nongcun zhong yin hunyin wenti jixu fasheng zisha beisha qingkuang de baogao' de zhishi" [Directives from the CC on the publication of the "Report from the CCWMC regarding the post-Marriage Law period in the countryside, where marital problems have continued to produce instances of suicide or murder."]. In *ZFWN*, E11–31.

CC.1954 [1997]. "Liu Shaoqi zhaokai jiezhi shengyu wenti zuotanhui" [Liu Shaoqi Holds Symposium on Birth Control Issues]. In ZJSQ, 471.

CC. 1958 [1960]. "Resolution on Some Questions Concerning the People's Communes." In *Contemporary China 3 (1958–59)*, edited by E. S. Kirby, 213–33. Hong Kong: Hong Kong University Press.

CCTV. 2021. "Ta shi zhonggong lishi shang di yi wei nü zhongyang weiyuan, 30 jisui jiu bei chengwei 'ge ming de lao zumu'" [In CCP history, the first female member of the central committee, who at thirty years of age became the "paternal grandmother of the revolution"]. *Juzi zhoutou* [Orange Isle]. https://doi.org/http://www.juzizhoutou.net/hongqi/bdyx/2021-01-06/8770.html. Accessed November 23, 2021.

CCWMC. 1939 [1991]. "Zhonggong zhongyang fuwei guanyu muqian funü yundong de fangzhen he renwu de biaozhi xin" [Letter of instruction from the CCWMC on the current goals and responsibilities of the Chinese women's movement]. In *ZFYLZ (1937–1945)*, 138–46.

Central People's Government Administrative Council. 1951 [1988]. "Central People's Government Administrative Council's Instructions on the investigation of the implementation of the Marriage Law [Zhongyang renmin zhengfu zhengwuyuan guanyu jiancha hunyinfa zhi hang qingkuang de zhishi] "In ZFYWZH, 2: 121–26.

Chan, Alfred L. 2001. *Mao's Crusade: Politics and Policy Implementation in China's Great Leap Forward*. Oxford, UK: Oxford University Press.

Chan, Anita. 1985. *Children of Mao: Personality Development and Political Activism in the Red Guard Generation*. London: Macmillan.

Chan, Anita, Richard Madsen, and Jonathan Unger. 1992. *Chen Village Under Mao and Deng: The Recent History of a Peasant Community in Mao's China*. Berkeley: University of California Press.

Chan, Anita, Richard Madsen, and Jonathan Unger. 2009. *Chen Village Under Mao and Deng: Revolution to Globalization*. 3rd ed. Berkeley: University of California Press.

Chang, Parris. 1975. *Power and Policy in China*. University Park: Pennsylvania State University Press.

Chappell, Louise and Fiona Mackay. 2017. "What's in a Name? Mapping the Terrain of Informal Institutions and Gender Politics." In *Gender and Informal Institutions*, edited by Georgina Waylen, 23-44. New York: Rowman and Littlefield.

Charrad, Mounira M. 2001. *States and Women's Rights: The Making of Postcolonial Tunisia, Algeria, and Morocco*. Berkeley: University of California Press.

Charrad, Mounira M. 2010. "Women's Agency Across Cultures: Conceptualizing Strengths and Boundaries." *Women's Studies International Forum* 33: 517–22.

Charrad, Mounira M. 2011. "Central and Local Patrimonialism: State-Building in Kin-Based Societies." *Annals of the American Academy of Political and Social Science* 636 (1): 49–68.

Chen Hanfei. 2014. "Fa shenti: 1950 nian hunyinfa de biaoda yu shijian" [The body of law: expression and practice of the 1950 Marriage Law]. *Funü yanjiu lun cong* [Collection of women's studies] 5 (125): 63–70.

Chen Jian. 1994. *China's Road to the Korean War: The Making of the Sino-American confrontation*. New York: Columbia University Press.

Chen, Tina Mai. 2003. "Female Icons, Feminist Iconography? Social Rhetoric and Women's Agency in 1950's China." *Gender & History* 15 (2): 268–95.

Chen, Tina Mai. 2011. "Peasant and Woman in Maoist Revolutionary Theory, 1920s-1950s." In *Reform, Revolution, and Radicalism in Modern China, Essays in Honor of Maurice Meisner*, edited by Catherine Lynch, Robert Marks and Paul Pickowicz, 55–77. Lanham, MD: Lexington Press.

Chen Yixin. 2011. "Under the Same Maoist Sky: Accounting for Death Rate Discrepancies in Anhui and Jiangxi." In *Eating Bitterness: New Perspectives on China's Great Leap Forward and Famine*, edited by Kimberley Ens Manning and Felix Wemheuer, 197–225. Vancouver: University of British Colombia Press.

Chen Yun. 1957 [1988]. "Bixu tichang jiezhi shengyu" [The imperative to promote birth control]. In *ZFYWZH*, 2: 293–95.

Cheng Tiejun and Mark Selden. 1994. "The Origins and Social Consequences of China's Hukou System." *China Quarterly* 139: 644–68.

Chesneaux, Jean. 1972. "Secret Societies in China's Historical Evolution." In *Popular Movements and Secret Societies in China 1840–1950*, edited by Jean Chesneaux, 11–13. Stanford, CA: Stanford University Press.

Chiang Yung-chen. 2006. "Womanhood, Motherhood and Biology: The Early Phases of The Ladies Journal, 1915–25." *Gender & History* 18 (3): 519–45.

Chin, Carol C. 2003. "Beneficent Imperialists: American Women Missionaries in China at the Turn of the Twentieth Century." *Diplomatic History* 27 (3): 327–52.

Chin, Carol C. 2006. "Translating the New Woman: Chinese Feminists View the West, 1905–15." *Gender & History* 18 (3): 490–518.

Chisholm, Amanda, and Hanna Ketola. 2020. "The Cruel Optimism of Militarism: Feminist Curiosity, Affect, and Global Security." *International Political Sociology* 14 (3): 270–85.

Chung Jae Ho. 1991. "The Politics of Prerogatives in Socialism: The Case of Taizidang in China." *Studies in Comparative Communism* 24 (1): 58–76.

Chung Yen-Lin. 2015. "The Unknown Standard-Bearer of the Three Red Banners: Peng Zheng's Roles in the Great Leap Forward." *China Journal* 74: 129–43.

Chung, Yuehtsen Juliette. 2002. *Struggle for National Survival: Eugenics in Sino-Japanese Contexts, 1896–1945*. New York: Routledge.

Clements, Barbara. 1997. *Bolshevik Women*. New York: Cambridge University Press.

Cohen, Myron. 1993. "Cultural and Political Inventions in Modern China: The Case of the Chinese Peasant." *Daedalus* 112 (2): 151–70.

Cohen, Myron. 2005. *Kinship, Contract, Community, and State: Anthropological Perspectives on China*. Stanford: Stanford University Press.

Collins, Patricia Hill and Sirma Bilge. 2020. *Intersectionality*, 2nd ed. Medford, MA: Polity Press.

Cong Xiaoping. 2007. *Teacher's Schools and the Making of the Modern Chinese Nation-State, 1897–1937*. Vancouver: University of British Colombia Press.

Cong Xiaoping. 2016. *Marriage, Law, and Gender in Revolutionary China, 1940–1960*. Cambridge: Cambridge University Press.

Connell, R.W. 1990. "The State, Gender, and Sexual Politics: Theory and Appraisal." *Theory and Society* 19 (5): 507–44.

Cothran, Boyd, Joan Judge, and Adrian Shubert. 2020. "Introduction." *Women Warriors and National Heroes: Global Histories,* edited by Boyd Chothran, Joan Judge and Adrian Shubert, 1–20. London: Bloomsbury Academic.

Crane, Hillary. 2004. "Resisting Marriage and Renouncing Womanhood: The Choice of Taiwanese Buddhist Nuns." *Critical Asian Studies* 36 (2): 265–84.

Crane, Hillary. 2011. "Resistance through Transformation? The Meanings of Gender Reversals in a Taiwanese Buddhist Monastery." In *Women and Gender in Contemporary Chinese Societies: Beyond Han Patriarchy*, edited by Shanshan Du and Ya-chen Chen, 185–200. Lanham, MD: Lexington Press.

Crenshaw, Kimberlé Williams. 1991. "Mapping the Margins: Intersectionality, Identity Politics, and Violence Against Women of Color." *Stanford Law Review* 43 (6): 1241–99.

Dal Bó, Ernesto, Pedro Dal Bó, and Jason Snyder. 2009. "Political Dynasties." *The Review of Economic Studies* 76: 115–42.

David, Mirela. 2018. "Female Gynecologists and their Birth Control Clinics: Eugenics in Practice in 1920s-1930s China." *Canadian Bulletin of Medical History* 35 (1): 32–62.

Davin, Delia 1976. *Woman-work: Women and the Party in Revolutionary China*. Oxford: Oxford University Press.

della Porta, Donatella. 1995. *Social Movements, Political Violence, and the State: A Comparative Analysis of Italy and Germany*. New York: Cambridge University Press.

Deng Liqun, Ma Hong, and Wu Heng. 1986. *Dangdai Zhongguo de weisheng shiye* [Health services in contemporary China]. 2 vols. Beijing: Zhongguo shehui kexue chubanshe.

Deng Xiaoping. 1954 [1997]. "Deng Xiaoping dui Deng Yingchao lai xin de pishi" [Deng Xiaoping's comment regarding Deng Yingchao letter]. In *ZJSQ* 146.

Deng Yanhua and Kevin J. O'Brien. 2013. "Relational Repression in China: Using Social Ties to Demobilize Protesters." *China Quarterly* 215: 533–52.

Deng Yingchao. 1937 [1991]. "Duiyu xian jieduan funü yundong de yijian" [Opinion on the current stage of the women's movement]. In *ZFYLZ* (1937–1945), 8–14.

Deng Yingchao. 1938 [1991]. "Lun nü canzheng yuan de zeren" [Responsibilities of women government officials]. In *ZFYLZ [1937–1945)]*, 76–78.

Deng Yingchao. 1939 [1991]. "Kangri minzu tongyi zhanxian zhong de funü yundong" [The women's movement in the anti-Japanese National United Front]. In *ZFYLZ (1937–1945)* 164–75.

Deng Yingchao. 1942 [1985]. "Tan nannü qingnian de lianai, hunyin wenti" [Speaking on the question of youth love and marriage]. In *Lao gemingjia de lianai, hunyin he jiating shenghuo* [Love, marriage, and family life of elder revolutionaries], edited by Zhao Zhangan, Lan Wei, and Zhang Tianruo, 1–7. Beijing: Gongren chubanshe.

Deng Yingchao. 1942 [1987]. "Women duiyu haizi he muqin de taidu" [Our attitude toward children and mothers]. In *Jinian yu huiyi Deng Yingchao* [Commemorating and remembering Deng Yingchao], 182–86. Beijing: Renmin ribao chubanshe.

Deng Yingchao. 1943 [1988]. "Luetan funü yu canzheng" [Discussing women and political Involvement]. In *CCDYKK*, 80–81.

Deng Yingchao. 1948 [1988]. "Dang yao jiaqiang lingdao, nü ganbu yao zi wo piping" [The party has to strengthen its guidance, while women cadres have to be self-critical]. In *CCDYKK*, 142–50.

Deng Yingchao. 1949 [1988]. "Zhongguo funü yundong dangqian de fangzhen renwu baogao—zai Zhongguo funü di yici quanguo daibiao dahui shang de gongzuo baogao" [Report on the present tasks of the direction of the Chinese Women's Movement—Work report at the first All-China women's representative meeting]. In *ZFYWZH* 2: 5–9.

Deng Yingchao. 1950 [1988]. "Guanyu zhonghua renmin gongheguo hunyin fa de baogao" [Report on the PRC's Marriage Law]. In *CCDYKK*, 169–85.

Deng Yingchao. 1951 [1988]. "Xin Zhongguo funü qianjin zai qianjin" [New women of China advance and advance again]. In *ZFYWZH* 2: 130–33.

Deng Yingchao. 1953 [1988]. "Si nian lai zhongguo funü yundong de jiben zongjie he jinhou renwu" [A general summary of the last four years of the Chinese Women's Movement and future tasks]. In *CCDYKK*, 230–34.

Deng Yingchao. 1954 [1997]. "Fu: Deng Yingchao gei Deng Xiaoping de xin" [Attachment: letter from Deng Yingchao to Deng Xiaoping]. In *ZJSQ*, 146.

Deng Yingchao. 1956 [1988]. "Jinyibu fahui funü canjia shengchan de jijixing, baohu funü ertong de jiankang he anquan" [Further develop women's enthusiasm for participation in production, [while] protecting the health and safety of women and children]. In *CCDYKK*, 278–83.

Deng Yingchao. 1964 [1988]. "Yi Mao Zedong sixiang wei zhidao, yanjiu fuyun lishi ziliao" [With Mao Zedong Thought as our guide, explore the historical documents of the women's movement]. In *CCDYKK*, 304–7.

Deng Yingchao. 1989. "Deng Yingchao zhi shoudu tongxue shimin de xin" [Deng Yingchao's letter to the students and citizens of the capital]. *Renmin ribao* [People's Daily], May 23, 1989, 1.

Deng Yingchao. 1989 [2019]. "Deng Yingchao tongzhi zai zhonggong zhongyang zhengzhi ju kuoda huiyi shang de fa yan (zhaiyao) [Comrade Deng Yingchao's statements at the expanded meeting of the Political Bureau of the CC (summary)]." In *Zui hou de mimi—Zhonggong shisan jie si zhong quanhui 'liusi' jielun wendang* [The last secret—The fourth plenary session of the 13th CC of the CCP 'June 4th' conclusion documents], edited by Cai Yongmei, 211–12. Hong Kong: New Century Publishing.

Deng Yingchao and Meng Qingshu. 1938 [1991]. "Women duiyu zhanshi funü gongzuo de yijian" [Our view on wartime women-work]. In *ZFYLZ* [1937–1945], 44–53.

Deutsch, Sandra McGee. 1991. "Gender and Sociopolitical Change in Twentieth-Century Latin America." *Hispanic American Historical Review* 71 (2): 259–306.

Diamant, Neil J. 2000. *Revolutionizing the Family: Politics, Love, and Divorce in Urban and Rural China. 1949–1958.* Berkeley: University of California Press.

Diamant, Neil J. 2001a. "Making Love "Legible" in China: Politics and Society during the Enforcement of Civil Marriage Registration, 1950–66." *Politics & Society* 29 (3): 447–80.

Diamant, Neil J. 2001b. "Between Martyrdom and Mischief: The Political and Social Predicament of CCP War Widows and Veterans, 1949–66." In *Scars of War: The Impact of Warfare on Modern China*, edited by Diana Lary and Stephen MacKinnon, 162–87. Vancouver: University of British Colombia Press.

Diamond, Norma. 1975. "Collectivization, Kinship and the Status of Women in Rural China." *Bulletin of Concerned Asian Scholars* 7 (Jan-Mar): 25–32.

Diamond, Norma. 1983. "Household, Kinship and the Status of Women in Taitou Village, Shandong Province." In *Agricultural and Rural Development in China Today*, edited by Randolph Barker and Beth Rose, 78–96. Ithaca, NY: International Agricultural Program, New York State College of Agricultural Life Sciences, Cornell University.

Dikötter, Frank. 2010. *Mao's Great Famine: The History of China's Most Devastating Catastrophe, 1958–1962.* New York: Walker & Co.

Dillon, Nara. 2007. "New Democracy and the Demise of Private Charity in Shanghai." In *Dilemmas of Victory: The Early Years of the People's Republic of China*, edited by Jeremy Brown and Paul G. Pickowicz, 80–102. Cambridge, MA: Harvard University Press.

Ding, Iza. 2022. *The Performative State: Public Scrutiny and Environmental Governance in China.* Ithaca: Cornell University Press.

Ding Ling. 1942 [1989]. "Thoughts on March Eight." In *I Myself Am a Woman*, edited by Tani E. Barlow with Gary J. Bjorge, 317–21. Boston: Beacon Press.

Dittmer, Lowell. 1995. "Chinese Informal Politics." *China Journal* 34 (July): 1–34.

Dixon, John. 1981. *The Chinese Welfare System, 1949–1979*. New York: Praeger Publishers.

Dixon, John, and David Macarov, eds. 1992. *Social Welfare in Socialist Countries*. New York: Routledge.

Domenach, Jean-Luc. 1995. *The Origins of the Great Leap Forward*. Translated by A. M. Berrett. Boulder, CO: Westview Press.

Dong Bian. 1958 [1988]. "Zai quanguo funü gongzuo huiyi shang de fayan" [Speech on the occasion of the National Conference on Women-Work]. In *ZFYWZH*, 2: 363–65.

Dong Bian. 1991. "Keqin kejing de Shen dajie" [Dearest elder sister Shen]. In *Nü jie wenhua zhanshi Shen Zijiu* [Shen Zijiu: female culture warrior], edited by Dong Bian, 158–65. Beijing: Zhongguo funü chubanshe.

Dong Bian, Cai Asong, and Tan Deshan, eds. 1992. *Women de hao dajie Cai Chang* [Our good elder sister, Cai Chang]. Beijing: Zhongyang wenxian chubanshe.

Dong Lan. 2011. *Mulan's Legend and Legacy in China and the United States*. Philadelphia: Temple University Press.

Dou, Eva. 2021. "China Seeks to Reduce Abortions, as Beijing Pushes for More Children." *Washington Post*. https://www.washingtonpost.com/world/ asia_pacific/china-abortion-women/2021/09/27/bdba51fa-1f60-11ec-a8d9-0827a2a4b915_story.html Accessed July 6, 2022.

Drucker, Alison R. 1979. "The Role of the YWCA in the Development of the Chinese Women's Movement, 1890–1927." *Social Service Review* 53 (3): 421–40.

Duara, Prasenjit. 1998. "The Regime of Authenticity: Timelessness, Gender, and National History in Modern China." *History and Theory* 37 (3): 287–308.

DuBois, Ellen Carol, and Katie Oliviero. 2009. "Circling the Globe: International Feminism Reconsidered, 1920 to 1975." *Women's Studies International Forum* 32 (1): 1–3.

Edgerton-Tarpley, Kathryn. 2004. "Family and Gender in Famine: Cultural Responses to Disaster in North China, 1876–1879." *Journal of Women's History* 16 (4): 119–47.

Edwards, Louise. 1994. *Men and Women in Qing China: Gender in The Red Chamber Dream*. New York: E. J. Brill.

Edwards, Louise. 2002. "Coopting the Chinese Women's Suffrage Movement for the Fifth Modernisation—Democracy." *Asian Studies Review* 26 (3): 285–307.

Edwards, Louise. 2003. "Liu-Wang Liming." In *BDCW*, 374–76.

Edwards, Louise. 2008. *Gender, Politics, and Democracy: Women's Suffrage in China*. Stanford, CA: Stanford University Press.

Edwards, Louise. 2012. "Women Sex-spies: Chastity, National Dignity, Legitimate Government and Ding Ling's 'When I Was in Xia Village.'" *China Quarterly* 212 (December): 1059–78.

Edwards, Louise. 2020. "Commemorating China's Wartime Spies: Red Agents Guan Lu and Jiang Zhuyun, and the Problem of Female Fidelity." *Women Warriors and National Heroes: Global Histories*, edited by Joan Judge and Adrian Shubert, 217–32. London: Bloomsbury Collections.

Eisenstadt, Shmuel Noah. 1973. *Traditional Patrimonialism and Modern Neopatrimonialism*. Beverly Hills, CA: Sage.

Eisenstein, Hester. 1996. *Inside Agitators: Australian Femocrats and the State*. Philadelphia: Temple University Press.

Endicott, Mary Austin, and Jim Endicott. 1953. *Five Stars Over China: The Story of Our Return to New China*. Toronto: Self-Published.

Enloe, Cynthia. 1989. *Bananas, Beaches, and Bases: Making Feminist Sense of International Politics.* Berkeley: University of California Press.

Epstein, Israel. 1993. *Woman in World History: Life and Times of Soong Ching Ling (Mme. Sun Yatsen).* Beijing: New World Press.

Evans, Harriet. 1997. *Women and Sexuality in China: Female Sexuality and Gender since 1949.* New York: Continuum.

Evans, Harriet. 2008. *The Subject of Gender: Daughters and Mothers in Urban China.* Lanham, MD: Rowman & Littlefield.

Evans, Peter B. 1995. *Embedded Autonomy: States and Industrial Transformation.* Princeton, NJ: Princeton University Press.

Eyferth, Jacob. 2015. "Liberation from the Loom? Rural Women, Textile Work, and Revolution in North China." In *Maoism at the Grassroots: Everyday Life in China's Era of High Socialism,* edited by Jeremy Brown and Matthew D. Johnson, 131–53. Cambridge, MA: Harvard University Press.

Fang Hongjiao and Zhou Jintao. 2008. "Minguo shiqi guomindang gaocen zhengzhi nüxing de zhengzhi quxiang yu shenfen—Song Qingling, He Xiangning wei xushu zhongxin" [The political orientation and identity of high-level GMD political women of the Republican Era—Song Qingling and He Xiangning as the narrative center]. In *Shehui kexue ji kan* [Social Science Journal] 3 (176): 133–40.

Fang Weizhong and Jin Chongji, eds. 2001. *Li Fuchun chunzhuan* [Biography of Li Fuchun]. Beijing: Zhongyang wenxian chubanshe.

Fang Xiaoping. 2017. "Bamboo Steamers and Red Flags: Building Discipline and Collegiality among China's Traditional Rural Midwives in the 1950s." *China Quarterly* 230: 420–43.

Fei Honghuan. 1998. "Zhou Enlai hunlianguan chutan" [Zhou Enlai's Perception of Marriage and Love]. *Dang de wenxian* [Documents of the Party] 3 (1): 57–61.

Ferlanti, Federica. 2012. "The New Life Movement at War: Wartime Mobilisation and State Control in Chongqing and Chengdu, 1938–1942." *European Journal of East Asian Studies* 11 (2): 187–212.

Fernea, Elizabeth W. 2003. "Family Feminism or Individual Feminism? Different Histories, Different Paths to Gender Equity." *Hawwa Journal of Women in the Middle East and Islamic World* 1 (2): 131–51.

Ferree, Myra Marx. 1992. "The Political Context of Rationality: Rational Choice Theory and Resource Mobilization." In *Frontiers in Social Movement Theory,* edited by Aldon D. Morris and Carol McClurge Mueller, 29–52. New Haven, CT: Yale University Press.

Ferree, Myra Marx. 2004. "Soft Repression: Ridicule, Stigma, and Silencing in Gender-Based Movements." In *Authority in Contention,* edited by Daniel J. Myers and Daniel M. Cress, 138–55. Boston: Elsevier.

Feuerwerker, Yi'tsi Mei. 2003. "Ding Ling." In *BDCW,* 138–44.

Fleschenberg, Andrea. 2009. "A Leader-in-Waiting—Female Political Leadership in Burma." In *The Gender Face of Asian Politics,* edited by Aazar Ayaz and Andrea Fleschenberg, 138–62. Oxford: Oxford University Press.

Fong, Vanessa 2004. "Filial Nationalism among Chinese Teenagers with Global Identities." *American Ethnologist* 31 (4): 631–48.

Forster, Keith. 1997. "Localism, Central Policy, and the Provincial Purges of 1957–1958: The Case of Zhejiang." In *New Perspectives on State Socialism in China,* edited by Timothy Cheek and Tony Saich, 191–233. New York: Routledge.

Friedman, Edward, Paul Pickowicz, and Mark Selden. 2005. *Revolution, Resistance and Reform in Village China.* New Haven, CT: Yale University Press.

Friedman, Edward, Paul Pickowicz, Mark Selden, and Kay Ann Johnson. 1991. *Chinese Village, Socialist State*. New Haven, CT: Yale University Press.

Frödin, Olle Jonas. 2012. "Dissecting the State: Towards a Relational Conceptualization of States and State Failure." *Journal of International Development* 24 (3): 271–86.

Fu Hualing. 2014. "Mediation and the Rule of Law: The Chinese Landscape." In *Formalisation and Flexibilisation in Dispute Resolution*, edited by Joachim Zekoll, Moritz Bälz, and Iwo Amelung, 108–29. Boston: Brill.

Fu Lien-Chang. 1953. "Learning from Advanced Soviet Medicine. *Chinese Medical Journal* 7 (4): 241–47.

Fukuyama, Francis. 2013. "What Is Governance?" *Governance: An International Journal of Policy, Administration, and Institutions* 26 (3): 347–68.

Funnell, Victor. 1970. "The Chinese Communist Youth Movement, 1949–1966." *China Quarterly* 42 (April–June): 105–30.

Gao Hua. 2018. *How the Red Sun Rose: The Origins and Development of the Yan'an Rectification Movement, 1930–1945*. Translated by Stacy Mosher and Jian Guo. Hong Kong: Chinese University Press.

Gao Wangling. 2011. "A Study of Chinese Peasant 'Counter-Action.'" In *Eating Bitterness: New Perspectives on China's Great Leap Forward and Famine*, edited by Kimberley Ens Manning and Felix Wemheuer, 272–94. Vancouver: University of British Colombia Press.

Gao Wenqian. 2007. *Zhou Enlai: The Last Perfect Revolutionary*. Translated by Peter Rand and Lawrence R. Sullivan. New York: Public Affairs.

Gao Xiaoxian. 2006. "'The Silver Flower Contest': Rural Women in 1950s China and the Gendered Division of Labour." *Gender & History* 18 (3): 594–612.

Gao Yunxiang. 2006. "Nationalist and Feminist Discourses on Jianmei (Robust Beauty) during China's 'National Crisis' in the 1930s." *Gender & History* 18 (3): 546–73.

Ghodsee, Kristen. 2019. *Second World, Second Sex*. Durham, NC: Duke University Press.

Ghosh, Arunabh. 2020. *Making It Count: Statistics and Statecraft in the Early People's Republic of China*. Princeton, NJ: Princeton University Press.

Gill, Graeme. 2011. *Symbols and Legitimacy in Soviet Politics*. New York: Cambridge University Press.

Gilmartin, Christina K. 1990. "Violence Against Women in Contemporary China." In *Violence in China: Essays in Culture and Counterculture*, edited by Jonathan N. Lipman and Stevan Harrell, 203–25. Albany: State University of New York Press.

Gilmartin, Christina K. 1995. *Engendering the Chinese Revolution: Radical Women, Communist Politics, and Mass Movements in the 1920s*. Berkeley: University of California Press.

Gilmartin, Christina K. 2003. "Wang Huiwu." In *BDCW*, 534–35.

Glosser, Susan L. 2003. *Chinese Visions of Family and State, 1915–1953*. Berkeley: University of California Press.

Goffman, Erving. 1963. *Stigma: Notes on the Management of Spoiled Identity*. Englewood Cliffs, NJ: Prentice-Hall.

Gold, Thomas, Doug Guthrie, and David Wank. 2002. "An Introduction to the Study of Guanxi." In *Social Connections in China: Institutions, Culture, and the Changing Nature of Guanxi*, edited by Thomas Gold, Doug Guthrie and David Wank, 3–20. New York: Cambridge University Press.

Goldstein, Joshua S. 1998. "Scissors, Surveys, and Psycho-Prophylactics." *Journal of Historical Sociology* 11 (2): 153–84.

Goodman, David. 2000. "Revolutionary Women and Women in the Revolution." *China Quarterly* 163 (September): 915–42.

Goodwin, Jeff. 1997. "The Libidinal Constitution of a High-Risk Social Movement: Affectual Ties and Solidarity in the Huk Rebellion, 1946 to 1954." *American Sociological Review* 62 (1): 53–69.

Goodwin, Jeff, and Steven Pfaff. 2001. "Emotion Work in High-Risk Social Movements: Managing Fear in the U.S. and East German Civil Rights Movement." In *Passionate Politics: Emotions and Social Movements*, edited by Jeff Goodwin, James M. Jasper, and Francesca Polletta, 282–302. Chicago: University of Chicago Press.

Gorski, Philip S. 2003. *The Disciplinary Revolution: Calvinism and the Rise of the State in Early Modern Europe*. Chicago: University of Chicago Press.

Gould, Deborah B. 2009. *Moving Politics: Emotion and Act Up's Fight Against AIDS*. Chicago: University of Chicago Press.

Grammatico, Karin. 2010. "Populist Continuities in "Revolutionary" Peronism? A Comparative Analysis of the Gender Discourses of the First Peronism (1946–1955) and the Montoneros." In *Gender and Populism in Latin America: Passionate Politics*, edited by Karen Kampwirth, 122–39. University Park: Pennsylvania State University Press.

Greenhalgh, Susan, and Edwin A. Winckler. 2005. *Governing China's Population: From Leninist to Neoliberal Biopolitics*. Stanford, CA: Stanford University Press.

Gu Xiulian. 2013. *20 Shiji Zhongguo funü yundong shi (zhongjuan)* [The history of the twentieth-century women's movement in China. Vol. 2]. Beijing: Zhongguo funü chubanshe.

Guo Huayi. 2004. "Deng Yingchao." In *TR*, 77–107.

Guo, Vivienne Xiangwei 2019. *Women and Politics in Wartime China: Networking Across Geopolitical Borders*. London: Routledge.

Guy, Donna J. 2009. *Women Build the Welfare State: Performing Charity and Creating Rights in Argentina, 1880–1955*. Durham, NC: Duke University Press.

Haggis, Jane. 1998. "'Good Wives and Mothers' or 'Dedicated Workers'? Contradictions of Domesticity in the 'Mission of Sisterhood,' Tranvancore, South India." In *Maternities and Modernities: Colonial and Postcolonial Experiences in Asia and the Pacific*, edited by Kalpana Ram and Margaret Jolly, 81–113. New York: Cambridge University Press.

Hercus, Cheryl. 1999. "Identity, Emotion, and Feminist Collective Action." *Gender & Society* 13 (1): 34–55.

Hershatter, Gail. 1997. *Dangerous Pleasures: Prostitution and Modernity in Twentieth-Century Shanghai*. Berkeley: University of California Press.

Hershatter, Gail. 2011. *The Gender of Memory: Rural Women and China's Collective Past*. Vol. 8. Berkeley: University of California Press.

Hicken, Allen. 2011. "Clientelism." *American Review of Political Science* 14: 289–310.

Hill, Patricia R. 1996. *The World Their Household: The American Woman's Foreign Mission Movement and Cultural Transformation, 1870–1920*. Ann Arbor: University of Michigan Press.

Hillman, Ben. 2014. *Local State Networks and Party-State Resilience in Rural China*. Stanford, CA: Stanford University Press.

Hochschild, Arlie Russell. 1975. "The Sociology of Feeling and Emotion: Selected Possibilities." In *Another Voice*, edited by Marcia Millman and Rosabeth Moss Kanter, 80–307. Garden City, NY: Anchor Books.

Hochschild, Arlie Russell. 1983 [2012]. *The Managed Heart: Commercialization of Human Feeling.* Berkeley: University of California Press.

Hoffman, David L. 2011. *Cultivating the Masses: Modern State Practices and Soviet Socialism, 1914–1939.* Ithaca, NY: Cornell University Press.

Honig, Emily. 1986. *Sisters and Strangers: Women in the Shanghai Cotton Mills, 1919–1949.* Stanford, CA: Stanford University Press.

Honig, Emily. 1996. "Christianity, Feminism, and Communism: The Life and Times of Deng Yuzhi." In *Christianity in China: from the Eighteenth Century to the Present,* edited by Daniel H. Bays, 243–62. Stanford, CA: Stanford University Press.

Honig, Emily. 2015. "The Life of a Slogan." In *Gender and Chinese History: Transformative Encounters,* edited by Beverly Jo Bossler, 185–207. Seattle: University of Washington Press.

Hou Rui. 2020. "Maintaining Social Stability without Solving Problems: Emotional Repression in the Chinese Petition System." *China Quarterly* 243: 635–54.

Hou Xiaojia. 2016. *Negotiating Socialism in Rural China: Mao, Peasants, and Local Cadres, in Shanxi, 1949–1953.* Ithaca, NY: Cornell University Press.

Htun, Mala. 2003. *Sex and the State: Abortion, Divorce, and the Family Under Latin American Dictatorships and Democracies.* New York: Cambridge University Press.

Hu Yongheng. 2017. "Desperate Fighting: Divorce Petitions of Soldiers' Spouses in the Communist Base Areas during the War of Resistance." *Journal of Modern Chinese History* 11 (2): 303–22.

Huang Biping. 2004. "Cai Chang." In *TR,* 43–75.

Huang Daoxuan. 2019. "Disciplined Love: The Chinese Communist Party's Wartime Restrictions on Cadre Love and Marriage." *Journal of Modern Chinese History* 13 (1): 61–75.

Huang Jing. 2000. *Factionalism in Chinese Communist Politics.* New York: Cambridge University Press.

Huang, Phillip. 2005. "Divorce Law Practices and the Origins, Myths, and Realities of Judicial 'Mediation' in China." *Modern China* 31 (2): 151–203.

Huang Qizao. 1997. "Zhongguo funü de guanghui kaimo" [A glorious model for Chinese women]. In *QJ,* 124–27.

Hubbard, Joshua A. 2018. "The 'Torch of Motherly Love': Women and Maternalist Politics." *Twentieth-Century China* 43 (3): 251–69.

Hunan sheng weitonggao. 1927 [1991]. "Hunan sheng weitonggao (di yishisi hao), guanyu Hunan funü de xian zhuang ji jinhou yundong de fangzhen" [Hunan provincial committee (notice number fourteen), the situation of women in Hunan Province and guidelines for later movements]." In *ZFYLZ (1927–1937),* 8–10.

Hunt, Lynn. 1992. *The Family Romance of the French Revolution.* Berkeley: University of California Press.

Hunter, Jane. 1984. *The Gospel of Gentility.* New Haven, CT: Yale University Press.

Ibrahim, Jibrin. 2004. "The First Lady Syndrome and the Marginalisation of Women from Power: Opportunities or Compromises for Gender Equality." *Feminist Africa* 3 (September): 48–69.

Jacka, Tamara. 1997. *Women's Work in Rural China: Change and Continuity in an Era of Reform.* New York: Cambridge University Press.

Jasper, James M. 1997. *The Art of Moral Protest: Culture, Biography, and Creativity in Social Movements.* Chicago: University of Chicago Press.

Jasper, James M. 1998. "The Emotions of Protest: Affective and Reactive Emotions in and around Social Movements." *Sociological Forum* 13 (3): 397–424.

Ji Rong, ed. 1992. *Zhongguo funü yundong shi* [The history of the Chinese women's movement]. Changsha: Hunan chubanshe.

Jia Shucun. 2012. "Feng Yuxiang jituan yu Li Dequan jiazu" [The Feng Yuxiang group and Li Dequan clan]. *Shoudu shifan daxue xuebao* (*Shehui kexue ban*) [Journal of Capital Normal University (Social Sciences Edition)] 207 (4): 15–20.

Jiang Xinhui and Yunyun Zhou. 2021. "Coalition-Based Gender Lobbying: Revisiting Women's Substantive Representation in China's Authoritarian Governance." *Politics and Gender*: 1–33.

Jin Feng. 1993. *Deng Yingchao zhuan* [Biography of Deng Yingchao]. 2 vols. Beijing: Renmin chubanshe.

Jin Qiu. 1999. *The Culture of Power: The Lin Biao Incident in the Cultural Revolution.* Stanford, CA: Stanford University Press.

Jin Yihong. 2006. "Rethinking the 'Iron Girls': Gender and Labour during the Chinese Cultural Revolution." *Gender & History* 18 (3): 613–34.

Johnson, Kay Ann. 1983. *Women, the Family, and Peasant Revolution in China.* Chicago: University of Chicago Press.

Johnson, Tina Phillips. 2011. *Childbirth in Republican China: Delivering Modernity.* Lanham, MD: Lexington Books.

Johnson, Tina Phillips, Elizabeth Littell-Lamb, and Kimberley Ens Manning. 2018. "Maternalist Internationalism: Women's Leadership in China's Cold War Struggles (1949–1995)." *Chinese Women in World History*, Taiwan.

Joseph, Suad. 2011. "Political Familism in Lebanon." *The Annals of the American Academy of Political and Social Science* 636 (1): 150–63.

Judd, Ellen R. 1989. "Niangjia: Chinese Women and Their Natal Families." *Journal of Asian Studies* 48 (3): 525–44.

Judd, Ellen R. 1998. "Reconsidering China's Marriage Law Campaign: Toward a De-orientalised Feminist Perspective." *Asian Journal of Women's Studies* 4 (2): 8–26.

Judge, Joan. 2001. "Talent, Virtue and the Nation: Chinese Nationalisms and Female Subjectivities in the Early Twentieth Century." *American Historical Review* 106 (3): 765–803.

Judge, Joan. 2008. *The Precious Raft of History: The Past, the West, and the Woman Question in China.* Stanford, CA: Stanford University Press.

Kampen, Thomas. 2000. *Mao Zedong, Zhou Enlai, and the Evolution of the Chinese Communist Leadership.* Copenhagen: NIAS Publishing.

Kampwirth, Karen. 2002. *Women and Guerrilla Movements: Nicaragua, El Salvador, Chiapas, Cuba.* University Park, PA: Pennsylvania State University Press.

Kampwirth, Karen. 2004. *Feminism and the Legacy of Revolution: Nicaragua, El Salvador, and Chiapas.* Athens: Center for International Studies, Ohio University.

Kampwirth, Karen. 2010. "Populism and the Feminist Challenge in Nicaragua: The Return of Daniel Ortega." In *Gender and Populism in Latin America: Passionate Politics*, edited by Karen Kampwirth, 162–79. University Park: Pennsylvania State University Press.

Kaplan, Caren, Norma Alarcón, and Minoo Moallem, eds. 1999. *Between Woman and Nation: Nationalisms, Transnational Feminisms, and the State.* Durham, NC: Duke University Press.

Kang Keqing. 1949 [1997]. "Guanyu ertong baoyu gongzuo de yijian" [Thoughts on child welfare work]. In *Kang Keqing Wenji* [Anthology of Kang Keqing's Writings], edited by ACWF, 23–28. Beijing: Zhongguo funü chubanshe.

Kang Keqing. 1952 [1997]. "Heping dui haizi yiweizhe shenme" [What peace means to children]. In *Kang Keqing Wenji* [Anthology of Kang Keqing's Writings], edited by ACWF, 69–73. Beijing: Zhongguo funü chubanshe.

Kang Keqing. 1958. "Wei shenme yao qiangdiao haizi quan tuo, xiao xuesheng zhuxiao?" [Why emphasize that young children should board in nurseries, and that primary school pupils live at school?]. *WW* 21: 9–11.

Kang Keqing. 1977 [1988]. "Mao zhuxi shuailing women zou funü chedi jiefang de daolu" [Chairman Mao leads us on the path of complete women's emancipation]. In *ZFYWZH*, 2:430–37.

Kang Keqing. 1993. *Kang Keqing huiyi lu* [Kang Keqing's memoirs]. Beijing: Jiefang jun chubanshe.

Kang Keqing. 1997. "Jiechu de shehui huodongjia—Li Dequan tongzhi" [A brilliant activist—comrade Li Dequan]." In *QJ*, 118–23.

Kang Wenqing. 2022. "Seeking Pleasure in Peril: Male Same-Sex Relations during the Cultural Revolution." *Positions-East Asia Cultures Critique* 30 (1): 61–84.

Kantola, Johanna. 2006. *Feminists Theorize the State*. New York: Palgrave Macmillan.

Keith, Molly. 1949. "How This Pamphlet Came to Be Written." In *British Woman in China*, edited by Marian Ramelson, 2–3. London: British Committee, Women's International Democratic Federation.

Kennelly, Jacqueline Joan. 2009. "Youth Cultures, Activism, and Agency: Revisiting Feminist Debates." *Gender and Education* 21 (3): 259–72.

Key, Ellen Karolina Sofia. 1911. *Love and Marriage*. New York: Putnam.

King, Richard. 2011. "Romancing the Leap: Euphoria in the Moment before Disaster." In *Eating Bitterness: New Perspectives on China's Great Leap Forward and Famine*, edited by Kimberley Ens Manning and Felix Wemheuer, 51–71. Vancouver: University of British Colombia Press.

Kingdon, John W. 2003. *Agendas, Alternatives, and Public Policies*. 2nd ed. New York: Longman.

Kipnis, Andrew B. 1997. *Producing Guanxi: Sentiment, Self, and Subculture in a North China Village*. Durham, NC: Duke University Press.

Klatch, Rebecca E. 2004. "The Underside of Social Movements: The Effects of Destructive Affective Ties." *Qualitative Sociology* 27 (4): 487–509.

Klein, Donald W., and Anne B. Clark. 1971. *Biographic Dictionary of Chinese Communism, 1921–1965*. 2 vols. Cambridge, MA: Harvard University Press.

Ko, Dorothy. 1994. *Teachers of the Inner Chambers: Women and Culture in Seventeenth-Century China*. Stanford: Stanford University Press.

Koikari, Mire. 2008. *Pedagogy of Democracy: Feminism and the Cold War in the U.S. Occupation of Japan*. Philadelphia, PA: Temple University Press.

Koven, Seth, and Sonya Michel. 1990. "Womanly Duties: Maternalist Politics and the Origins of Welfare States in France, Germany, Great Britain, and the United States, 1880–1920." *American Historical Review* 95 (4): 1076–1108.

Koven, Seth, and Sonya Michel. 1993. "Introduction." In *Mothers of a New World: Maternalist Politics and the Origins of Welfare States*, edited by Seth Koven and Sonya Michel, 1–42. London: Routledge.

Krohn-Hansen, Christian, and Knut G. Nustad. 2005. "Introduction." In *State Formation: Anthropological Perspectives*, edited by Christian Krohn-Hansen and Knut G. Nustad, 3–26. Ann Arbor: Pluto Press.

Kueh, Y. Y. 2006. "Mao and Agriculture in China's Industrialization: Three Antitheses in a 50-year Perspective." *China Quarterly* 187 (September): 700–723.

Kuhonta, Erik Martinez, Dan Slater, and Tuong Vu. 2008. *Southeast Asia in Political Science: Theory, Region, and Qualitative Analysis.* Stanford, CA: Stanford University Press.

Kung, James Kai-Sing, and Shuo Chen. 2011. "The Tragedy of the Nomenklatura: Career Incentives and Political Radicalism During China's Great Leap Famine." *American Political Science Review* 105 (1): 27–45.

Kutcher, Norman. 1999 [2009]. *Mourning in Late Imperial China: Filial Piety and the State.* New York: Cambridge University Press.

Kwok Pui-Lan. 1992. *Chinese Women and Christianity: 1860–1927.* Atlanta, GA: Scholar's Press.

Kwok Pui-Lan. 1996. "Chinese Women and Protestant Christianity at the Turn of the Twentieth Century." In *Christianity in China: From the Eighteenth Century to the Present,* edited by Daniel H. Bays, 194–208. Stanford, CA: Stanford University Press.

Ladd-Taylor, Molly. 1993. "Toward Defining Maternalism in U.S. History." *Journal of Women's History* 5 (2): 110–13.

Ladd-Taylor, Molly. 1994. *Mother-Work: Women, Child Welfare, and the State, 1890–1930.* Vol. 159. Champaign: University of Illinois Press.

Lampton, David M. 1977. *The Politics of Medicine in China: The Policy Process, 1949–1977.* Boulder, CO: Westview Press.

Lampton, David M. 1992. "A Plum for a Peach: Bargaining, Interest, and Bureaucratic Politics in China." In *Bureaucracy, Politics, and Decision Making in Post-Mao China,* edited by Kenneth G. Lieberthal and David M. Lampton, 33–91. Berkeley: University of California Press.

Lan Hua R. and Vanessa L. Fong, eds. 1999. *Women in Republican China: A Sourcebook.* New York: M. E. Sharpe.

Lanzona, Vina A. 2009. *Amazons of the Huk Rebellion: Gender, Sex, and Revolution in the Philippines.* Madison: University of Wisconsin Press.

Latourette, Kenneth Scott. 1967. *A History of Christian Missions in China.* New York: Russell and Russell.

Lead Party Group of the ACDWF. 1953. "Quanguo fulian dangzu guanyu jidujiao nü qingnian hui xiang zhongyang de baogao; Zhonghua funü jiezhi hui quanguo zongjie gaikuang" [The ACDWF's Lead Party Group's report to the CC on the YWCA; Overview of the National Association of the WCTU] 1031–1–6. CMA.

Lee Ching Kwan and Yang Guobin. 2007. "Introduction: Memory, Power, and Culture." In *Re-envisioning the Chinese Revolution: The Politics and Poetics of Collective Memories in the Reform Era,* edited by Lee Ching Kwan and Yang Guobin, 1–20. Stanford, CA: Stanford University Press.

Lee Haiyan. 2007. *Revolution of the Heart: A Genealogy of Love in China, 1900–1950.* Stanford, CA: Stanford University Press.

Lee, Lily Xiao Hong. 2003a. "Deng Yuzhi." In *BDCW,* 135–37.

Lee, Lily Xiao Hong. 2003b. "He Xiangning." In *BDCW,* 200–204.

Lee, Lily Xiao Hong. 2003c. "Jiang Qing." In *BDCW,* 258–64.

Lee, Lily Xiao Hong 2003d. "Shi Liang." In *BDCW,* 450–55.

Lee, Lily Xiao Hong. 2003e. "Song Qingling." In *BDCW,* 466–74.

Lee, Lily Xiao Hong, and Sue Wiles. 1999. *Women of the Long March.* St. Leonards: Allen and Unwin.

Leese, Daniel. 2011. *Mao Cult: Rhetoric and Ritual in China's Cultural Revolution.* New York: Cambridge University Press.

Lei Jieqiong. 1990. "Huainian Yang Chongrui yishi [In memory of Dr. Yang Chongrui]." In *Yang Chongrui boshi—Danchen bainian jinian* [Dr. Yang Chongrui—remembrance on the occasion of the 100th anniversary of her birth], edited by Yan Renqing, 1–3. Beijing: Beijing yike daxue he Zhongguo xiehe yike daxue lianhe chubanshe.

Lei Zhifang. 1990. "Wo guo jihua shengyu de tuohuangzhe" [A Pioneer For China's Birth Control]." In *Yang Chongrui boshi—Danchen bainian jinian* [Dr. Yang Chongrui—remembrance on the occasion of the 100th anniversary of her birth], edited by Yan Renying, 15–19. Beijing: Beijing yike daxue he Zhongguo xiehe yike daxue lianhe chubanshe.

Li Baoguang. 1992. "Shenqing huainian Cai dajie" [Fondly remembering elder sister Cai]. In *WHDCC*, 72–78.

Li, Danke. 2010. *Echoes of Chongqing: Women in Wartime China*. Champaign: University of Illinois Press.

Li Dequan. 1943 [1991]. "Zhanshi funü wenti" [Problems of women during wartime]. In *ZFYLZ (1937–1945)*, edited by Wang Menglan, 728–32. Beijing: Zhongguo funu chubanshe.

Li Dequan. 1952. "Health for All the People." *China Reconstructs* January 1 (1): 14–20.

Li Dequan. 1955 [1999]. "Zai shijie muqin dahui shang de fayan" [Speech given at the World Mother's Conference]." In *ZFWN*, *E13–15*.

Li Dequan. 1957 [1965]. "Birth Control and Planned Families." In *Communist China, 1955–1959: Policy Documents with Analysis*, edited by Harvard University Joint Auspices of the Center for International Affairs and the East Asian Research Center, 295–99. Cambridge, MA: Harvard University Press.

Li Dequan. 1959. "Guanxin funü jiankang baochi wangsheng ganjin" [Take care of women's health in order to protect their exuberant spirit]." *Women of China* 3: 1–2.

Li Dequan. 1960. "Liji ba chu hai mie bing yundong tui xiang xin gaochao" [Immediately push the campaign of eliminating pests and diseases to a new climax]. *WW* 2: 2–3.

Li Fuchun and Bo Yibo. 1957 [1992]. "Jiu muqian jianshe zhong de wenti gei Mao Zedong de baogao" [A report submitted to Mao Zedong on current issues with construction]." In *Li Fuchun xuanji* [Li Fuchun's Anthology], 190–96. Beijing: Zhongguo jihua chubanshe.

Li Honghe. 2014. "Xin zhongguo chengli chuqi de jiu chanpo gaizao" [The reform of old midwives in the earliest period of the founding of New China]. *Zhonggong dang shi yanjiu* [CCP Historical Research] (6): 64–73.

Li Honghe and Li Anshan. 2015. "Xin zhongguo chengli chuqi Li Dequan de yiliao weisheng sixiang he shijian tanxi" [An analysis of the medical thought and practical analysis of Li Dequan]." *Zhongguo Pudong ganbu xueyuan xuebao* [The Pudong China Cadre Institute Journal]. 9 (3): 59–65.

Li Wei. 1997. "Cai Chang jiaowang yishi" [Anecdotes of Cai Chang]. *Renwu* [Personages] 1 (101).

Li Wei and Wilson Wong. 2020. "Advocacy Coalitions, Policy Stability, and Policy Change in China: The Case of Birth Control Policy, 1980–2015." *Policy Studies Journal* 48 (3): 645–71.

Li Yingtao. 2007. "Women, Marriage, and International Relations." In *Bonds across Borders*, edited by Priscilla Roberts and He Peiqun, 159–75. Newcastle, UK: Cambridge Scholars Publishing.

Li Yinhe. 2006. "Regulating Male Same-Sex Relationships in the People's Republic of China." In *Sex and Sexuality in China*, edited by Elaine Jeffreys, 82–101. London: Routledge.

Li Zhisui. 1994. *The Private Life of Chairman Mao*. New York: Random House.

Li Zhuanjun and Zhang Zhi. 2007. "Li Dequan." In *Zhonggongdang shi renwu zhuan* [Biographies of personages from CCP history, Vol. 86], edited by Zhongguo zhonggongdang shi renwu yanjiu hui [The research committee on historical personages of the CCP], 271–340. Beijing: Zhongyang wenxian chubanshe.

Lieberthal, Kenneth G. 1992. "Introduction: The 'Fragmented Authoritarianism' Model and Its Limitations." In *Bureaucracy, Politics, and Decision-Making in Post-Mao China*, edited by Kenneth G. Lieberthal and David M. Lampton, 1–31. Berkeley: University of California Press.

Lieberthal, Kenneth G. 1993. "The Great Leap Forward and the Split in the Yan'an Leadership 1958–1965." In *Politics of China 1949–1989*, edited by Roderick MacFarquhar, 87–147. New York: Cambridge University Press.

Lieberthal, Kenneth G. 1995. *Governing China: From Revolution through Reform*. New York: W. W. Norton.

Lieberthal, Kenneth G., and Michel Oksenberg. 1988. *Policy Making in China: Leaders, Structures, and Processes*. Princeton, NJ: Princeton University Press.

Lim Kha-ti [Lin Qiaozhi]. 1953. "Painless Childbirth." *China Reconstructs* 2 (3): 375–83.

Lim Kha-ti [Lin Qiaozhi]. 1959. "Obstetrics and Gynecology in Past Ten Years." *Chinese Medical Journal* 79 (5): 375–83.

Lim, Louisa. 2014. *The People's Republic of Amnesia: Tiananmen Revisited*. New York: Oxford University Press.

Lin Qiaozhi. 1964. "Biyun, rengong liuchan he shuluanguan jieza shu de ji ge wenti" [Issues with contraception, abortion, and tubal ligation]. *Renmin junyi* [The People's Military Medicine] (5): 32–37.

Littell-Lamb, Elizabeth. 2010. "Localizing the Global: The YWCA Movement in China, 1899 to 1939." In *Women and Transnational Activism in Historical Perspective*, edited by Kimberly Jensen and Erika Kuhlman, 63–87. Dordrecht, Netherlands: Republic of Letters Publishing.

Littell-Lamb, Elizabeth. 2011. "Caught in the Crossfire: Women's Internationalism and the YWCA Child Labor Campaign in Shanghai, 1921–1925." *Frontiers: A Journal of Women's Studies* 32 (3): 134–66.

Liu Dongxiao. 2006. "When Do National Movements Adopt or Reject International Agendas? A Comparative Analysis of the Chinese and Indian Women's Movements." *American Sociological Review* 71 (6): 921–42.

Liu, He Lydia, Rebecca E. Karl, and Dorothy Ko, eds. 2013. *The Birth of Chinese Feminism: Essential Texts in Transnational Theory*. New York: Columbia University Press.

Liu Heng. 1984. "Qishi funü jiushi qishi ni ziji de muqin" [Discriminating against women means discriminating against your own mother]. *People's Daily*, January 19, 1984.

Liu Jialin. 1958. "Youguan funü xuanchuan gongzuo de ji ge wenti" [Several questions regarding women's propaganda work]. *WW* 16: 13–20.

Liu Jiaquan. 1988. *Song Qingling zhuan* [The Biography of Song Qingling]. Beijing: Beijing chubanshe.

Liu Jucai. 1995. *Li Dequan de gushi* [Stories about Li Dequan]. Shijiazhuang: Hebei shaonian ertong chubanshe.

Liu, Judith, and Donald P. Kelly. 1996. "'An Oasis in a Heathen Land': St. Hilda's School for Girls, 1928–1936." In *Christianity in China: From the Eighteenth*

Century to the Present, edited by Daniel H. Bays, 228–42. Stanford, CA: Stanford University Press.

Liu Shaoqi. 1946 [1984]. "Directive on the Land Question." In *Selected Works of Liu Shaoqi*, 372–78. Beijing: Foreign Languages Press.

Liu Shaoqi. 1954 [1997]. "Tichang jieyu" [Promote Birth Control]. In *ZJSQ*, 146–47.

Liu Shaoqi. 1958 [1965]. "The Present Situation, the Party's General Line for Socialist Construction and Its Future Tasks." In *Communist China, 1955–1959: Policy Documents and Analysis*, edited by Harvard University Joint Auspices of the Center for International Affairs and the East Asian Research Center, 417–49. Cambridge, MA: Harvard University Press.

Liu Weifang. 2008. "Zhongguo funü yundong 'da yuejin' shimo" [The story of the Chinese women's movement's through the GLF]." *Zhonghua nüzi xueyuan xuebao* [Chinese Women's Studies Institute Journal] 20 (5): 104–5.

Liu Yu. 2006. "Why Did It Go So High? Political Mobilization and Agricultural Collectivization in China." *China Quarterly* 187 (September): 737–42.

Liu Yu. 2010. "Maoist Discourse and the Mobilization of Emotions in Revolutionary China." *Modern China* 36 (3): 329–62.

Liu Zhi. 1992. "Cai dajie he women lian xin" [Our hearts are one with elder sister Cai]. In *WHDCC*, 112–17.

Lombardo, Emanuela, and Maxime Forest. 2015. "The Europeanization of Gender Equality Policies: A Discursive-Sociological Approach." *Comparative European Politics* 13 (2): 222–39.

Lombardo, Emanuela, Petra Meier, and Mieke Verloo, eds. 2009. *The Discursive Politics of Gender Equality: Stretching, Bending, and Policy-Making*. New York: Routledge.

Lü Xiaobo. 2000. *Cadres and Corruption: The Organizational Involution of the Chinese Communist Party*. Stanford, CA: Stanford University Press.

Lu Yong and Miao Yonghe, eds. 2000. *Jiangsu shengzhi—shehui tuanti zhi—funü tuanti pian* [Gazetteer of Jiangsu province—social groups annals—women's groups chapter]. Beijing: Fangzhi chubanshe.

Lubman, Stanley. 1967. "Mao and Mediation: Politics and Dispute Resolution in Communist China." *California Law Review* 55: 1284–1359.

Luciak, Ilja A. 2001. *After the Revolution: Gender and Democracy in El Salvador, Nicaragua, and Guatemala*. Baltimore: Johns Hopkins University Press.

Luo Qiong. 1936 [2000]. "Cong 'xianqi liangmu' dao 'xianfu liangfu'" [From good wives, wise mothers to good husbands, wise fathers]. In *Luo Qiong wenji* [The collected works of Luo Qiong], edited by Luo Qiong, 142–44. Beijing: Zhongguo funü chubanshe.

Luo Qiong. 1957 [1988]. "Tongguo baokan jingchang jinxing funü xuanchuan gongzuo" [Frequently promote women-work through journals]. In *ZFYWZH*, 2:276–81.

Luo Qiong. 1980 [1988]. "Guanyu guanche yi shengchan wei zhongxin de funü gongzuo fangzhen wenti (diyao)" [On the issue of carrying out production-centered women-work (excerpts)]. In *ZFYWZH*, 2:554–64.

Luo Qiong. 1983 [1997]. "Xuexi Cai dajie kaichuang funü jiefang xin jumian de geming jingshen" [Learning from elder sister Cai's pioneering women's liberation, (and the) revolutionary spirit of the new situation]. In *QJ*, 60–70.

Luo Qiong. 1989 [2000]. "Xiang Shen Zijiu dajie zhushou de shike" [Celebrating the birthday of elder sister Shen Zijiu]. In *LQW*, 209–19.

Luo Qiong. 1992. "*Cai dajie de jiaohui mingke xintou*" [Elder sister Cai's teachings are engraved in my heart]. In *WHDCC*, 45–52.

Luo Qiong. 1993. "Yili zai funü jiefang lingyu de fengbei" [A towering and monumental contribution in the field of women's liberation]. In *Huainian Deng Yingchao dajie* [In commemoration of elder sister Deng Yingchao], edited by Huang Qicao, 230–45. Beijing: Zhongguo funü chubanshe.

Luo Qiong. 1998a [2000]. "Deng Xiaoping tongzhi zai zhongyao de lishi shike dui funü gongzuo de zhiyin" [In crucial moments, comrade Deng Xiaoping always guided women-work]. In *LQW*, 49–67.

Luo Qiong. 1998b [2000]. "Liu Shaoqi tongzhi dui funü gongzuo de zhidao sixiang ji chenggong shijian" [On the guiding spirit and successful implementation of comrade Liu Shaoqi's ideas on women-work]. In *LQW*, 16–32.

Luo Qiong. 2002. "Luo Qiong tan xin Zhongguo di yi bu 'hunyin fa' qicao qianhou" [Luo Qiong discusses drafting the first "Marriage Law" in New China]. *Renmin ribao* [The People's Daily (Overseas edition)], March 22, 2002.

Luo Qiong, Huang Ganying, and Yang Yun. 1986 [1997]. "Zhe zhuo de wei zuguo de fazhi jianshe fendou: daonian Han Youtong tongzhi" [Struggling for the legal construction of the country: remembering comrade Han Youtong]. In *QJ*, 325–37.

Luo Qiong and Zuo Songfen. 1997. "Kangri jiuguo de nü junzi funü qunzhong de liangshi yiyou—yi Shi Liang dajie" [An Anti-Japanese war national salvation gentleman, good friend, and teacher of the women masses—remembering elder sister Shi Liang]. In *QJ*, 111–17.

Luo Yinan. 2021. "Re-Examining Theories on Factionalism in the Maoist Period: The Case of the Lushan Conference of 1959." *Modern China* (January): 1–32.

Luo Yuansheng. 2004. "Shuai Mengqi." In *TR*, 229–66.

Lüthi, Lorenz. 2008. *The Sino-Soviet Split: Cold War in the Communist World*. Princeton, NJ: Princeton University Press.

Ma Shexiang, ed. 2013. "*Mao Zemin furen Zhu Danhua fangtanlu*" [Interviews with Mao Zemin's spouse Zhu Danhua]. Beijing: Renmin wenxue chubanshe [People's literature publishing house].

Ma Yinchu. 1957 [1997]. "Xin renkou lun" [New population theory]. In *ZJSQ*, 551–57.

MacFarquhar, Roderick. 1983. *The Origins of the Cultural Revolution: The Great Leap Forward, 1958–1960*. Vol. 2. New York: Oxford University Press.

Mackay, Fiona. 2014. "Nested Newness, Institutional Innovation, and the Gendered Limits of Change." *Politics & Gender* 10 (4): 549–71.

MacKinnon, Stephen. 2001. "Refugee Flight at the Outset of the Anti-Japanese War." In *Scars of War: The Impact of Warfare on Modern China*, edited by Diana and Stephen MacKinnon Lary, 118–34. Vancouver: University of British Colombia Press.

Mahmood, Saba. 2005. *Politics of Piety: The Islamic Revival and the Feminist Subject*. Princeton, NJ: Princeton University Press.

Mair, Peter, and Case Mudde. 1998. "The Party Family and Its Study." *Annual Review of Political Science* 1 (1): 211–29.

Mann, Michael. 1986. "The Autonomous Power of the State: Its Origins, Mechanisms, and Results." In *States in History*, edited by John A. Hall, 109–36. Oxford: Basil Blackwell.

Mann, Susan L. 2005. "Biographies of Exemplary Women." In *Hawai'i Reader in Traditional Chinese Culture*, edited by Victor H. Mair, Nancy S. Steinhardt, and Paul R. Goldin, 607–13. Honolulu: University of Hawai'i Press.

Manning, Kimberley Ens. 2005. "Marxist Maternalism, Memory, and the Mobilization of Women in the Great Leap Forward." *China Review* 5 (1): 83–110.

Manning, Kimberley Ens. 2006a. "The Gendered Politics of Woman-work: Rethinking Radicalism in the Great Leap Forward." *Modern China* 32 (3): 349–84.

Manning, Kimberley Ens. 2006b. "Making a Great Leap Forward? The Politics of Women's Liberation in Maoist China." *Gender & History* 18 (3): 574–93.

Manning, Kimberley Ens. 2007. "Communes, Canteens, and Crèches: The Gendered Politics of Remembering the Great Leap Forward." In *Re-Envisioning the Chinese Revolution: The Politics and Poetics of Collective Memories in Reform China*, edited by Ching Kwan Lee and Guobin Yang, 93–118. Stanford, CA: Stanford University Press.

Manning, Kimberley Ens. 2010. "Embodied Activisms: The Case of the Mu Guiying Brigade." *China Quarterly* 204 (December): 850–69.

Manning, Kimberley Ens. 2011. "The Gendered Politics of Woman-Work: Rethinking Radicalism in the Great Leap Forward." In *Eating Bitterness: New Perspectives on China's Great Leap Forward and Famine*, edited by Kimberley Ens Manning and Felix Wemheuer, 72–106. Vancouver: University of British Colombia Press.

Manning, Kimberley Ens. 2017. "Attached Advocacy and the Rights of the Trans Child." *Canadian Journal of Political Science* 50 (2): 579–95.

Manning, Kimberley Ens. Forthcoming. "Ideological Intimacies: Grassroots Women's Leadership and the One-Child Policy." In *Oxford Handbook of East Asian Gender History*, edited by Barbara Molony, Hyaeweol Choi and Janet Theiss. Oxford: Oxford University Press.

Manning, Kimberley Ens, Cindy Holmes, Annie Pullen Sansfaçon, Julia Temple Newhook, and Anne Travers. 2015. "Fighting for Trans* Kids: Academic Parent Activism in the 21st Century." *Studies in Social Justice* 9 (1): 118–35.

Manning, Kimberley Ens, and Felix Wemheuer. 2011a. *Eating Bitterness: New Perspectives on China's Great Leap Forward and Famine*. Vancouver: University of British Colombia Press.

Manning, Kimberley Ens, and Felix Wemheuer. 2011b. "Introduction." In *Eating Bitterness: New Perspectives on China's Great Leap Forward and Famine*, edited by Kimberley Ens Manning and Felix Wemheuer, 1–27. Vancouver: University of British Colombia Press.

Mao Zedong. 1927 [1959]. "Report on an Investigation of the Peasant Movement in Hunan." In *Selected Works of Mao Zedong*, 21–59. London: Lawrence & Wishart.

Mao Zedong. 1933 [1995]. "Investigation of Changgang Township." In *Mao's Road to Power: Revolutionary Writings Vol. 4*, edited by Stuart Schram, 584–85. Armonk, NY: M. E. Sharpe.

Mao Zedong. 1936 [1992]. "To Feng Yuxiang." In *Mao's Road to Power: Revolutionary Writings, Vol. 5*, edited by Stuart Schram, 460–61. Armonk, NY: M. E. Sharpe.

Mao Zedong. 1939 [1991]. "Mao Zedong zai yan'an zhongguo nüzi daxue kaixue dianli shang de jianghua' [Mao Zedong's address at the opening of the Yan'an China Women's University]. In *ZFYLZ (1937–1945)*, 149–50.

Mao Zedong. 1942 [1996]. "Commentary G: Speech at the Yan'an Forum on Literature and Art (2 and 23 May 1942)." In *The Rise to Power of the Chinese Communist Party*, edited by Tony Saich, 1122–32. Armonk, NY: M. E. Sharpe.

Mao Zedong. 1948 [1991]. "Zhonggong zhongyang guanyu jiu yue huiyi de tongzhi (jielu)" [Notice on the September meeting, from the Central Committee of the CCP (excerpts)]. In *ZFYLZ (1937–1945)*, 289.

Mao Zedong. 1955 [1986]. "The Debate Over Agricultural Cooperativization and the Present Class Struggle." In *The Writings of Mao Zedong 1949–1976: Volume 1, September 1945-December 1955*, edited by Michael Y.M. Kau and John K. Leung, 629–54. Armonk, NY: M. E. Sharpe.

Mao Zedong. 1956 [1992]. "Speech at the Second Plenum of the Eighth Central Committee (November 15, 1956)." In *The Writings of Mao Zedong 1949–1976: Volume 2, January 1956-December 1957*, edited by John K. Leung and Michael Y.M. Kau, 158–95. Armonk, NY: M. E. Sharpe.

Mao Zedong. 1956 [1957]. "Women Joining in Production Solve the Labour Shortage." In *Socialist Upsurge in China's Countryside*, edited by the General Office of the Central Committee of the Chinese Communist Party, 285–86. Beijing: Foreign Languages Press.

Mao Zedong. 1957 [1992]. "Forward to: The Situation in the Summer of 1957." In *The Writings of Mao Zedong: Volume 2*, edited by John K. Leung and Michael Y.M. Kau, 653–62. Armonk: M. E. Sharpe.

Mao Zedong. 1958 [1989]. "Talks at the Wuchang Conference (November 21–23, 1958)." In *The Secret Speeches of Chairman Mao: From the Hundred Flowers to the Great Leap Forward*, edited and. translated by Roderick MacFarquhar et al., 456–65. Cambridge, MA: The Council of East Asian Studies, Harvard University.

Mao Zedong. 1961 [1974]. "Untitled Poem." In Mao Tse-Tung Unrehearsed; Talks and Letters: 1956-71, edited by Stuart Schram and translated by Joan Chinnery and Tieyun, 339. Hammondsworth: Penguin Books.

Marx, Karl. 1978. "The Eighteenth Brumaire of Louis Bonaparte." *The Marx-Engels Reader*, 2nd ed., edited by Robert C. Tucker, 594–617. New York: W. W. Norton.

McCoy, Alfred W., ed. 2009. *An Anarchy of Families: State and Family in the Philippines*. Madison: The University of Wisconsin Press.

McElderry, Andrea. 1986. "Woman Revolutionary: Xiang Jingyu." *China Quarterly* 105 (March): 95–122.

McElderry, Andrea. 2003. "Xiang Jingyu." In *BCDW*, 577–79.

Meijer, Marinus J. 1971. *Marriage Law and Policy*. Hong Kong: Hong Kong University Press.

Meisner, Maurice J. 1986. *Mao's China and After: A History of the People's Republic*. New York: Collier Macmillan.

Meng Guangli. 1991. He Xiangning. In *Zhonggong dangshi renwu Zhuang* [Biographies of Communist Party Historical Figures], edited by Zhonggong dangshi renwu zhuan yanjiuhui [Communist Party Historical Figures' Research Society]. Xi'an: Shaanxi renmin chubanshe.

Merkel-Hess, Kate. 2016. "A New Woman and Her Warlord: Li Dequan, Feng Yuxiang, and the Politics of Intimacy in Twentieth-Century China." *Frontiers of History in China* 11 (3): 431–57.

Mertha, Andrew. 2009. "Fragmented Authoritarianism 2.0: Political Pluralization of the Chinese Policy Process." *China Quarterly* 200 (December): 1–18.

Migdal, Joel S. 2001. *State in Society: Studying How States and Societies Transform and Constitute One Another*. New York: Cambridge University Press.

Mitchell, Timothy. 1991. "The Limits of the State: Beyond Statist Approaches and Their Critics." *American Political Science Review* 85 (1): 77–96.

Mitter, Rana. 2004. *A Bitter Revolution: China's Struggle with the Modern World*. New York: Oxford University Press.

Mitter, Rana, and Helen Schneider. 2012. "Introduction: Relief and Reconstruction in Wartime China." *European Journal of East Asian Studies* 11 (2): 179–86.

MOH Lead Party Group. February 1954 [1997]. "Zhongyang weishengbu dangzu guanyu jiezhi shengyu wenti xiang dang zhongyang de baogao" [A report from the MOH Lead Party Group submitted to CC on the problem of contraceptive methods]. In *ZJSQ*, 1–3.

MOH Lead Party Group. 1955 [1999]. "Weisheng bu dangzu guanyu jiezhi shengyu wenti de baogao" [MOH CCP Group report regarding problems of birth control]. In *ZFWN*, E13–78.

MOH Lead Party Group. 1958 [1997]. "Guanyu jieyu gongzuo de baogao" [Report regarding birth control work]. In *ZJSQ*, 125–28.

Moon, Bruce E., and William J. Dixon. 1985. "Politics, the State, and Basic Human Needs: A Cross-National Study." *American Journal of Political Science* 29 (4): 661–94.

Morgan, Kimberly J. 2006. *Working Mothers and the Welfare State: Religion and the Politics of Work-Family Policies in Western Europe and the United States.* Stanford, CA: Stanford University Press.

Mueggler, Erik. 2001. *The Age of Wild Ghosts: Memory, Violence, and Place in Southwest China.* Berkeley: University of California Press.

Mullender, Audrey, and David Ward. 1991. *Self-Directed Groupwork: Users Take Action for Empowerment.* London: Within and Birch.

Murphy, Michelle. 2012. *Seizing the Means of Reproduction: Entanglements of Feminism, Health, and Technoscience.* Durham, NC: Duke University Press.

Nathan, Andrew J. 1973. "A Factionalism Model for CCP Politics." *China Quarterly* 53 (January-March): 33–66.

Nathan, Andrew J. 2001. "Introduction: The Documents and their Significance." In *The Tiananmen Papers*, compiled by Liang Zhang, edited by Andrew J. Nathan and Perry Link, xv–xlv. New York: Public Affairs.

Nieto-Valdivieso, Yoana Fernanda. 2017. "The Joy of the Militancy: Happiness and the Pursuit of Revolutionary Struggle." *Journal of Gender Studies* 26 (1): 78–90.

O'Brien, Kevin J., and Lianjiang Li. 1999. "Campaign Nostalgia in the Chinese Countryside." *Asian Survey* 39 (3): 375–93.

O'Connor, Julia, Ann Shola Orloff, and Sheila Shaver. 1999. *States, Markets, Families: Gender, Liberalism, and Social Policy in Australia, Canada, Great Britain and the United States.* New York: Cambridge University Press.

Oi, Jean Chun. 1989. *State and Peasant in Contemporary China: The Political Economy of Village Government.* Berkeley: University of California Press.

Oksenberg, Michel. 1974. "Methods of Communication within the Chinese Bureaucracy." *China Quarterly* 57 (January-March): 1–39.

Olick, Jeffrey K. 2003. *States of Memory: Continuities, Conflicts, and Transformations in National Retrospection.* Durham, NC: Duke University Press.

Ong, Lynette H. 2022. *Outsourcing Repression: Everyday State Power in Contemporary China.* New York: Oxford University Press.

Ono, Kazuko. 1989. *Chinese Women in a Century of Revolution, 1850–1950.* Stanford, CA: Stanford University Press.

Ou Mengjue. 1947 [1991]. "Yi feng gongkai de xin—tan Dongbei funü gongzuo" [An open letter to discuss women-work in the Northeast]. In *ZFYLZ*, 128–31.

Ou Mengjue. 1983. "Wo zui jingpei de Cai Chang tongzhi" [My most respected comrade Cai Chang]. In *Funü yundong de xianqu—Cai Chang* [Forerunner of the women's movement—Cai Chang], 29–45. Beijing: Zhongguo funü chubanshe.

Pan, Lynn. 2015. *When True Love Came to China.* Hong Kong: Hong Kong University Press.

Pantsov, Alexander V., and Steven I. Levine. 2013. *Mao: The Real Story.* New. York: Simon and Schuster.

Parish, William L., and Martin King Whyte. 1978. *Village and Family in Contemporary China*. Chicago: University of Chicago Press.

Passerini, Luisa, ed. 1992. *Memory and Totalitarianism*. Oxford: Oxford University Press.

Pateman, Carole. 1988. *The Sexual Contract*. Stanford, CA: Stanford University Press.

Pateman, Carole. 1989. *The Disorder of Women: Democracy, Feminism, and Political Theory*. Stanford, CA: Stanford University Press.

Patil, Vrushali. 2013. "From Patriarchy to Intersectionality: A Transnational Feminist Assessment of How Far We've Really Come." *Signs: Journal of Women in Culture and Society* 38 (4): 847-67.

Peng Dehuai. 1941 [1991]. Xie gei "Huabei funü" [Written for Huabei women]. In *ZFYLZ (1937–1945)*, 494–96.

Peng Dehuai. 1943a [1991]. "Chongxin renshi funü gongzuo" [A new assessment of women-work]. In *ZFYLZ (1937–1945)*, 672–74.

Peng Dehuai. 1943b [1991]. "Zai Jinjiluyu si qu dangwei fuwei lianxi huiyi bianmu shi de jiangyan" [Speech at the closing of the joint conference between the Party Committee and the Women Committee of the Fourth District of Jinjiluyu]. In *ZFYLZ (1937–1945)*, 675–83.

Peng Dehuai. 1958. "Zhonggong zhongyang zhengzhi ju weiyuan Peng Dehuai tongzhi daibiao dang zhongyang zai quanguo funü jianshe shehui zhuyi jiji fenzi daibiao huiyi shang de zhici" [Member of the CCP's Politburo representing the CC, Comrade Peng Dehuai's address at the conference of women delegates for the construction of socialist activism]. *WW* 24: 2–3.

The People's Daily. 1957. "Xuduo yixuejia fabiao yijian, bu tongyi fangkuan rengong liuchan de xianzhi" [Many medical scientists express their opinion, objecting to the relaxation of restrictions on abortion]. May 26, 1957, 2nd Ed.

"The People's Relief Administration of China." 1952. *China Reconstructs* 1 (1): 47–48.

Perkins, Dwight H. 1966. *Market Control and Planning in Communist China*. Cambridge, MA: Harvard University Press.

Perry, Elizabeth J. 1980. *Rebels and Revolutionaries in North China, 1845–1945*. Stanford, CA: Stanford University Press.

Perry, Elizabeth J. 1994. "Labor Divided: Sources of State Formation in Modern China." In *State Power and Social Forces*, edited by Joel Migdal, 143–73. New York: Cambridge University Press.

Perry, Elizabeth J. 2002a. *Challenging the Mandate of Heaven: Social Protest and State Power in China*. Armonk, NY: M. E. Sharpe.

Perry, Elizabeth J. 2002b. "Moving the Masses: Emotion Work in the Chinese Revolution." *Mobilization* 7 (2): 111–28.

Phatanothai, Sirin, with James Peck. 1994. *The Dragon's Pearl*. New York: Simon and Schuster.

Pitcher, Anne, Mary H. Moran, and Michael Johnston. 2009. "Rethinking Patrimonialism and Neopatrimonialism in Africa." *African Studies Review* 52 (1): 125–56.

Plotkin, Mariano Ben. 2003. *Mañana es San Perón: A Cultural History of Perón's Argentina*. Wilmington, DE: Scholarly Resources.

Plum, M. Colette. 2006. "Unlikely Heirs: War Orphans during the Second Sino-Japanese War, 1937–1945." PhD Diss., Stanford University.

Plum, M. Colette. 2011. "Orphans in the Family: Family Reform and Children's Citizenship during the Anti-Japanese War, 1937–45." In *Beyond Suffering: Recounting War in Modern China*, edited by James Flath and Norman Smith, 186–206. Vancouver: University of British Colombia Press.

Plum, M. Colette. 2015. "Inscribing War Orphans' Losses into the Language of the Nation in Wartime China, 1937–1945." *Childhood, Youth, and Emotions in Modern History,* edited by Stephanie Olsen, 198–220. New York: Palgrave Macmillan.

Polachek, James M. 1983. "The Moral Economy of the Kiangsi Soviet (1928–1934)." *Journal of Asian Studies* 42 (4): 813–14.

Polletta, Francesca. 1998. "Contending Stories: Narrative in Social Movements." *Qualitative Sociology* 21 (4): 419–46.

Polletta, Francesca. 2008. "Culture and Movements." *Annals of the American Academy of Political and Social Science* 619: 78–96.

Pringle, Rosemary, and Sophie Watson. 1992. "'Women's Interests' and the Post-Structuralist State." In *Destabilizing Theory*, edited by Michele Barrett and Anne Phillips, 53–73. Stanford: Stanford University Press.

Pringsheim, Klaus H. 1962. "The Functions of the Chinese Communist Youth Leagues (1920–1949)." *China Quarterly* 12 (October-December): 75–91.

Pullen Sansfaçon, Annie, and Kimberley Ens Manning. 2015. "Maximising Research Outcomes for Trans Children and Their Families in Canada: Using Social Action and Other Participatory Methods of Inquiry." In *Lesbian, Gay, Bisexual, and Trans Health Inequalities*, edited by Julie Fish and Kate Kargan, 223–36. Bristol, UK: Policy Press.

Purdey, Jemma, Edward Espinall, and Muhammad Uhaib As'ad. 2016. "Understanding Family Politics." *South East Asia Research* 24 (3): 420–35.

Qi Zhongheng. 1958 [1997]. "Weisheng bu buzhang zhuli Qi Zhongheng zai quanguo jieyu gongzuo huibao huiyi shang de zongjie fayan (jielu)" [Vice-Minister of Health Qi Zhongheng's concluding remarks at the birth control meeting (excerpt)]. In *ZJSQ*, 289–91.

Qiao Peihua. 2009. *Xinyang shijian* [The Xinyang incident]. Hong Kong: Kaifang chubanshe.

Qinghua xiao you zong hui (Tsinghua Alumni Association). February 11, 2014. "Yan Renying: Cong linchuang dao baojian de niepan." https://www.tsinghua.org.cn/info/1951/18047.htm. Accessed May 30, 2022.

Ramphele, Mamphela. 1996. "Political Widowhood in South Africa: The Embodiment of Ambiguity." *Daedalus* 125 (1): 99–117.

Ray, Rayka. 1999. *Fields of Protest: Women's Movements in India*. Minneapolis: University of Minnesota Press.

Read, Benjamin L. 2012. *Roots of the State: Neighborhood Organization and Social Networks in Beijing and Taipei*. Stanford, CA: Stanford University Press.

Reddy, William M. 2009. "Historical Research on the Self and Emotions." *Emotion Review* 1 (4): 302–15.

Reed, Jean-Pierre. 2004. "Emotions in Context: Revolutionary Accelerators, Hope, Moral Outrage, and Other Emotions in the Making of Nicaragua's Revolution." *Theory and Society* 33 (6): 653–703.

Reid, Susan E. 2005. "The Krushchev Kitchen: Domesticating the Scientific-Technological Revolution." *Journal of Contemporary History* 40 (2): 289–316.

Remick, Elizabeth J. 2014. *Regulating Prostitution in China: Gender and Local Statebuilding 1900–1937*. Stanford, CA: Stanford University Press.

Ren Fen, ed. 1989. *Zhongguo funü yundong shi* [The history of the Chinese women's movement]. Shijiazhuang: Beifang funü ertong chubanshe.

Riley, Denise. 1988. *Am I That Name? Feminism and the Category of 'Women' in History*. Minneapolis: University of Minnesota.

Robnett, Belinda. 1997. *How Long? How Long? African-American Women in the Struggle for Civil Rights*. New York: Oxford University Press.

Roces, Mina. 2010. "Asian Feminisms: Women's Movements from the Asian Perspective." In *Women's Movements in Asia: Feminisms and Transnational Activism*, edited by Mina Roces and Louise Edwards, 1–20. New York: Routledge.

Rofel, Lisa. 1999. *Other Modernities: Gendered Yearnings in China After Socialism*. Berkeley: University of California Press.

Rogaski, Ruth. 2004. *Hygenic Modernity: Meanings of Health and Disease in Treaty-Port China*. Berkeley: University of California Press.

Rong Xia. 2010. *Funü zhidao weiyuanhui yu kangri zhanzheng* [The new life movement Women's Advisory Council and the War of Resistance]. Beijing: Renmin Press.

Rosen, Stanley. 1995. "Women and Political Participation in China." *Pacific Affairs* 68 (3): 315–41.

Ross, Heidi A. 1996. "'Cradle of Female Talent': The McTyeire Home and School for Girls, 1892–1937." In *Christianity in China: From the Eighteenth Century to the Present*, edited by Daniel H. Bays, 209–27. Stanford, CA: Stanford University Press.

Ruf, Gregory A. 1998. *Cadres and Kin: Making a Socialist Village in West China, 1921–1991*. Stanford, CA: Stanford University Press.

Rupp, Leila J. 1994. "Constructing Internationalism: The Case of Transnational Women's Organizations, 1888–1945." *American Historical Review* 99 (5): 1571–1600.

Rupp, Leila J. 1998. *Worlds of Women: The Making of an International Women's Movement*. Princeton, NJ: Princeton University Press.

Ryūichi, Narita. 1998. "Women in the Motherland: Oku Mumeo through Wartime and Postwar." In *Total War and Modernization*, edited by Yasushi Yamanouchi, J. Victor Koschmann, and Narita Ryūichi, 137–58. Ithaca, NY: Cornell University East Asia Series.

Sabatier, Paul A. 1988. "An Advocacy Coalition Framework of Policy Change and the Role of Policy-Oriented Learning Therein." *Policy Sciences* 21 (2–3): 129–68.

Sageman, Marc. 2004. *Understanding Terror Networks*. Philadelphia: University of Pennsylvania Press.

Saich, Tony. 2021. *From Rebel to Ruler: One Hundred Years of the Chinese Communist Party*. Cambridge, MA: Belknap Press of Harvard University Press.

Sakamoto, Hiroko. 2004. "The Cult of 'Love and Eugenics' in May Fourth Movement Discourse." *Positions: East Asia Cultures Critique* 12 (2): 329–76.

Sasaki, Motoe. 2016. *Redemption and Revolution: American and Chinese New Women in the Early Twentieth Century*. Ithaca: Cornell University Press.

Schmalzer, Sigrid. 2021. "Beyond Bias: Critical Analysis and Layered Reading of Mao-Era Sources." *Positions: Asia Critique* 29 (4): 759–82.

Schmidt, Vivien A. 2010. "Taking Ideas and Discourse Seriously: Explaining Change through Discursive Institutionalism as the Fourth 'New Institutionalism.'" *European Political Science Review* 2 (1): 1–25.

Schneider, Helen M. 2011. *Keeping the Nation's House: Domestic Management and the Making of Modern China*. Vancouver: University of British Colombia Press.

Schneider, Helen. 2012. "Mobilising Women: The Women's Advisory Council, Resistance and Reconstruction during China's War with Japan." *European Journal of East Asian Studies* 11 (2): 213–36.

Schneider, Leander. 2014. *Government of Development: Peasants and Politicians in Postcolonial Tanzania*. Bloomington: Indiana University Press.

Schoenhals, Michael. 1992. *Doing Things With Words in Chinese Politics*. Berkeley: University of California Press.

Schram, Stuart R. 1974. *The Political Thought of Mao Tse-tung*. New York: Praeger.

Searle, Eleanor. 1988. *Predatory Kinship and the Creation of Norman Power, 840–1066*. Berkeley: University of California Press.

Selden, Mark. 1988. *The Political Economy of Chinese Socialism*. Armonk, NY: M. E. Sharpe.

Selden, Mark. 1995. *China in Revolution: The Yenan Way Revisited*. Armonk, NY: M. E. Sharpe.

Shambaugh, David. 1997. "Building the Party-State in China, 1949–1965: Bringing the Soldier Back In." In *New Perspectives on State Socialism in China*, edited by Timothy Check and Tony Saich, 125–50. New York: M. E. Sharpe.

Shang Mingxuan and Tang Yulin, eds. 1990. *Song Qingling zhuan* [The Biography of Song Qingling]. Beijing: Beijing chubanshe.

Shao Lizi. 1954 [1997]. "Zai diyi jie quanguo renmin daibiao dahui diyici huiyi shang de fayan (jielu)" [Speech from the first meeting of the first session of the National People's Congress (excerpt)]. In *ZJSQ* 529.

Shao Wenjie, ed. 1984. *Henan shengzhi; Funü yundong zhi* [Provincial gazetteer of Henan; annals of the Women's Movement]. Zhengzhou: Qinzhou xinhua shoudian gujiu bu.

Shen Zijiu. 1935 [1991]. "Nüzi de zisha" [Suicide Amongst Women]. In *Nüjie wenhua zhanshi shen zijiu* [Shen Zijiu: Champion of Women's Rights], edited by Dong Bian, 223–26. Beijing: Zhongguo funü chubanshe.

Sheridan, James E. 1966. *Chinese Warlord: The Career of Feng Yu-hsiang*. Stanford, CA: Stanford University Press.

Shi Chengli. 1988. *Zhongguo jihua shengyu huodong shi* [The history of China's birth planning activities]. Urumqi: Xinjiang renmin chubanshe.

Shi Liang. 1987. *Shi Liang zishu* [Shi Liang's Memoirs]. Beijing: Zhongguo wenshi chubanshe [Chinese Literary and Historical Press].

Shih, Victor, Christopher Adolph, and Liu Mingxing. 2012. "Getting Ahead in the Communist Party: Explaining Advancement of Central Committee Members in China." *American Political Science Review* 106 (1): 166–87.

Shuai Mengqi. 1957 [1988]. "Jianku fendou, wending tigao" [Struggle arduously, rise with stability]. In *ZFYWZH*, 2: 288–91.

Shue, Vivienne. 1980. *Peasant China in Transition*. Berkeley: University of California Press.

Shue, Vivienne. 1988. *The Reach of the State: Sketches of the Chinese Body Politic*. Stanford, CA: Stanford University Press.

Skocpol, Theda. 1992. *Protecting Soldiers and Mothers: The Political Origins of Social Policy*. Cambridge, MA: Belknap Press of Harvard University Press.

Smith, Amanda. 2013. "Thought Reform and the Unreformable: Reeducation Centers and the Rhetoric of Opposition in the Early People's Republic of China." *Journal of Asian Studies* 72 (4): 937–58.

Smith, Ewan. 2021. "On the Informal Rules of the Chinese Communist Party." *China Quarterly*: 1–20.

Smith Finley, Joanne. 2021. "Why Scholars and Activists Increasingly Fear a Uyghur Genocide in Xinjiang." *Journal of Genocide Research* 23 (3): 348–70.

Snow, Edgar. 1938 [1978]. *Red Star Over China*. New York: Bantam.

Snow, Helen Foster. 1939 [1977]. *Inside Red China*. New York: Da Capo Press.

Snow, Helen Foster. 1967. *Women in Modern China*. The Netherlands: Mouton and Co.

Snow, Helen Foster. 1972. *The Chinese Communists: Sketches and Autobiographies of the Old Guard*. Westport, CT: Greenwood.

Snow, Helen Foster. 1984. *My China Years*. New York: William Morrow.

Solomon, Richard H. 1969. "Mao's Effort to Reintegrate the Chinese Polity: Problems of Authority and Conflict in Chinese Social Processes." In *Chinese Communist Politics in Action*, edited by Doak A. Barnett, 271–360. Seattle: University of Washington.

Song Qingling. 1939 [1991]. "Guanyu yuanzhu youji dui zhanshi di huyu" [A call to assist guerrilla fighters]. In *ZFYLZ (1937–1945)*, 243–47.

Song Qingling. 1958 [1988]. "Zai ertong jie xiang muqinmen shuo ji jihua" [A few words to mothers on Childrens' Day]. In *ZFYWZH*, 2: 365–66.

Song Shaopeng. 2006. "The State Discourse on Housewives and Housework in the 1950s in China." *Berliner China-Hefte/Chinese History and Society* 31: 49–62.

Song Shaopeng. 2015a. "Geming shiguan de heli yichan—Weirao Zhongguo funü shi yanjiu de taolun" [A reasonable legacy of the revolutionary view of history—A discussion of the research on Chinese women's history]. *Wenhua Zongheng* [Cultural Aspects] 8: 50–55.

Song Shaopeng. 2015b. "Zhongguo nüxing shenfen rentong de lishi he xianshi—cong "nü de guan" shijian tan qi" [The history and reality of Chinese women's identity: from the 'Nü De Guan' incident]. *Wenhua Zongheng* [Cultural Aspects] 1: 100–107.

Song Yiwu. 2013. *The Biographical Dictionary of the People's Republic of China*. Jefferson, NC: McFarland and Company.

Soong Chiang May-ling (Song Meiling). 1940. *This Is Our China*. New York: Harper and Brothers.

Soong Ching Ling (Song Qingling). 1942 [1953]. *The Chinese Women's Fight for Freedom*. Beijing: Foreign Languages Press.

Soong Ching Ling (Song Qingling). 1952a. "Protect the Children!" *China Reconstructs*, March–April 1: 2–3.

Soong Ching Ling (Song Qingling). 1952b. "Welfare Work and World Peace." *China Reconstructs*. February 1: 1–2.

Spakowski, Nicola. 2005. "Women's Military Participation in the Communist Movement of the 1930s and 1940s: Patterns of Inclusion and Exclusion." In *Women in China: The Republican Period in Historical Perspective*, edited by Mechtild Leutner and Nicola Spakowski, in Berliner China-Studien, 129–71. Münster, Germany: Lit Verlag.

Spakowski, Nicola. 2018. "Socialist Feminism in Postsocialist China." *Positions: Asia Critique* 26 (4): 561–92.

Spakowski, Nicola. 2022. "Women Labour Models and Socialist Transformation in early 1950s China." *International Review of Social History* 67 (S30): 131–54.

Spence, Jonathan D. 1990. *The Search for Modern China*. New York: W. W. Norton.

Stacey, Judith. 1983. *Patriarchy and Socialist Revolution in China*. Berkeley: University of California Press.

Steinmetz, George. 2011. "Bourdieu, Historicity, and Historical Sociology." *Cultural Sociology* 5 (1): 45–66.

Steinmüller, Hans. 2015. "'Father Mao' and the Country-Family: Mixed Feelings for Fathers, Officials, and Leaders in China." *Social Analysis: International Journal of Anthropology* 59 (4): 83–100.

Stephan, Rita. 2010. "Couple's Activism in Lebanon: The Legacy of Laure Moghaizel." *Women's Studies International Forum* 33 (6): 533–41.

Stetson, Dorothy M. MacBride, and Amy Mazur. 1995. *Comparative State Feminism.* Thousand Oaks, CA: Sage.

Stoler, Ann Laura. 2004. "Affective States." In *A Companion to the Anthropology of Politics*, edited by David Nugent and Joan Vincent, 4–20. Malden, MA: Blackwell.

Stranahan, Patricia. 1983. *Yan'an Women and the Communist Party.* Berkeley: Institute of East Asian Studies, University of California, Berkeley Center for Chinese Studies.

Strauss, Julia. 2002. "Paternalist Terror: The Campaign to Suppress Counterrevolutionaries and Regime Consolidation in the People's Republic of China, 1950–1953." *Comparative Studies in Society and History* 44 (1): 80–105.

Strauss, Julia. 2020. *State Formation in China and Taiwan: Bureaucracy, Campaign, and Performance.* Cambridge: Cambridge University Press.

Stueck, William, ed. 2013. *Rethinking the Korean War.* Princeton, NJ: Princeton University Press.

Su Ping. 1990. *Cai Chang zhuan* [The biography of Cai Chang]. Beijing: Zhongguo funü chubanshe.

Swartz, David L. 2013. "Metaprinciples for Sociological Research in a Bourdieusian Perspective." In *Bourdieu and Historical Analysis*, edited by Philip S. Gorski, 19–35. Durham, NC: Duke University Press.

Tang Shuiqing. 2011. "'Lihun fa' yu 'funü fa': 20 shiji 50 niandai chuqi xiangcun minzhong dui hunyin fa de wudu" [The 'divorce law' and 'women's law': the misreading of the Marriage Law in the early 1950s]. *Fudan Xuebao* [Fudan Journal] 6: 129–37.

Tanner, Murray Scot, and Michael J. Feder. 1993. "Family Politics, Elite Recruitment, and Succession in Post-Mao China." *Australian Journal of Chinese Affairs* 30 (July): 89–119.

Tarrow, Sidney. 2005. *The New Transnational Activism.* New York: Cambridge University Press.

Taylor, Kim. 2005. *Chinese Medicine in Early Communist China, 1945–63.* New York: Routledge Curzon.

Teiwes, Frederick C. 1967. *Provincial Party Personnel in Mainland China 1956–1966. Occasional Papers of the East Asian Institute.* New York: Columbia University.

Teiwes, Frederick C. 1979. *Politics and Purges in China.* Armonk, NY: M. E. Sharpe.

Teiwes, Frederick C. 1984. *Leadership, Legitimacy, and Conflict in China.* Armonk, NY: M.E. Sharpe.

Teiwes, Frederick C. 1990. *Politics at Mao's Court: Gao Gang and Party Factionalism in the Early 1960s.* Armonk, NY: M. E. Sharpe.

Teiwes, Frederick C. 1993. "The Establishment and Consolidation of the New Regime, 1949–1957." In *The Politics of China, 1949–1989*, edited by Roderick MacFarquhar, 5–86. New York: Cambridge University Press.

Teiwes, Frederick C., and Warren Sun. 1999. *China's Road to Disaster: Mao, Central Politicians and Provincial Leaders in the Unfolding of the Great Leap Forward 1955–1959.* London: Sharpe.

Terrill, Ross. 1984. *The White-Boned Demon: A Biography of Madame Mao Zedong.* 1st ed. New York: Morrow.

Tetreault, Mary Ann. 1992. "Women and Revolution: A Framework for Analysis." In *Gendered States: Feminist (Re)Visions of International Relations Theory*, edited by V. Spike Peterson, 99–121. Boulder, CO: Lynne Rienner.

Thane, Pat. 1993. "Women in the British Labour Party and the Construction of State Welfare, 1906–1939." In *Mothers of a New World: Maternalist Politics and the*

Origins of Welfare States, edited by Seth Koven and Sonya Michel, 343–77. New York: Routledge.

Thapar-Björkert, Suruchi, and Louise Ryan. 2002. "Mother India/Mother Ireland: Comparative Gendered Dialogues of Colonialism and Nationalism in the Early 20th Century." *Women's Studies International Forum* 25 (3): 301–13.

Thaxton, Ralph A. 1997. *Salt of the Earth: The Political Origins of Peasant Protest and Communist Revolution in China*. Berkeley: University of California Press.

Thaxton, Ralph A. 2008. *Catastrophe and Contention in Rural China: Mao's Great Leap Forward Famine and the Origins of Righteous Resistance in Da Fo Village*. New York: Cambridge University Press.

Thaxton, Ralph A. 2011. "How the Great Leap Forward Famine Ended in Rural China: 'Administrative Intervention' versus Peasant Resistance." In *Eating Bitterness: New Perspectives on China's Great Leap Forward and Famine*, edited by Kimberley Ens Manning and Felix Wemheuer, 251–71. Vancouver: University of British Colombia Press.

Thomas, Gwynn. 2011. "The Legacies of Patrimonial Patriarchalism: Contesting Political Legitimacy in Allende's Chile." *Annals of the American Academy of Political and Social Science* 636 (1): 69–87.

Thomas, Jakana L., and Kanisha D. Bond. 2015. "Women's Participation in Violent Political Organizations." *American Political Science Review* 109 (3): 488–506.

Thorborg, Marina. 1978. "Chinese Employment Policy in 1949–78 with Special Emphasis on Women in Rural Production." In *Chinese Economy Post Mao: A Compendium of Papers*, 535–604. Washington, DC: U.S. Government Printing Office.

Thornton, Patricia. 2007. *Disciplining the State: Virtue, Violence, and State-Making in Modern China*. Cambridge, MA: Harvard University Asia Center Monograph.

Tong, James. 2003. "The Gender Gap in Political Culture and Participation in China." *Communist and Post-Communist Studies* 36 (2): 131–50.

Towns, Ann E. 2010. *Women and States: Norms and Hierarchies in International Society*. New York: Cambridge University Press.

Tripp, Aili Mari, Isabel Casimiro, Joy Kwesiga, and Alice Mungwa, eds. 2009. *African Women's Movements: Changing Political Landscapes*. New York: Cambridge University Press.

Trotsky, Leon. 1925 [1973]. *Women and the Family*. New York: Pathfinder Press.

Tyrrell, Ian R. 1991. *Woman's World/Woman's Empire: The Woman's Christian Temperance Union in International Perspective, 1800–1930*. Chapel Hill, NC: University of North Carolina Press.

Unger, Jonathan. 2002. *The Transformation of Rural China*. Armonk, NY: M. E. Sharpe.

Van der Klein, Marian, and Rebecca Jo Plant. 2012. "Introduction: A New Generation of Scholars on Maternalism." In *Maternalism Reconsidered: Motherhood, Welfare and Social Policy in the Twentieth Century*, edited by Marian Van der Klein, Rebecca Jo Plant, Nichole Sanders, and Lori R. Weintrob, 1–21. New York: Berghahn Books.

Viterna, Jocelyn. 2013. *Women in War: The Micro-Processes of Mobilization in El Salvador*. New York: Oxford University Press.

Vogel, Ezra F. 2011. *Deng Xiaoping and the Transformation of China*. Cambridge, MA: Harvard University Press.

Vu, Tuong. 2010. "Studying the State Through State Formation." *World Politics* 62 (1): 148–75.

Wai, Zubairu. 2012. "Neo-Patrimonialism and the Discourse of State Failure in Africa." *Review of African Political Economy* 39 (131): 27–43.

Walder, Andrew. 1986. *Communist Neo-Traditionalism: Work and Authority in Chinese Industry*. Berkeley: University of California Press.

Wang Bing. 2003. "Yang Chongrui." In *BDCW*, 611–13.

Wang Liping and Julia Adams. 2011. "Interlocking Patrimonialisms and State Formation in Qing China and Early Modern Europe." *Annals of the American Academy of Political and Social Science* 636 (1): 164–81.

Wang Menglan, ed. 1990. *Deng Yingchao geming huoding qi shi nian dashiji* [Seventy years of Deng Yingchao's revolutionary activities]. Beijing: Zhongguo funü chubanshe.

Wang Shiwei. 1942 [1996]. "The Wild Lily." In *The Rise to Power of the Chinese Communist Party*, edited by Tony Saich, 1103–8. Armonk, NY: M. E. Sharpe. Original edition, Jiefang Ribao [Liberation Daily], March 13 & 27, 1942.

Wang Xingjuan. 1997. *Li Min, He Zizhen yu Mao Zedong* [Li Min, He Zizhen and Mao Zedong]. Beijing: Zhongguo wenlian chuban gongsi.

Wang Yanhong, Zhou Yanzhi, and Liu Zhilan. 2007. "Xin Zhonguo di yi bu 'hunyin fa' qicao shimo" [The beginning and end of the drafting of the first "Marriage Law" in new China]. *Zongheng* [Aspect] 2.

Wang Yanni. 2011. "An Introduction to the ABCs of Communization: A Case Study of Macheng County." In *Eating Bitterness: New Perspectives on China's Great Leap Forward and Famine*, edited by Kimberley Ens Manning and Felix Wemheuer, 148–70. Vancouver: University of British Colombia Press.

Wang Yuhua. 2021. "State-in-Society 2.0: Toward Fourth-Generation Theories of the State." *Comparative Politics* 54 (1): 175–98.

Wang Zheng. 1999. *Women in the Chinese Enlightenment: Oral and Textual Histories*. Berkeley: University of California Press.

Wang Zheng. 2005. "'State Feminism'? Gender and Socialist State Formation in Maoist China." *Feminist Studies* 31 (3): 519–51.

Wang Zheng. 2017. *Finding Women in the State: A Socialist Feminist Revolution in the People's Republic of China, 1949–1964*. Berkeley: University of California Press.

Wang Zijin, Liu Yuebin, and Chang Zonghu. 2002. *Zhongguo shehui fuli shi* [A History of Chinese Social Benefits]. Beijing: Zhongguo shehui chubanshe.

Ward, Matthew. 2016. "Rethinking Social Movement Micromobilization: Multi-Stage Theory and the Role of Social Ties." *Current Sociology Review* 64 (6): 853–74.

Ward, Michael D., Katherine Stovel, and Audrey Sacks. 2011. "Network Analysis and Political Science." *Annual Review of Political Science* 14: 245–64.

Waylen, Georgina, ed. 2017. *Gender and Informal Institutions*. New York: Rowman and Littlefield.

Weakland, John H. 1958. "Family Imagery in a Passage by Mao Tse-Tung: An Essay in Psycho-Cultural Method." *World Politics* 10 (3): 387–407.

Weber, Max. 1946. *From Max Weber: Essays in Sociology*. Translated by H. H. Gerth and C. Wright Mills. New York: Oxford University Press.

Wedeen, Lisa. 1999. *Ambiguities of Domination: Politics, Rhetoric, and Symbols in Contemporary Syria*. Chicago: Chicago University Press.

Wedeen, Lisa. 2010. "Reflections on Ethnographic Work in Political Science." *Annual Review of Political Science* 13: 255–72.

Wei Hong. 2004. "He Zizhen." In *TR*, 3–42.

Wei Li, and Lucian W. Pye. 1992. "The Ubiquitous Role of the Mishu in Chinese Politics." *China Quarterly* 132 (December): 913–36.

Weigelin-Schweidrzik, Susanne. 2003. "Trauma and Memory: The Case of the Great Famine in the People's Republic of China (1959–1961)." *Historiography East and West* 1 (1): 39–67.

Wemheuer, Felix. 2010. "Dealing with Responsibility for the Great Leap Famine in the People's Republic of China." *China Quarterly* 201 (March): 176–94.

Wemheuer, Felix. 2011. "'The Grain Problem is an Ideological Problem': Discourses of Hunger in the 1957 Socialist Education Campaign." In *Eating Bitterness: New Perspectives on China's Great Leap Forward and Famine*, edited by Kimberley Ens Manning and Felix Wemheuer, 107–29. Vancouver: University of British Colombia Press.

Wemheuer, Felix. 2012. "Dining in Utopia: An Intellectual History of the Origins of the Public Dining." In *Hunger and Scarcity under State-Socialism*, edited by Mathias Middell and Felix Wemheuer, 277–301. Leipzig: Leipzier Universitätsverlag GmbH.

Wemheuer, Felix. 2014. *Famine Politics in Maoist China and the Soviet Union*. New Haven, CT: Yale University Press.

Wemheuer, Felix. 2019. *A Social History of Maoist China: Conflict and Change, 1949–1976*. Cambridge: Cambridge University Press.

Wen, Guanzhong James, and Gene Chang. 1997. "Communal Dining and the Chinese Famine of 1958–1961." *Economic Development and Cultural Change* 46 (1): 1–34.

White, Tyrene. 2006. *China's Longest Campaign: Birth Planning in the People's Republic, 1949–2005*. Ithaca, NY: Cornell University Press.

Whiting, Allen S. 1968. *China Crosses the Yalu: The Decision to Enter the Korean War*. Stanford, CA: Stanford University Press.

Wiles, Sue. 2003a. "Cai Chang." In *BDCW*, 21–25.

Wiles, Sue. 2003b. "Ge Jianhao." In *BDCW*, 173–75.

Wiles, Sue. 2003c. "He Zizhen." In *BDCW*, 206–8.

Wiles, Sue. 2003d. "Liu Qingyang." In *BDCW*, 358–60.

Wilkinson, J. Norman. 1974. "'The White-Haired Girl': From 'Yangko' to Revolutionary Ballet." *Educational Theatre Journal* 26 (2): 164–74.

Wilkinson, Patrick. 1999. "The Selfless and the Helpless: Maternalist Origins of the U.S. Welfare State." *Feminist Studies* 25 (3): 571–97.

Wilson, Dick. 1984. *Zhou Enlai: A Biography*. New York: Viking Penguin.

Witke, Roxane. 1967. "Mao Tse-tung, Women, and Suicide." *China Quarterly* 31 (July–September): 128–47.

Witke, Roxane. 1970. "Transformation of Attitudes Towards Women During The May Fourth Era of Modern China." PhD. diss., University of California, Berkeley.

Witke, Roxane. 1977. *Comrade Chiang Ch'ing*. Boston: Little, Brown.

Wolf, Margery. 1985. *Revolution Postponed: Women in Contemporary China*. Stanford, CA: Stanford University Press.

Wong, Joseph. 2004. *Healthy Democracies: Welfare Politics in Taiwan and South Korea*. Ithaca, NY: Cornell University Press.

Wong Yin Lee. 2003. "Deng Yingchao." In *BDCW*, 131–35.

Wou, Odoric Y.K. 1994. *Mobilizing the Masses: Building Revolution in Henan*. Stanford, CA: Stanford University Press.

Wright, Guowei. 2009. "Lin Qiaozhi: The Pulse of a Quiet Faith." In *Salt and Light: Lives That Shaped Modern China*, edited by Carol Lee Hamrin and Stacey Bieber, 114–32. Eugene, OR: Pickwick.

Wu Yiching. 2014. *The Cultural Revolution at the Margins*. Cambridge, MA: Harvard University Press.

Xu Guangping. 1957 [1999]. "Zai shoudu ge jie funü jinian 1957 nian 'san ba' guoji funü jie da hui shang jiang hua" [Speech at the 1957 "March 8th" International Women's Day Conference for women from all walks of life in the capital]. In *ZFWN*, E15–127.

Xun Zhou. 2020. *The People's Health*. Montreal: McGill University Press.

Yan Yunxiang. 1996. *The Flow of Gifts: Reciprocity and Social Networks in a Chinese Village*. Stanford, CA: Stanford University Press.

Yan Yunxiang. 2001. "Practicing Kinship in Rural North China." In *Relative Values: Reconfiguring Kinship Studies*, edited by Sarah Franklin and Susan McKinnon, 224–45. Durham, NC: Duke University Press.

Yan Yunxiang. 2003. *Private Life under Socialism: Love, Intimacy, and Family Change in a Chinese Village, 1949–1999*. Stanford, CA: Stanford University Press.

Yang Dali L. 1996. *Calamity and Reform in China: State, Rural Society and Institutional Change Since the Great Leap Famine*. Stanford, CA: Stanford University Press.

Yang Dali L., Xu Huayu, and Tao Ran. 2014. "A Tragedy of the Nomenklatura? Career Incentives, Political Loyalty and Political Radicalism during China's Great Leap Forward." *Journal of Contemporary China* 23 (89): 864–83.

Yang, Dennis Tao. 2008. "China's Agricultural Crisis and Famine of 1959–1961: A Survey and Comparison to Soviet Famines." *Comparative Economic Studies* 50: 1–29.

Yang Guobin. 2000. "Achieving Emotions in Collective Action: Emotional Processes and Movement Mobilization in the 1989 Chinese Student Movement." *Sociological Quarterly* 41 (4): 593–614.

Yang Jie. 2014. "Introduction." In *The Political Economy of Affect and Emotion in East Asia*, edited by Yang Jie, 3–28. London: Routledge.

Yang Jie. 2015. *Unknotting the Heart: Unemployment and Therapeutic Governance in China*. Ithica: Cornell University Press.

Yang Jisheng. 2012. *Tombstone: The Great Chinese Famine, 1958–1962*. Translated by Stacy Mosher and Guo Jian and edited by Edward Friedman, Guo Jian and Stacy Mosher. New York: Farrar, Straus, and Giroux.

Yang, Mayfair Mei-hui. 1994. *Gifts, Favors, and Banquets: The Art of Social Relationships in China*. Ithaca, NY: Cornell University Press.

Yang Nanying, ed. 1991. *Zhonghua quanguo funü lianhehui si shi nian (1949–1989)* [Forty years of the ACWF]. Beijing: Zhongguo funü chubanshe.

Yang Nianqun. 2004. "Disease Prevention, Social Mobilization and Spatial Politics: The Anti Germ-Warfare Incident of 1952 and the 'Patriotic Health Campaign.'" *Chinese Historical Review* 11 (2): 155–82.

Ying Hu. 2009. "'How Can A Daughter Glorify the Family Name?' Filiality and Women's Rights in the Late Qing." *Nan Nü* 11: 234–69.

Yip Ka-che. 2001. "Disease and the Fighting Men: Nationalist Anti-Epidemic Efforts in Wartime China, 1937–1945." In *China in the Anti-Japanese War, 1937–1945*, edited by David P. Barrett and Larry N. Shyu, 171–88. In Studies in Modern Chinese History. New York: Peter Lang.

Yong Xin Xianwei. 1931 [1991]. "Xiangganbianjiang qu funü gongzuo jue'an" [Legal decision on women-work in the Hunan-Jiangxi Border District]. In *ZFYLZ (1927–1937)*, 157–60.

Young, Helen Praeger. 2001. *Choosing Revolution: Chinese Women Soldiers on the Long March*. Champaign: University of Illinois Press.

Yun Xia. 2013. "Engendering Contempt for Collaborators: Anti-Hanjian Discourse Following the Sino-Japanese War of 1937–1945." *Journal of Women's History* 25 (1): 111–34.

Zarrow, Peter. 1988. "He Zhen and Anarcho-Feminism in China." *Journal of East Asian Studies* 47 (4): 796–813.

Zeng Zhi. 1992. "Mianhuai Cai Chang dajie" [In memory of elder sister Cai Chang]. In *WHDCC*, 29–32.

Zeng Zhi. 1993. "Huiyi Deng Dajie guanxin wo de ji jianshi" [Remembering elder sister Deng who took care of some matters for me]. In *Huainian Deng Yingchao Dajie* [Cherishing the memory of elder sister Deng], edited by Shu Mei Zhang, 53–60. Beijing: Zhongguo funü chubanshe.

Zeng Zhi. 2011. *Baizhan guilai ren ci shen: Zeng Zhi huiyi lu* [Battle-scarred and coming home: The memoirs of Zeng Zhi]. Beijing: People's Literature Publishing House.

Zhang Chengjie. 2010. "1950 Nian 'Hunyin fa' ji qi yinfa de shehui bianqe" [The "1950 Marriage Law" and the social changes it generated]. *Jiangsu daxue xuebao, shehui kexue xuebao* [Journal of Jiangsu University, Social Sciences Edition] 12 (5): 34–52.

Zhang Liang. 2001. "Reflections on June Fourth." In *The Tiananmen Papers*, edited by Andrew J. Nathan and Perry Link. New York: Public Affairs.

Zhang Lihua, Ru Haitao, and Dong Naiqiang. 1992. "Jiangui sishi nian funü tushu gaikuang" [A survey of forty years of books on women]. In *Zhongguo funü lilun yanjiu shinian* [Ten Years of Women's Studies in China, 1981–1990], edited by Xiong Yumei, Liu Xiaocong, and Qu Wen, 592–605. Beijing: Zhongguo funü chubanshe.

Zhang Ling. 2013. "Kangzhan shiqi sichuan sheng fuyou weisheng shiye pingxi" [Analysis of maternal and child health services in Sichuan Province during the Anti-Japanese War]. *Xinan daxue xuebao* [South-West University Journal] 39 (1): 151–57.

Zhang Naihua. 1996. "The All-China Women's Federation, Chinese Women and the Women's Movement: 1949–1993." PhD Dissertation, Michigan State University.

Zhang, Qian Forrest. 2014. "The Strength of Sibling Ties: Sibling Influence on Status Attainment in a Chinese Family." *Sociology* 48 (1): 75–91.

Zhang Qingping. 2005. *Lin Qiaozhi*. Beijing: Baihua Wenyi Chubanshe.

Zhang Tianshe. 2017. "Feng Yuxiang Sulian qijian yu Sidalin huimian wenti kaobian" [Doubt about Feng Yuxiang's Meeting with Stalin during his visit to the Soviet Union]. *Tangdu xuekan* [Tangdu Journal] 33 (1): 107–12.

Zhang Yun. 1952 [1996]. "Guanyu dangqian funü gongzuo wenti de baogao" [Report on current issues in women-work]. In *ZYW*, 126–35.

Zhang Yun. 1953 [1996]. "Wei guanche hunyin fa da yundong shouxian zuo hao fulian ganbu benshen de sixiang zhunbei" [In order to implement the Marriage Law Campaign first adequately prepare the basic thinking of Women's Federation cadres]. In *ZYW*, 136–39.

Zhao Jinping. 2003a. "Li Dequan." In *BDCW*, 302–3.

Zhao Jinping. 2003b. "Shen Zijiu." In *BDCW*, 448–50.

Zhao Jinping. 2003c. "Zhang Yun." In *BDCW*, 699–701.

Zhao Zhangan, Lan Wei, and Zhang Tianruo. 1985. *Lao geming jia de lian'ai, hunyin he jiating shenghuo* [Love, marriage, and family life in the families of revolutionary elders]. Beijing: Gongren chubanshe.

Zheng Chaolin. 1997. *An Oppositionist for Life: Memoirs of the Chinese Revolutionary Zheng Chaolin*. Translated by Gregor Benton and edited by Gregor Benton. New Jersey: Humanities Press.

Zhonghua quanguo funü lianhehui funü yanjiusuo [Research Institute of All China's Women's Federation] and Shaanxi sheng funü lianhehui yanjiushi [Research Office of Shaanxi Provincial Women's Federation], eds. 1991. *Zhongguo funü tongji ziliao, 1949–1989.* [Statistics on Chinese women, 1949–89]. Beijing: Zhongguo tongji chubanshe.

"Zhonghua suwei'ai gongheguo hunyin tiaoli" [Chinese Soviet Republic Marriage Act]. 1931 [1991]. In *ZFYLZ (1927–1937)*, 151–54.

Zhou Enlai. 1939 [1991]. "Zhou Enlai zai Yan'an Zhongguo nüzi daxue kaixue dianli shang de jianghua (1939 nian 7 yue 20 ri) (jielu)" [Zhou Enlai's speech at the opening ceremony of the Chinese Women's University in Yan'an (July 20, 1939) (excerpt)]. In *ZFYLZ (1937–1945)*, 151.

Zhou Enlai. 1942 [1991]. "Lun xian qi liang mu yu muzhi" [On "Good Wives, Wise Mothers" and Motherhood]. In *ZFYLZ (1937–1945)*, 608–11.

Zhou Enlai. 1953 [1988]. "Zhongyang renmin zhengfu zhengwuyuan: guanyu guanche hunyinfa de zhishi" [Central People's Government's Administrative Council: Directives on how to implement the Marriage Law]." In *ZFYWZH*, 153–55.

Zhou Enlai. 1953 [1997]. "Zhou Enlai guanyu renkou he jihua shengyu de lunshu" [Zhou Enlai discusses population issues and birth planning]. In *ZJSQ*, 133.

Zhou Enlai and Deng Yingchao. 1944, 1947, 1954 [1998] "Zhou Enlai, Deng Yingchao wanglai shuxin si feng" [Four letter correspondence between Zhou Enlai and Deng Yingchao]. *Dang de Wenxian* [Party Literature] 1: 24–27.

Zhu Chengxia. 1939 [1991]. "Dabieshan yi nian lai de funü gongzuo" [A year of women-work in Dabieshan]. In *ZFYLZ (1937–1945)*, 214–27.

Zhu De. 1948 [1991]. "Zai jiefangqu funü gongzuo huiyi shang de jianghua" [A speech given at the women-work meeting in the liberated areas]. In *ZFYLZ (1945–1949)*, 276–80.

Zweig, David. 1989. *Agrarian Radicalism in China, 1968–1981*. Cambridge, MA: Harvard University Press.

Zylan, Yvonne. 2000. "Maternalism Redefined: Gender, the State, and the Politics of Day Care, 1945–1962." *Gender & Society* 14 (5): 608–29.

Index

www.ingramcontent.com/pod-product-compliance
Lightning Source LLC
Chambersburg PA
CBHW030856270326
41929CB00008B/446